International Law and the Rise of Nations

The State System and the Challenge of Ethnic Groups

Edited by
Robert J. Beck and Thomas Ambrosio

CHATHAM HOUSE PUBLISHERS
SEVEN BRIDGES PRESS, LLC

NEW YORK · LONDON

Seven Bridges Press, LLC
135 Fifth Avenue,
New York, NY 10010-7101

Copyright © 2002 by Chatham House Publishers of Seven
Bridges Press, LLC

Publisher: Ted Bolen
Managing Editor: Katharine Miller
Production Services: Bytheway Publishing Services, Inc.
Cover design: Tim Mayer
Printing and Binding: Victor Graphics, Inc.

Library of Congress Cataloging-in-Publication Data

International law and the rise of nations : the state system and
the challenge of ethnic groups / [edited by] Robert J. Beck and
Thomas Ambrosio.
     p. cm.
   Includes index.
   ISBN 1-889119-30-X (pbk)
     1. International law.   2. National state.   3. Sovereignty.   4.
International relations and culture.   I. Beck, Robert J., 1961–
. II. Ambrosio, Thomas, 1971–   .
   KZ3900 .I57 2002
   341—dc21

                                             00-012974

Manufactured in the United States of America
10   9   8   7   6   5   4   3   2   1

International Law and
the Rise of Nations

We wish to dedicate this book
to our beloved spouses,
Bernadette and Beth

Contents

Acknowledgments

THIS BOOK HAS its origins in the University of Virginia's Department of Government and Foreign Affairs, where Bob taught for eight years and Tom pursued his doctoral studies. After several successful pedagogical collaborations in International Law and International Organization, we resolved to undertake a joint scholarly project when the appropriate opportunity arose. That occasion was afforded by a course first offered by Tom in the summer of 1998, "Nationalism and Ethnicity." Select elements of Tom's syllabus, we judged then, might serve as the basis of a unique and compelling collection of essays.

In compiling this volume, we sought out the contributions of several scholars with University of Virginia connections: Inis L. Claude, Michael Fowler, and Julie Bunck. Throughout the course of our project, we benefited significantly from the advice and encouragement of many other colleagues in International Law, History, and International Relations. These include Michael Barnett, Mark Bradley, Barry Buzan, Paul Diehl, Nejat Dogan, Andrew Hurrell, Christopher Joyner, Keith Krause, Lorna Lloyd, David Martin, Jeffrey Morton, Nicholas Onuf, Timothy Schorn, Claudena Skran, Joel Trachtman, and Jutta Weldes. Hurst Hannum thoughtfully reviewed and approved our proposed editorial changes to his featured essay. Nathaniel Berman and Bruce Cronin provided invaluable feedback on our characterizations of their contributions. For their constructive suggestions on his essay, "Britain and the 1933 Refugee Convention," Bob wishes particularly to thank Anthony Clark Arend, Bruce Cronin, John Duffield, Guy Goodwin-Gill, Hurst Hannum, Jeff Legro, John Owen, Alfred Rubin, and Michael Schechter. Tom is indebted to Allen Lynch, Paul Shoup, and John Echeverri-Gent for their patience and help in guiding his exploration of the irredentism phenomenon.

The selection and organization of works for conclusion here was done jointly drawing on Tom's original syllabus. We together wrote the focus essays, compiled the bibliographies, and edited the featured texts. Bob wrote the Introduction and Tom the Conclusion. Cheryl Kirby-Stokes provided essential production assistance, greatly simplifying our editorial process. We are most grateful to Ted Bolen and Bob Gormley for their consistent, enthusiastic support of our project. Finally, we wish to dedicate this volume to our cherished spouses, Bernadette Gjud Beck and Beth Ambrosio, whose encouragement and understanding have been unfailing.

Foreword

Inis L. Claude Jr.

FOR TWO CENTURIES or so the ethnic factor—the enthusiasms, affinities, cleavages, loyalties, rivalries, demands, and exclusions associated with and generated by nationalism—has had a significant effect on both domestic and international politics. Its impact has been variable in nature and intensity; it has shattered empires and consolidated states, nourished political communities and inspired genocide, facilitated cooperation and inflamed antagonisms. Nationalistic fervor has waxed and waned; it has sometimes seemed capable of being stifled or at least tamed, while at other times it has appeared uncontrollable. Nationalism has profoundly affected our thinking about the character of the global system by giving rise to the quite divergent ideals of the nation-state, incorporating all of a nation and no other population, the nation-state-cum national minorities, in which a tolerant and generous majority and loyal minorities co-exist happily and confidently, and the multinational state, jointly owned and operated by two or more national entities enjoying equality of status.

Clearly, all of this has both direct and indirect effects upon international law. By increasing the incidence and multiplying the cruelties of war, both internal and international, nationalism has inspired and necessitated fresh attention to both *jus in bello* and *jus ad bellum*. Giving rise to the claim of right of national self-determination, the ethnic factor has both strengthened and undermined the doctrine of sovereignty: to accord legitimacy to the demand for national self-determination is to endorse the right of an ethnic group to achieve sovereign status (and if one has the right to acquire sovereignty, one surely has the right to exercise and defend it), but it is also to lend support to secessionist and perhaps even irredentist attacks upon the territorial integrity of sovereign states. The recent and continuing decline in the legal and political repute of the norm of non-intervention is surely attributable in large measure to the domestic crises engendered by ethnic ambitions and animosities; a revised and enlarged doctrine of humanitarian intervention has come to the fore. After World War I, a limited scheme of internationally guaranteed rights for members of national minorities was imposed upon specified states, overriding their protests based upon the doctrine of sovereignty. After World War II, this scheme was abandoned in favor of subsuming minority rights under the general rubric of human rights applicable to all persons. Since the end of the Cold War, we have completed the circle: international intervention on behalf of persecuted and endangered national minorities has once again become the dominant, and virtually only, form of international human rights activity.

The changes in international law that have occurred, those that are brewing, and those that may be required, in response to the impact of the ethnic factor are the subject matter of this timely and important volume. We who are concerned about the future of world order have good reason to read and ponder its pages.

Introduction

AMONG THE MOST significant consequences of the Cold War's end have been the resurgence of "nations" and the attendant challenges that such nations pose for global order and international law. For at least two and a half centuries after the Peace of Westphalia, the political world was largely defined by states and a state system or systems. After World War I, however, and especially since the late-1980s, nations have proved of increasing political salience, and the state system has been compelled to attempt some accommodation of them within its legal framework.

Our volume recounts the story of the often contentious relationship between "nation" and "state." In its three substantive sections, we explore in turn three principal themes: the "rise of nations," the international legal challenges that such nations pose, and the international legal responses that have been offered to the rise of nations phenomenon.

We do not propose or endorse here a single definition of "nation," a term "mired in difficult disputations."[1] As Hutchinson and Smith have observed, "[q]uestions of definition have bedeviled our field of study, and there is no agreement among scholars about 'subjective' and 'objective' factors in the definition of nations, or about the relationship of nations and nationalism to ethnicity on the one hand, and statehood on the other."[2] Even so, a nation may reasonably be construed as a politicized or "self-aware" ethnic group,[3] and most of the works featured in this volume are generally informed by such an understanding. A "state," meanwhile, though itself not an uncontested concept, may nevertheless be construed as it has been commonly defined: "an entity that has a defined territory and a permanent population, under the control of its own government, and that engages in, or has the capacity to engage in, formal relations with other such entities."[4]

This compilation seeks to impart a broad historical perspective, placing the rise of nations within the context of international systemic change. Our focus is primarily on the twentieth century and on formal legal rules. Nevertheless, we do not suggest that the "rise of nations" has been confined to the twentieth century, or even to the post–Cold War period. Indeed, two of our featured essays consider in some detail the immediate post-Napoleonic period. Furthermore, although the rise of nations serves as our work's fundamental organizing premise, we do not contend here that the histories of either international law or nationalism have been linear, continuous, or strictly progressive. A number of our selections, perhaps most conspicuously that of Nathaniel Berman, depict a historically contingent, discontinuous "international law of nationalism."

Our volume features a unique collection of essays from prominent International Law (IL) and International Relations (IR) scholars. We have deliberately assembled an interdisciplinary anthology, guided by the convictions that "the study of nations . . . cannot be confined to a single disciplinary perspective"[5] and that lawyers and political scientists can profitably collaborate.[6] Several contributions have been prepared specifically for inclusion in this book. In "The Nation Neglected," for example, Michael Ross Fowler and Julie Marie Bunck offer a compelling interpretation of the 1814–1914 period. Robert J. Beck uses archival evidence to show how a state sovereignty understanding, not a "national sovereignty" one, framed interwar Britain's refugee policy deliberations. In "Irredentism: Self-Determination and Interstate War," Thomas Ambrosio considers the international legality of forcible attempts by states to unify nations under the guise of self-determination.

For each of this volume's three substantive sections, brief focus essays are offered. Each such essay introduces its associated section's four selected readings, placing them in thematic and scholarly context. It concludes by providing bibliographic suggestions.

In at least three notable respects our work seeks to distinguish itself from existing ones on the general theme of nationality/ethnicity. First, ours does not concentrate on international security or ethnic conflicts per se, though its subject necessarily has important security implications. Instead, our focus is on formal *legal* rules and their application. Second, case studies do not predominate our volume. Several of our selections, however, consider specific cases in some detail, including: British policymaking toward the first multilateral treaty designed to protect refugees, post–World War II irredentism, and settler infusions in Tibet and Israel's Occupied Territories. Lastly, our volume does not seek to provide a general treatment of sovereignty in international law. Although issues of state sovereignty figure prominently in any discussion of the challenges posed by the rise of nations, this book concentrates on nations' particular relationship(s) to sovereignty—not on sovereignty's more general character.

Our volume commences with Thomas Franck's provocative essay, "Clan and Superclan: Loyalty, Identity, and Community in Law and Practice." For two compelling reasons we have chosen this work by an eminent international lawyer to introduce our anthology. First, Franck offers here an elegant characterization of the post–Cold War world, one of simultaneous integration and fragmentation, of interdependence and schismatic movements. What we are now witnessing, Franck underscores, "is not an irresistible centrifugal trend to a world of rampant tribalist nationalism, nor, for that matter, to rampant centripetal globalism, but to paradoxical elements of both tendencies." Second, Franck's essay illumines the "most basic terms needed to discuss social organization": nation and state. Commonly, but unhappily linked in usage, these concepts lie at "the core of today's bloodiest public political conflicts and the most passionate private struggles for identity and self-definition."

Franck acknowledges the necessity to define such key terms. "Classification," he concedes, "is essential." Still, he reminds us that categories like "nation" and "state" are in some respects arbitrary, artificially separating "phenomenon that are actually distinguished only by degrees of difference." Nation, for Franck, connotes "an affinity group that has placed certain values high on its agenda: shared genealogical origins, language and historic myths, as well as cultural and, perhaps, religious compatibility." The term "infers a popular preference for 'likes being with like,' and a high degree of social conformity." A multicultural state, meanwhile, stands in sharp contrast, reflecting "quite different social values: a civil society sharing a preference for the civic virtues of liberty and material well-being, as well as a desire to associate for protection and security." In advancing his "inductively derived theory of personal identity," Franck ultimately eschews strictly formal definitions. Instead, he fruitfully explores "the unstated values and assumptions that underpin the lexicon of nationalism."

Some may wish to challenge Franck's contention that "there [is] virtually no such thing as a real 'nation,'" or that a new "'right' to personal self-determination" may be emerging. Still, it is difficult to deny the thoughtfulness of his analysis or, even more so, to dispute the significance of his essay's subject. Franck's basic question has inspired our volume, too: "What is going on here . . . in Somalia, Slovakia, Quebec and Kazakhstan?"

NOTES

1. Gidon Gottlieb, *Nation Against State: A New Approach to Ethnic Conflicts and the Decline of Sovereignty* (New York: Council on Foreign Relations, 1993), x.
2. John Hutchinson and Anthony D. Smith, eds., *Nationalism* (Oxford: Oxford University Press, 1994), 15.
3. Walker Connor, "A Nation is a Nation, is a State, is an Ethnic Group, is a . . . .," Ibid., 45.
4. *Restatement (Third), Foreign Relations Law of the United States*, Section 201. See also Article 1 of the Montevideo Convention of 1933 on Rights and Duties of States, *League of Nations Treaty Series* 165: 19.

5. Hutchinson and Smith, *Nationalism*, 3.

6. For a discussion of the challenges to and benefits of IL-IR interdisciplinarity, see Robert J. Beck, Anthony Clark Arend, and Robert Vander Lugt, eds., *International Rules: Approaches from International Law and International Relations* (Oxford: Oxford University Press, 1996); Anthony Clark Arend, *Legal Rules and International Society* (Oxford: Oxford University Press, 1999); Kenneth Abbott, "Modern International Relations Theory: A Prospectus for International Lawyers," *Yale Journal of International Law* 14 (1989): 335-411; Anne-Marie Slaughter Burley, "International Law and International Relations Theory: A Dual Agenda," *American Journal of International Law* 87 (1993): 205-39; and Steven R. Ratner and Anne-Marie Slaughter, "Appraising the Methods of International Law: A Prospectus for Readers," *American Journal of International Law* 93 (1999): 291-301.

Clan and Superclan: Loyalty, Identity and Community in Law and Practice

Thomas M. Franck

> *There are many countries in our blood, aren't there, but only one person. Would the world be in the mess it is if we were loyal to love and not to countries?*
>
> —GRAHAM GREENE, *OUR MAN IN HAVANA*

IN BOSNIA, THE vaunted ideal—a multivariegated state of Muslims, Orthodox Serbs and Catholic Croats living in a tolerant civil society—has virtually been extinguished by a torrent of blood and tears. In Belgium, itself a less than two-hundred-year-old product of Catholic rebellion against Orange-Protestant Holland, the Flemish Catholics of Flanders have all but parted ways with the French Catholics of Wallonia, leaving an ethnically stressed Brussels paradoxically ensconced as capital of a "United Europe." What is going on here, or in Somalia, Slovakia, Quebec and Kazakhstan?

The question, of course, is not new. Since the fall of communism, the subject is on everyone's mind. Commentators have tended to frame the issue in terms of two plausible explanations. The first argues that we are witnessing a mere historic "blip," a detour on the road to a grander, more rational world order, one that arranges trade, communications, health and environmental protection by transnational sectoral regimes. On the other side of this dialectic

Reprinted from Thomas M. Franck, "Clan and Superclan: Loyalty, Identity and Community in Law and Practice," *American Journal of International Law* 90, no. 3 (July 1996): 359–83. Reproduced with permission from 90 AJIL 359 (1996) © The American Society of International Law.

about the meaning of contemporary events are those who argue that genetics (or language, religion and culture) are still the most substantial human commonalities and that to defy this immutable truth—by constructing ever wider, more remote and deracinated regimes based on other utilities—is, quite simply, Sisyphean.[1]

This essay accepts some aspects of both theses. It recognizes that some nationalisms do not end in blood and tears, and that, for some persons, self-identification is best achieved by loyalty to a nation, tribe or ethnie.[2] It also credits the seemingly contrary notion that, for many persons, personal loyalty and identity now tend to cluster around other magnets: the civil society, the transnational corporation, the global religion, a Socialist International, even the Internet. In historical terms, both nationalism and transnational regimes have long bid (sometimes competitively) for the adherence of persons. Indeed, in the past, persons have often had multiple or compound identities.

What is new is a growing consciousness of a personal right to compose one's identity. This explanation sees current developments neither exclusively in terms of the inexorable emergence of global and regional regimes nor in terms of a nationalist determinism. Rather, it posits the emergence of a world in which each individual will freely choose a personal identity constructed out of a broad array of building blocks: a world in which self-determination evolves from a plural to a singular entitlement, from a right of peoples to one of persons.

Admittedly, this optic is not one directed primarily toward present surface reality. It may, however, provide a glimpse of underlying tendencies that the post-Communist world's messy, seemingly irreconcilable surface realities obscure. The purpose of this essay is to sketch out the sociohistorical phenomenology on which such an explanatory theory is based, and to test it out on at least one contemporary set of legal phenomena: the attitude of states toward multiple nationality as a right of individuals. If we indeed are witnessing the emergence of a new "right" to personal self-determination, one would expect to see some evidence of it in state practice. While it is far from preemptive, the mere fact that some such evidence is now beginning to appear makes these indicators of state behavior particularly important as deductive confirmation of the inductively derived theory of personal identity that this essay advances.

I. IDENTITY IN THE POST-COLD WAR ERA

With the end of colonialism and of the Cold War, empires have receded and been replaced by independent states; and independent states have been challenged by constituent tribal, national or ethnic entities seeking secession. We can discern a powerful wave of global localism breaking over the cliffs of the state system.

The idea of the state as a multicommunal civil society is thus challenged from below by schismatic movements. Meanwhile, a parallel phenomenon of growing interdependence is also challenging the state as insufficient to meet the needs of the third millennium. In response, states are moving into closer association, delegating parts of their sovereignty to supranational authorities dealing with environmental issues such as ozone depletion; extreme violations of human rights; and threats to international peace, international liquidity and trade.

The paradox of these moves by societies simultaneously pursuing greater centrifugalism *and* centripetalism—greater divergence *and* convergence—casts a bright beam of light on the global crises of personal identity. Since the Reformation, the Peace of Westphalia and the writings of Hugo Grotius, the state has been the alpha and omega of personal identity. One is Canadian or American or Rwandan or Indonesian. All persons and corporate entities have a nationality, which describes their singular and total identity as recognized by the international legal and political system.

This simple, unidimensional system for defining identities and loyalties is under pressure from the same forces as are challenging the supremacy of the state. While many Canadians, Americans and Europeans now have more than one nationality, most Rwandans think of themselves only as Hutu or Tutsi. In Europe, a new European identity is competing with historical nationalisms, even as Bretons turn against their French identity. In 1995, seventy thousand blue helmets served the United Nations command—more than in all but a handful of national armies. Clearly, something is happening. But what is it, and how will it affect our future?

II. TRIBE, NATION, STATE

Despite the tendency to refer to countries as "nation-states," there are very few states that consist of a single nation or ethnie. At the core of today's bloodiest public political conflicts and the most passionate private struggles for identity and self-definition lies the conflict between these two concepts: the nation and the state. To understand and address the public and private aspects of this conflict, one must begin by uncoupling those two terms, which stand for such opposed values and prognoses of humanity's destiny.

Hegel locates the source of this profound conflict squarely at the center of his definition of a nation. "Nations," he wrote, "may have had a long history before they finally reach their destination—that of forming themselves into states."[3] But, Hegel believed, the natural destiny of each nation is to make itself a state. This progression, Ernest Gellner says, is not borne out historically and, he warns, "we must not accept the myth."[4] To Gellner, the proposition is not only historically false, but also anthropologically absurd and politically disastrous. "Nations" according to Gellner, "are not inscribed into the nature of things, they do not constitute a political version of the doctrine of natural kinds. Nor were national states the manifest ultimate destiny of ethnic or cultural groups." To this, Professor E. J. Hobsbawm adds: "Nations, we now know . . .

are not as Bagehot thought, as old as history. The modern sense of the word is no older than the eighteenth century."[5]

Before that, there were amorphous cultures, ethnie, but these usually saw no reason to pursue an exclusivist agenda of social organization, let alone to become nation-states. Moreover, these ethnie, with few exceptions, were themselves amalgams of smaller groups.[6] A turning point came with the superimposition of modern nationalism, specifically in France, on the amorphous grouping that was the prenationalist state. That development, however, is neither (as Hegel thought) a necessary working out of a historic destiny, nor the prevalent state of things now, or at any time in the past. As Gellner puts it, nations are not "the bricks of which mankind is made up."[7]

Nevertheless, after World War I, the Wilsonian world of self-determining nation-states seemed to acquire a verisimilitude that at times encouraged the belief that it was both "natural" and "just" for each "people" to have a state of its own, partly echoing earlier demands for this sort of justice advanced by Bismarck and Mazzini. John Maynard Keynes remarked despairingly of the Versailles peace negotiations, that this Wilsonian dogma "exalts and dignifies the divisions of race and nationality above the bonds of trade and culture, and guarantees frontiers but not happiness."[8] In 1975, in the Western Sahara Advisory Opinion, the International Court of Justice seemed to acknowledge the supremacy of a people's legal right to self-determination, echoing the United Nations General Assembly's sweeping Resolutions 1514 (XV) and 1541 (XV), even while changing the moniker of those entitled to achieve statehood from "a nation" to "a people." Needless to say, this did nothing to clarify who those entitled—a "people"—are; nor did it resolve the policy issue beneath the Wilsonian entitlement that had troubled Lord Keynes.

A. The Underlying Values

The purpose of this discourse is not to join, let alone resolve, these troublesome perplexities.[9] It is, rather, to seek first some terminological clarity by examining the unstated values and assumptions that underpin the lexicon of nationalism, and then to think about the future direction of an era in which the thesis of nationalism and antithesis of globalization might be expected to produce a third-millennium synthesis that will permit humanity to find self-definition and will enable law to locate the socio-structural matrix within which it will be expected to operate.

Let us begin by trying to define for ourselves these most basic terms needed to discuss social organization, personal identity and loyalty: *nations* and *states*. They represent profoundly different historical facts and manifest quite different social priorities, which it will be necessary to examine with clarity, since the usages of both terms are eminently confusing.

The two terms, unhappily, are commonly linked in usage. Hegel, for example, stipulated that the "nation state is mind in its substantive rationality and immediate actuality and is therefore the absolute power on earth."[10] For our purpose of clarification, however, the term nation-state must first be disaggregated to permit both its components to be analyzed in the light of practice. The term nation or tribe suggests an affinity group that has placed certain values high on its agenda: shared genealogical origins, language and historic myths, as well as cultural and, perhaps, religious compatibility. It infers a popular preference for "likes being with like," and a high degree of social conformity. In sharp contrast, the multicultural state reflects quite different social values: a civil society sharing a preference for the civic virtues of liberty and material well-being, as well as a desire to associate for protection and security. There are currently ample examples of each, although the distinction, of course, is one of degree.

States, such as the United States, may deliberately foster myths of a shared "melting-pot" nationhood. In pursuit of unity, states may even become aggressively nationalist, inventing a nationhood based on imagined commonalities of history, genetics, religion and culture. France is a more single-minded, yet also not wholly successful, example of a multinational state inventing itself as a nation-state. *Le Monde* recently had to remind its readers, in this "Year of King Clovis," that the occasion celebrates a national myth: "un catechisme scolaire, d'origine a la fois royaliste et republicaine, entretient dans notre pays l'image d'une nation intemporelle, eternelle, preexistant a sa propre histoire." It pointed out that whoever this first French king was, he probably spoke proto-German, but certainly not proto-French. Many states, however, manifestly have not become nation-states—Canada, Nigeria, Switzerland, India and Belgium are examples—and they remain multiethnic or multinational civil societies. These tend to be not as socially tight-knit as uniethnic nation-states, but they emphasize their diversity as a source of strength, rather than their genetic, historical and cultural unity.

Nations and tribes are quite similar in emphasizing their peoples' common genes, history and culture. They share the mythology of an ennobling past that largely determines the destiny they pursue. The civil society of a compounded state, instead, tends to share a vision of a glorious self-invented future: much as nineteenth-century Americans touted their "manifest destiny" but not their manifest history. In this they differed from another immigrant-settler people, the Afrikaners of South Africa, who perceived themselves as a tribe or nation.

Today, a person's loyalty system is increasingly likely to be a compound of subjectively chosen external references: to family, culture, religion, ideals, institutions, the state and even to humanity. These identity-shaping compounds are complex and dynamic, creating the possibility of conflict in the psyche. In particular, there may be a conflict, latent or virulent, between loyalty to nation or tribe and loyalty to the state. Since very few states consist of only one ethnie, the way persons apportion their loyalty among these various external references determines, in large measure, who they are.

National or tribal values may be seen to predominate when a person's identity is shaped primarily by historical considerations: common myths, past glories or defeats, injustices suffered or overcome, grievances nourished and burnished. Common language, culture, genealogy and religion project the romanticized past onto the future. Individuals and groups who define themselves in this way are likely to want to live among others of the same ethnie: to eat the food, listen to the music, and dance to the rhythms that are believed to have delighted their ancestors. Statist values, in contrast, do not reflect this same reverence for the past, substituting the diverse citizens' futurist aspirations.

Both a nation-tribe and a civil society organized as a multiethnic state can run amok with jingoism, but the sources of their respective jingoisms are different. Nations tend to become aggressive as a manifestation of ethnic xenophobia (Hitler's German nation, Hirohito's Japan), while civil states do so in pursuit of universal ideals and mercantilist expansion (Napoleon's empire-state, the nineteenth-century United States).

The sinews of a civil society are usually less tensile than those of a nation-state or tribe. The civil society's optimism about its citizens' common future is more contingent and less rooted than is the pride of a tribe or nation based on a gloriously imagined racial, historic and cultural past. Nevertheless, statist identity, based on the vision of a shining future or manifest destiny, may emerge to bind the civil society into a cohesive force. This happened during the Industrial Revolution in Britain, the French Revolution and the Italian risorgimento. Something like it may even have happened in Tito's Yugoslavia. Sometimes, as in Britain, this statist civil awakening happens in connection with technological innovations that generate, and ultimately may satisfy, a revolution of social expectations. At other times, a state is called into being at the behest of charismatic leaders—Napoleon, Bismarck, Garibaldi—who succeed in forging a diverse rabble into a questing citizenry by iron will or iron wheels. Such forging may go on until the state becomes a nation: as when the Jewish tribes wandered the Sinai until they cohered as a militant nation-state, albeit one later to split again into tribes. Or it may not happen at all, leaving a civil state that is no more than the merest hollow political forum for constituent factions and classes waging war by other means.

We speak deliberately of forging a nation, but, as with all else about the terminology of personal identity, this usage is not free of controversy. Nations usually pretend to be genetically based manifestations of historical social forces. They do not perceive themselves as being forged out of anything but, rather, as being the true elements of history. Not so the state, which rarely claims to be a state of nature but, in most instances, perceives itself as an invented civil society of persons bound together by ideals, a constitution and a common enterprise.

The belief in a mythology of humanity's "state of nature" may be historically inaccurate, but quite accurately revealing of profound personal values of the believer. Myth tellers seem to have settled on several universal stories. The first describes humanity as composed of solitary persons who join together for certain limited contractarian purposes, such as security, division of labor and economies of scale. . . . This conception contrasts with a second, quite different and decidedly determinist myth about the origins of socialization, one that emphasizes the power of concentric circles of familial and genetic kinship. Common language, culture, religion and values, from this perspective, are the product of associations mandated by blood and genetics, not the other way around. To Hegel, an extreme example, this blood tie dictates all personal identity and must determine the contours of communities organized as states, "the absolute power on earth" that demands of persons "absolute obedience, renunciation of personal opinions and reasoning, in fact complete absence of mind."[11] Rebutting this view are most modern sociologists and historians, who tend to believe that there "is no firm sociological mooring to the nation, not in language, not in religion, and not in ethnicity."[12] This antideterminist view, however, does not necessarily predispose acceptance of its voluntarist antithesis.

We will turn later in this essay to some of the other, more recent theories of nationalism. What makes the voluntarist and determinist stories of interest is not that either is demonstrably true but, rather, that both are told more to illustrate a point of view than to report actual history. Both are inventions important not for what they tell us about the nature of humanity but for what they tell us about the inventors and retailers of these theories of "the nature of man." Of interest is why some persons prefer one myth of personal identity that portrays the individual in isolation as "natural," while others choose one of the archetypal myths. Of interest, too, is the choice *among* archetypal myths: why, for example, some choose the story of Adam and Eve, which proposes the "natural" commonality of a bonded all-embracing humanity, while others prefer less universal archetypes as are embodied, for example, in the Norse saga. The Adam and Eve story, adumbrated in the tale of Abel and Cain and of Jacob and Esau, accounts for nations as an aberrational aftermath of ego—"the fall of man"— while much folklore takes a far more benevolent, proud view of the origins of particular ethnie and nations.

If the persuasiveness of these two stories of the "natural state of humanity"—the voluntarist and the determinist—is undermined by what we now know about our origins, so is that of yet a third story: the modern liberal myth of an emerging common human destiny. This speaks of a *historical* imperative for ever-greater unities: not quite a reunion of the family of Adam and Eve, but a working out of the common strands of everyone's humanity. The modernist-humanist faith perceives nations, tribes, states and other forms of identity based on groups as mere transitory phases in an inexorable progression from the primitive clan to the federation of humankind. Immanuel Kant and Clarence K. Streit visualized such a progression and, in 1965, Robert Hutchins's Center for the Study of Democratic Institutions published a proposed global constitution.

The formation of multinational states after World War I seemed to presage the inevitable coming of such a new postnational era. Yugoslavia, Czechoslovakia and the Soviet Union are examples of multinational states conceived in the higher cosmopolitan consciousness of the state as stepping-stone from national to global thinking. Indeed, the much-earlier multinational empires—the Roman, Austro-Hungarian and Ottoman—seemed to show that nations could live together under a common associational umbrella, a transnational consciousness.

It now appears, however, that the liberal-modernist perception of human sociopolitical convergence is also a myth, one expressing the myth teller's social values but not literally or historically accurate, not supportable by evidence. Indeed, history sometimes seems to build a momentum in the opposite direction, away from an ever-broader convergence. The multinational states formed after World War I have disintegrated with the end of the Cold War, just as the earlier empires gave way to the Reformation or the nationalist aftermath of the French Revolution. Today, a less confident view of history's inexorable march to ever-widening circles of sociopolitical union appears warranted. It may be that groups form, join or even integrate with others, and then, under certain circumstances, part. Neither union nor dissolution seems quite so self-evidently "natural" or inevitable in the cacophony of today's world. As Professor Linda Colley has observed, "Historically speaking, most nations have always been culturally and ethnically diverse, problematic, protean and artificial constructs that take shape very quickly and come apart just as fast. . . ."[13]

A possible condition making for dissolution is the failure of the association's inceptive dream that spiritual and material rewards would flow from the enlarged political space. Even that, however, is conjecture. We do know that there is no evidence to support the claim of any particular political configuration—the multinational state, the nation-state, the city-state, the multistate organization, or any other—to be the "natural" order of things, to reflect some ineluctable human destiny. Rather, what appears to be operating is a continual ebb and flow of differing, little-understood imperatives that at various times and circumstances rearrange the self-image of persons and thereby provoke revision of the boundaries of political communities.

Yet it is also essential to remember that we are speaking of arbitrary definitional categories that artificially separate—designate as discrete—phenomena that are actually distinguished only by *degrees* of difference. While staking out and insisting upon categorical boundaries, one should not lose sight of the fluid realities. Behind the words are value preferences, and these do not come in impervious categories.

B. The Definitional Categories and the Realities They Obscure

Words categorize, and categories obscure both the interpenetration between the values expressed in words and the dissimilarities within the categories arbitrarily established. Yet classification is essential. In the view of Philip Allott, a "legal relation is heuristic because it simplifies actual reality for computational purposes. Actual reality, as it presents itself in human consciousness, is infinitely complex, uncertain and dynamic. In order to make legal relations operationally effective, as instruments of social transformation, they must exclude much of actual reality."[14] The words *nation* and *nationalism* are prime examples. Hobsbawm has noted that the criteria for defining a nation "—language, ethnicity or whatever—are themselves fuzzy, shifting and ambiguous, and as useless . . . as cloud-shapes are compared to landmarks. This, of course, makes them unusually convenient for propagandist and programmatic, as distinct from descriptive purposes."[15] It also makes it possible today to speak, straight-faced, of retaining the "sovereignty" of the state of Bosnia while conceding the special status of the Republic of Srpska and recognizing its "links" with the Federal Republic of Yugoslavia.

People's preferences, fortunately, are far more calibrated and flexible than language. Consider the "German-speaking people," be they residents of Berlin, Vienna or Zurich. Quite aside from the subjective preference of the denizens of these great German-speaking cities, each might well appear to the naked eye as a *civitas* of a Germanic *nation*. The key indicator of a nation is its common language and culture. Yet we also know that, to the historically trained eye, this linguistic affinity is not a natural given. It has evolved through a synthesis of persons whose tribal origins and language may have been Visigoth, Prussian, Rhenish, Alsatian, Westphalian, Hannoverian, Saxon, Bohemian, Frisian, Sorb, Bavarian, Tyrolean, Celt, Slavic or Danish. These languages, to the extent they have survived, even today show differences from one another. German, like almost every living language, is to a degree synthetic. Germany, moreover, is only in a mythic sense the manifestation of an eternal genetic or cultural unity. This dissonance between actual anthropological history and its subjective political perception demonstrates the elasticity, if not the meaninglessness, of the term nation as commonly used today.

Somewhat the same is true of Great Britain. Although the French may still refer to those across the English Channel and, sometimes also to others across the North Atlantic, as "les anglo-saxons," that designation, of course, has but passing contemporary relevance to the ethnic heritage of the inhabitants of England, let alone those of Scotland, Wales and Northern Ireland. Great Britain is actually a melting pot of nations, if not quite as recently and evidently so as the United States, Australia or Canada. For centuries Frisians, Scots, Celts, Picts, Angles, Danes, Saxons and Normans, and now Afro-Caribbeans and various Asian peoples, have more or less synthesized to create a political community.

This community still operates primarily as a civil society, albeit one that has some identifiable characteristics: integrated educational, religious and social institutions; some shared values; common speech patterns; and, perhaps, a degree of coherence in self-image. But Britain is not really a nation; it is, quite simply, a state.

As for the English language, the British speak a tongue that has incorporated elements of Saxon, German, Celtic, Latin, Scots, Pictish and Norman French. Britain, the quintessential "Anglo-Saxon" nation, has nothing remotely approximating a uniform "blood" pedigree; and, of course, some of its constituent components are less genetically merged than the English. The Welsh, Scots, Manx and Channel Islanders, as well as recent immigrants, still retain some backward-looking sense of their "national" separateness and, in some instances, may still harbor a forward-looking wish to secede from Great Britain in a quest to regain their separate imagined sociopolitical identities.

England, too, has had a life of the popular imagination. William Blake, at the beginning of the nineteenth century, imagined the New Jerusalem in England's—not Britain's—"green and pleasant land," evidencing a belief that Christ's feet may have walked "upon England's mountains green." And, to friend and foe alike, the English were a formidable nation long after the United Kingdom became a state encompassing it. Schoolchildren still learn that Napoleon Bonaparte, at Rochefort in 1815, said with a mixture of bitterness and awe, "Wherever wood can swim, there I am sure to find this flag of England." We know what he meant, although the flag of England was the cross of St. George, little used except by Anglican churches. It is all so confusing because the concept of nation is so vague and misleading.

Germany and Britain are in no way unusual in being imaginary nations. Throughout the world, despite the power of the nationalist and self-determination movements, there are today almost no "nations" in the pure ethnic, genetic or cultural sense. There are, of course, Scottish nationalists; but the "Scots" in fact are highlanders or lowlanders, a merger of culturally, linguistically, religiously and historically distinct clans. Even the relatively exclusive Jewish "nation" is a mixture of European, Middle Eastern and African genetic stock. Many Jews do perceive themselves as constituting a "nation" and manifested that perception in creating Israel. Yet in Israel, too, people's varied and mixed ethnic origins are clearly apparent in social and political contexts. The concept of a unique Jewish nation also ignores not only the conversions to Judaism around the Black Sea and in East Africa, but also the historical synthesis of the tribes of Judah and Benjamin that once made up Judea, and the twelve tribes that constituted ancient Israel before the division of the kingdom. Of course, none of this should lead us to ignore the facts that Israelis do speak a common language and that most share myths of a common history and culture.

Israel demonstrates something else about nationhood. As inhabitants of a

Jewish state in a region of Arab states, Israelis also share a common sense of danger, which, in turn, requires a degree of cohesion. Such cohesion probably cannot simply derive from being a civic association of immigrants but, rather, may necessitate emphasizing the nation as the basis of the state. Danger may be one of the historic factors that forge nation-states. Faced with the fall of France and the onslaught of German V-2 rockets in World War II, the British found themselves reacting as a state with at least some of the indices of a nation: a surprising degree of pride in an imagined ethnic and heroic history; and a future destiny rooted in a shared, exclusive national past, when the British—not the English or Scottish—navy ruled the waves, and the British—not the Ulster or Welsh—grenadiers were the greatest "of all the world's great heroes." But this ethos prevailed only for a time and only to a degree. With the decline in both Britain's fortunes and the dangers to its security after World War II, the internal nations have reemerged as significant forces for devolution or disintegration and for reinvention of the ethnic self on the divided, and rather disappointed if still sceptered, isle.

Thus the picture becomes even more complex. If almost no "nation" is pure in the genetic sense of "common blood," what is a nation, other than a synthesis of other, earlier, vanished or submerged "nations" (or "tribes" or "clans"), which, in some instances and to some degree, can be deconstructed by forces we barely understand—as recently happened with such vengeful force when the seemingly homogeneous Somali nation (tribe) broke up into murderous "clans"?

Whatever people may wish to imagine about their past, deconstructing their myths has dangers but also holds some promise. It gives us a closer approximation of who we were, a useful first step in self-definition. When the Romans met their northern neighbors in Gaul, they reported encountering not peoples corresponding with the modern French or Germans, but warring clans. If we can live with the truth about who we were, we may have taken a first step toward discovering who we are becoming.

For one thing, we may discover that our identities have been much more mutable than we imagined. Distinctly different tribes or nations, for historic reasons and to different degrees, do sometimes merge their identities and submerge their origins, opting to become partly or entirely assimilated into a larger tribe/nation identity. This happened to the clans of Scotland and an efficient merger of various provincial Germanic and some Frisian elements made plausible the notion of a Dutch nation-state. China is a nation-state that has to a significant extent merged its quite distinct ethnie. In modern times, this process of social merger and synthesis has accelerated through the technological supremacy of the state, with its ability to instill a sense of community among diverse peoples through means that Professor Benedict Anderson has identified as "census, map and museum."[16] The extent to which the merger occurs is always a matter of degree and, longitudinally, of time. In the far northeastern marches of Holland, some Frisians still remain Frisian in language and custom. There is still a South Moluccan identity in Indonesia, but it appears to be fading.

There are other forms of mutability. A nation may decide against merging with others but join, instead, in a multinational state based not on a synthesized ethnie but on a compact establishing what Professor Gellner has called a civil society.[17] In Canada, Belgium, Switzerland and India, and increasingly in the United States, some of the citizenry's various genetic, linguistic, historical and cultural components have endured, yet have permitted the emergence of a state, albeit one without a homogeneous national identity. All Sikhs are Indian citizens, but they are not part of an Indian nation. The citizens of India have imagined a shared civil society in a coherent political state, but not necessarily a shared culture, language, religion or nation. They have nevertheless succeeded in having a state, in part by inventing and defending their civil society, thereby bypassing the assimilationist effort needed to synthesize the fiction of a nation-state.

Such civil society-based states—with their compacts between the constituent ethnie, tribes and nations but little fusion of identities—may sometimes disintegrate under the pressure of a suddenly resurgent centrifugal tribalism or nationalism. The composite populace may even revert, as in the former Yugoslavia, to ancient hostilities. Then, some missionaries of resurgent tribalism, deploying genocide, may even recreate true "nation-states" by cleansing territory of any lingering traces of multiethnicity. Fortunately, this occurs only in the most extreme cases.

The extent to which a civil society permits ethnie and nationalities to coexist, or conduces to their gradual self-perceived merger, or ends in failure and stress if not outright dissolution, is always a matter of degree, varying with the circumstances and over time. Vocabulary rarely allows for this fluidity and shading, and, by falsifying the past, vocabulary may actually block the future.

III. CONCEPTUAL COMPLEXITY: IDENTITY AND LOYALTY

A. Multireferences of Identity

These are times when nations and nationalism do seem to be the building blocks of society and history. Such a determinist prognosis, however, runs aground on an obdurate fact that makes the current neo-tribal nationalist revival even more astonishing. This is, after all, also the era of enlightened internationalism. Even as Serbs, Bosnians, Tamils and Chechens fight to the death (primarily the death of others, of course) for the right to unite "likes with like" and to sever their political links with the "alien others," it becomes apparent that their sought-after independence is a chimera in yet another sense. Not only is there virtually no such thing as a real "nation," but there is also no such thing as real "independence." Even the best-established states can daily be observed yielding more and more of their sovereignty to regional and global systems of governance.

They do this not necessarily out of an evolving sense of human kinship but in recognition of functional necessity. Even the newly cleansed ethnic nations of the former Yugoslavia undoubtedly will find themselves scrambling to surrender chunks of their precious sovereignty to the European Union, which manages migration for its member governments, as well as credit policies, trade, competition policy and aspects of foreign relations. Without membership in multistate systems, such new nation-states as Serbia, Croatia and Georgia would soon find themselves becoming a sort of tribal theme park, their foreign trade and industry atrophying. Moreover, for their defense, they are also likely to want to join the North Atlantic Treaty Organization or some other regional military superestablishment. What is currently being witnessed, therefore, is not an irresistible centrifugal trend to a world of rampant tribalist nationalism, nor, for that matter, to rampant centripetal globalism, but to paradoxical elements of both tendencies.

. . . The likely prognosis is that there is unlikely to be a single trend. Instead, we now have a dynamic dialectic in which countervailing tendencies contend and coexist. This, too, is not historically unprecedented. Gellner points out that, on the one hand, there have always been

> city states, tribal segments, peasant communes and so forth, running their own affairs . . . and on the other, large territories controlled by a concentration of force at one point. A very characteristic political form is, of course, one which fuses these two principles: a central dominant authority co-exists with semi-autonomous local units.[18]

The modern analog of this tendency is the European Union's policy of subsidiarity, which seeks to reinforce the role in governance of towns, counties and intra- and interstatal regional authorities. The effect is to diversify the objects of personal loyalty. To this, Hobsbawm adds that "we cannot assume that for most people national identification—when it exists—excludes or is always or ever superior to, the remainder of the set of identifications which constitute the social being."[19] Some of these identifications may be subnational or substatist, while others will transcend those units of governance. In the words of Professor Colley, "Identities are not like hats. Human beings can and do put on several at a time."[20]

When communities of persons find themselves—their identities—pushed toward integration into larger communities and simultaneously feel a powerful pull toward self-definition in terms of smaller communities of "likes," the consequence may, but certainly need not, be a kind of collective schizophrenia and loss of centered identity. The very same circumstances can also be liberating, generating a bracing, creative accommodation of multiple loyalties, a sense of belonging to concentric circles of identity and community. Human beings for millennia have defined themselves in terms of loyalty to more than one system of social and political organization: as subjects of the emperor or king; communicants of a transnational church; members of a family, clan and nation; and perhaps members of an artisan or professional guild or of a secret order or society. Historically, the eternal question—who am I?—has more often than not been answered in terms of multiple external references, to which loyalty was felt to be owed. In the eighteenth century, "I" could have been a Magyar, a Hungarian, a subject of the Habsburg emperor, a burgher of Szeged, a Calvinist, a Freemason, a printer and a member of the extended family Nagy.

This complex system of personal loyalty relationships would have been supported by a mixture of nature and nurture: "I" would see myself as both the subject of my temporal liege lord and a sheep of my spiritual pastor: first, because that appeared to be the "natural" order of things, and, second, because both my liege lord and my pastor feed and protect me, respectively, in body and soul, in the here and the hereafter.

Nature and nurture continue today to be the active ingredients in loyalty formation. To understand the dynamic forces creating the dominant loyalties, in any era, it is necessary to examine this prevailing pull of nature and nurture.

B. Loyalty Systems

Throughout history, loyalty systems have been rigidly enforced by nature and nurture: by social habits that were legitimated as being rooted in "the nature of things" and reinforced by the extending or withholding of services and benefits. Nature and nurture, when they operate effectively, buttress the status quo of the belief system. Even so, loyalties have also evolved. This evolution has taken two directions. There have been transformations, first, in the references of loyalty and, second, in attitudes toward multiple loyalties.

1. Loyalty References. Historically, humans have defined themselves in terms of loyalty to a person or persons (the emperor, king, prince or pope) and to an institution or institutions (empire, state, nation, church, transnational orders, guilds or organizations).

In the West, this has meant, for much of the time, that loyalty was owed, first, to a Roman emperor and empire and, later, to a Germanic successor, the Holy Roman emperor and Empire. Both the Roman and the Holy Roman Empires, as well as the Ottoman and Muscovite dynasties, usually permitted a substantial degree of local autonomy to princes, tribes, nations or religious minorities, which consequently coexisted with imperium as a subsidiary loyalty reference.

Second, for most of Western history, loyalty was also due to the pope in Rome and "his" church, or to the Orthodox church and its patriarch in Constantinople, or to other "Western" religious institutions. Most persons had little difficulty accommodating both loyalties even when, as happened frequently, the loyalty references were not fully aligned.

During the sixteenth and seventeenth centuries, a third, new loyalty object began to contend for popular acceptance: the state. "State," however, described neither an empire nor a nationality, but a territory "owned" by a king or queen. It became the prevalent form of post-Westphalian political organization except in a few surviving empires and the exceptional civic republics like Geneva and the towns of the Hanseatic League. Moreover, loyalty during this early statist period was still owed by the subject not to the state but, personally, to its monarch. That personage, by the seventeenth century, had created a claim to fealty by defeating the claims of neighboring rival princes, and by undermining and overcoming the claims of emperor and pope. The ruler, particularly in post-Reformation Europe, won the right to demand the exclusive loyalty of his or her subjects: one person, one liege.

The previously common accommodation of multiple loyalties thus generally ceased in late Tudor England and in the Sun King's France, when the state became sovereign and the sovereign became the state. Within these new personalized states or fiefdoms, the individual's loyalty to the sovereign was real, not symbolic of a communal "national" identity. Between ruler and ruled, and among the ruled, there was little sense of community. The sovereign and the elite surrounding the scepter usually spoke Latin, French or German, whereas the populace spoke Gaelic, Czech or Magyar. Even in France, most people spoke the dialects of Brittany, Normandy or the Languedoc, while the court and the surrounding Ile-de-France spoke French.

The answer to the question—who am I?—in these circumstances had become simpler than in the days of empire and universal church: I am the vassal of my king or queen, a subject of the sovereign's state. Yet nationalism, let alone ethnic or racial solidarity, played little, if any, part in this loyalty system, based as it was on an exclusive, personalized subordination of the person to the state sovereign. "I" was identified by my personal duty and reward relation to the royal government, not by any consociation with my neighbors. I did not perceive myself as a denizen of a *gemeinschaft*. My personal liege, the king, was almost certainly of an ethnie unrelated to mine except in the remotest sense.

In the remaining empires of this period—the Habsburg and Ottoman, in particular—there was also little sense of *national* cohesion, although the system tolerated and encouraged some degree of self-rule in its component minority ethnie. These ethnie, however, did not think of themselves as nations. For example, Professor Bernard Lewis reports that, until the nineteenth century the Turks thought of themselves primarily as Muslims; their loyalty belonged, on different levels, to Islam and to the Ottoman house and state. The language a man spoke, the territory he inhabited, the race from which he claimed descent, might be of personal, sentimental or social significance. . . . [But] the very concept of a Turkish nationality was submerged—and this despite the survival of the Turkish language and the existence of what was in fact though not in theory a Turkish state. . . .

The Turkish national idea, in the modern sense, [only] first appears in the mid-nineteenth century.[21]

When nationalism attracted the Turks, it drew its impetus, as did parallel developments in the Austrian and Hungarian parts of the Habsburg Empire, from the French Revolution. But it drew its romantic ideological inspiration from Germany. The alien other was conceived in genetic-ethnic mythology. "Even today, [in] . . . the secular Republic," Lewis notes, "a non-Muslim in Turkey may be called a Turkish citizen, but never a Turk."[22]

Two late eighteenth-century revolutions—the American and the French—ended the personalization of loyalty, but not its exclusivity. After 1789, it became possible to answer the question—who am I?—by reference to a radically new object of loyalty: I am no subject, I am an American or French citizen. Citizenship repudiated and repealed the idea of the subject, rejected the idea of personalized sovereignty and substituted the notions of equality, fraternity and liberty. The state became the nation: not the nation of ethnic compatibility but the nation of kindred ideals. Thus, a Citizen Paine could claim the nationalities of Britain, the United States and France; the Marquis de Lafayette could become, in effect, an American revolutionary; Montesquieu could be co-opted to inspire the cause of both revolutions; and the Dutchman Hugo de Groot could appear in Paris as the ambassador of Sweden.

The move in terminology from subject to citizen denotes a tectonic shift in the loyalty system, creating for the first time, at least since the early Athenian and Roman republics, a theory of horizontal, as opposed to vertical, loyalty. Loyalty, in this ideological revolution, was to be owed by the people to themselves, conjoined in liberty, equality and fraternity to constitute a new sovereign: the "nation." In this historical context, however, nation meant something entirely different from its current usage.

Both in the United States of 1776 and in the France of 1789, the term nation was used to mean nothing more or less than the citizenry. The nation of the United States consisted of territory, citizens and formally shared ideals of liberty and equality, at least for free white men. A decade later, a transformed polity emerged on the sovereign territory of the French king. It, too, was defined by a common loyalty not to a sovereign but to the citizenry and the ideals of liberty, equality and fraternity. In both instances, this new nationality was based on shared republican ideals and not on the commonality of blood or a shared history and culture. Even though the common republican ideals were to be implemented within a defined territory, they were thought to have the universal validity guardedly claimed for them by Immanuel Kant.

That sort of late eighteenth-century concept of the nation and of nationalism was far removed from the statist, personalized loyalty references that preceded it, and even further from the concepts that late in the nineteenth century appropriated the terms nation and nationalism but twisted them into new loyalty patterns based on exclusive and xenophobic loyalty to myth-history, race, language, ethnie and culture.

The French nation that emerged in 1789 was not even remotely related conceptually to the German nation created and led a century later by Prussia. French nationalism, at its origin, was a political phenomenon, not an ethnic, cultural, historical or linguistic one. It created what today we think of when we describe a civil society in a nonsectarian, multinational state. The point of the revolution was to take the state away from the sovereign and create a new nation of shared political ideals, from the top down. To support this new state, its government deliberately set about spreading a national language, culture and identity.

This was no mean task. In 1789, fewer than half the citizens of France actually spoke French and only about one in ten spoke it "correctly," as a first language. The task of the new French republic was to use the opening created by a new regime of liberty and equal opportunity to entice the citizenry into new national schools, libraries and museums that would dazzle them—Burgundians, Haut Savoyards, Basques and Bretons—with the beauties and benefits of acquiring the patina of French language and culture hitherto common primarily in the Ile-de-France. "To be precise," Hobsbawm tells us,

> the advance guard of middle-class nationalism fought its battle along the line which marked the educational progress of large numbers of "new men" into areas hitherto occupied by a small elite. The progress of schools and universities measures that of nationalism, just as schools and especially universities became its most conscious champions. . . .[23]

This was nationalism created top-down. Top in this context signifies a new and much broader-based elite of officialdom, professionals, educators and intellectuals: often combined in a single "Renaissance" person. They invented the nation. To this end, they also invented myths, but they were, at least at first, relatively benign and outward looking. Almost a century later, Massimo d'Azeglio, the former prime minister of Piedmont, is said to have observed after the reunification: "We have made Italy: now we have to make Italians."[24] The "nations" created in America, France and Italy were invented to instill a sense of unity based on common loyalty to the democratic, republican institutions of the state. It is in those three countries, rather than in Germany, that Kant's republican prescriptions[25] were put into practice to invent—top-down—a liberal nationalism as loyalty reference for the citizenry of new republics. Nationalism was not the reason these states came to exist. Nationalism was a necessary condition for transforming the preexisting oligarchic states into the revolutionary demos whose new equality of rights and entitlements could be actualized only if the citizenry also shared a bonding, equalizing language, education and culture.

In America, however, the further influence of John Locke could be seen in defining the nation. Emphasizing values conspicuously absent from revolutionary France, Locke insisted that the power of government and the sway of majorities be limited. By negotiating tangible institutional and legal barriers to centralized majoritarian tyranny, the established Anglicans of Virginia, the Puritans of Massachusetts, the Quakers of Pennsylvania and the disestablishmentarians of Rhode Island were persuaded to act on Lockean principles. They agreed to preserve the powerful autonomy of their several states, entrench property rights as the requisite of personal liberty, and sharply limit the powers of the federal government. What resulted was a state of states, but it, too, was united by a common loyalty to values, principles and an optimistic materialism. Here, too, the decapitation of personal sovereignty had led to the invention of a fair substitute: the sovereignty of immutable citizens' rights.

The nationalism of 1776 and 1789, in sum, was political, territorial and inclusionary, even though it was also in a special sense xenophobic. Its underlying, unifying principles were not thought to be unique to one people but, rather, of universal applicability, deriving their logic from a new myth of "common sense" or "understanding" that was implicit in the "nature of mankind." These principles were creative both in inventing a community where there had been none and in basing that community on a horizontally egalitarian loyalty system, rather than a vertical, hierarchic one. To the extent it defined itself through enmity to an alien other, that other was not the British (in the case of revolutionary America) or Germans (in the case of revolutionary France). On the contrary, America had strong Whig allies in Britain and the French Revolution found enthusiastic echoes in Frankfurt. The alien other, certainly at first, was not a foreign nation, ethnie or culture, but monarchy, privilege, oppression and inequality of opportunity: the transnational forces ranged against the American and, far more, the French Revolutions.

If this sort of self-identification was a far cry from that of the people in Tudor, Stuart and even early Hannoverian England or Bourbon France, it was a farther one from the twentieth-century nationalisms of Hitler's Germany or the Serbs of Bosnia. Buried deep beneath the later-conceived, illiberal, romantic

contemporary usage of the term nationalism there lie these profoundly different, distinctly antithetical antecedents.

In the nineteenth and early twentieth centuries, the terms nation and nationalism took on new definitions first assigned them in the eighteenth century
by Johann Gottfried Herder, the German romanticist who popularized the idea
of the German Volk. In the words of Professor Hans Kohn:

> Its roots seemed to reach into the dark soil of primitive times and to have
> grown through thousands of hidden channels of unconscious
> development, not in the bright light of rational political ends, but in the
> mysterious womb of the people, deemed to be so much nearer to the
> forces of nature.[26]

Like Jean-Jacques Rousseau, Herder stressed the purity of the instinctive, natural person over the rational, deductive one, thereby creating (if unintention-
ally) the elevation of the group over the individual and of blood and genes over
the intellect. Nature took on quite a different meaning when used in this pan-
theistic way to glorify cultural primitivism and blood origins, as opposed to the
earlier deductive usage of the term to assert the natural rights of individuals to
life, liberty and the pursuit of happiness.

Herder's ideas did not attain much currency until more than a century after his death. Even then, they were more distorted than applied in the unpropi-
tious circumstances of the political collapse of the defeated German, Austro-
Hungarian, Russian and Ottoman Empires. The failure of those crumbling,
decadent regimes to provide nurture to their peoples, together with the inspiration of the French and Russian regicide, unleashed a frantic effort to uncover in
nature a new reference to which loyalty could be directed in the hope of thus
achieving the hitherto unrealized expectation of psychic and material rewards.

Late nineteenth- and twentieth-century romantic nationalism and its tribal
definition of the nation are everywhere evident in the sociopolitical phenomena
dominating the end of the second millennium. When we now speak of the nation, we must do so in the realization that it is the German romantic, not the
American or French liberal-rationalist, idea that has carried the day, both lexi-
cally and politically. No amount of demythologization of ethnic theories of pure
nations prevents some of the world's peoples from seeking to organize around
febrile Fichtean myths of consanguinity. In popular parlance, America is only a
state, Germany a nation (which also, after a hiatus, was again able to regain
statehood). But whatever fragmentation and suppression the German nation-
state may have endured after its defeat in 1945, its people never for a moment
ceased to think of themselves as a nation. The powerful pull of loyalty exerted
by the imagined nation demonstrates that, even in the age of science, a loyalty
system based on romantic myths of shared history and kinship has a capacity to

endure that may be the envy of a state with the most liberal civil society and patriotic citizenry.

At the end of the twentieth century, tenacious loyalty to tribe and the ethnic nation has clearly endured. This phenomenon has had to be accommodated in the vocabulary of identity definition. It deserves a term that does not cause it to be confused with loyalty to the liberal civil society or with patriotism directed at a multiethnic secular state. This tribal nationalism, however, while still resilient, has not triumphed over other loyalty systems, which also endure.

The modern state continues to generate the loyalty of patriotic adherence to civil society born in the American and French Revolutions. At the end of the twentieth century, moreover, still another concept of loyalty is emerging, another kind of self-identification, a new notion of community. Transnational loyalties are reappearing and multiple loyalties are once again being tolerated. To the traditional transnational references such as churches, "the working class" or the "invisible college of international lawyers" (the guild) are being added such newcomers as the transnational corporation, transnational political parties, and supranational political institutions. Evidence of this new concept can be seen as French, British, Italians and Danes vote to elect their members of the European Parliament, or take property and human rights claims against their own governments to the European Court of Human Rights, or carry their European passports across unguarded national frontiers. In the words of Hedley Bull, in the twentieth century,

> there has been a retreat from the confident assertions, made in the age of Vattel, that the members of international society were states and nations, towards the ambiguity and imprecision on this point that characterized the era of Grotius. The state as a bearer of rights and duties, legal and moral, in international society today is widely thought to be joined by international organizations, by non-state groups of various kinds operating across frontiers, and—as implied by the Nuremberg and Tokyo War Crimes Tribunals, and by the Universal Declaration of Human Rights—by individuals.[27]

This new layered loyalty directed by persons to multiple loyalty references is not confined to the unification movement in Europe. Something comparable is evident in the sight of troops, police and election monitors from a dozen states of North and South America patrolling Haiti's, Nicaragua's and El Salvador's stumbling efforts to conform to agreed hemispheric standards of democracy. A new ethos is expected of the six thousand civil servants of the United Nations who, by Article 100 of the UN Charter, are required to give primary loyalty to the United Nations system.[28] The seventy thousand UN blue helmets recently deployed around the world are national contingents, but they operate under the

Secretary-General's command. Daily they manifest the potential and the perils of layered loyalty. Increasingly, individuals from many states and ethnie are seeking and receiving spiritual and material nurture from transnational sources; and this is causing them to redefine themselves by reference to a more complex loyalty system.

2. Exclusive/Inclusive Loyalty Compacts.
What does this latest transformation of loyalty patterns portend? Are we on the verge of a new stage of human evolution in which loyalty to the state is transformed into a higher loyalty to humanity, symbolized by global (or regional) institutions of government, commerce, education and communications? There is some evidence that we are. Global communications, the emergence of English as a worldwide lingua franca, the personal career mobility and information networks created by transnational corporations, the common humanitarian endeavors of global organizations (e.g., peacekeeping, malaria eradication, ozone protection) and the codification of universal codes of rights and duties are nurturing some persons' fledgling identification with a common humanity. This emergence of transnational loyalty references is as functionally inevitable today as the emergence of liberal states in direct response to the dictates of industrial revolution and overseas expansions in the late eighteenth century. Now, as then, new challenges require new social formations. In many areas of endeavor—commerce, defense, environmental protection, health, entertainment, education—human needs and wants cannot any longer be satisfied by, or in, the state alone. Increasingly, as human nurturing is provided by transnational institutions, some flow of personal loyalty in that direction will also come to seem "natural." Adam and Eve will be rediscovered and the sin of a humanity divided will be redeemed. Well, maybe.

Whatever its prospects now, the current development of transnational cultures, politics and loyalties has long been foreseen by prescient observers of social evolution. Kant, writing in late eighteenth-century Prussia, foresaw a universal world order based on law in a cosmopolitan and universal republican federation of liberal states. He rejoiced in the coming of the Weltbürger—citizens of the world—and railed against "the demand of fools in Germany for national pride." Kant's disciple Friedrich Schiller (1759–1805) dramatized his mentor's idea of Weltbürgertum (world citizenry), adding *allgemeine Menschenliebe* (general love of humanity) as the personal loyalty appropriate to post-Enlightenment civilization. This is restated with great passion in Schiller's "Ode to Joy," which, set to music by Beethoven in his Ninth Symphony, has now emerged from the concert hall to become the European national anthem. That such passionate longing for a new universalist loyalty to world citizenry and institutions, united in pursuit of liberty and freedom, should have been the central intellectual pursuit of eighteenth-century Germany's greatest philosopher and leading playwright starkly indicates the provenance of the idea of the long-awaited global loyalty system. Truly remarkable is only the costly and prolonged delay in giving the idea any political impetus.

IV. IDENTITY AS A PERSONAL ACT OF SELF-DETERMINATION

A. Multiple Loyalty References

Undoubtedly, new multilayered loyalty references are emerging, perceived both as natural and as nurturing. Yet any analysis concluding that Kant's vision has at last been implemented fails sufficiently to take into account countervailing evidence: the resurgence of rampant tribal nationalisms in Europe and in African-Asian lands after decolonization and the fall of communism. A celebration of triumphant Kantian humanism would also ignore the continuing evident vitality of the still-powerful, still-entrenched state system. In the words of Hedley Bull, "It would be going beyond the evidence to conclude that 'groups other than the state' have made such inroads on the sovereignty of states that the states system is now giving way. . . ."[29] Now, even more than in Kant's Prussia, it is primarily the state that collects taxes, provides education, licenses the professions, regulates commerce, polices the streets, and cares for the sick and hungry. Loyalty to the nurturing state is still an eminently logical fact of life, still considered "natural" except in those instances where the state fails to deliver.

A balanced view of tendencies at the end of the twentieth century reveals that powerful centripetal and centrifugal loyalties coexist with resilient statist patriotism. In this era, loyalty is likely to be perceived as less like a dollar to be bet on one's favorite racehorse, than a handful of birdseed to be distributed among several feeding stations. Thus, a person may be, to some degree, loyal to one's state, ethnic group, race, religion, city, business firm or professional association and family. One may feel loyalty to secret associations such as the Masons or Opus Dei, as well to local or transnational ideological formations such as the "Third International" and Christian Democracy. Some may even experience pulls of loyalty to the United Nations, the International Red Cross or the cause of Amnesty International or the Greenpeace movement.

Multiple loyalty, like much else in this essay, is not especially remarkable. As we have seen, it has been the rule rather than the exception in Western civilization. Each of the great empires tolerated it to some degree. Bull terms this "a structure of overlapping authorities and criss-crossing loyalties."[30] What is remarkable is the extent to which a person's loyalty system today, for the first time in history, has become a matter of personal choice. In the early Mediterranean empires, as also in the more recent Ottoman and Habsburg Empires, multiple loyalty references were the rule, rather than the exception: but these loyalties were imposed on persons by virtue of who they were and where they lived. They were not freely chosen.

. . . Except during the latter part of the nineteenth and most of the twentieth centuries, it was normal for persons thus to define themselves by multiple loyalties: the seventeenth-century Munich householder was a Bavarian loyal to his king, but he was also a subject of the Holy Roman emperor, a faithful communicant of the church of Rome, and someone who might dimly identify with "the Germanic peoples." Only rarely did this multiplicity pose a quandary, and ordinarily only as regards the loyalty of an unfortunate member of the elite who, like Lord Chancellor Sir Thomas More of England, had to choose personally between King Henry VIII and the Bishop of Rome at a moment when they were on a collision course. Normally, the need to make such difficult choices was obviated by external realities: persons' loyalty was, quite simply, dictated by where they lived, what religion their liege lord practiced, the language their family spoke at home, the education they had received, the career they followed—and all these usually stood in a hierarchic harmony, a harmony achieved by the utter surrender of free will in matters of personal identity.

B. Multiple Citizenship
In the latter half of the twentieth century, this free will has been claimed by citizens, the right to create their own identities on the basis of personal choice and commitment.

The response of a legal system to a citizen's claim to "dual nationality" is an excellent indicator of that society's tolerance not merely for multiple loyalty but for the right of individuals to choose their affiliations. In many countries, most notably the United States, this response has shifted radically.

[Franck enters into a detailed discussion here of citizenship and dual nationality in the United States and other Western countries—eds.]

Most western European states, as well as Canada, New Zealand and the United States, now permit multiple nationality, which is symbolic of a new tolerance for an individual's "layered" loyalty and identity. Certainly, dual nationality is still far from universally applauded. However, even where attitudes have traditionally been wholly negative, they appear to be changing and these changes respond to a change in political attitudes and social values. The Council of Europe's Convention on the Reduction of Cases of Multiple Nationality and Military Obligations in Cases of Multiple Nationality, for example, was recently amended by a protocol that repeals earlier prohibitions on dual nationality. It allows the parties to provide that nationality of origin may be retained where a person "acquires the nationality of another Contracting Party on whose territory either he was born and is resident, or has been ordinarily resident for a period of time beginning before the age of 18," or "in cases of marriage," or where the "parents are nationals of different Contracting Parties."[31]

As we have seen, a relaxed attitude to layered loyalty is not new, but when it occurred in the past it was *imposed*, not *chosen* by the individual subject. Today, there is a conscious shift in attitude, reflected in citizenship law, that makes it acceptable, betimes even admirable, for the individual (or, for that matter, the corporation) to design a complex identity expressive of values and preferences transcending monolithic loyalty to only one political or ethnic community. As Professor George Fletcher has observed, "We typically find ourselves in a set of intersecting circles of loyalty commitment. In the United States and indeed in virtually every modern culture, we are . . . caught in the intersection of at least a half-dozen circles of loyal attachment."[32] That this is normal, and that it may even be useful to mitigate the simplistically stark boundaries between unilinear loyalty systems of "nations" and "peoples," is being recognized in various legal systems' search for a new accommodation with the concept of dual or multiple nationality.

V. CONCLUSIONS

For some, the growing internationalism of recent years has provoked anomie, xenophobia, a white-knuckled clinging to the flotsam and jetsam of identity that floats to the surface whenever a ship of state founders. Oddly, too, the international system, by reserving status, voice and rewards only for those ethnie and tribes that have achieved statehood, further conduces to virulent secessionist nationalism. With the crumbling of empires and the emergence of immature democracy, ancient blood feuds and tribal hatreds have been unleashed by unscrupulous politicians to aggrandize themselves. Some hope or fear that this is a trend: back to the future.

Others, however, see a quiet tide running in the opposite direction: a tendency toward a newly assertive global claim to personal self-determination, a growing trend toward autochthonous self-identification, an opening up of yet-unbroached possibilities of layered and textured loyalties. It is at least possible that such an invitation to self-definition and self-realization may soon be widely and enthusiastically accepted. It is conceivable that many, in future, actually will shed the drab single-hued identities deterministically front-loaded onto their lives by the accidents and myths of birth and blood.

This does not mean that persons are about to become more self-sufficient, individualistic or atomistic in relation to others. The need for community appears to be as strong as ever, even among those who sit at home, alone, night after night, surfing the Internet. The trend toward self-identification does suggest, however, that some significant and growing part of humanity is seeking community with others based on commonalities that are neither genetic nor territorial. It may also be that the right to personal self-determination will at first be exercised primarily by professional, commercial or intellectual elites, small in number but wielding disproportionate influence on the way society and identity are structured and defined.

Already, states see public uses for their citizens' layered loyalties. In an increasingly interdependent world, these personal ties often are eagerly exploited by foreign offices, businesses, educational institutions, churches and the communications industry. The fact that, in 1996, the Foreign Minister of Bosnia also happened to be an American citizen, if it raised eyebrows, did so in subtle appreciation of its potentially beneficial implications. Citizen Paine redux![33] But whereas Paine was an exceptional phenomenon, the multiple national today is becoming quite ordinary. Even where formal citizenship is not involved, there may be multiple loyalty: it is no longer considered derisory for American citizens to be involved in representing and promoting before Congress or the State Department the parochial interests of Ireland, Israel or South Africa as states to which, in addition to their loyalty to America, they feel a special attachment.

Transnational corporations, too, openly distribute their loyalty among the various countries in which they strive to operate as good citizens. To help them, the states in which they are incorporated, headquartered or owned adopt laws that accommodate such multiple loyalty, for example, not only by encouraging Rupert Murdoch to change—or add to—his citizenships to suit his worldwide business convenience, but by seeking to create rules to mitigate conflict between various state regulatory and taxation regimes.

What is new about all this, in sum, is not the reemergence—and tolerance—of multiple loyalty references, but the acceptance of a right of persons (and other entities, including transnational corporations) to compose their own identity by constructing the complex of loyalty references that best manifest who they want to be. In that sense, we have entered an era of freely imagined identities, one in which personal choice is no longer circumscribed by accidents or manipulations of genetics, class, place or history. Individuals may opt to delegate their new legal and social empowerment to some single, "natural" objective imperative: their parents' religion, their place of birth, their social or professional caste. But they need not do so: increasingly, by national law and international usage, they are being freed to design their own identities. It is an awesome responsibility, the ultimate freedom, and a promising reconfiguration of the internal dynamics of the international system.

NOTES

1. An excellent example of this dialogue between liberal nationalists and transnational regime theorists is found in Foreign Affairs. Michael Lind, *In Defense of Liberal Nationalism*, FOREIGN AFF., May/June 1994, at 87; and Gidon Gottlieb, *Nations Without States*, id. at 100.
2. For a discussion of "ethnie," see Anthony D. Smith, THE ETHNIC ORIGINS OF NATIONS (1986).
3. G.W.F. Hegel, LECTURES ON THE PHILOSOPHY OF WORLD HISTORY 134 (H. B. Nisbet trans., 1975).
4. Ernest Gellner, NATIONS AND NATIONALISM 49 (1983).
5. E.J. Hobsbawm, NATIONS AND NATIONALISM SINCE 1780 3 (2d ed. 1990).
6. See John A. Armstrong, NATIONS BEFORE NATIONALISM 4, 284 (1982).
7. Gellner, *supra* note 4, at 48.
8. John Maynard Keynes, *A Revision of the Treaty*, reprinted in 3 THE COLLECTED WRITINGS OF JOHN MAYNARD KEYNES 1, 8 (D. Moggridge ed., 1972).

9. See, e.g., Nathaniel Berman, *"But the Alternative Is Despair": European Nationalism and the Modernist Renewal of International Law*, 106 HARV. L. REV. 1792 (1993); Nathaniel Berman, *Modernism, Nationalism, and the Rhetoric of Reconstruction*, 4 YALE J.L. & HUMAN. 351 (1992); Nathaniel Berman, *A Perilous Ambivalence: Nationalist Desire, Legal Autonomy, and the Limits of the Interwar Framework*, 33 HARV. INT'L L.J. 353 (1992).

10. G.W.F. Hegel, PHILOSOPHY OF RIGHT 213 (T. M. Knox trans., 1942) (1821).

11. *Id.* at 211–12.

12. John A. Hall, *Nationalism: Classified and Explained*, DAEDALUS, Summer 1993, at 1, 4.

13. Linda Colley, BRITONS 5 (1992).

14. Philip Allott, *The International Court and the Voice of Justice*, in FIFTY YEARS OF THE INTERNATIONAL COURT OF JUSTICE 17, 19–20 (Vaughan Lowe & Malgosia Fitzmaurice eds., 1995).

15. Hobsbawm, *supra* note 5, at 6.

16. Benedict Anderson, IMAGINED COMMUNITIES 163 (rev. ed. 1991).

17. Ernest Gellner, CONDITIONS OF LIBERTY: CIVIL SOCIETY AND ITS REVIVAL (1994).

18. Gellner, *supra* note 4, at 13.

19. Hobsbawm, *supra* note 5, at 11.

20. Colley, *supra* note 13, at 6.

21. Bernard Lewis, THE EMERGENCE OF MODERN TURKEY 2 (1961).

22. *Id.* at 15.

23. E.J. Hobsbawm, THE AGE OF REVOLUTION: 1789–1848, at 166 (1962).

24. Quoted in Hugh Seton-Watson, NATIONS AND STATES 107 (1977).

25. Immanuel Kant, *On Perpetual Peace*, in KANT'S POLITICAL WRITINGS 105 (Hans Reiss ed., 1970) (1795).

26. Hans Kohn, THE IDEA OF NATIONALISM: A STUDY OF ITS ORIGINS AND BACKGROUND 331 (1944).

27. Hedley Bull, THE ANARCHICAL SOCIETY—A STUDY OF ORDER IN WORLD POLITICS 39 (1977).

28. In the *Bernadotte* case, the International Court of Justice recognized that the United Nations must have legal standing to pursue claims on behalf of its Secretariat's personnel, so that individual civil servants will not need to look to their states of citizenship for protection of their interests. Reparation for injuries suffered in the service of the United Nations, 1949 ICJ REP. 174 (Advisory Opinion of Apr. 11).

29. Bull, *supra* note 27, at 275.

30. *Id.* at 255.

31. Second Protocol amending the Convention on the Reduction of Cases of Multiple Nationality and Military Obligations in Cases of Multiple Nationality, Nov. 2, 1993, paras. 5–7, amending Art. 1, Eur. TS No. 149. The Protocol amends Eur. TS No. 43, June 5, 1963.

32. George P. Fletcher, LOYALTY 155 (1993).

33. Paine had, betimes, English, American and French citizenship and, after the Polish revolution of 1791, considered also applying for Polish citizenship. John Keane, TOM PAINE: A POLITICAL LIFE 446 (1995).

PART I
The Rise of Nations

Part I: Introduction

AT THE DAWN of the twenty-first century, the international salience of national groups can scarcely be doubted. It was not always this way, of course. On the contrary: In the story of the international system's evolution—a nonlinear, discontinuous history arguably commencing with the Peace of Westphalia—"nations" figure only modestly for the first two and a half centuries.

The essays featured here jointly recount the "rise of nations" story. Each contribution to Part I has its own particular substantive concentration and employs a distinct scholarly approach to the study of international rules.[1] All share the fundamental view, however, that international law reflects a dynamic social/historical context, though the essays express this thesis with different disciplinary vocabulary.

In "The Nation Neglected: The Organization of International Life in the Classical State Sovereignty Period," Michael Ross Fowler and Julie Marie Bunck focus on the state system(s) of the 1814–1914 period. In an analysis typical of International Relations' "English School,"[2] they argue that the century between the Congress of Vienna's opening and World War I's outbreak "proved a watershed era in delineating sovereignty's chief entitlements and responsibilities and in refining sovereignty's implications and exposing its limitations." They contend, further, that "the manner in which these fundamental issues regarding law and power were answered formed patterns that remain useful in explaining how similar issues have been approached in more recent times." A central theme of Fowler and Bunck's survey of the age of imperialism is that Europeans applied ambiguous criteria then for the attainment of "sovereign" status. In deciding who might join their "Eurocentric club," state leaders were particularly driven by economic, military and political factors and the desire for international stability. Considerations of nation and nationality, thus, were routinely subordinated to statist ones.

Like that of Fowler and Bunck, the essay of J. Samuel Barkin and Bruce Cronin reflects an appreciation of the social dimensions of international politics and a view that various "understandings of sovereignty" have obtained over time. It differs, however, among other things, in its theoretical approach, Constructivist,[3] and its broader historical attention: the periods after the Napoleonic Wars, World War I, World War II, and the Cold War. Barkin and Cronin contend that a historical tension has existed between two interpretations of sovereignty and its rules: "*state sovereignty*, which stresses the link between sovereign authority and a defined territory, and *national sovereignty*, which emphasizes a link between sovereign authority and a defined population." These two understandings, they suggest, differ fundamentally "in the source of their legitimation as independent entities," thereby changing the environment in which states interact. In eras like the post–Napoleonic order when state sovereignty has prevailed, nationalist claims have been subordinated to the preservation of "stable, effective states with strong institutions." Conversely, during periods such as that after World War I when sovereign "legitimation derives primarily from nationalist principles," states have supported changes in territorial borders to reflect better the national self-determination principle. Though it has much in common with that of Fowler and Bunck, the Barkin and Cronin interpretation arguably portrays greater historical variability in sovereignty understandings.

Robert J. Beck's essay concentrates on a far narrower time frame than do Part I's first two selections. In "Britain and the 1933 Refugee Convention," Beck traces the evolution of British policy toward the first multilateral treaty designed to protect refugees: the October 28, 1933, Convention Relating to the International Status of Refugees. Drawing on the Barkin and Cronin distinction between national and state sovereignty, Beck uses archival evidence to show how a "state sovereignty" understanding framed the British decision not to participate in drafting the treaty but also those decisions later to sign and to ratify the formal agreement. Here, he offers an empirical challenge to Barkin and Cronin's national sovereignty depiction of the post–World War I period. In interwar Britain's refugee policy deliberations, at least, Beck finds national sovereignty considerations to have been "conspicuously absent."

In Part I's final selection, Nathaniel Berman argues that the "international law of nationalism" is historically contingent.[4] Understandings of both international authority and the protagonists of nationalist conflict, he posits, have changed over time. So, too, have understandings changed of the *relationship* between international authority in its various incarnations and the nationalist protagonists in their protean forms. Such changed understandings, Berman submits, have reflected shifting and contestable "cultural projections" emanating from the centers of international power, as well as the acceptance, rejection, or reappropriation of these cultural projections by the parties in conflict. For example, in different situations, such distinctions as those between "nation" and "minority," "civilized" and "uncivilized," and "European" and "non-European," have been construed and applied by international authority in consequentially disparate ways. Berman thus depicts a discontinuous history—a story featuring multiple international communities and nationalisms. This heterogeneity, he contends, is obscured by conventional accounts of doctrinal or institutional progress. Berman traces five major incarnations of the international law of nationalism—from pre–World War I until post-1989. He concludes that it is impossible to devise a "neutral approach innocent of differential cultural projections and unimplicated in the partisan imposition of power."[5] Whether or not one accepts Berman's methodology, his analysis merits the close attention of scholars and policymakers.

NOTES

1. On the scholarship of "international rules," see Robert J. Beck, Anthony Clark Arend, and Robert Vander Lugt, eds., *International Rules: Approaches from International Law and International Relations* (Oxford: Oxford University Press, 1996); and Anthony Clark Arend, *Legal Rules and International Society* (Oxford: Oxford University Press, 1999).

2. Focusing on "state systems" (i.e., "systems of states" or "international systems"), the "English School" of the International Relations discipline emphasizes the social nature and implications of international politics, and thus, the potentially significant role played by international rules and institutions in fostering order. Among the first generation of English School scholars are Hedley Bull, Herbert Butterfield, and Martin Wight. Scholars disagree whether or not to include C.A.W. (Charles) Manning and E.H. Carr as founding fathers. Prominent second generation scholars of the English School include James Mayall and Alan James. Tim Dunne and Ole Wæver are notable young "ES" scholars.

    Representative works that address the international system's historical evolution include: Hedley Bull, *The Anarchical Society* (New York: Columbia University Press, 1977); Hedley Bull and Adam Watson, eds., *The Expansion of International Society* (Oxford: Clarendon Press, 1984); C.A.W. Manning, *The Nature of International Society* (London: LSE, 1962; 2nd edition, London: Macmillan, 1975); James Mayall, *Nationalism and International Society* (Cambridge: Cambridge University Press, 1990); and Adam Watson, *The Evolution of International Society: A Comparative Analysis* (New York: Routledge, 1992).

    Recent noteworthy works on the English School include: Kai Alderson and Andrew Hurrell, eds., *Hedley Bull on International Society* (London: Macmillan, 2000); Barry Buzan, "From International System to International Society: Structural Realism and Regime Theory Meet the English School," *International Organization* 47 (1993): 327–52; Tony Evans and Peter Wilson, "Regime Theory and the English School of International Relations: A Comparison," *Millennium: Journal of International Studies* 21 (1992): 329–51; Rick Fawn and Jeremy Larkin, eds., *International Society After the Cold War* (London: Macmillan, 1996); Alan James, "System or Society," *Review of International Studies* 19 (1993): 269–88; B.A. Roberson, ed., *International Society and the Development of International Relations Theory* (London: Pinter, 1998); Martin Shaw, "Global Society and Global Responsibility: The Theoretical, Historical and Political Limits of 'International Society,' " *Millennium: Journal of International Studies* 21 (1992): 421–34; and Ole Wæver, "Four Meanings of International Society: A Trans-Atlantic Dialogue," in Roberson, ed., *International Society and the Development of International Relations Theory*.

    For an excellent bibliographic compilation on the English School, see: http://www.ukc.ac.uk/politics/englishschool/bibliography.htm

3. Prominent book-length works of Constructivist International Relations scholarship include: Martha Finnemore, *National Interests in International Society* (Ithaca, NY: Cornell University Press, 1996); Peter J. Katzenstein, ed., *The Culture of National Security: Norms*

and Identity in World Politics (New York: Columbia University Press, 1996); Audie Jeanne Klotz, *Norms in International Relations: The Struggle Against Apartheid* (Ithaca, NY: Cornell University Press, 1996); Friedrich Kratochwil, *Rules, Norms, and Decisions: On the Conditions of Practical and Legal Reasoning in International Relations and Domestic Affairs* (Cambridge: Cambridge University Press, 1991); Nicholas Onuf, *World of Our Making: Rules and Rule in Social Theory and International Relations* (Columbia: University of South Carolina Press, 1989); John Gerard Ruggie, *Constructing the World Polity: Essays on International Institutionalization* (London: Routledge, 1998); Jutta Weldes, *Constructing National Interests: The United States and the Cuban Missile Crisis* (Minneapolis: University of Minnesota Press, 1999); and Alexander Wendt, *Social Theory of International Politics* (Cambridge: Cambridge University Press, 1999).

   Among the most useful article-length works: Jeff Checkel, "The Constructivist Turn in International Relations Theory," *World Politics* 50 (1998): 324–48; Martha Finnemore and Kathryn Sikkink, "International Norm Dynamics and Political Change," *International Organization* 52 (1998): 887–918; Nicholas Onuf, "Constructivism: A User's Manual," in *International Relations in a Constructed World* Vendulka Kubalkova, Nicholas Onuf, and Paul Kowert, eds., (London: M.E. Sharpe, 1998), 58–78; John Ruggie, "What Makes the World Hang Together? Neo-Utilitarianism and the Social Constructivist Challenge," *International Organization* 52 (1998): 855–86; and Alexander Wendt, "Anarchy is What States Make of It: The Social Construction of Power Politics," *International Organization*, 46(1992): 391–425.

4. Professor Berman resists attempts to label his scholarship, preferring that it be judged on its substance. Even so, his essay might arguably be categorized as "New Stream" or "Critical" International Law. It shares with such work, *inter alia*: a concentration on legal discourse and the ideational structures that underly such discourse; a concern for "identity" and "authority"; a tendency to focus on "oppositions" or "poles"; and a rejection of law as an objective enterprise.

   On the "New Stream" approach to International Law, see Beck, Arend, and Vander Lugt, eds., *International Rules*, 227–52.

5. Despite this conclusion, Professor Berman embraces faith in law's power to provide a shared discursive and institutional framework for contending nationalists and internationalists in particular contexts.

For Further Reading

Bull, Hedley, and Adam Watson, eds. *The Expansion of International Society*. Oxford: Clarendon Press, 1984.

Buzan, Barry, and Richard Little. *International Systems in World History: Remaking the Study of International Relations*. Oxford: Oxford University Press, 2000.

Emerson, Rupert. *From Empire to Nation: The Rise to Self-Assertion of Asian and African Peoples*. Boston: Beacon Press, 1967.

Ferguson, Yale H., and Richard W. Mansbach. *Polities: Authority, Identities, and Change*. Columbia: University of South Carolina Press, 1996.

Fowler, Michael Ross, and Julie Marie Bunck. *Law, Power, and the Sovereign State: The Evolution and Application of the Concept of Sovereignty*. University Park: Pennsylvania State University Press, 1995.

Hashmi, Sohail H., ed. *State Sovereignty: Change and Persistence in International Relations*. University Park: Pennsylvania State University Press, 1997.

Held, David et al. *Global Transformations: Politics, Economics and Culture*. Stanford, CA: Stanford University Press, 1999.

Hinsley, F.H. *Nationalism and the International System*. London: Hodder and Stoughton, 1973.

Hinsley, F.H. *Sovereignty*. New York: Basic Books, 1966.

Jackson, Robert. *Quasi-States: Sovereignty, International Relations, and the Third World*. Cambridge Studies in International Relations, vol. 12. Cambridge: Cambridge University Press, 1993.

Jackson, Robert H., and Alan James, eds. *States in a Changing World: A Contemporary Analysis.* Oxford: Clarendon Press; New York: Oxford University Press, 1993.

James, Alan. *Sovereign Statehood: The Basis of International Society.* Key Concepts in International Relations, no. 2. London; Boston: Allen & Unwin, 1986.

Krasner, Stephen D. *Sovereignty: Organized Hypocrisy.* Princeton, NJ: Princeton University Press, 1999.

Mayall, James. *Nationalism and International Society.* Cambridge: Cambridge University Press, 1990.

Sakamoto, Yoshikazu, ed. *Global Transformation: Challenges to the State System.* Tokyo: United Nations University Press, 1994.

Sellers, Mortimer, ed. *The New World Order: Sovereignty, Human Rights, and the Self-Determination of Peoples.* Washington, DC: Berg, 1996.

Shinoda, Hideaki. *Re-Examining Sovereignty: from Classical Theory to the Global Age.* Basingstoke: Macmillan, 2000.

Smith, Tony. *The Pattern of Imperialism: The United States, Great Britain, and the Late-Industrializing World Since 1815.* Cambridge: Cambridge University Press, 1981.

Spruyt, Hendrik. *The Sovereign State and Its Competitors: An Analysis of Systems Change.* Princeton, NJ: Princeton University Press, 1994.

Watson, Adam. *The Evolution of International Society: A Comparative Analysis.* New York: Routledge, 1992.

The Nation Neglected: The Organization of International Life in the Classical State Sovereignty Period

Michael Ross Fowler and Julie Marie Bunck

THE FRENCH *SOUVERAIN* and English derivative *sovereignty*[1] initially referred to a ruler's supremacy over other possible authorities within a society. European monarchs trumpeted their domestic, or internal, sovereignty to counter potential competing claims to their subjects' allegiance by the nobility, their royal rivals, and on occasion the church. Later, representative governments co-opted a term that had originally connoted a ruler's absolute supremacy in order to assert the broad powers that their citizens had delegated to them.[2] And, whatever the form of political regime, declarations of internal sovereignty in multination states frequently served to warn national minorities that a central authority stood prepared to defend the state against subversion, secession, and revolution.[3]

Eighteenth-century Europeans started to use sovereignty in an external sense as well. Unlike the political development of civilizations in Asia, the Americas, and the Middle East, a multiplicity of European nationalities had, since the Roman Empire, preserved differing levels of independence by gaining access to new military technologies such that no one power could subjugate the rest.[4] Thus, while European boundaries regularly shifted and the fortunes of Europe's particular power centers waxed and waned, the efforts of various leaders to unify the continent consistently failed as countervailing power was brought together against the state with European imperial pretensions.[5]

As contacts between their variegated political communities increased in frequency and complexity, Europeans began referring to sovereignty when focusing on two matters: the relative independence of one European polity interacting with others and the absence of any greater human authority over and above that of the state. A sovereign state was generally thought to be able to make its own decisions about vital domestic and international affairs, at least in the sense that no other political community had official authority over it.[6] In this way the new notion of external sovereignty came to coexist with the older conception of internal sovereignty.[7]

During the nineteenth century the growth of British, French, Spanish, Dutch, Portuguese, German, and Belgian colonial empires through Asia, the Middle East, and eventually Africa forcibly brought large swaths of the globe into subservient relations with the Western world.[8] However, Europeans also succeeded in a distinct venture: having their own quite singular and avowedly statist system of international relations adopted by the rest of the world. While imperial conquest played an important part in extending the European international system, it was by no means the only factor. Various significant political communities in Asia, the Middle East, and the Americas were either never colonized by Europeans or successfully overthrew such colonization. And, these polities, too, eventually took their places as recognized sovereign states within the Eurocentric international system.

Throughout this period Europeans regularly subordinated the position of nations[9] to that of states.[10] This was in large part a consequence of European political development and the sheer numbers of European nationalities. In the mid-nineteenth century, for instance, the Austrian state alone included Germans, Poles, Italians, Croats, Serbs, Rumanians, Slovenes, Magyars, Ruthenians, Czechs, and Slovaks. Thus, to the extent that nineteenth-century European leaders focused on such a disturbing prospect, the notion that each of their nationalities might attempt to gain its own state raised visions of truly extravagant political fragmentation.

Indeed, the potential loss of power by the leaders of dominant nations within multination states was very likely to bring about fierce resistance and considerable instability and economic dislocation. If leaders of multination states would not willingly countenance such a radical reorganization of European political life, their governments were similarly disinclined to encourage such notions in other regions of the world. Hence, Europeans naturally preferred to export a statist, rather than a nationalist, organizing model for international affairs.

As Europe became the veritable pivot of international relations, references to the external sovereignty of states multiplied. And, the extensive use of the term raised certain significant theoretical questions, questions that the international community would continue to grapple with during the twentieth century. For instance, just what constitutes the sovereign state? That is, what criteria would political communities have to meet in order to become recognized sovereigns? Further, just what does sovereign status confer? That is, under what circumstances and in what manner would sovereign status assist a state, and when would it prove ineffectual?

The 1814–1914 period, which might be termed an era of classical state sovereignty, witnessed the international community's repeated and conspicuous subordination of nation and nationality considerations to those of states and sovereign governments. Indeed, it is our contention that the one hundred years between the opening of the Congress of Vienna and the outbreak of the First World War, apart from being an age of imperialism, proved a watershed era in delineating the chief entitlements and responsibilities of sovereignty and in refining its implications and exposing its limitations. Furthermore, the manner in which these fundamental issues regarding law and power were answered formed patterns that remain useful in explaining how similar issues have been approached in more recent times.

I. GAINING SOVEREIGN STATUS

In 1800 four principal systems of states dominated the conduct of international affairs: the Chinese, European, Indian, and Islamic.[11] In a system of states the states are sufficiently linked that, as one source puts it, "the behavior of each [has] to factor into the political calculations of the others."[12] In fact, the globe was already too small and human endeavors too great for these systems to function wholly separately. The Ottoman Empire, for instance, had been a significant ally, rival, and trading partner of Western states for generations, and at the zenith of its power had authority over almost a third of the European continent.[13]

Nonetheless, compared with its chief rivals, the European system was unique. Although the corpus of international law was substantially smaller than today, by 1800 Western leaders had accepted that the sovereign members of their Eurocentric statist society were separate and juridically equal units[14] and had started to promulgate laws regarding war, the seas, treaty-making, and diplomatic privileges and immunities. It is notable as well that European governments attempted to manage their international affairs via reciprocal diplomatic dealings. While temporary assignments were the essence of diplomacy elsewhere, the Europeans established permanent missions in one another's capitals. This, too, helped to transform Europe, in Emmerich de Vattel's phrase, from a "heap of detached parts" into a political system.[15]

On account of the singular development of political relations on the continent, sovereign statehood and sovereign equality, international law and diplomatic reciprocity, became central features of the European conduct of international affairs alone. In contrast, those in charge of the traditional fulcrums of the other systems tended to view their states as the centers of potentially unlimited political universes.[16] Not only were the other polities in their systems thought to be gravitating about the focal point of greatest power and civilization, but all peoples beyond their systems were presumed to belong to lesser communities, to be resisted and, it was hoped, subsumed before their corrupting influence spread too far.

And yet, the same centralized authority that made the Chinese, Turks, and Indians appear formidable in comparison with decentralized Europe also brought, as one historian noted, "a uniformity of belief and practice, not only in official state religion but also in such areas as commercial activities and weapons development. . . . Possessing fewer obstacles to change, European societies entered into a constantly upward spiral of economic growth and enhanced military effectiveness which, over time, was to carry them ahead of all other regions of the globe."[17]

Well before the outbreak of the First World War the European system of sovereign states had decisively overwhelmed its rivals. Not only had a global economy coalesced, largely dependent on European centers of international trade and finance, but alternative systems of states had plainly faded in relevance. The Ottoman Empire had been thoroughly dismantled. Britain's imperial grip on India had tightened. And, the Western community of states had forced China and Japan, which both had been pursuing policies of seclusion a hundred years earlier, to open themselves to foreign trade.[18] At length, each joined the European system, and by the outset of the twentieth century the Japanese had gained general recognition not only as a power to contend with in Asia but as a "civilized," or perhaps more accurately "Europeanized," nation.

In this way a global international system had started to take shape on the European model, molding together the regional congeries of states that had hitherto existed.[19] Indeed, by 1914 the shape of the global society that would definitively supplant the international system of states after the Second World War was plainly visible. That is, states had begun to "establish by dialogue and consent common rules and institutions for the conduct of their relations, and [to] recognize their common interest in maintaining these arrangements."[20]

That this was an era of tremendous European expansion, stimulated by its industrial revolution, military strength, imperialist doctrines, and prolific birth rates, is thus of transcendent importance.[21] While in the first quarter of the century the United States consolidated itself, and the Spanish Empire in Latin America and the Caribbean dissolved, the resulting "European settler states" generally underscored, rather than threatened, European primacy in international affairs.[22] So, too, did the growth of westernized political elites in many non-European communities later in the century.[23]

Of course, gaining sovereign statehood and a recognized place in the European international system was never a prerequisite for participating in international relations with Europeans. In order to advance their commercial and other interests, European governments (and trading companies acting, more or less, on their behalf) had long been willing to negotiate formal agreements with many different political entities without regard to such early twentieth-century concepts as legal personality and the formal criteria of statehood.[24] Indeed, for generations European states had negotiated treaties and other agreements with various rulers in India, such as the Rajah of Assam and the Nizam of Hyderabad, and with tribes in Africa,[25] the Americas, and the East Indies.[26]

Nevertheless, as the nineteenth century progressed, the recognition by Europeans of the status of non-Europeans as sovereign states was an important step toward more complete participation by non-Europeans in what remained in important respects a Eurocentric international system. Hence, the non-Western world did not typically resist gaining sovereign statehood. Rather, from the nineteenth century forward it tended to embrace sovereignty eagerly, with particular passion during twentieth-century decolonization.

This was in part a consequence of the fact that the intense nationalism that so marked nineteenth-century Europe was by no means wholly confined to Britain and the continent. And, aspirations to advance the national cause, either by independence or by unification, eventually led political communities inside and outside Europe toward the goal of sovereign statehood and, hence, toward greater participation in international society.

In this regard, non-Westerners readily discerned that their state's interests could be promoted, if often in a defensive manner, by taking part in the Eurocentric system.[27] Various aspects of the expanding law of nations, from neutrality to freedom of the seas to international arbitration, proved attractive to many governments. Agreeing to exchange diplomats and to protect their persons helped Western and non-Western states alike to carry out foreign policies. Non-Europeans also found that respect for an apparently impartial body of international laws could be touted in an effort to persuade reluctant constituents at home that the Europeans were not "lawless barbarians."[28]

Indeed, with time, adopting this European approach to international relations could be turned to the advantage of non-Westerners even more emphatically.[29] As one authority noted, capturing control of sovereign states eventually enabled non-Western polities to combat external dominance, control economic resources, establish relations with foreign states, ally with friends and divide enemies, and expound their views to the outside world.[30] Once recognized as sovereign, states of quite modest influence could exert a strength when combined that they lacked when functioning independently. For all of the above reasons sovereignty and sovereign equality could be conceived as leveling concepts that might, under particular circumstances, benefit the weak against the strong in international affairs.[31]

Furthermore, gaining sovereign status did not frontally assault the divergent value systems of the non-European states. It did not compel the Chinese, Ottomans, Indians, Japanese, and others to renounce whatever superiority they might perceive in domestic social, cultural, and religious matters. Indeed, non-Westerners could hope to use recognition of sovereignty to erect international "No Trespassing" signs to protect diversity, not to threaten it.

Finally, while characteristically striving not to be entangled in distant wars, non-European peoples nonetheless saw considerable advantages in maintaining and cultivating a range of commercial and cultural ties with Britain and the continent.[32] Not only did citizens of various newly independent states, particularly in the Americas, frequently have strong ethnic or religious ties with Europe, but consumers around the globe were interested in Western products. By 1860 the United Kingdom boasted a third of the world's merchant marine. It alone produced half or more of the world's iron and coal and controlled one fifth of international commerce and two fifths of the trade in manufactured goods.[33] By 1913 Britain, Germany, France, the Netherlands, Belgium, and Switzerland accounted for more than half of the world's exports, with the European settler states of the United States, Canada, and Australia accounting for an additional 18.5 percent.[34]

For their part, nineteenth-century Europeans did not simply countenance the recognition of the sovereign status of distant states. Rather, they frequently encouraged it and did so without the discrimination on religious, cultural, or racial grounds that one might have expected to encounter in this age.[35] One important reason that the Europeans embraced the idea of sovereign status for certain non-European political communities was that the term sovereignty, in both its external and internal dimensions, had long connoted duties as well as rights. As Sun Yat-sen, Provisional President of China, declared in 1912: "[W]e will try our best to carry out the duties of a civilized nation so as to obtain the rights of a civilized nation."[36]

Sixteen years later, the eminent Swiss jurist Max Huber wrote: "Territorial sovereignty . . . involves the exclusive right to display the activities of a State. This right has as corollary a duty: the obligation to protect within the territory the rights of other States, in particular their right to integrity and inviolability in peace and war, together with the rights which each State may claim for its nationals in foreign territory."[37] In fact, states that joined the European system were thereupon bound by the principles of international law, even those principles developed before the states had gained independence or otherwise attained sovereign status.[38]

Some Europeans viewed recognition of the sovereign status of non-European states as a natural part of the spread of their civilization. Others saw it in light of the need for rapidly industrializing states to gain stable sources of raw materials and sales outlets for manufactured goods. They believed extending sovereign status to non-European states would benefit commerce, particularly since a state could recognize another as sovereign and nonetheless negotiate extremely favorable, indeed sometimes downright abusive, terms of trade with it. Still other Europeans perceived the chance to ally with newly sovereign states against their Old World rivals.[39] After a disputed assertion of independence, colonists naturally turned to other European powers to counterbalance the military force of the imperial state from which they were trying to secede.[40]

All this suggests that gaining sovereign statehood was emphatically not a product of legal argument before disinterested courts of justice. Rather, politicians and diplomats made decisions about sovereign status with close reference to the economic, military, and political contexts. One consequence was that, as Europeans came to recognize certain non-European societies as sovereigns but not others, it became evident that the criteria for attaining sovereignty were ambiguous. While plainly a sovereign state had to include people, territory, and a government, neither numbers nor size nor type of regime were employed in any systematic manner to distinguish sovereign from nonsovereign political actors.[41]

In particular, sovereign status was not awarded on the basis of the nationalist credentials of a political community. That is, Europeans did not single out particularly unified, or wealthy, or long-lived nations to recognize as sovereign states. Indeed, the characteristics of the populations of those nineteenth-century polities that gained recognition of their sovereignty varied considerably. And, although certain single-nation states, such as Japan,[42] were hailed as recognized sovereign states, the international community more frequently declared multi-nation states to be sovereign. At the Congress of Berlin in 1878, for instance, Romania, Serbia, and Montenegro gained sovereign status after each explicitly agreed to protect the rights of religious minorities.[43]

Furthermore, despite the ancient use of sovereignty to describe domestic political supremacy, sovereign statehood in practice did not hinge on the relative strength of central and local governments. It seemed clear that a state was not going to be recognized as sovereign if its government wholly lacked continuity and the ability to ensure some minimal level of domestic order. However, just how orderly and continuous the government of an aspirant political community had to be in order to gain sovereign status had not been carefully considered, much less resolved, by 1814 or even by 1914.[44]

Indeed, certain nineteenth-century decisions foreshadowed the fact that to date the international community has never applied a very stringent strength-of-government criterion to decisions regarding sovereign status. For example, during the nineteenth century, various influential states recognized Haitian sovereignty even in the midst of exceptional strife even by the standards of that traditionally tumultuous society.[45] Of even greater significance, Western powers intent on trading with China chose not to deny that state's sovereignty despite considerable internal turmoil.

During the nineteenth century, then, Europeans began to organize the international relations of distant polities, though without any special focus on the cohesiveness of particular ethnic groups and certainly without any declaration that every nation had a right to its own state. And, as the European international system expanded at the expense of other systems, it became clear that in order to qualify as a sovereign state in the eyes of Europeans, a political entity had to meet some criterion other than people, territory, and a government. That essential element was related to two different concepts, each of which emerged from state practice in this era:[46] the notions of *de facto* independence and *de jure* independence.

The idea of *de facto* independence was that to attain sovereignty a political entity had to demonstrate some form of internal and external political independence. And, the aspirant state had to assert that independence in practice, not merely claim it.[47] An aspiring sovereign state might thus formally declare its independence and forcibly defy all others who might wish to challenge it. The Americans opened this path, declaring their independence in 1776 and, seven years later, gaining acknowledgment of the defeat of the British challenge. Many other states would follow this approach, though more would do so in the twentieth century than in the nineteenth.

It soon became evident, however, that certain ambiguities complicated the *de facto* independence equation. Some posited that a legitimate authority had to exercise that *de facto* independence. Others reasoned that attempting to assess legitimacy would be ill-advised and advocated using sovereignty simply to describe reality.[48] People also differed on just how *de facto* independent a political entity must be to qualify as sovereign. What about the influence over a state wielded by a great power? Or, how about opposing forces that controlled some portion of a state's territory?

A competing view focusing on *de jure* independence, that is, legal or constitutional independence from other states,[49] thus eventually gained adherents. The *de jure* approach proved particularly useful for assessing situations in which a state was gaining independence in a nonviolent manner. Rather than engage in revolution or secessionist civil war, many political communities took an evolutionary approach to attaining sovereign status. They gradually shed their dependence on a larger power and eventually negotiated a mutually agreeable independent posture, often retaining some formalistic link such as membership in a greater power's commonwealth. In the nineteenth century the Brazilians[50] and Canadians[51] blazed this trail, and it became the most heavily traveled for colonies attaining their independence.[52]

Political entities that gained *de facto* and *de jure* independence were widely recognized as sovereign. However, from time to time a political entity seemed to obtain one but not the other.[53] For instance, despite Japanese efforts to create the sovereign state of Manchukuo in northern Asia, only five states accorded it recognition. Its claim to *de jure* independence failed in the face of a total lack of *de facto* independence.[54]

In the 1814–1914 period a particular entity was thus called sovereign when the international community of the time determined that it had gained, or perhaps regained,[55] sovereign status.[56] That decision came about through a highly politicized process, dominated by the European powers, in which recognized sovereign states opted to treat another state as sovereign on account of its independence from superior authority.[57]

This suggests that the constitutive theory of recognition, the notion that the act of recognition actually "creates" the sovereign state, better describes the European practice in creating an international system in the nineteenth century than the opposing declaratory theory, the notion that recognition merely acknowledges the fact of a state already in existence. Modern international lawyers prefer to think in declaratory terms, in part because the constitutive theory has been roundly denounced as "an instrument of European dominance."[58] Furthermore, there is, as one scholar put it, "an element of absurdity in the claim that states such as China, Egypt, or Persia, which existed thousands of years before states came into being in Europe, achieved rights to full independence only when they came to pass a test devised by nineteenth-century Europeans."[59]

Nonetheless, while extending invitations to a Eurocentric club of sovereign states was neither a wholly logical nor evenhanded approach to managing certain international affairs, it remains a reasonably apt analogy for what actually happened. The nineteenth century saw a European system of states overwhelm alternative systems. In due course European states, and their settler state offshoots, applied the European concept of sovereign statehood to non-Europeans. They did so in a constitutive manner. And, acceptance by other states might be derived from a strong showing of *de jure* independence or *de facto* independence or both. But, ultimately the international community, made up of other recognized sovereign states, decided the point at which a political entity had gained sovereignty.

II. THE CONSEQUENCES OF GAINING SOVEREIGN STATUS

If the method of arriving at sovereign statehood was ambiguous and controversial, so too were the consequences of gaining sovereign status.[60] A key issue in international affairs in the nineteenth and early twentieth centuries was whether sovereignty would be chiefly employed as a legal concept that aimed to provide an identical set of rights and duties to each and every qualified state, or whether its principal use would be as a political idea expressing the extent to which a state was free to make its own decisions about internal and external affairs.[61] These distinct uses of the term *sovereignty* reflected two broad trends in international affairs.

In 1814, after the Russians and British had managed to check the "unbridled sovereignty"[62] of Napoleon, the Congress of Vienna initiated a new era in Europe's management of international affairs. At Vienna the leading states orchestrated what became a continuing series of consultations[63] among themselves aimed at promoting order by discussing and, when possible, resolving both routine and potentially inflammatory affairs on the continent and beyond.[64]

While the Concert of Europe prolonged a conservative status quo and either ignored or sought to bottle up potent forces of nationalism and liberalism, it did succeed in minimizing destructive wars on the continent, with peace prevailing among the strongest powers from 1815 to 1854 and again from 1871 to 1914. And, the Concert was duly sensitive to the relative power of the participants, with the stronger states accepting more responsibilities and seizing more weight in decision making than did their weaker neighbors. One might have supposed, then, that the implications of sovereign statehood within an international system dominated by European powers would also be closely attuned to differing levels of power.

At the same time, however, a legalistic and egalitarian trend in international affairs was also visible. The Congress of Vienna itself stimulated the growth of international law. Not only was the peace settlement considered a single instrument that each signatory could uphold and none was to infringe in whole or in part, but the Congress went on to enunciate rules regarding diplomatic privileges and immunities and free navigation on international rivers. Then, over the course of the nineteenth century European states of great, moderate, and negligible strengths were invited to various of the ensuing congresses.

Equally important, the geographic scope of the participants at international conferences of various stripes steadily expanded.[65] European states alone participated at the Congress of Vienna; however, Ottoman representatives attended the Paris Peace Conference of 1856. In the 1870s Chinese delegates took part in the Universal Postal Union, the International Institute of Agriculture, and the Association for the Reform and Codification of the Law of Nations.[66] The Hague Conference of 1899 brought together European, Ottoman, and Chinese diplomats with those of the United States, Mexico, Japan, Persia, and Siam. By the second Hague conference of 1907, attended by representatives of forty-four states, sixteen Latin American states had joined the deliberations, including Haiti and the Dominican Republic.

As the roster of invitees increased, the principle of sovereign equality, that is, one state, one vote, became established as the procedural norm in international organizations.[67] This strong countercurrent of equality, especially when paired with the spread of democracy and the liberal political tradition, suggested that the meanings of sovereignty might develop in a legalistic and egalitarian manner, rather than one so reliant on power calculations.

Just as the international community was feeling its way toward decisions regarding sovereign status, it also found it necessary to determine how sovereignty ought to be applied, that is, what practical benefits sovereign status conferred on states. A split soon developed between two modes of applying the term. Some people thought of sovereignty as something absolute, that could be won or lost; others took sovereignty to be something variable, that could be augmented or diminished. In metaphorical terms, a chunk approach to sovereignty contrasted with a basket approach.[68]

The chunk theorists conceived of sovereignty as a set of rights and duties that was handed over to duly qualified states in monolithic form, rather like identical chunks of stone. Sovereignty was something a political entity either lacked or fully possessed, and a state, by virtue of its sovereign status, possessed a set of identical rights and obligations. Chunk thinkers conceded that, as a practical matter, what different states could do with their sovereignty was likely to differ dramatically based on circumstances, and power, and the content of the treaties the state had signed.[69] However, the chunk school firmly maintained that sovereign rights and duties did not differ from one state to the next.

In contrast, the basket school did not associate sovereignty with formal juridical equality so much as with degrees of political inequality. Since one state might well be "more sovereign" than another, the term might better be conceived as a basket of attributes. Thus, in 1890 theorist Sir Henry Maine observed: "[T]his indivisibility of sovereignty . . . does not belong to International Law. The powers of sovereigns are a bundle or collection of powers, and they may be separated one from another."[70]

The chunk approach viewed the equality of sovereign states as a statement of Western ideals and the actual practice of states as a secondary matter.[71] In contrast, basket theory focused on how states actually acted when faced with the need to apply the sovereignty concept. This more politicized approach empirically investigated a state's attributes and treated it accordingly. A great power had more in its basket: more sovereign attributes and corresponding entitlements and responsibilities, than did a small, neutral or weak state. The basket thinkers thus conceived of sovereignty as essentially a variable, relative phenomenon and concluded that the sovereignty of states would naturally increase or decrease over time.

As the European international system came to be adopted globally during the nineteenth century, these two uses of sovereignty repeatedly clashed as people tried to apply the concept to actual international problems.[72] Of many possible examples,[73] the use of the term sovereignty with respect to China illustrates these conceptual tensions.

The commercial interests of the European powers and the United States plainly favored encouraging a stable and territorially intact China.[74] Western states long referred to and treated China as a sovereign primarily in order to cultivate these interests, though the size of China's territory and population, its ancient civilization, and its periods of considerable military strength doubtless amounted to secondary factors. Thus, in the nineteenth century the Western states signed treaties with China as a sovereign associate, Chinese diplomats participated in international conferences as representatives of a recognized sovereign state, and Chinese nationals consistently conducted China's foreign relations. Indeed, up until the Opium War with Britain, Chinese rulers even set the conditions on which their people would be permitted contact with Europeans.[75]

Starting with the Treaty of Nanking,[76] however, the Western powers wrested new arrangements from China's rulers, featuring the highly favorable rights to trade and the foreign diplomatic representation that forced China to accept sustained contact with the outside world. Britain acquired Hong Kong to serve as a trading clearinghouse, and all the European powers gained freedom of navigation on inland rivers and the use of five, then fifteen, and eventually sixty-nine designated treaty ports.[77]

When domestic turmoil followed in the "vast and increasingly chaotic Chinese Empire,"[78] threatening these new "Open Door" commercial arrangements, nine stronger foreign powers acted in concert to extract a total of 36 concessions from China. In particular, territories were leased from China in perpetuity to be, in effect, sublet to foreign nationals and fortified and defended by foreign states. Indeed, the terms of the treaties even banned the Chinese from residing in these areas.[79] Eventually, foreign officials went so far as to manage China's low tariffs and its postal service and to exclude foreign nationals from the administration of justice in Chinese courts.

This provoked more internal strife aimed at eliminating the foreign presence "root and branch." In turn, Western powers and Japan[80] forcibly intervened in China once again and in the Boxer Protocol of 1901 gained more exacting protection of the life, liberty, and property of foreigners in China. They also created a new type of right of passage, creating an access zone from Peking to the sea, and banning within it all military forces—even those of China.[81] In the meantime, substantial commerce flowed in and out of China.

The Chinese felt betrayed: China was a sovereign state and yet the chunk of sovereign rights and duties to which the Chinese felt entitled had been withheld in important respects. Hence, Chinese diplomats periodically objected to the Western approach of labeling China sovereign, yet allocating to the Chinese sovereign rights that differed fundamentally from those the Western powers themselves enjoyed. After bowing to Japanese demands in May 1915, Yuan Shih-k'ai, president of the Chinese republic, declared that China's sovereignty had to be "consolidated" by force.[82] Before the Paris Peace Conference concluding the First World War, the Chinese government submitted a position paper stating that "interested Powers . . . out of their sincere regard for the sovereign rights of China" ought to renounce spheres of influence or interest in China and revise all agreements conferring preferential rights and privileges and territorial advantages.[83] When European powers proved unreceptive, China refused to sign the Treaty of Versailles.[84]

According to the dominant interpretation of sovereignty at the time, however, the Chinese had simply been accorded a lesser basket of sovereign rights and duties than those enjoyed by more fully sovereign states. And, in this regard the Chinese had not been singled out. In certain respects China's unequal treaties followed the pattern set by European powers in the earlier treaties of capitulation with the Ottoman Empire.

Indeed, various states signed treaties that not only conferred markedly greater benefits on the stronger party, but that contained provisions that plainly diminished a state's control over its territory, such as providing for extraterritorial jurisdiction for the citizens of the stronger state within the territory of the weaker.[85] In the 1850s Japan experienced its own set of unequal treaties. Then, in 1876 the Japanese ended the seclusion of Korea by imposing a like treaty on the Koreans.[86] Eventually, the Japanese joined in signing unequal treaties with the Chinese.

The effect of the unequal treaties lingered far longer in China than in Japan, however, since the Japanese convinced the international community that Japan had become a civilized nation. Among other important acts, the Japanese had invited outside consultants in a range of subjects, had wholly revamped their legal system, had "meticulously" observed international law in the Sino-Japanese War of 1895, and had actively participated in the suppression of the Boxer Revolution in 1900–1901.[87]

The imposition of unequal treaties and their eventual renegotiation underscores the primacy of basket thinking in the 1814–1914 period. The treaties plainly contemplated the possibility that the state being treated as a lesser sovereign entity might become more sovereign. Once that state was able to carry out additional sovereign duties, stronger states, explicitly or implicitly, promised to accord it additional sovereign rights. For instance, when China's government was sufficiently stable and powerful to be able to secure the rights of foreign nationals, in other words when China had become in that sense more fully sovereign, the troops would no longer be needed to ensure the protection of foreigners. At that point, the forces would be removed.

Similarly, Western powers justified the extraterritorial provisions that excused foreign nationals from China's courts on the grounds that the Chinese administration of justice did not, in substance or procedure, meet the norms of the international community. Whenever China adopted a more civilized legal system, the extraterritorial provisions would become an anachronism. And, in fact, as domestic legal systems developed more complex procedures and more widely accepted principles, Western powers did eliminate extraterritorial provisions vis-à-vis China and other sovereign states.[88]

Reliance on a basket approach to sovereignty can also be seen in the affairs of newly independent countries at the beginning of the twentieth century. After the Spanish-American War brought independence to Cuba, the international community treated the island as sovereign. Nonetheless, the United States oversaw the insertion of the Platt Amendment in the Cuban constitution, restricting Cuba's freedom of action. For instance, the amendment stipulated that Cuba could not contract public debts in sums beyond its revenues and gave the United States the right to intervene to maintain a government adequate to protect life, liberty, and individual property on the island.

Because Cuba lacked certain attributes, a stronger power removed a right commonly associated with fully sovereign states: that of nonintervention in its affairs. Nonetheless, Cuba's peers opted to treat the state as retaining its sovereign status. Again, this suggests that in the early twentieth century the international community, and the United States in particular, treated Cuba as possessing a different brand of sovereignty than that found in more powerful states.

During much the same period Panama agreed in the Hay-Varilla Treaty of 1903 to grant to the United States "in perpetuity" the use, occupation, and control of the Canal Zone, providing the United States within that Zone all the rights, power, and authority that the United States would possess if it were sovereign. In fact, international servitudes of various sorts were consistent with a basket approach to sovereignty and had been recognized as legally binding. That is, a sovereign state might contract for the right to exercise some type of authority for some substantial period within another sovereign's territory.[89] In the eighteenth and nineteenth centuries Western states had created servitudes among themselves dealing with fishing and transit rights, maintaining coal deposits for steamships, and exploiting such natural resources as timber, minerals, and even hay.

However, American control over the Canal Zone seemed of a different order of magnitude and, hence, throughout the twentieth century chunk and basket thinkers clashed over how it ought to be interpreted.[90] One prominent theorist, writing in the chunk tradition, observed: "The actual inequality of states and their dependence upon each other has no relevance for the legal status called sovereignty. Panama is as sovereign a state as the United States, although in the choice of its policies and laws it is much more limited than the United States."[91]

In contrast, basket thinkers found the extent to which Panama depended on American military protection to break away from Colombia to be analytically significant. From the basket perspective, the United States extracted the Canal Zone deal from Panamanians who had no choice but to agree or watch their new state collapse. Hence, the Canal Zone always diminished Panamanian sovereignty since a Great Power scrutinized Panama's basket of sovereign attributes and thereupon compelled a weak, newly created state to relinquish control over its territory. Indeed, the basket approach has characterized the manner in which most Panamanians have viewed sovereignty and explains why Panamanian leaders in December 1999 publicly hailed the act by the United States of relinquishing control over the Canal as a development that brought fuller sovereignty to their state.

III. CONCLUSION

Sovereignty has had remarkable lasting power because of its adaptability and usefulness. As an international system expanded rapidly from Europe to the globe, exporting the concept of the sovereign state promoted international order. As an organizing concept it helped people to determine who was officially responsible in what territories and who was formally entitled to control the activities of which groups. It thus formed an important foundation for a greatly enlarged domain of international politics.

In the nineteenth century European leaders found concepts that promoted a stable international order to be especially attractive. During this era nationalism showed its revolutionary face, as nationalists ignored the current order in favor of advancing the cause of their nation by moral claims to legitimacy. In contrast, "sovereigntyism" was inherently stabilizing: Focusing on the state and its rights and responsibilities underscored the value of promoting a growing community of states. Sovereignty thus provided an important counterpoise to nationalism in a period marked by the clashes between forces of revolution and forces of order.

More particularly, European leaders in this age were intent on upholding a stable, conservative order, quelling the revolutionary sentiments that welled up in Europe from 1820 to 1833 and especially 1848 to 1849 and curbing the antimonarchical trends so evident in the New World. It is thus not surprising to see how deeply enamored they became of the concept of sovereignty. As one scholar noted, "[A]s is customary when men have finally adopted a fundamental idea, the solution of all problems and the adjustment to all new developments were made to conform to it."[92]

Virtually all of Europe was soon divided into sovereign states or their antithesis—neutral areas. Indeed, Europeans went so far as to apply the sovereignty concept to the Holy See by establishing a sovereign Vatican city-state.[93] As European influence spread abroad, even such distant political communities as the natives of New Zealand—who had neither a philosophical tradition of sovereignty nor even the historical experience of a united state—were advised to adopt the mold of the sovereign state as the United Tribes of New Zealand.[94]

It is not beyond debate as to whether transplanting the alien idea of sovereign statehood to foreign societies and then treating those entities for certain purposes as sovereign equals was the most sensible approach for the strongest set of powers to take in managing international relations. Nonetheless, it was an approach with redeeming features, notable among them its encouragement of the development of independent centers of political power.

In any event, by exporting the device of the sovereign state around the globe without regard to widely varying cultural, historical, and philosophical circumstances, nineteenth-century leaders set a pattern that their twentieth-century counterparts adopted wholeheartedly. It is thus not surprising that the resolution of questions regarding sovereign statehood in the 1814–1914 period parallels the resolution of certain similar issues in more recent times.

For instance, the rejection of the purported sovereign status of the various "homeland" states created by South Africa paralleled the rejection of the Manchukuo bid for sovereignty orchestrated by Japan. And, more broadly, the international community still seems to issue or withhold invitations to join a circle of recognized sovereigns. This helps to explain why the new states of the former Soviet Union and the other European empires that disintegrated in the latter part of the twentieth century attached considerable importance to recognition decisions.

As for the related issue of what sovereignty delivers to a state, the continued popularity of a basket approach to sovereignty may be viewed as a reaction to the shortcomings of the concept of sovereign statehood. When according states an identical chunk of rights and duties would elevate egalitarian ideals over the maintenance of order, states regularly opted to conceive of sovereignty in basket terms. In this sense basket thinkers were correct in claiming that their approach more accurately reflected the manner in which the international community actually behaved.

For instance, after major twentieth-century conflicts the victors did not hesitate to impose peace treaties that strictly circumscribed the freedom of action of defeated states. After World War II the international community did not attempt to strip Japan and Germany of formal sovereign status, nor did it treat Iraq in such a manner after the Persian Gulf War. Instead, these countries retained their sovereignty but were compelled to accept treaty terms that dramatically narrowed their policy options. To the basket theorist it is plain that the defeated country lacked the full complement of rights enjoyed by the victors.

Of course, the argument that nineteenth-century thinking about sovereignty has retained its relevance in the twentieth century ought not be overstated. After the Second World War the many newly sovereign states helped to shape the evolving international society. International norms changed, and various legal principles that had centrally benefitted European states at the expense of Third World states were revamped. For instance, rules changed dramatically regarding the use of force, the expropriation of natural resources, and the validity of treaties agreed on under duress.

More particularly, recognition of the principle of self-determination changed the tenor of the debate over the sovereign status of aspirant political communities. It is worth noting, however, that through the twentieth century the international community unequivocally endorsed, in practice, *colonial* self-determination: that is, the right of a nation caught in a subservient colonial relationship to break away from an empire and form its own state. The more sweeping notion of *national* self-determination—that is, the right of nations within multination states to attain their own sovereign state—gained a measure of rhetorical legitimacy but, as a practical matter, was applied quite erratically.[95] Should such a principle gain common currency in the twenty-first century, it would threaten a range of multinational and binational states, just as it would have in the nineteenth century. For this reason as well, the experience of those grappling with the sovereignty concept in the 1814–1914 period retains its relevance today.

NOTES

1. The German term *souveranetat* came into use considerably later, being introduced in the middle of the eighteenth century. It took on particular political significance in 1806 with the establishment of the Rhine Confederation. See F.H. Hinsley, *Sovereignty*, 2d ed. rev. (Cambridge: Cambridge University Press, 1986), 137.

2. In 1791 Tom Paine wrote in the *Rights of Man*: "Monarchical sovereignty, the enemy of mankind and the source of misery, is abolished, and sovereignty is restored to its natural and original place, the nation." F.H. Hinsley, *Power and the Pursuit of Peace: Theory and Practice in the History of Relations Between States* (Cambridge: Cambridge University Press, 1963), 92. The French Constitution of 1791 declared: "[S]overeignty is one and indivisible, inalienable, and imprescriptible." See Michael Ross Fowler and Julie Marie Bunck, *Law, Power, and the Sovereign State: The Evolution and Application of the Concept of Sovereignty* (University Park: The Pennsylvania State University Press, 1995), 66.

3. Although declarations of internal sovereignty by a central government often had these antinationalist overtones, national minorities frequently responded by trying to turn the concept of sovereignty against their oppressors.

4. See Paul Kennedy, *The Rise and Fall of the Great Powers: Economic Change and Military Conflict from 1500 to 2000* (New York: Random House, 1987), 22.

5. See generally Hendrik Spruyt, *The Sovereign State and Its Competitors: An Analysis of Systems Change* (Princeton: Princeton University Press, 1994).

6. Hugo Grotius defined sovereignty as "that power whose acts are not subject to the control of another, so that they may be made void by the act of any other human will." Quincy Wright, *Mandates Under the League of Nations*, p. 278, citing Grotius, *De jure belli ac pacis*, I (1625), c. 3, secs. 7, 16, 17; II, c. 5, sec. 31.

7. It is certainly true that "a conceptual tool used indiscriminately has its analytical edge irreparably dulled." Inis L. Claude Jr., "The Peace-Keeping Role of the United Nations," in *The United Nations in Perspective*, ed. E. Berkeley Tompkins (Stanford, CA: Hoover Institution Press, 1972), 49. In the case of sovereignty, however, its internal and external forms were by no means wholly distinct philosophical notions. As Hinsley wrote: "The idea that there is a sovereign authority within the [domestic] community carried with it . . . the idea that this authority is one among other authorities ruling in other communities in the same sovereign way: a state which claims to be free of limit and control within its community is bound in logic to concede the same freedom to other states in theirs." Hinsley, 158.

8. Paul Kennedy noted: "In the year 1800, Europeans occupied or controlled 35 percent of the land surface of the world; by 1878 this figure had risen to 67 percent, and by 1914 to over 84 percent." Kennedy, 150.

9. For purposes of this essay we are inclined to merge objective and subjective approaches to nationhood by defining a nation as a group that believes in its own identity and exhibits certain, though not necessarily all, of the following characteristics. It usually desires self-government, speaks a common language, shares customs, possesses some historical continuity, distinguishes itself from other like groups, and believes in its own distinct racial origins.

10. We use "state" to mean a legal governing entity that forms a self-contained political community in that it possesses final political authority over a people and territory.
11. See generally David Gillard, "British and Russian Relations with Asian Governments in the Nineteenth Century," in *The Expansion of International Society*, eds. Hedley Bull and Adam Watson (Oxford: Clarendon Press, 1984), 87.
12. See Hedley Bull and Adam Watson, "Introduction," in *The Expansion of International Society*, eds. Hedley Bull and Adam Watson (Oxford: Clarendon Press, 1984), 1. Ian Brownlie usefully added: "The word 'system' . . . implies a more or less common set of forms, procedures, and political techniques for managing transactions and more general relations between states." Ian Brownlie, "The Expansion of International Society: The Consequences for the Law of Nations," in *The Expansion of International Society*, eds. Hedley Bull and Adam Watson (Oxford: Clarendon Press, 1984), 357.
13. In our view the history of Ottoman contacts with Europe suggest that it might sometimes be viewed as part of the European system and sometimes as distinct from it. For instance, while neither marriage pacts nor sea trade alone necessarily brought the Ottoman Empire into the European system, such contacts eventually became more extensive and were paired with military alliances. While traditionally an ally of France, between 1790 and 1810 the Ottoman Empire allied itself for different periods with Sweden, Prussia, Britain, and Russia. See Thomas Naff, "The Ottoman Empire and the European States System," in *The Expansion of International Society*, eds. Hedley Bull and Adam Watson (Oxford: Clarendon Press, 1984), 148, 161–62.
14. This key contribution to the law among nations, derived from the work of the eighteenth-century jurist Emerich de Vattel, had certainly influenced the actions of governments to that extent. Vattel's most influential treatise was *Le Droit des gens; principes de la loi naturelle, appliques a la conduite et aux affaires des nations et des souverains* (1758). From the 1760s forward, the British, French, and American governments regularly referred to this first handbook of international law, with other governments following suit later in the century. See Hinsley, *Sovereignty*, 200–201.
15. Ibid., 194, citing Vattel, book III, ch. iii, sect. 47.
16. This had been true of the Roman Empire as well. See ibid., 161.
17. Kennedy, xvii.
18. Japan passed the edict of 1791, laying out rules to govern how foreign vessels approaching Japan and foreigners who nonetheless landed in the country should be treated. This was followed by an even stricter and more unconditional repulsion edict in 1825.
19. See Hedley Bull, "The Emergence of a Universal International Society," in *The Expansion of International Society*, eds. Hedley Bull and Adam Watson (Oxford: Clarendon Press, 1984), 117.
20. See Bull and Watson, "Introduction," 1. Since by 1914 so much of Africa and the Middle East had neither participated in a dialogue nor consented to common rules and institutions nor even been merged into a global economy in a meaningful way, we would date the emergence of an international society somewhat later than does Bull, who wrote: "By the First World War . . . a universal international society of states clearly existed which covered the whole world and included representatives of the Americas, Asia, and Africa as well as of Europe." Bull, "The Emergence of a Universal International Society," 123. Note that Bull later qualified this statement as follows: "The greater part of Asia, Africa, and Oceania comprised colonial dependencies: the universal international society was one of states, but not everywhere of peoples or nations." Ibid., 125.
21. See Michael Howard, "The Military Factor in European Expansion," in *The Expansion of International Society*, eds. Hedley Bull and Adam Watson (Oxford: Clarendon Press, 1984), 33–42. Europe's population was approximately 187 million in 1800, 266 million in 1850, and 460 million in 1914. In contrast Asia's population stood at approximately 700 million in 1850. See Kennedy, 146. For similar estimates see Joseph Strayer, Hans W. Gatzke, and E. Harris Harbison, *The Mainstream of Civilization,* 2d ed. rev. (New York: Harcourt Brace Jovanovich, 1974), 545, 577.
22. An exception was the Monroe Doctrine proclamation that, while the United States would

not interfere with existing European colonies, European states were not to extend their political control to any portion of the Western hemisphere. As Adam Watson observed: "[The Monroe Doctrine] remains something to be wondered at, in the century of confident and irresistible European imperialism and expansion all over the Eastern hemisphere." Adam Watson, "New States in the Americas," in *The Expansion of International Society*, eds. Hedley Bull and Adam Watson (Oxford: Clarendon Press, 1984), 138.

23. See Adam Watson, "European Expansion," in *The Expansion of International Society*, eds. Hedley Bull and Adam Watson (Oxford: Clarendon Press, 1984), 30. Although the growth of a Western elite started as early as the 1790s in the governing circles of the Ottoman Empire, it achieved particular momentum in the middle of the nineteenth century. See Naff, 151, 163.

24. See Brownlie, "The Expansion of International Society," 361. The 1933 Montevideo Convention on the Rights and Duties of States was a major step toward changing prior diplomatic practices in this regard.

25. Treaties were made with the Basutos and Somalis as well as many other political communities. See ibid., 364, and Bull, "European States and African Political Communities," 114.

26. The *Island of Palmas* case, to cite one well-known example, explored the history and ambiguities of Spanish and Dutch contacts in the East Indies. *Island of Palmas* [U.S./Neth.], 2 *R. Int'l Arb. Awards* 829 (1928).

27. One Japanese authority noted: "[T]he Meiji Government used international law both to defend Japan against Western interference in her domestic affairs and as a means of breaking up China's suzerainty over Korea. The Japanese were to achieve this through the use of force, but they also tried to make use of the basic conceptual tools of the Western theory of international relations embodied in international law, such as sovereign equality, independence, and non-intervention, to which the Chinese idea of suzerainty was opposed." Hidemi Suganami, "Japan's Entry into International Society," in *The Expansion of International Society*, eds. Hedley Bull and Adam Watson (Oxford: Clarendon Press, 1984), 195.

28. See ibid., 195.

29. Hinsley perceptively observed: "[Sovereignty's] function in the history of politics has been either to strengthen the claims of power or to strengthen the ways by which political power may be called to account." Hinsley, *Sovereignty*, 25.

30. Hedley Bull, "The Revolt Against the West," in *The Expansion of International Society*, eds. H. Bull and A. Watson (Oxford: Clarendon Press, 1984), 224.

31. By 1864 Wheaton's *Elements of International Law* had been translated into Chinese and distributed in China, and over time Chinese officials used international law concepts such as sovereignty and duress in relation to the "unequal treaties" that had been signed with the West. See Gerrit W. Gong, "China's Entry into International Society," in *The Expansion of International Society*, eds. Hedley Bull and Adam Watson (Clarendon: Oxford University Press, 1984), 181.

32. See Watson, "New States in the Americas," 138.

33. For Britain's preeminence in the 1860–1870 period see Kennedy, 151, and Evan Luard, *The Management of the World Economy* (New York: St. Martin's Press, 1983), 64.

34. Luard, 64. In 1913 Japan had a mere 2 percent share of world exports; India accounted for 5 percent, Brazil 2 percent, and Indonesia 1.6 percent. Ibid.

35. The early recognition of the sovereign statehood of Haiti, Liberia, Siam, and Ethiopia underscores this assertion.

36. Gong, 181.

37. *Island of Palmas*, at 839.

38. Hinsley, *Sovereignty*, 208.

39. In his famous statement of 1826 British Foreign Secretary George Canning told the House of Commons: "[I]s . . . [the balance of power] not a standard perpetually varying, as civilization advances and as new nations spring up and take their place among established

political communities? . . . I resolved that if France had Spain it should not be Spain with the Indies. I called the New World into existence to redress the balance of the Old."

40. See Watson, "New States in the Americas," 135.

41. For a more extensive version of this argument see generally Michael Fowler and Julie Bunck, "What Constitutes the Sovereign State?" *Review of International Studies* 22 (1996): 381–404. For an alternative view see Alan James, *Sovereign Statehood: The Basis of International Society* (London: Allen & Unwin, 1986), especially chapter 2, "Definition."

42. One may question even Japan's claim to be a single-nation state in the nineteenth century as the Ainu and, after being colonized in 1879, the Okinawans arguable formed separate nations.

43. Daniel Philpott, "Ideas and the Evolution of Sovereignty," in *State Sovereignty: Change and Persistence in International Relations*, ed. Sohail Hashmi (University Park: The Pennsylvania State University Press, 1997), 36.

44. For a parallel conclusion about the somewhat analogous process of entering international society see Watson, "European Expansion," 24. One might also note that how orderly a government must be in order to its retain sovereign status is a question that even twentieth-century leaders, with all their experience with problems of internal disorder, have yet to answer satisfactorily.

45. See Watson, "New States in the Americas," 133.

46. Inis Claude perceptively observed: "Concepts are rarely products of pure cogitation; they generally derive from practice, from the trial and error of effort. We reflect upon our experiences and thus develop concepts to explain and justify, to make sense of, what we have done." Inis L. Claude Jr., "The New International Security Order: Changing Concepts," *The Naval War College Review* (1994): 9.

47. For elaboration of the following examples see Watson, "New States in the Americas," 128–32.

48. For instance, after the War of 1812 the United States Supreme Court unanimously reasoned that legitimacy is irrelevant to determining sovereign status and that sovereignty should be equated with *de facto* possession and control. See our discussion of *United States v. Rice*, 15 U.S. (4 Wheat) 391, 392 (1819) in Fowler and Bunck, "What Constitutes the Sovereign State?" 385–86.

49. In the early twentieth century international lawyer Westel Woodbury Willoughby formulated "the one and final test of sovereignty" as follows: "[T]he presence or absence of sovereignty in a given political entity depends upon whether or not that entity has such complete control over its own legal competence that it cannot against its own legal will, be legally bound in any way whatsoever by the legal will of another political body." Westel W. Willoughby, *The Fundamental Concepts of Public Law* (New York: Macmillan, 1924), cited in Vernon A. O'Rourke, *The Juristic Status of Egypt and the Sudan* (Baltimore: Johns Hopkins University Press, 1935), 21.

50. While Napoleon's conquest of Iberia and the consequent paralysis of imperial Spain's government precipitated revolutions in Latin America, it also brought about a Portuguese government-in-exile in Brazil. In the 1820s John VI returned from Rio de Janeiro to Lisbon, leaving behind his son Peter whom the Brazilians soon proclaimed Emperor Peter I. In 1824 Portugal and the United States recognized the independence of Brazil, followed by the major European powers. In 1889 Peter II abdicated, and the Brazilian Republic was born. See Watson, "New States in the Americas," 129.

51. While the British forcibly suppressed the Canadian rebellions of the 1830s, they also continued to increase powers of self-government in stages so as to avoid the total rupture of relations that had occurred with their former American colonists. See ibid., 131.

52. One might note, however, that the cooperative route to independence depended in most instances on the fact that cooperative colonists might become uncooperative unless satisfactory terms were offered them. That is, the fact that the violent route to independence had already been taken by others had in some sense broken the will of the imperial state to retain its empire. See Bull, "The Revolt Against the West," 225.

53. For an early twentieth-century dispute involving territories of the former Ottoman Empire

and the clashing of *de facto* and *de jure* interpretations of sovereignty see our account of *Lighthouses in Crete and Samos [Greece v. Fr.], PCIJ* (Ser. A/B), No. 71, at 94 (1937) in Fowler and Bunck, *Law, Power, and the Sovereign State*, 55–57.

54. For the whimsical case of a British sea captain, James George Meads, who sailed through the South China Sea in the 1870s, claiming the small islands and reefs now known as the Spratley Islands in the name of his own republic see Fowler and Bunck, *Law, Power, and the Sovereign State*, 54. While documents were duly filed and a foreign minister designated, the republic—like Manchukuo—never amounted to more than a paper creation in the eyes of the international community.

55. Writing of the entry of non-European states into international society, Bull and Watson noted the conflict: "between the view . . . taken by European powers at the time, that it was a process of admission to an exclusive club with rigorous qualifications for membership drawn up by the original or founding members, and the view taken later by many Third World states that it was not so much an admission as a readmission to a general international society of states or peoples whose independence had been wrongfully denied." Bull and Watson, "Introduction," 8. Of course, various political communities explicitly regained sovereignty, among them Vietnam, Poland, and Abyssinia-cum-Ethiopia.

56. Quincy Wright put it as follows: "[M]ost governments, courts, and jurists assumed that a state, whether it had long existed in fact, like Turkey, or had recently become a *de facto* state through successful revolution, like the United States, could not become a member of the Family of Nations and a state *de jure* except through admission to that circle by states already in it." Quincy Wright, *The Existing Legal Situation as It Relates to the Conflict in the Far East* (New York: Institute of Pacific Relations, 1939), 26–27.

57. The community of states that had already gained sovereign status might express its acceptance of the entry of another in various ways. The language used in signing treaties with another state could signal its acceptance, as could inviting representatives of a state to participate in international conferences on the basis of sovereign equality. Most often, however, other sovereigns made known their view concerning an aspiring sovereign state by either formally recognizing its existence or withholding such an official declaration.

58. Bull, "The Emergence of a Universal International Society," 122.

59. Ibid., 123.

60. As one early twentieth-century authority noted: "The word sovereignty holds various conflicting connotations and by no means arouses identical patterns in the minds of different students." O'Rourke, 10.

61. See the similar thought expressed in Barry Buzan, *People, States, and Fear: The National Security Problem in International Relations* (Chapel Hill: University of North Carolina Press, 1983), 41.

62. Watson, "European Expansion," 25.

63. These included the Congress of Paris in 1856, the two London conferences in 1871 and 1912–13, the two Berlin congresses in 1878 and 1884–85, and the two Hague conferences in 1899 and 1907.

64. Here we have in mind the role played by conferences of European states in managing the colonial competition, especially in Africa. See Hedley Bull, "Europe and Africa," in *The Expansion of International Society*, eds. Hedley Bull and Adam Watson (Oxford: Clarendon Press, 1984), 109. For a comprehensive list of European congresses and conferences, omitting only ambassadorial and technical meetings, see Hinsley, *Power and the Pursuit of Peace*, 214.

65. Bull, "The Emergence of a Universal International Society," 123.

66. Gong, 181.

67. See generally Robert A. Klein, *Sovereign Equality Among States: The History of an Idea* (Toronto: University of Toronto Press, 1974).

68. For a more detailed exposition of this theory, which was originally formulated by Inis Claude, see our chapter 3, "How Is Sovereignty Applied in Theory?" in *Law, Power, and the Sovereign State*, 63–82.

69. See, for instance, the statement of Chief Justice John Marshall: "The world being composed of distinct sovereignties, possessing equal rights and equal independence, whose mutual benefit is promoted by intercourse with each other . . ., all sovereigns have consented to a relaxation in practice . . . of that absolute and complete jurisdiction within their respective territories which sovereignty confers." *Schooner Exchange v. M'Faddon & Others*, 11 U.S. (7 Cranch) 116, 136 (1812).

70. Sir Henry Maine, *International Law* (London: J. Murray, 1890), 58, cited in F.A. Vali, *Servitudes of International Law: A Study of Rights in Foreign Territory*, 2d ed. rev. (New York: Frederick A. Praeger, 1958), 300. Various other scholars followed Maine's lead. For instance, Hans Blix observed: "As ownership is described as a bundle of rights, sovereignty may perhaps be described as a bundle of competences." Hans Blix, *Sovereignty, Aggression, and Neutrality* (Stockholm: Almquist & Wiksell, 1970), 11–12.

71. It may be that chunk theory interprets sovereignty in such a way as to try to contribute to a more just international order.

72. Bull put this development somewhat differently, writing: "In the gradations of independence recognized by the European powers in the extra-European world, the spectrum of positions intermediate between full sovereignty and the status of a colony . . . there could be seen the survival, alongside the concept of a society of equally sovereign states, of the older and historically much more ubiquitous concept of international relations as the relations between suzerains and vassals." Bull, "The Emergence of a Universal International Society," 125–26.

73. For a more detailed exposition of this thesis, see Fowler and Bunck, *Law, Power, and the Sovereign State*, 83–125.

74. See Gillard, 89.

75. Watson, "European Expansion," 29.

76. In the two years following the Nanking Treaty Western powers and China signed the Treaty of the Bogue, the Treaty of Wanghia, and the Treaty of Whampoa.

77. As one authority noted: "The treaty ports became the permanent residences of increasing numbers of Westerners, the centres for trade and commerce, the home stations of the Western gunboats, and the sites of consulates and military barracks, all protected as semi-autonomous units with their own tax and legal-judicial systems and thereby exempt from Chinese jurisdiction." Gong, 176.

78. Watson, "European Expansion," 31.

79. Raymond Aron, *Peace and War: A Theory of International Relations*, trans. Richard A. Howard and Annette Baker-Fox (New York: Frederick A. Praeger, 1967), 742. This led to the notorious sign outside certain Shanghai parks: "No Dogs or Chinese."

80. Hedley Bull observed: "The Japanese did not respond to the Dowager Empress's request to the Mikado for Asian unity against the West, but joined in the defence of the international society of states, to membership of which they graduated." Bull, "The Revolt Against the West," 220.

81. See Wright, *Existing Legal Situation*, 33, 36. The World Court found that such rights of passage did not violate international law. See *Right of Passage over Indian Territory [Port. v. India]*, 160 ICJ 6 (Judgment) and the discussion in Fowler and Bunck, *Law, Power, and the Sovereign State*, 86–88.

82. Kevin P. Lane, *Sovereignty and the Status Quo: The Historical Roots of China's Hong Kong Policy* (Boulder, CO: Westview Press, 1990), 18, citing John V.A. MacMurray, *Treaties and Agreements with and Concerning China, 1894–1919* (New York: Oxford University Press, 1921), 1,215.

83. See "Questions for Readjustment, Submitted by China to the Peace Conference," *The Chinese Social and Political Science Review* 5A (1920): 116. See also Lane, *Sovereignty and the Status Quo*, 21–22.

84. Similar requests made by Chinese diplomats at the Washington Conference of 1921 were tabled and rejected. Not until the Anglo-Chinese Treaty of 1930 did China begin to recover leased territories. See Fowler and Bunck, *Law, Power, and the Sovereign State*, 96–97.

85. Egypt, the Persian Gulf states, even Russia signed treaties similar in important respects. See Bull, "Revolt of the West," 218–220.

86. See Suganami, 192.

87. Ibid., 192. Suganami later noted: "This institutional Westernization helped Japan to attain the position of equality with the Western Powers because the revision of 'unequal' treaties had been made conditional upon her internal law reforms on the Western model." Ibid., 197.

88. Bull noted: "Turkey achieved the elimination of extraterritorial jurisdiction through the Treaty of Lausanne in 1923 . . .; Egypt through the Anglo-Egyptian Treaty of 1936; China through agreement with the United States and Britain in 1943. In the Persian Gulf . . . extraterritorial jurisdiction continued until the British withdrawal in 1971." Bull, "The Revolt Against the West," 220.

89. See generally Vali, and Helen Dwight Reid, *International Servitudes in Law and Practice* (Chicago: University of Chicago Press, 1932), and Fowler and Bunck, *Law, Power, and the Sovereign State*, 99–102.

90. Indeed, international relations theorists and persons active in international affairs have continued to think either in terms of a basket approach to sovereignty or a chunk approach in regard to various issues. For instance, for the chunk school Alan James contended that no state is 82 percent sovereign or 57 percent sovereign. Taking the basket approach, Quincy Wright declared: "Sovereignty in international law is . . . a variable term. Each international person differs to some extent from every other in its capacity in law or in fact to establish normal legal relations with others. The line between a fully sovereign and a partly sovereign state is not precise and is continually changing with the development of international relations. Limitations which were yesterday considered impairments of sovereignty are today normal and vice versa." Wright, *Mandates Under the League of Nations*, 294.

91. Hans J. Morgenthau, *Politics Among Nations: The Struggle for Power and Peace* (New York: Alfred A. Knopf, 1948), 248.

92. Hinsley, *Sovereignty*, 204–5.

93. Ibid., 205.

94. Ibid., 206. Note that not all tribal societies were deemed to have the requisite social structure necessary to enter treaty relations. As one authority noted, Africa's Zulu tribe qualified, while Australia's aborigines did not. Brownlie, "The Expansion of International Society," 362.

95. Inis L. Claude Jr., "The United States and Changing Approaches to National Security and World Order," *Naval War College Review* 48 (1995): 48.

The State and the Nation: Changing Norms and the Rules of Sovereignty in International Relations

J. Samuel Barkin and Bruce Cronin

THE INTERNATIONAL RELATIONS literature regularly embraces sovereignty as the primary constitutive rule of international organization.[1] Theoretical traditions that agree on little else all seem to concur that the defining feature of the modern international system is the division of the world into sovereign states. Despite differences over the role of the state in international affairs, most scholars would accept John Ruggie's definition of sovereignty as "the institutionalization of public authority within mutually exclusive jurisdictional domains."[2] Regardless of the theoretical approach however, the concept tends to be viewed as a static, fixed concept: a set of ideas that underlies international relations but is not changed along with them. Moreover, the *essence* of sovereignty is rarely defined; while legitimate authority and territoriality are the key concepts in understanding sovereignty, international relations scholars rarely examine how definitions of populations and territories change throughout history and how this change alters the notion of legitimate authority.

Definitions of sovereignty tend to focus on its legal content; this content changes little, therefore sovereignty is seen as fixed. The institutionalization of

Reprinted from J. Samuel Barkin and Bruce Cronin, "The State and the Nation: Changing Norms and the Rules of Sovereignty in International Relations," *International Organization* 48, no. 1 (winter 1994): 107–30. © 1994 by the IO Foundation and the Massachusetts Institute of Technology.

authority within mutually exclusive domains is, however, as much a function of its legitimacy as of its legal content. Thus an institutional, as opposed to a purely legal, understanding of sovereignty must address the legitimization of the nation-state system as well as its formal definition. As we argue below, understandings of legitimacy tend to change from era to era. This study examines the concept of sovereignty as a variable by exploring some of the circumstances under which the political legitimation of the nation-state changes over time. In doing so we will argue that the rules of sovereignty are neither fixed nor constant, but rather are subject to changing interpretations.[3] Specifically we hold there has been a historical tension between state sovereignty, which stresses the link between sovereign authority and a defined territory, and national sovereignty, which emphasizes a link between sovereign authority and a defined population. The two types fundamentally differ in the source of their legitimation as independent entities, thereby altering the environment through which states relate to each other.

During periods when international norms legitimize state rather than national sovereignty, the international community and its institutions will tend to defend the rights of established states against nationalist claims of domestic ethnic groups. On the other hand, when the norms of the international order favor national over state sovereignty, the international community will be more sympathetic to pleas for national self-determination, often at the expense of established states. The legitimizing principles are called into question during major systemic crises, such as world wars or widespread political upheavals, because the new dominant coalition often sees the previous emphasis on one form of sovereignty as the cause of the crisis. The coalition then creates a postwar order that reflects this belief. This dynamic occurs because it is impossible to completely satisfy the statist and nationalist principles simultaneously. Therefore, the new system tends to generate its own crisis, leading to a reevaluation of the normative principle.

This argument will be highlighted in four brief plausibility probes, ranging in time from the post-Napoleonic settlement to the present. We argue consequently that sovereignty should be viewed as a variable rather than as a constant and therefore that the state as a basic analytic unit should be scrutinized in international relations theory.[4]

I. Sovereignty as a Variable

For realism, sovereignty is a necessary constant; it is the fundamental assumption from which the realist notion of anarchy is derived.[5] Institutional approaches similarly take sovereignty as it given. According to Stephen Krasner for example, the "historical legacy of the development of the state system has left a powerful institutional structure (sovereignty), one that will not be dislodged easily, regardless of changed circumstances in the material environment."[6] Janice Thomson and Krasner further argue that sovereignty is not only a constant but is unlikely to change at all in the near future.[7] Even those theoretical traditions that focus on the role of rules and norms in providing order to the international system tend to approach sovereignty in a static way. Hedley Bull, for example, argues that "an independent political community which merely claims a right to sovereignty (or is judged by others to have such a right), but cannot assert this right in practice, is not a state properly so-called."[8] The questions of the basis upon which such a right is asserted, what constitutes a legitimate claim, and how this standard has been applied throughout history are all left unexplored.

From this brief overview it is apparent that the bulk of the international relations literature generally does not account for any variation in the legitimation of sovereignty through the course of modern history. It is often not appreciated fully that sovereignty is a social construct, and like all social institutions its location is subject to changing interpretations. In other words, while the specific expression of sovereignty may remain constant, that which is considered to be sovereign changes. This inflexibility in the study of sovereignty has unduly constrained the usefulness of the concept for theories of international organization. The way in which political actors define the political and geographic boundaries of legitimate authority over territory and populations strongly affects the principles on which the international system will function. At a minimum it stipulates how sovereignty may be created or transferred, historically the primary issue following a world war or other major upheaval in the system. In particular it defines how state succession is to be regulated, such as when large states break apart into smaller units or when several sovereign units combine into one.

How important are rules of sovereignty in creating and maintaining order in the international system? A realist may argue that sovereignty is based less on a set of principles than on the ability of a political group to establish domestic control over its territory and defend it from external attack. As Robert Art and Robert Jervis point out, the anarchic environment of international politics not only allows every state to be the final judge of its own interests but also requires that each provide the means to attain them.[9] Yet the very foundation of the nation-state system—its diplomatic procedures, treaties, international laws, wars, and all other institutions that provide for communication and interaction among states—rests on the mutual recognition among government leaders that they each represent a specific society within an exclusive jurisdictional domain. Diplomatic recognition and legitimation are prerequisites for participation in the system as a full member. The type of legitimacy, Inis Claude argues, is essentially a political rather than a legal or moral function.[10] Thus a nationalist group claiming to represent a population and territory that takes military action in support of its claim is considered terrorist; as such, it is generally condemned and opposed (often militarily) by the world community. At the same time a state, however much it is disliked, is recognized as having the right to defend its claims with military force.

Changes in the content and understanding of sovereignty can greatly affect the ways in which states are constrained or enabled to act in their international relations. As Anthony Giddens points out, the sovereignty of the nation-state does not precede the development of the state system. State authorities were not originally empowered with an absolute sovereignty destined to become confined by a growing network of international connections. Rather, the development of state sovereignty depended (and still depends) on a monitored set of relations between states. "'International relations' are not connections set up between preestablished states," Giddens argues, "which could maintain their sovereignty without them: they are the basis upon which nation-states exist at all."[11]

II. SOVEREIGNTY: THE STATE AND THE NATION

Sovereignty in international relations has been ascribed to two different types of entities: states, defined in terms of the territories over which institutional authorities exercise legitimate control, and nations, defined in terms of "communities of sentiment" that form the political basis on which state authority rests.[12] While they are institutionally and structurally alike, these two ideal types differ fundamentally in the source of their legitimation as sovereign entities. In this article we present the concepts of "state" and "nation" as ideal types to examine the ramifications of differing interpretations of the source of legitimate authority within a defined political boundary. In practice there is a continuum from statist to national legitimation of sovereignty, and nation-states always show some characteristics of both.

Since the seventeenth century the state has been recognized as the supreme power within a defined juridical border.[13] This ended both the Church's transnational claims to political authority and the overlapping jurisdictions of nobles, kings, and clerics that characterized the late medieval system. As Ruggie points out, the distinction between internal and external political realms, separated by clearly demarcated boundaries, is a modern phenomenon; it is the constitutive basis of the nation-state system.[14] State sovereignty—institutional authority within a set of clearly demarcated boundaries—is self-justifying; historical possession legitimates continued jurisdiction. In much of Europe, its origins can be traced to the legal titles and dynastic ties that provided monarchs with a claim to the territory that eventually provided the basis for the modern state. In this way state legitimation is similar to the legitimation of property in many systems of law; possession, in the absence of claims by others, leads to ownership.

Modern concepts of the nation began to develop a century after this juridical understanding of the state. The distinguishing feature of modern nationalism is the claim that nations should be politically self-determining and that group sentiment (national solidarity) should serve as the sole criterion in defining the nation.[15] The nation-state is accordingly legitimated to the extent that it represents the political aspirations of a particular nation. Legitimation stems not from the boundaries but from the community of sentiment.

Since the evolution of modern nationalism, there has been a tension between two opposing principles: state sovereignty, which stresses the link between sovereign authority and a defined set of exclusive political institutions, and national sovereignty, which emphasizes a link between sovereign authority and a defined population.[16] State sovereignty emphasizes the integrity of borders based on historical possession, national frontiers, and viability. If we follow this logic, the viability of a state is based on the ability of established institutions to exercise authority over the population. This control is best assured by stable, effective states with strong institutions rather than by newly defined nations that may lack administrative competence and social stability. Thus from the perspective of the stability of the international system, international norms should favor the stability of sovereign states over the unpredictability of sovereign nations. Since most countries contain some type of minority population, a sovereignty based on national claims can be seen as potentially destabilizing for all states. In addition, since there is no international authority capable of enforcing treaties and agreements, long-standing states based on stable institutions and historic control of territory can better ensure compliance than those based on principles of nationality. This is reinforced by the fact that juridical borders can be fixed objectively, whereas national identification, being inherently subjective, cannot be fixed in the same way.

[States] . . . relate to each other in terms of common practices, norms, and rules where such rules provide the basis for making judgments of just and unjust international conduct, for advancing claims of rights, and for seeking redress when rules are violated.[17] States are concerned with their social as well as their physical well-being, in particular the legitimation of their own authority and of the system as a whole. As Claude argues, legitimation requires that "power be converted into authority, competence be supported by jurisdiction, and possession be validated as ownership."[18] The maintenance of legitimacy requires that states conform with the international community's conception of justice. This conception changes from era to era, and thus there can be no single standard from which to judge what is just. According to Claude, however, there is a tendency for a single concept of legitimacy to become generally dominant in a particular era. Statist principles, reflecting a legitimation that is founded on bases ranging from the balance of power to dynastic conservatism, have dominated at times. However, "the modern era has also seen the establishment of national self-determination as the basis of legitimate statehood, and the global extension of the reach of this legitimizing principle has been one of the most significant developments of recent decades."[19] To the extent that this is true, modern states should be expected to be sympathetic to the idea of international borders based on nationality, as this helps to legitimize the state system and by extension their own role within it. Consequently, when disjunctures become apparent between juridical boundaries and nationalist sentiments, a society of nation-states in which legitimation derives primarily from nationalist principles should support altering those borders to better reflect the principle of national self determination.

These two ideals clearly cannot be simultaneously fulfilled in all circumstances, particularly when national claims infringe on the currently recognized borders of existing sovereign states. Should the state emphasis predominate in the understanding of sovereignty over the national emphasis, then international borders will be seen as territorially determined, and the international community can be expected to defend the interests of established states over nationalist aspirations. On the other hand, should the national emphasis predominate, then states will be seen as tied to specifically defined populations and territorially malleable to suit the evolution of nations. The international community will then be more sympathetic to nationalist claims, often at the expense of established states. This tension is always present within the international system, but it becomes particularly acute during periods when the international order undergoes rapid change.

Historically, understandings of sovereignty tend to be redefined during and following the conclusion of major wars or in the aftermath of widespread political upheavals. Such understandings are a reflection of the norms and principles that underlay the legitimation of the nation-state following a particular era. According to Robert Gilpin, a necessary "component of the governance of an international system is a set of rights and rules that govern or at least influence the interactions among states."[20] These rules, Gilpin argues, are negotiated at the conclusion of great wars, where the negotiated treaties serve as the constitution of the state system.

It is our contention that the legitimation of the nation-state in a particular era is determined largely by the principles around which the winning coalition unites during the course of a great war, as well as in its aftermath, as the dominant coalition constructs a new international order. These principles cannot be objectively deduced solely from the nature of the states and the distribution of capabilities, but must also be induced from the process of building the coalition and the intersubjective consensus among the members of the coalition as to the cause of the war.[21] We base this proposition on the premise that norms and principles are at least partially derived through political interaction, rather than from an objective notion of self-interest. Since the very nature of the nation-state system contains elements of both nationalism and statism, one cannot know *a priori* which principle will be adopted by a particular coalition.

Furthermore, we argue that this consensus is itself partially created as a reaction to a perceived overemphasis on either the state or the nation during the previous period. The tension between state legitimation and national legitimation can never be completely resolved; as discussed above, the ideals of state and nation are often contradictory, and the realization of both can rarely be simultaneously achieved. When an international order focuses legitimacy on one, tensions often arise in the other. Thus, postwar settlements will tend to favor one over the other, and the emphasis is often reevaluated during the creation of a new international order. Consequently, we suggest that the resolution of the state/nation tension depends on which emphasis is seen as more destabilizing during the construction of an international order. The precise content of postwar settlements cannot be determined through general theory; they are historically unique. Rather, we argue that the general emphasis of legitimacy oscillates between state and nation. Stated in dialectical terms, the legitimacy of the nation-state is a synthesis of statist and nationalist forms of legitimation. The potential contradictions of these two forms drive a process in which the content of legitimacy develops in a crisis and changes to favor one form over the other.

We will now briefly examine four historical cases as a plausibility probe for this approach. The four eras examined are ones in which definitions of sovereignty were focused alternately on the state and the nation. In doing so we will highlight how the relevant actors viewed the nature of the international system at the time, their concept of a legitimate nation-state, and the determination of state borders. The periods that will be studied include the aftermath of the following wars: the Napoleonic Wars, World War I, World War II, and the Cold War.

III. State Sovereignty and the Post-Napoleonic Order

One of the earliest challenges to the Westphalian concept of sovereignty came about in the years following the French Revolution. From 1792 to 1815, France attempted to export its revolution (and territorial control) throughout Europe, bringing with each conquest the ideas of nationhood, republicanism, and liberty. These ideas directly threatened the principles on which most European monarchies were based. In addition, following the French withdrawal from the territories conquered during the Napoleonic Wars, more than half of Europe was without government. The Hapsburg dynasty that had ruled much of the region was reorganized into a modern state. Consequently, the old continental system of principalities, dynasties, and states was replaced by a more rationalized system of modern states. The principles on which this new system would be legitimized were therefore of utmost importance.

Following the defeats of Napoleon in 1814 and 1815, an international order was constructed by the victorious coalition that lasted at least until 1848 and to a lesser extent through 1856. This order was based in large part on the principles that united a rather diverse group of states in opposition to Napoleon: the parliamentary monarchy of Britain and the absolute monarchies of Austria, Prussia, and Russia. Although the members of the Grand Alliance had conflicting interests, both geopolitical and military, they eventually agreed to a set of principles that defined and legitimized their war against Napoleon. These principles defined how sovereignty would be interpreted after the war. Furthermore, as will be shown below, it was through interaction among the victorious states and France that the "legitimist" principle was developed, favoring dynastic claims of territory over national claims by newly liberated peoples throughout Europe.

British Foreign Secretary Lord Castlereagh's stated objective was the liberation of Europe from French control and a return to a continental balance of power. He believed that the cause of the Napoleonic Wars was a coupling of nationalism with Jacobinism (a form of French radicalism that advocated the spread of liberty, equality, and nationhood by force of arms and internal repression). Austrian minister Klemens von Metternich also saw republicanism and nationalism as the causes of the war. Unlike Castlereagh however, he sought to define the war aims of the anti-French coalition based on two key conservative principles: the sanctity of treaties and the legitimacy of sovereigns. French nationalism contained several elements that threatened these aims. First, the Jacobin concept of nation included the idea of citizenship and peoplehood. According to the Declaration of the Rights of Man and Citizen, "the source of all sovereignty resides essentially in the nation." This was partially reflected in Napoleon's use of a conscript army, rather than a professional aristocratic military, something that was unheard of in even the most autocratic states. Second, Jacobinism was militantly patriotic; the French language, flag, and national anthem were incorporated into a series of domestic rituals designed to rally the nation around Jacobin ideals. As historian Carlton Hayes explains, "To the Jacobins 'the people' has become 'the nation', a mystical entity, an absolute sovereign."22

While the nationalism of the French Revolution was based more on historic ties than on a sense of ethnic or linguistic solidarity, the French Revolution added to the traditional definition of the nation the requirement of citizenship rights. Thus while French nationalism did not require a common language, it did instill a conception of Frenchness throughout the population. This population was now loyal to "France" as an abstraction rather than to the state, which was previously synonymous with the monarchy. Consequently the notion of nationality, if not specifically of ethnicity, was introduced. It is telling that this notion affected even the loyalists; in 1789, twelve hundred members of the French National Guard took an oath declaring that they were no longer Dauphinois, Provençaux, or Languedociens, but only Frenchmen.

Both Austria and Russia agreed that the war was a struggle for equilibrium, that such an equilibrium would be based on a European society of states, and that the order would essentially be conservative in character. In short, the war against Napoleon had three specific aims: to restore a balance of power, to stop the spread of French radical ideas, and to prevent liberal revolutions in Europe.

Although Czar Alexander was more sympathetic to the ideas of constitutionalism and self-determination, in the end Metternich's legitimizing principle was accepted by all as the *raison d'être* of the coalition. It favored the state over the nation. There would be a conservative European society of states, not nations, in which all postwar borders would be defended by collective force. Unlike the aftermath of World War I (see below), the post-Napoleonic period saw a decrease in the number of states in Europe, brought about through the incorporation of smaller territories into existing states. Even France was allowed to retain some of the non-French territories it had acquired during the war. The views of Austrian Emperor Francis II on how a new legitimate nation-state could be created is contained in his statement to Czar Alexander: "A Prince can, if he wishes, cede a part of his country and all of his people" to create such a state. "If he abdicates then his rights are passed on to his legitimate heirs."[23]

The peace settlements concluded at the first Peace of Paris (1814) and the Treaty of Vienna (1815) clearly reflected the value of the state over the nation. The claims of ancient nations, such as Poland, were all but ignored. The Belgians, Norwegians, and Poles were placed under foreign rule; Belgium was incorporated into Holland and Norway, into Sweden. Germany and Italy remained fragmented and disunited by design, even though Britain preferred a united Germany to help maintain a balance of power in Central Europe. In resolving the Polish question, Austria retained Galicia and Tarnopol and Prussia was given Posen and Thorn. The remainder of the Duchy of Warsaw came under the authority of the czar of Russia. In addition, Prussia obtained two-thirds of Saxony. During the Congress of Vienna, territories were bartered among the sovereigns. When one sovereign lost a contested territory, he was "compensated" with another. The use of the term "souls" rather than "citizens" to describe the populations a sovereign would receive in compensation symbolized the view that states existed apart from their people.

While many political scientists have come to view this simply as balancing dynamics at work, it is apparent that the territorial balance of power was in fact only one of the principles for which the war was fought. The creation of the Holy Alliance in 1815 and the adoption of "legitimist" principles articulated by Metternich and French Minister Talleyrand-Perigord demonstrated that the principle of the "legitimate state" was as important as the principle of maintaining a balance. Czar Alexander proposed a fraternal association of sovereigns guided by the precepts of Christianity and dynastic solidarity rather than by traditional diplomacy. The important point for our purposes here is the fact that the association was a compact among rulers, not among nations or peoples.

The British position also reflected the legitimizing principles of the war at least as much as its own security interests. If one evaluated British interests on the basis of security alone, there would be little reason for them to support a territorial settlement that denied nationhood to the dispossessed peoples of Europe. Britain had no territorial ambitions on the Continent; in Europe, British interests merely required that no single power be too strong. Metternich's assertion that Europe was a society of states was the basis for his belief that community interests made the notion of sovereignty less than absolute. According to Metternich, when domestic social unrest makes it impossible for a government to meet its treaty obligations that bind it to other countries, "the right to intervene belongs as clearly and indisputably to every government which finds itself in danger of being drawn into the revolutionary maelstrom, as it does to any individual who must put out a fire in his neighbor's house if it is not to spread to its own."[24] This principle was put into force a number of times, as the Holy Alliance subsequently intervened to prevent liberal revolution throughout Europe.

As a result of this settlement, there were few interstate wars between 1815 and 1856 and none involving more than one great power. On the other hand, rebellions, mostly nationalist in character, occurred regularly within the German principalities, the Netherlands, the Italian states, Greece, Poland, France, Spain, and ultimately within the Austrian Empire itself. At the same time, until after the Crimean War the great powers allowed only two border changes in the European state system: the independence of Belgium and Greece. All other rebellions were put down by collectively sanctioned force.

IV. WORLD WAR I AND THE TRIUMPH OF THE NATION

While the structural conditions of the international system during and after World War I were quite similar to those of the early nineteenth century, the international order constructed at the end of the Napoleonic Wars differed considerably from that of the post-Versailles period. In both cases empires collapsed, territories were redistributed, and the victorious states were committed to restoring a balance of power on the Continent by reducing the strength of the enemy.[25] In addition, the end of both conflicts was followed by domestic unrest that spread throughout the Continent. Rioting and revolutionary agitation threatened a number of well-established regimes in Europe during both eras. While the feared ideology of the early nineteenth century was French liberalism/Jacobinism, after World War I socialism, in particular Bolshevism, played this role.

Yet although both the Congress of Vienna and the conference at Versailles dealt to a large degree with the question of a European balance, the nineteenth-century settlement resulted in a *reduction* of countries and a restoration of traditional great power borders, while the post-World War I order led to an *increase* in countries and a breakup of traditional empires. The question of what to do with the territories conquered by France a century earlier was resolved by restoring sovereignty to traditional authorities, yet the collapse of the post-World War I empires led to a proliferation of new state formations based largely on the principle of nationality. One factor that can explain this difference is the varying conceptions of sovereignty and nationhood brought about by competing beliefs over the causes of war and the basis of order in the international system.

Although none of the main antagonists entered the war with a set of political principles in mind, the analysis and program of U.S. President Woodrow Wilson predominated by the end of the war. During the course of World War I, there was little discussion about goals and principles other than military objectives. In fact, apart from territorial questions, there was little to distinguish the two sides, particularly if one considers their views of what a postwar international order would look like. Within the Allied coalition, agreement was restricted primarily to military questions. Animosities between Britain and France, which dated back to the era of Louis XIV, remained strong. Italy's membership in the alliance was primarily opportunistic; Britain and France simply offered Italy a better deal. French Prime Minister Clemenceau clearly wanted Germany rendered incapable of fighting another large-scale war, much as the Grand Alliance wished to strip France of that ability a century earlier. Clemenceau argued that the cause of the war was German power and that the containment of Germany after the war was France's chief goal. British Prime Minister Lloyd George's primary interest was in dividing up the remnants of the German and Hapsburg empires and ensuring that neither Germany nor France dominated the Continent.

It was not until the intervention of Woodrow Wilson that the Allied cause developed a unified purpose. A statement of principles became necessary for the Allies to differentiate themselves from the Central Powers, particularly since the rationale behind the war was not immediately clear to either the Russian or U.S. populations. According to Wilson, this was a war to end all wars. The purpose of fighting the war was to eliminate the very causes of war itself: the balance of power, the system of alliances, and the denial of self-determination and democracy to peoples throughout the world. He diagnosed as a major cause of World War I the lack of congruence between nations and states and the existence of autocratic governments. For Wilson a legitimate nation-state was one that represented a defined national population and whose government was accountable to its people.

In his well-known Fourteen Points address to Congress, Wilson articulated a *raison d'être* for the Allied coalition. While the first five points dealt primarily with general diplomatic principles, points six through thirteen were addressed to specific territorial questions, all of which were applications of the principle of self-determination. In addition to these fourteen points, Wilson added four principles which included the tenets that "people and provinces must not be bartered about from sovereignty to sovereignty as if they were chattels or pawns in a game" and that all territorial questions had to be settled "in the interests of the populations concerned."[26] These statements can be seen as a direct reference to how the Congress of Vienna bartered the newly liberated territories among the victorious states without taking into consideration principle of nationality. One could argue that the intensity of nationalist feelings that developed in the latter part of the nineteenth century could be traced directly to the overemphasis on creating a perfect equilibrium following the defeat of Napoleon. While Wilson's idealism was not necessarily shared by either Britain or France, they eventually agreed to accept his principles as the basis on which to build an international order following the end of the war. Clemenceau initially attacked Wilson as hopelessly naive, holding to his belief in the balance of power. However in 1918 the French position changed when the foreign ministry issued a proposal for a postwar settlement agreeing that peace must rest on three principles, including national self-determination and the protection of minority rights.

Lloyd George also came to accept Wilson's basic principles during the course of the war. In 1918 he spoke at a London trade union conference and argued that a just and lasting peace would require the restoration of sanctity of treaties, the settlement of territorial disputes on the basis of national self-determination, and the creation of an international organization to limit armaments and diminish the probability of war. Even Germany, on the verge of defeat, turned to the United States rather than Britain or France to negotiate peace based on Wilsonian principles. In a note sent to the United States on 7 October 1918, Germany said, "The German government accepts as the basis for its negotiations, the program laid down by the President of the United States."[27]

Although the first five of Wilson's fourteen points were essentially eliminated in secret talks between Wilson, Clemenceau, and Lloyd George prior to the conference at Versailles, those that dealt primarily with the principle of nationalism, including Wilson's four principles, were left intact. Like the Congress of Vienna a century earlier, the conference at Versailles divided up historically disputed territories among the victors: France was given Alsace and Lorraine, Britain and France were granted "mandates" over German colonies and the territories of the former Ottoman Empire, and Italy received some islands off the Dalmatian coast. Yet unlike at Vienna, the conference at Versailles was attended by representatives from dozens of dispossessed nations and peoples who were allowed to press their claims before the assembled powers. Additionally, in resolving the disposition of the Austrian, German, and Russian empires, the principle of national sovereignty was clearly the guide. The various Balkan Slavic groups were united to form a new state, Yugoslavia. Romania was expanded to include those parts of the Austrian Empire where a majority of Romanians lived, and Hungary became an independent state. The Czechs and Slovaks were united into the new state of Czechoslovakia, and what was left of the old Hapsburg Empire became independent Austria. Estonia, Latvia, and Lithuania were granted independence. Istria and Trentino, both Italian-speaking areas, were brought into Italy. Finally, plebiscites were held in a number of small regions, including Schleswig-Holstein, Upper Silesia, and Saarland, so that the inhabitants could decide for themselves what country they wanted to join.

The principle of self-determination was put to its greatest test over the question of how to deal with Germany's former colonies and Turkey's former territories. While the British were leery about setting a precedent that could threaten their empire by granting colonial independence, Wilson stood by his wartime principle that people should not be bartered about from sovereignty to sovereignty. The victorious powers struck a compromise solution in the Treaty of Sèvres: the colonies would be freed from colonial control by the great powers by placing them under the protective wing of the League of Nations. The League of Nations in turn would appoint various nations as guardians.

V. WORLD WAR II AND ITS AFTERMATH

The accepted interpretation of the main cause of World War II was very different from that of World War I. Whereas World War I was seen after the fact as old alliance politics gone out of control, World War II was viewed both during its course and after as a fight against fascism. There are several components of fascist ideology, but one crucial component that serves to differentiate fascism from other totalitarianisms is a particularly virulent strain of nationalism. Opposition to such expansionist nationalism served as an effective banner under which to unite the Allies for two reasons. First, it matched the popular impression of the prime cause of the war. Second, it was acceptable to all of the Allies, a group of states whose political systems and ideologies had little else in common.

Nationalism was perceived as a primary cause of the war; it had provided the pretext for the German occupations of Austria, Czechoslovakia, and Poland that led to the outbreak of war. It was seen as one of the most objectionable aspects of fascist ideology. While self-determination remained a legitimate political goal, nationalisms that were xenophobic and expansionist came to be seen as an unacceptable threat to international peace. Nationalism had previously been associated with the desire of people to be free. Fascism associated nationalism with the desire of some people to dominate or dislocate others. This led to a conceptual separation of "the self-determination of peoples" from nationalism as the legitimate basis for the state.[28]

The self-determination of peoples implies that everyone as an individual has a right to his or her own government and to participate in that government. The term "peoples" does not, however, imply any specific basis for delineating national boundaries.[29] As long as all of the people within the boundaries have equal access to the government and the government does not try to control any peoples outside of those boundaries, the requirements of self-determination have been fulfilled. Nationalism, on the other hand, does imply a specific basis for delineating state boundaries. The state should match the nation. Should members of the nation live outside of the state, an expansionist nationalism would have the state expand to wherever those nationals live. In areas where members of more than one nationality live, interstate conflict becomes both likely and virulent. The normative acceptance by the winning coalition, the Allies, of the self-determination of peoples as the legitimate basis for the state reflected their perception that it was nationalism that had caused the war in the first place.

This normative acceptance is reflected in the document intended to be the primary basis for postwar international relations, the Charter of the United Nations (UN). The [first article of the] Charter affirms as the first purpose of the UN the maintenance of international peace and security. It defines this as the prevention of the violation of established state borders by the forces of other states.[30] This clearly establishes the priority of the integrity of established state borders over the integrity of national or nationalist groups. The charter also affirms the principle of the self-determination of peoples, but not of nations, and the principle of noninterference in the domestic affairs of other states.[31] This suggests that it is their people as individuals, not the "nation" as a separate entity, that states represent. As long as a state adequately represents its people as individuals, other states cannot legitimately claim to represent some of these people as members of its "nation."[32]

The emphasis in the UN Charter on noninterference in the domestic affairs of other states is markedly different from the emphasis on international justice to be found in the League of Nations Charter.[33] This is reflected in the academic response to international relations to be found in the periods following World Wars I and II. The dominant trend in the study of international relations after World War I, idealism, stressed the value of international equity and justice in the long term over the value of stability and *raison d'état* in the short term. Nationalism was seen as the source of the legitimacy of states, and therefore states might be changed to better reflect the ideal of state as nation. The dominant trend in the same field of study following World War II, realism, was in some ways the opposite. It argued for the return of Realpolitik. States were seen as legitimized by the representation of their populations, whoever made up that population. It therefore was the role of the state to act in the interest of itself and its population, rather than to act toward some long-term internationalist ideal in a manner that might rebound to the detriment of the immediate national interest.

The intersubjective understanding of the winning coalition that state borders had a legitimacy apart from national groups had a marked effect on the pattern of borders in Europe following the war. Despite the animosities shown by many Soviet nationalities to Russian domination during the war, the Soviet state was allowed to grow. At the same time, the German nation was divided into two states in order to ease interstate conflict, a pattern that was soon to be repeated in Korea and Vietnam.[34] Many borders in Eastern Europe, such as those between the Soviet Union and Poland, Czechoslovakia, and Romania, were altered in ways that were politically convenient but ethnically nonrepresentative. These changes were officially recognized by the international community. Finally, the emphasis on juridical borders rather than the populations within them is strongly suggested by the solution to the problem that had led to the war in the first place: German ethnically motivated expansionism in Eastern Europe. Instead of expanding the borders of the German state to encompass ethnic Germans in Eastern Europe, millions of ethnic Germans were evicted en masse from Poland and Czechoslovakia so that their borders with Germany would no longer be threatened.

The understanding of the winning coalition as to the legitimate basis of sovereignty had a distinct effect on postwar international relations as well. One particular area in which this effect can be seen is the process of decolonization. The norm of the self-determination of peoples clearly speaks against colonial empires, and these came to be seen as increasingly illegitimate and unacceptable through the late 1940s and 1950s. For the most part however, decolonization did not proceed along nationalist lines. Rather, the borders of new states tended to match the arbitrarily chosen borders of colonial territories. This is particularly clear with respect to the decolonization of Africa. By retaining colonial rather than traditional borders as the basis for the creation of new states, the colonial powers and the UN sought to maximize the viability of the new states, rather than ethnic or tribal ties. In so doing it reflected the accepted norm that the legitimacy of states was based on good government,[35] not national self-determination.[36]

Once again, the reification of state borders in Europe and the Third World provided a basis for the "rules of the game" that helped to stabilize relations among states, particularly between the two blocs. Despite great differences in ideology and domestic institutions, the United States, the Soviet Union, and the European states rarely supported secessionist movements either in Europe or in the Third World.

VI. SOVEREIGNTY AFTER THE COLD WAR

After World War II, realism seemed an appropriate response to the excesses of nationalism. However, as the Cold War progressed and the balance of terror and the concept of mutually assured destruction developed, the dangers of nationalism receded in both popular perceptions and the perceptions of decision makers. The Cold War was a war about legitimating political and economic ideologies, not one about legitimating the state. The end of the Cold War has seen it reaction against realpolitik and against noninterference in the domestic affairs of other states, and for the role of the West in promoting its political and economic ideals internationally. This has led to a change in both the discourse concerning legitimacy in foreign affairs and the conduct of foreign affairs.

The international norm following World War II as discussed above was to reify the state in its existing borders. This allowed for gross abuses by governments of their populations, including in extreme instances a country committing ethnic genocide without a substantive response from the international community. Internal imperialism—the domination of one ethnic group over others within an established state—was also tacitly accepted by other states due to the emphasis on the integrity of juridical borders and the norm of nonintervention. While the international community may not have condoned these actions, neither did it advocate restructuring borders to prevent it. The predominance of *raison d'état* that resulted from this reification led to a popular discontent within the "winning coalition" with an international milieu that was perceived as increasingly unable to cope with the threats of nuclear weapons on the one hand and looming environmental disaster on the other. These factors increasingly weakened the legitimacy of sovereignty understood as the inviolability of states. As the political discourse in international relations increasingly reflects this change, foreign policies are beginning to reflect it as well.

The end of the Cold War has not to date resulted in the sort of official documentation by the winning coalition that marked the end of previous hegemonic conflicts. There is therefore no formal document that expresses the understanding of this coalition as to the nature of the legitimacy of sovereignty. However, there have been substantial changes in the forms of discourse in which discussions of international relations have taken place. As little as four or five years ago, alterations in the borders of Eastern Europe were perceived, both popularly and officially, as potential threats to the peace. Now such changes are considered either neutrally, as in the case of Czechoslovakia, or positively, as in the case of the former Soviet Union or Yugoslavia. The recent action of the UN in excommunicating Yugoslavia for something that twenty years ago may have been considered purely domestic actions exemplifies this change.

The increasing degree to which some Western countries, such as Belgium, Canada, and Spain, feel that they must make concessions to domestic ethnic minorities also reinforces the contention that the understanding of the legitimate basis of the state is changing. If these concessions are to be found within the winning as well as the losing coalitions, they cannot be explained by reference to power politics. Some of these alterations, such as the reunification of Germany and the breakup of the Soviet Union, may reflect the changed security environment after the end of the Soviet military threat to Western Europe. Others, however, do not. The unification of Yemen and the recent talks by the Korean governments suggest that after decades of ideological animosity, they have abruptly come to view the "nation" as having priority over the "state." The demise of Yugoslavia certainly owes as much to a relatively sudden loss of perceived legitimacy, both in the eyes of the international community and in the eyes of Yugoslavia's constituent populations, as to the changed security environment.

The reaction in the United States and Western Europe to the breakup of the Soviet Union also cannot convincingly be traced strictly to security considerations. American and Allied policy toward the Soviet Union until 1989 was to firmly support the central government for both security and ideological reasons. The security reason was that a strong central government would be necessary to preside over troop withdrawals and arms reductions effectively, and the ideological reason was support for President Gorbachev and his reforms. This policy changed rather abruptly to support for the breakup of the Soviet Union into its constituent republics; the international perception of the central government devolved from that of a force for the maintenance of order to an institution of ethnic imperialism. This perceptual shift can be explained better through an examination of changes in understandings of state legitimation than changes in the security environment.

There are exceptions to the resurgence in the legitimacy of nationalism. Two in particular are useful for illustrative purposes, South Africa and Iraq. The international community is explicitly committed to majority rule in a united South Africa. There are two reasons for this. The first is that this commitment predates by decades the end of the Cold War, and therefore the international discourse on South Africa is to some extent fixed in the norms of the Cold War. In other words, because this discourse has been strongly institutionalized, it displays some of the stickiness and continuity characteristic of formal institutions.[37] The second reason is the perception that a breakup of South Africa would not serve the purpose of national self-government generally so much as the purposes of the white minority specifically.

The current policy of the United States and its allies toward Iraq displays a commitment to maintaining the integrity of the country even though there are active secessionist movements within it.[38] This policy results explicitly from balance-of-power considerations, an indication that while recent changes in the interpretation of sovereignty have altered the realpolitik of the cold war, they have not eliminated it entirely. It is worth noting, however, that the U.S. government has explicitly addressed the issue of the integrity of Iraq.[39] During the cold war it would likely have been simply assumed that this integrity would be maintained. The fact that the U.S. government has felt it necessary to address the issue at all, and its efforts to demonstrate that most Iraqis do not want their country broken up, indicates that the change in the understanding of sovereignty underlying discourse in international relations has indeed taken root.

VII. Conclusion

A brief examination of how political actors have defined sovereign authority through the course of modern history demonstrates that the rules of sovereignty vary, and thus the concept is neither fixed nor constant. Rather it is subject to changing interpretations that alter the environment in which states relate to each other. These changes in turn affect the ways in which states are constrained and enabled to act in their international relations. The case studies strongly indicate that while some international orders emphasize the state, others emphasize the nation and that this emphasis tends to oscillate between the two. We find that structural variables alone cannot account for these differences. The Grand Alliance operated within an international environment in 1815 similar to that faced by the Allies in 1919. Yet their solutions to the dilemmas differed considerably. Twenty-five years later, the winning wartime coalition adopted territorial policies similar to those embraced by the Grand Alliance a century earlier. Now there are strong indications that the emphasis has swung toward the national legitimation of sovereignty and away from the sovereignty of the state. We have tried to show that this occurs because our understanding of sovereign authority is intersubjective, largely based on the principles and beliefs that a dominant coalition comes to adopt in the process of constructing an international order.

One of the problems faced by political leaders is that state and national sovereignty can be internally contradictory. The stability of a system of sovereign states rests on the adherence by most states most of the time to a set of rules and common practices.[40] It also relies on a form of legitimacy that allows for mutual expectations. While stability is best assured through fixed, competent states with entrenched authoritative institutions, legitimacy requires a belief that the institutional forms are appropriate and right; in short, that they are just. Legitimacy is eroded when people no longer accept the principles that suggest why they ought to obey the existing authorities.

The dilemma arises when political leaders consider how the principle of self-determination would be put into practice: at what point is a people capable of organizing and administering a government that can ensure domestic welfare and guarantee compliance with international rules? As Kalevi Holsti argues, self-determination applied universally could result in the proliferation of conditionally viable and ineffective states.[41] It could also ignite domestic and regional confrontations in cases where conflicts of state interests do not necessarily exist. As nationalist norms expand their role as a legitimate basis of conflict resolution, such conditionally viable states and regional confrontations are appearing with increasing frequency. This can raise some important policy questions that are currently being discussed only in an ad hoc fashion: where to draw the line between legitimacy and viability and when nationally motivated regional confrontation constitutes an unacceptable threat to stability elsewhere.

From this pliable understanding of sovereignty, one can argue that "objective" material factors, such as polarity, are by themselves insufficient to understand the stability of the international system. Understandings as to what constitutes the legitimate basis of sovereignty have a significant impact on the patterns of global conflict. When an understanding predominates that sovereignty is based on the principle of nationality, efforts to alter state boundaries to reflect nationalist sentiments have a certain legitimacy. Wars may result from efforts to coordinate state boundaries with national groups when such a coordination would come at the expense of another state. For example, the German invasion of Czechoslovakia in 1938 was seen as having some legitimacy by the international community, but that was seen by the losing state, in this case Czechoslovakia, as being at its expense. When an understanding predominates that sovereignty is of a more juridical nature, then states are less likely to attempt to alter national borders in response to national or ethnic conflicts. These conflicts do not necessarily disappear, but they are more likely to be played out within countries than between them. Since juridical states cannot legitimately interfere in the domestic affairs of other states, ethnic conflicts will more often be decided by internal violence—the use of violence by states against elements of their own populations. Bosnia is a good example. As long as the international community recognized an intact Yugoslavia, any ethnic conflict between Serbs and members of other ethnicities in Bosnia was a purely internal Yugoslav affair. Once the international community recognized Bosnia as a separate state under the banner of national self-determination, the same conflict became an interstate war.

The degree of violence—defined as the total physical harm that comes to people—is not necessarily greater with any given understanding of sovereignty. However, when sovereignty is understood to stem from the nation, this violence is more likely to occur between and among states than when sovereignty is understood to be more juridical, in which case state violence is more likely to be internal than interstate. This affects the legitimation and thus the practice of external intervention, which can in turn affect the outcome. This can be clearly seen when comparing the actions of the international community to Iraq's violent suppression of Kurdish nationalism in the 1980s with its declaration of so-called safe zones in 1991.

As the contemporary world shifts from bipolarity, neorealists would suggest that some change should be expected in the degree of stability of the international system.[42] The analysis of sovereignty suggested here indicates that the contemporaneous shift in the predominant understanding of sovereignty will also serve to destabilize the system. This does not mean that the overall level of violence to which the people of the world are subjected will necessarily increase. It does mean, however, that a new category of causes of interstate conflict has been legitimated.

Finally, in arguing that sovereignty should not be understood as a strictly static concept, this article suggests that the state as a basic analytic unit should be scrutinized more than has often been the case in the international relations literature. The sovereign state has often been seen as a fixed entity, both from without and from within. From without, neorealists and neoliberal institutionalists alike take the sovereign state as a given. From within, theories of the domestic sources of foreign policy often assume a fixed sovereignty as the backdrop for domestic political activity. However, both structural theories and theories of domestic sources might benefit by allowing that sovereignty itself, as a basic unit of international relations theory, changes over time and that changing understandings of sovereignty can and do affect international relations.

NOTES

1. Constitutive rules can be defined as concepts that create and define new forms of behavior (x counts as y in context c). They are standardized, relatively unchanging practices that constitute a vocabulary for international communication. See p. 455 of David Dessler, "What's at Stake in the Agent-Structure Debate?" *International Organization* 43 (Summer 1989), pp. 441–73.

2. See p. 143 of John Ruggie, "Continuity and Transformation in the World Polity: Toward a Neorealist Synthesis," in Robert O. Keohane, ed., *Neorealism and Its Critics* (New York: Columbia University Press, 1986), pp. 131–57.

3. The "rules of sovereignty" are defined as a set of principles, by which the international community recognizes the legitimacy of authoritative control over a specified population and territory.

4. We are not suggesting that the state/national distinction is the only or even the most important element of change in the legitimation of sovereignty. We suggest only that it is an important one that can illustrate one way in which understandings of sovereignty can change.

5. Morgenthau sees sovereignty primarily in terms of its legal definition and without reference to its legitimation. Sovereignty is supreme authority to create and enforce laws within a given territory. Therefore for Morgenthau sovereignty is conceptually fixed and indivisible. See Hans J. Morgenthau, *Politics Among Nations: The Struggle for Power and Peace,* 6th ed. (New York: Alfred A. Knopf, 1985). For Waltz the relevant issue concerning sovereignty is whether states remain independent; the principles on which state authority is legitimized are not important. See Kenneth Waltz, *Theory of International Politics* (Reading, Mass.: Addison-Wesley, 1979), especially chap. 5. For Gilpin sovereign authority is derived from one's ability to maintain order and control within stable borders. "Within the territory it encompasses," Gilpin argues, "the state exercises a monopoly of the legitimate use of forces and embodies the idea that everyone in the territory is subject to the same law or set of rules." Robert Gilpin, *War and Change in World Politics* (Cambridge, England: Cambridge University Press, 1981), p. 17.

6. See p. 90 of Stephen D. Krasner, "Sovereignty: An Institutional Perspective," *Comparative Political Studies* 2 (April 1998), pp. 66–94.

7. Janice E. Thomson and Stephen Krasner, "Global Transactions and the Consolidation of Sovereignty," in Ernst-Otto Czempiel and James N. Rosenau, eds., *Global Changes and Theoretical Challenges: Approaches to World Politics for the 1990s* (Lexington, Mass.: Lexington Books, 1999), pp. 195–219.

8. Hedley Bull, *The Anarchical Society: A Study of Order in World Politics* (New York: Columbia University Press, 1977), p. 9.

9. See p. 3 of Robert Art and Robert Jervis, "The Meaning of Anarchy," in Robert Art and Robert Jervis, eds., *International Politics: Anarchy, Force, Political Economy, and Decision Making,* 2d ed. (Boston: Little, Brown, and Company, 1985).

10. See p. 370 of Inis L. Claude, Jr., "Collective Legitimization as a Political Function of the United Nations," *International Organization* 20 (September 1966), pp. 367–79.

11. Anthony Giddens, *The Nation-State and Violence* (Berkeley: University of California Press, 1987), p. 263.

12. The quotation is from Weber, who defines a nation as "a community of sentiment which would adequately manifest itself in a state of its own; hence, a nation is a community which normally tends to produce a state of its own." See Max Weber, *From Max Weber: Essays in Sociology,* Hans H. Gerth and C. Wright Mills, eds. (New York: Oxford University Press, 1981), p. 176.

13. The term "juridical" is being used here to refer to a formally stated and defined territorial boundary sanctioned by international law.
14. Ruggie, *supra* note 2, at 142–43.
15. For further discussions of nationalism and its development, see Ernest Gellner, *Nations and Nationalism* (Ithaca, N.Y.: Cornell University Press, 1983); Eric J. Hobsbawm, *Nations and Nationalism Since 1780* (Cambridge: Cambridge University Press, 1990); Benedict Anderson, *Imagined Communities: Reflections on the Origins and Spread of Nationalism* (London: Verso, 1983); and Anthony Smith, *Theories Of Nationalism* (New York: Holmes and Meier, 1983).
16. The idea of "national" sovereignty as it is used here should not be confused with ideas of "popular" sovereignty. National sovereignty is in fact a subset of popular sovereignty; it is a particular definition of who the people in "popular" are. There are two predominant ways of understanding popular sovereignty. One is that it means that the state should ultimately be responsible to the people as individual political beings. This has its roots in Lockean political theory and can result in such requirements of government as democracy and civil rights. The other way of understanding the concept is that it refers to the rights of a self-identifying group to govern itself as it separate political entity. This idea has its roots in different ways in both Rousseauian and Hegelian political theory and need not to be as democratically oriented as the first understanding. It is this approach to popular sovereignty that is compatible with national sovereignty as it is used here. This distinction follows the distinction between internal and external self-determination discussed by Lee Buchheit in *Secession: The Legitimacy of Self-Determination* (New Haven, Conn.: Yale University Press, 1978), pp. 13–16.
17. Terry Nardin, *Law, Morality, and the Relations of States* (Princeton, N.J.: Princeton University Press, 1983), p. 34.
18. Claude, *supra* note 10, at 367.
19. *Ibid.*, p. 369.
20. Gilpin, *supra* note 5, at 34.
21. There is a growing literature on the effects of intersubjective understandings on agency in international relations. The school of thought that stresses the importance of examining these understandings is sometimes referred to as "constructivist" or "reflectivist." For an introduction to this literature, see...Alexander Wendt, "Anarchy Is What States Make of It: The Social Construction of Power Politics," *International Organization* 46 (Spring 1992), pp. 391–426.
22. Carlton J. Hayes, *The Historical Evolution of Modem Nationalism* (New York: Russell and Russell, 1968), p. 69.
23. See Guglielmo Ferrero, *The Reconstruction of Europe: Talleyrand and the Congress of Vienna, 1814–1815* (New York: G. P. Putnam and Sons. 1941), p. 261.
24. Metternich is quoted in Kalevi Holsti, "Governance Without Government: Polyarchy in Nineteenth-century European International Politics," in James N. Rosenau and Ernst-Otto Czempiel, eds., *Governance Without Government: Order and Change in World Politics* (Cambridge, England: Cambridge University Press, 1992), p. 28.
25. The conclusion of World War I saw the collapse of four empires: German, Austro-Hungarian (Hapsburg), Ottoman, and Russian.
26. Ray Stannard Baker, *Woodrow Wilson and World Settlement*, vol. I (New York: Doubleday, Page and Co., 1922), p. 12.
27. Lloyd Ambrosius, *Wilsonian Statecraft: Theory and Practice of Liberal Internationalism During World War I* (Wilmington, Del.: Scholarly Resources, 1991), p. 12.
28. The quoted term is used throughout the Charter of the United Nations.
29. Of this dilemma Sir Ivor Jennings said, "On the surface it seems reasonable: let the people decide. It was in fact ridiculous because the people cannot decide until someone decides who are the people." Jennings is quoted in Buchheit, *supra* note 16, at 9.
30. Article 2, paragraph 4, and article 51.
31. Article 1, paragraph 2; and article 2, paragraph 7.
32. There is of course a tension here inasmuch as self-determination may serve in cases as an

expression of nationalist sentiment. This tension is recognized in practice by the UN but is often resolved in favor of the cohesion of existing states. [See Hannum's article in this volume—eds.]

33. For example, the Covenant of the League of Nations stipulates that "the Members of the League reserve to themselves the right to take such action as they shall consider necessary for the maintenance of right and justice" (article 15, paragraph 7). This reference to right and justice as a legitimate basis for state action is in marked contrast to the emphasis on international peace and security in the Charter of the UN.

34. In all three of these examples, "nations" were divided into two states, each in the sphere of influence of a different superpower. This willingness to subordinate national unity to superpower spheres of influence indicates that the termination of international conflicts was considered more important than national self-determination in these cases.

35. This is not meant to imply that there was any sort of consensus on what constituted "good government." The Western view of good government was based on individual welfare and political rights, whereas the communist view stressed social welfare and economic rights. The key point here is that both the individualist view and the class view are markedly different from a nationalist view, understood in the fascist sense.

36. Once again this refers to the view that sees the "nation" its something apart from the aggregate of the people that requires representation in its own right.

37. On the subject of the continuity of formal institutions in international relations, see Krasner, *supra* note 6, at 67, 74.

38. [i.e., the Kurds in the north and the Shiite Arabs in the south.]

39. Michael Gordon, "A Shield for Iraq," *The New York Times*, 20 August 1992, pp. Al.

40. Stability does not refer here to the absence of conflict but to the maintenance of the system intact without drastic changes in its form. This usage follows that of Waltz, *supra* note 5, at 161–63.

41. Kalevi Holsti, *Peace and War: Armed Conflicts and International Order 1648-1989* (Cambridge: Cambridge University Press, 1991), p. 352.

42. Waltz, *supra* note 5, at 204–10.

Britain and the 1933 Refugee Convention: National or State Sovereignty?

Robert J. Beck

> *[T]he interests of this country must predominate over all other*
> *considerations, but subject to this guiding principle each case will be*
> *carefully considered on its individual merits . . . [I]n accordance with the*
> *time-honoured tradition of this country no unnecessary obstacles are*
> *placed in the way of foreigners seeking admission.*

DRAFTED BY HOME Secretary Sir John Gilmour, this policy statement was approved by the British Cabinet on April 12, 1933.[1] Parliament had been seeking an answer to the query: "Will the Government . . . be prepared to consider the granting of asylum to German Jews on a self-supporting financial basis?" Gilmour's basic formula would be invoked by His Majesty's Government here and on many subsequent occasions. It reflected a factor that had regularly informed Britain's refugee policy-making in the 1930s: the government's statist understanding of sovereignty and of the sovereign's prerogatives and responsibilities. "National sovereignty" considerations, it will be shown, figured then only slightly, if at all, in Britain's refugee deliberations.

Reprinted from Robert J. Beck, "Britain and the 1933 Refugee Convention: National or State Sovereignty?" *International Journal of Refugee Law* 11 (1999): 597–624. Used by permission of Oxford University Press.

This essay traces the evolution of British policy toward the first multilateral treaty designed to protect refugees: the October 28, 1933 Convention Relating to the International Status of Refugees (1933 Convention). It begins by discussing two competing understandings of the sovereignty concept: "national sovereignty" and "state sovereignty." Next, it shows how the latter understanding framed British decisions not to participate in drafting the treaty but also those later to sign and to ratify it. By necessity, it also addresses Britain's relationship to the 1936 "Provisional Arrangement Concerning the Status of Refugees coming from Germany." Finally, it offers several broad conclusions—on international advocacy efforts, international norms scholarship, and national sovereignty—sustained by a review of inter-war Britain's refugee treaty policy-making.

Refugee policy *per se* merits scholarly attention for several reasons. The most obvious rationale is the immense human problem that refugee movements have posed since World War I. Tens of millions of persons have been driven from their home states in the past century, and recent UNHCR estimates suggest that as many as 21.5 million persons may now be considered "refugees." Not only does the magnitude of human suffering compel close examination by scholars, but also the significant geopolitical implications of the refugee phenomenon. As Gil Loescher has observed, perhaps with some hyperbole, "the flood of refugees from East to West Germany in 1989 . . . helped to bring down the Berlin Wall, expedited the unification of the two German states, and generated the most significant transformation in international relations since World War II."[2] The end of the Cold War, moreover, has engendered its own refugee flows of manifest political import, perhaps the most prominent ones thus far involving tribal/ethnic groups in Africa and the Balkans. Refugee policy warrants study, finally, because refugees "do not fit neatly into a state-centric paradigm." Falling "between the cracks of the state system," refugees pose a challenge both to "conventional ways of thinking about international politics"[3] and to those about international law.

Though one might productively examine more recent refugee policy-making, the inter-war period offers two conspicuous advantages for modern investigators. First, it was then that refugees emerged as an international issue and that the original international refugee regime was constituted. Many parallels exist between inter-war and contemporary refugees, moreover, and current international assistance programs have their origins then. Secondly, only recently have archival materials become available that shed light on the private views of decision-makers. Without such primary sources, the task of tracing government policy-making is substantially hindered.

Why concentrate, though, on *British*[4] refugee policy-making during the inter-war period? Several factors render the subject particularly compelling. First, before World War II the United Kingdom constituted one of only a very few "Great Powers." Though a declining hegemon, it remained a state of genuinely global reach and impact. Britain's influence extended to the refugee realm where, with France, it arguably exerted the most significant effect on inter-war international efforts. Secondly, the British Government administered Palestine then under a League of Nations Mandate that enjoined Britain to facilitate "Jewish immigration under suitable conditions." As the flow of Jews from Germany accelerated after January of 1933, His Majesty's Government was uniquely obliged to make decisions affecting simultaneously the fates of those Jewish refugees, of Palestine, and of the entire Middle East region. Finally, Britain, with Belgium, was one of only two states that became parties to *both* of the inter-war refugee conventions before the onset of the Second World War.[5] Britain thus constituted a conspicuous exception to the general state practice then of refusing to accept formal refugee-related limitations on sovereignty.

I. SOVEREIGNTY: NATIONAL AND STATE

"The actual content of sovereignty," Stephen Krasner submits, "has always been contested."[6] That "sovereignty" has engendered such persistent and spirited contention, by states and by scholars, is not surprising, for "the way in which political actors define the political and geographic boundaries of legitimate authority affects the principles on which the international system will function." Changes in how sovereignty is conceived "can greatly affect the ways in which states are constrained or enabled to act in their international relations."[7] What are states' jurisdictional limitations? States' lawful capacities? Their international duties, if any, as sovereigns? Surely, "the intensity of controversies about sovereignty suggests how important its internationalization is to political actors."[8]

In a provocative 1994 essay, reprinted in this volume, J. Samuel Barkin and Bruce Cronin argue that an "historical tension" has existed between two understandings (or "interpretations") of sovereignty and its rules: "*state sovereignty*, which stresses the link between sovereign authority and a defined territory, and *national sovereignty*, which emphasizes a link between sovereign authority and a defined population." These two types, they posit, "fundamentally differ in the source of their legitimation as independent entities, thereby altering the environment through which states relate to each other." In periods like the "post-Napoleonic order" when state sovereignty has prevailed, nationalist claims have been subordinated to the preservation of "stable, effective states with strong institutions." Conversely, during periods such as that after the First World War when sovereign "legitimation derives primarily from nationalist principles," states have supported changes in territorial borders to reflect better the "national self-determination" principle. Sovereignty's history, then, has been one of oscillation between an emphasis on state and one on nation. That variance, moreover, "cannot be objectively deduced" in realist fashion "solely from the nature of states and the distribution of capabilities." Rather, it must also be induced from processes of political interaction, ones featuring a significant intersubjective (i.e., shared, social) dimension. Though Barkin and Cronin concede that the "state/national distinction" may not be "the only or even the most important element of change in the legitimation of sovereignty," they nevertheless submit that it is "an important one."

Barkin and Cronin's typology, which appropriately underscores the dynamic, social, and ideational dimensions of sovereignty, may be employed profitably by scholars. Even so, to what extent is their characterization of the inter-war period empirically sustained? A general historical examination of post-WWI state practices suggests a number of conclusions. First, the "national sovereignty" depiction of the inter-war period by Barkin and Cronin is at least superficially supported. Certainly, at the Versailles Conference the representatives of dozens of dispossessed peoples were permitted in an unprecedented way to press their claims. Moreover, nationality considerations figured to some degree in the post-war dissolutions of the Austrian, German, and Russian empires, as they did in the attendant constructions of such new states as Yugoslavia and Czechoslovakia and such newly independent ones as Austria, Hungary, Estonia, Latvia, and Lithuania. Ironically, the inter-war period's mass refugee movements might well be interpreted as by-products of these efforts, and other less nobly intentioned ones, to effect nationality-based states.

Despite the inter-war currency of the "national self-determination" concept, the "state sovereignty" idea would seem still largely to have obtained then, especially with respect to the treatment of refugees, who quite often represented definable nationalities. If governments at times proved willing to redraw others' boundaries to promote "self-determination," and conveniently, their own securities, they nevertheless remained highly reluctant to render their state frontiers permeable. Furthermore, governments held fast to the view that only states into whose territories refugees had already flowed had a genuine "interest" in refugees, and hence, that states had no general, positive international obligation with respect to refugees, whatever their nationality. The "refugee problem" was deemed, in any case, merely an ephemeral one. As Claudena Skran has noted, "the solutions discussed and eventually implemented reflected the desire of governments to fit refugees back into the normal parameters of the [sovereign] state system."[9] In the inter-war period, consequently, sovereign legitimacy was not called into question when states assiduously monitored their own borders, and the sovereign's responsibility for non-nationals virtually ended at the frontier of its domain.

It is a relatively straightforward task to sketch generally, as has just been done here, the nature and political implications of a given international rule or principle during a particular historical period. The inherent danger posed by such an approach, however, is that by painting an ideational landscape with a broad brush, one may fail accurately to render its constitutive elements. To avoid miscasting the historic content and role of an international principle or rule, therefore, the scholar must turn to a close scrutiny of specific decision-making processes and strategic political interactions. Janice Thomson conceded in her article-length study of the decline of mercenarism that "examining the internal discussions leading up to the implementation of the [mercenarism] ban" would have helped "to illuminate the extent to which statesmen and others *actually* made a link between citizenship and foreign military service."[10] Unfortunately, thus far too little scholarship on international norms has concentrated on decision-making *per se*. This likely reflects the chief practical difficulty such historical research typically presents: either adequate documentary evidence does not exist, or it is not readily available.[11] Sufficient evidence remains of Britain's policy-making associated with the 1933 Convention, fortunately, to permit an assessment of the role of sovereignty understandings there. To such an appraisal, this essay will now turn.

II. BRITAIN AND THE 1933 CONVENTION

A. Origins of the Treaty

The October 28, 1933 Convention Relating to the International Status of Refugees represented the first binding multilateral instrument to afford refugees legal protection; it was, as well, the first international agreement to articulate the principle that refugees should not be returned involuntarily to their country of origin. The completed treaty never became applicable worldwide, and its scope remained confined to those already under League of Nations protection: Russian, Armenian, Assyrian, Assyro-Chaldean, and Turkish refugees. Despite these limitations, sixteen states ultimately became treaty parties or adherents. Moreover, even though many states parties made reservations to important articles, the 1933 Convention set standards for refugee treatment in several key issue areas and came to exert a significant influence on adherent state behavior.[12] State governments proved at first rather unenthusiastic about drafting the treaty and the British Government almost hostile; however, former refugees, private voluntary organizations (PVOs), and international refugee advocates all made important contributions to the process of its creation. Perhaps ironically, British private individuals occupied positions of prominence in the League system while the convention proposal was being mooted, including the League of Nations Secretary-General, Sir Eric Drummond, and Major Thomas Frank Johnson, Secretary-General of the Nansen International Office for Refugees.

Before the First World War, the international law of asylum had remained virtually uncodified. On the subject of refugees, meanwhile, customary law had stood silent as well. Accordingly, at the war's conclusion "refugee status" remained ambiguous, and one of the principal inter-war objectives of international refugee advocates would become international *legal* protection. Early efforts to secure this end included the Nansen Passport System that began in 1922, and subsequent special refugee "Arrangements" in 1924, 1926, and 1928. None of these arrangements, however, created legal obligations *per se*. Instead, each offered only non-binding recommendations to governments.

The informal 1928 Arrangement, in fact, had its origins in the first prominent proposal of a *formal* treaty. On September 7, 1927, a Russian refugee with international legal expertise urged that a refugee convention be concluded under the League's auspices. Jacques L. Rubinstein submitted his resolution on behalf of the Russian organizations represented on the Advisory Committee of Private Organizations, a non-governmental group then attached to High Commissioner for Refugees Fridtjof Nansen. Rubinstein's resolution was adopted and subsequently submitted by Dr. Nansen to the League Assembly, which in turn instructed Nansen to convene an inter-governmental conference. At the resultant June 28–30, 1928 meeting in Geneva, however, the majority of participating states proved unwilling "to contract formal obligations on behalf of the refugees." Consequently, "a formula was sought which would secure the maximum number of votes," and a non-binding Arrangement was thereby concluded.[13]

In 1931, Rubinstein's idea to draft a formal refugee treaty was revived. That August, the Inter-governmental Advisory Commission on Refugees convened in Geneva its fourth session. This special body of delegates from private organizations and fourteen states had been created by the League of Nations Council in 1928 to conduct a general survey of the League's refugee operations; after completing its May 1929 report, however, the group continued to advise the League's refugee agencies.[14] Now, among the proposals the Commission chose to endorse was that of its president, Monsieur E. de Navailles-Labatut, to establish a convention. That legal instrument would "stabilise the situation" of refugees upon the anticipated December 31, 1938 liquidation of the Nansen International Office.

In response to the Advisory Commission's August 1931 recommendation, the Twelfth League Assembly requested in its September 1931 session that the Governing Body of the Nansen Office, in consultation with the Commission, consider the advisability of preparing such a refugee treaty. To request Governing Body "consultation with the Commission," of course, was and would remain largely a formalism: the membership of the two bodies overlapped substantially. Typifying their interrelationship were the groups' compositions in 1933, when the Convention would be concluded. Fourteen of the Governing Body's twenty-two "members" or "substitute members" then also served on the Commission as government delegates, advisory members, or technical advisers. The Governing Body's remaining eight members and substitute members then included five PVO officials, the International Labour Organisation (I.L.O.) Director, the League Secretary-General, and one member of the Secretariat's Political Section.

On October 27, 1931, pursuant to a September 29 decision by the League Council, Secretary-General Eric Drummond transmitted all the Inter-governmental Advisory Commission's fourth session recommendations to "interested governments" for their reactions. The respondents manifested strikingly little interest in a refugee treaty, however.[15] The governments of Britain and twelve other states, for instance, offered *no* response whatsoever to the convention proposal, while not one state government was strongly supportive. By contrast, the Advisory Committee of Private Organizations, a non-governmental group that now reported to the Inter-governmental Advisory Commission, readily endorsed the Commission's convention proposal at the Committee's March 21, 1932 meeting.

At its April 1932 session, the Governing Body of the Nansen Office approved an exhaustive questionnaire on the "whole refugee problem." Addressed to the members of the Governing Body, the Inter-governmental Advisory Commission and the Advisory Committee of Private Organizations, the document would seek to ascertain whether a refugee convention would constitute "the best means of securing the stability of the situation of the refugees on the liquidation of the Office." On May 2, 1932, the formal list of queries was circulated, and it ultimately elicited twenty-six responses. In view of the modest sizes, policy predilections, and overlapping memberships then of the Governing Body, Advisory Commission, and Advisory Committee, the questionnaire process might well be characterized as a single group's exercise in "preaching" to itself, the already "converted."

The Sixth Committee of the League Assembly convened in the autumn of 1932. Serving as rapporteur then was Viscount Robert Cecil of Chelwood: president of the League of Nations Union, one of Britain's most prominent refugee advocates, and a consistent supporter of the refugee treaty effort.[16] Lord Cecil noted in his October 6 committee report that the body "was glad to learn that the Nansen Office [was] engaged upon the preparation of the Convention." The Committee "trust[ed] that the Governing Body, after consultation with the Inter-governmental Advisory Committee for Refugees, [might] be in a position in its next annual report to indicate the main lines of such a Convention." Cecil's report was adopted shortly thereafter by the Assembly in its thirteenth annual meeting.

On October 28, 1932, the Governing Body of the Nansen Office appointed a three-person "Committee of Experts" to "consider the advisability of a Convention to ensure the protection of refugees, and to consider certain questions raised regarding the application of the Arrangements of 1922, 1924, 1926, and 1928." Notably, only one member of the committee was a state government representative, Monsieur de Navailles, the resuscitator of Jacques Rubinstein's 1927 treaty initiative. The Deputy Director of Chancelleries and of the Litigation Department at the French Ministry of Foreign Affairs, de Navailles was both Vice President of the Nansen Office's Governing Body and President of the Inter-governmental Advisory Commission. Joining him were two refugees from Russia: Baron Boris Nolde, a Technical Adviser to the Commission and member of the Council of Former Russian Ambassadors; and Jacques L. Rubinstein, who was a member of the Central Commission for the Study of the Conditions of Russian Refugees and now a Governing Body deputy member. By January 9, 1933, the three experts had produced their report, informed by the results of the Nansen Office's May 1932 questionnaire.

On January 24, 1933, the Inter-governmental Advisory Commission convened its fifth official session. Britain was represented by its Consul in Geneva, Harold Patteson, who would be elected then a substitute member of the Governing Body. During the course of its meeting, the Commission reached several important treaty-related decisions. First, the group adopted the conclusions of the Committee of Experts report and agreed that a refugee convention was necessary. Given his presidency of the Commission, de Navailles was surely well placed to encourage this result. Secondly, the Commission decided to request preparation of a draft treaty by its president and by the Nansen Office Governing Body's president, who would be selected February 24 (Professor Georges Werner). Finally, subject to approval by the Governing Body, the Commission endorsed a "simplified procedure" for conclusion of a Convention that had been proposed by the Committee of Experts, a process departing from that earlier stipulated by the League's Twelfth Assembly.

The Advisory Commission's three principal recommendations were endorsed by the Nansen Office's Governing Body in its seventh session on April 26, 1933. Governing Body President Georges Werner would explain the "simplified procedure" in a formal May 18 communication to the League's members and its Council: "the Presidents of the Nansen International Office and of the Inter-governmental Advisory Commission would be instructed: (1) to prepare a draft convention for the purpose of ensuring the protection of refugees; (2) to communicate it, together with the experts report, to the Governments interested in the solution of the refugee problem; and (3) to invite these Governments to a small limited Conference for the purpose of drawing up and adopting a final text of the Convention, to be open to subsequent accessions." Judge Werner then listed those states that appeared "most interested" in solving the refugee problem based on "the number of refugees to whom they [had] extended hospitality." These states included thirteen of the fourteen with delegates on the Commission—Belgium, United Kingdom, Bulgaria, China, Czechoslovakia, Estonia, France, Germany, Greece, Latvia, Poland, Romania, and Yugoslavia—as well as Austria, Egypt, Finland, Lithuania, and Switzerland.

On May 22, 1933, Georges Werner appeared before the first meeting of the League Council's seventy-third session. Here he presented a report of the recent work of the Governing Body and the Inter-governmental Commission, urging that the Council endorse their proposals, including that for a simplified procedure. He argued that "it was necessary, in order to set on foot the Convention which everyone so greatly desired, to set up a procedure somewhat speedier than the ordinary procedure of the League of Nations." The Council thereafter adopted Werner's recommendations and requested the Presidents of the Governing Body and the Inter-governmental Advisory Commission to prepare a draft Convention for submission to a conference.

On Thursday morning, October 26, 1933, the Inter-governmental Conference on Refugees was convened in Geneva. Government representatives from fifteen states attended the three-day, five session meeting: Austria, Belgium, Bulgaria, China, Czechoslovakia, Egypt, Estonia, Finland, France, Greece, Latvia, Poland, Romania, Switzerland, and Yugoslavia. Conspicuously absent from the proceedings, however, were British, German, and Lithuanian government representatives. Perhaps equally striking was the presence and contribution there of several prominent refugees, none of whom represented state governments: L. Pachalian of the Central Committee for Armenian Refugees; and "Committee of Experts" members Nolde and Rubinstein. The pervasiveness of Nolde and Rubinstein's participation would be well illustrated by their dialogue's subsequent appearance on twenty-three of the official conference transcript's fifty-nine substantive pages. Rubinstein's high profile, in particular, likely reflected his central role in devising the draft convention. Monsieur de Navailles, with Rubinstein and Nolde the third member of the Committee of Experts, became by acclamation the President of the Inter-governmental Conference, in a development that probably was largely anticipated. The inter-war period's refugee-advocacy "epistemic community,"[17] if that group genuinely merits such a designation, was of very modest size and de Navailles represented one of its most prominent members.

By Saturday afternoon, October 28, 1933, the Inter-governmental Conference had agreed upon the final form of the Convention Relating to the International Status of Refugees. The "simplified procedure" strategy first advocated by Rubinstein, Nolde and de Navailles had successfully and rapidly yielded a treaty. Moreover, the final treaty closely followed the draft that had been penned by Rubinstein and his Inter-governmental Advisory Commission colleagues. On the treaty-making process *per se*, Rubinstein would offer these observations in a 1936 address at Chatham House:

> On this occasion [the October 1933 Conference] different tactics from those of 1928 were employed. There was no attempt to please everybody at the cost of sacrificing the text of the plan; the majority rule was not applied. All provisions supported by several votes were retained, and the governments regarding them as unacceptable were invited to make reservations. By these methods the adoption of the [first international] Convention [to protect refugees] was secured.

Judging it "an instrument of the first importance," Rubinstein urged that Britain sign the Convention. He recounted for his British audience the treaty's principal virtues:

> It betters the Nansen certificate system, it restricts abuses in the practice of expulsion, and it regulates certain points of private international law. Furthermore, it secures for refugees freedom of access to the law courts, and the most favorable treatment in respect of social life and assurance and of taxation; it exempts them from the rule of reciprocity, it provides for the optional institution of refugee committees in every country, and it secures certain modifications of the measures restricting unemployment.[18]

B. British Refugee Policy and the 1933 Intergovernmental Conference

Why was Jacques Rubinstein compelled in March of 1936 to plead publicly for British accession to the 1933 Convention? What had been the relationship between Great Britain and that treaty? And what role had understandings of "sovereignty," national and state, played in the deliberations of His Majesty's Government? For answers to these questions, one may productively begin with an examination of British policymaking at 1932's close. By then, the idea of drafting a refugee treaty had been reintroduced by Monsieur de Navailles, the Nansen Office Governing Body's exhaustive questionnaire on refugees had been circulated, and the Committee of Experts report was virtually complete. In its fifth formal session, moreover, the Inter-governmental Advisory Commission would very soon consider that important document's recommendations.

On Wednesday afternoon, December 21, 1932, Parliamentary Under Secretary of State Anthony Eden met in London with Lord Robert Cecil and Sir Walter Napier. Cecil had sought the interview to discuss with Eden the forthcoming Advisory Commission meeting in Geneva. In a background note prepared on December 20 for the Under Secretary, the Eastern Office's Angus Malcolm observed tersely that "the necessity for government co-operation [was] not quite clear." Furthermore, he conceded that "[w]e have no knowledge of a forthcoming meeting" of the Commission. "The Northern Dept.," he added, was "incline[d] to regard the transfer of these people to Soviet Armenia as unconsciously but none the less inhumane, & would not advise encouraging it." Britain, though, had apparently no positive duty as sovereign to discourage actively such "inhumane" practices by another sovereign, whatever national groups might be effected.

In the course of their December 21 meeting, Lord Cecil told Eden that "the problem [was] to persuade the French, Belgian, and Bulgarian [representatives] to accept" the proposed convention on refugees. Cecil further suggested that the "British representative might be able to do this." In these assertions, Lord Cecil was surely evincing optimism since he must have recognized the British Government's profound reluctance then to take an activist role in the refugee realm and to become party to any such treaty. Sir Walter Napier, meanwhile, provided Eden with a twelve-page essay he had drafted on "The Armenian Question." Appended to Napier's exposition was a "rough epitome of [a 16-article] Draft Refugee Convention," one that resembled the formal draft that would be debated ten months later in Geneva. The dismissive response to Napier's memo by Alexander Helm, Eastern Department official, suggested attitudes generally held in the Foreign Office: "the terms of the draft Convention (referred to in the last para of Sir W. Napier's memo and the text of which is apparently attached) hardly concern the Eastern Dept., I think." Here Helm was playing the sort of government "clerk" Lord Cecil would later decry as "earn[ing] his salary by making objections."

By May of 1933, the British Government had become no more enthused about the prospect of taking active measures on behalf of refugees abroad. When, for instance, the May 18 "Report of the Inter-Governmental Advisory Commission for Refugees on the Work of Its Fifth Session" was received in London, it elicited virtually no written reaction from the Foreign Office, even though the document was examined by a succession of officials, including: Ian Wilson-Young of the League of Nations Department; J.C. Sterndale Bennett of the Eastern Department; and Robert Maurice Hankey of the Central Department. "The remarks about expulsion on page 2," one counselor merely noted, "are presumably directed at the Persians, who are still in the habit of expelling Russian refugees back to Soviet territory."

Such blithe detachment then also informed Britain's policy toward Jewish refugees from Germany. Ever since the German exodus had commenced, the British Government had been compelled to consider whether this new refugee issue merited reference to the League of Nations. Petitions by individual and private organizations "were answered with a certain weary patience by Foreign Office officials who pointed out the incontrovertible fact that the refugees from Germany still possessed German passports, were not technically stateless, and therefore could not claim the protection of the Nansen Office."[19] After an internal review of the issue, the Foreign Office transmitted to the Home Office a formal letter. Here, it offered the legalism that the German refugees problem lay beyond the Nansen Office's authority. Moreover, it noted that "a suggestion by His Majesty's Government that the League should consider measures of assistance for German nationals leaving Germany would be regarded in that country as an act of unwarranted interference, and [Foreign Minister] Sir John Simon could not advise that it should be made." One sovereign ought not meddle in another's domestic affairs, or at least, not be vulnerable to such an accusation.

In July of 1933, the official spokesman of the British Jewish community in international affairs, Neville Laski, contacted Permanent Under Secretary Robert

Vansittart. In a letter and a personal call to Whitehall, the Chair of the Anglo-Jewish Association asked that Britain place on the League Assembly's September agenda the German refugee question. Laski's actions precipitated another review of Foreign Office policy, and in turn, an August 25, 1933 internal memorandum. Though prompted specifically by the German case, John Perowne's statement captured well his Government's general views then on its sovereign responsibilities and prerogatives with respect to refugees, and on the role to be played by international organization:

> The number of such refugees in the United Kingdom is still comparably small . . . but the competent authorities have no desire to see it increased . . . the Home Office, Colonial Office, Dominions Office and Ministry of Labour are especially anxious to avoid being placed in the position of having to turn down, or to act upon any immigration or settlement recommendations coming from such a source [the League]; and they do not want the matter referred to the League *at all* if that can be avoided . . . they are *a fortiori* averse from any suggestion that HM Government should . . . take the initiative.

The Foreign Office's reply to Mr. Laski was less direct, but still expressed the conviction that a state's interest in a given refugee problem depended on the extent to which its territorial boundaries had been crossed. It was not appropriate for Britain to raise the German refugee problem at the League, the missive explained, given the "very much smaller number of such refugees in this country than in most other countries concerned."

The same logic would drive the British Government's determination not to attend October's Inter-governmental Conference in Geneva: "Nansen refugees," those to be protected by the prospective refugee treaty, simply did not lie within Great Britain's borders in sufficient numbers to warrant such participation. Hence, Sir John Gilmour's Home Office, whose responsibilities included the admission of aliens, decided to decline the conference invitation. This decision greatly displeased Major Thomas Johnson, the Secretary-General of the Nansen Office, who nevertheless sought to respond to the "territorial/interest" argument on its own terms. In a September 29 letter, Ashley Clarke explained to Allen Leeper, Head of the League of Nations Department:

> Major Johnson . . . is, of course, perturbed at our decision not to be represented on the body which will consider the Convention. He advances as new reason to be considered the possibility that we may have a large body of Assyrians on our hands and that we may therefore be more affected by the general problem of the treatment of refugees than before. This does not seem to us to be a very substantial argument but

we pass it on to you in case you think that those concerned may wish to reconsider their opinion.

Clarke's letter from Geneva stimulated a lively response in London. John Nicholls of the League of Nations Department asked his colleagues on October 6, "Are you impressed by Major Johnson's new argument for participation? If so, we ought perhaps to refer the question back to the H.O. [Home Office] and C.O. [Colonial Office]." That same day, a colleague brusquely replied: "What is impressive is Major Johnson's capacity for finding himself work, often enough, during the last ten years, at the expense of the refugees themselves." On October 11, Alexander Helm observed that his Eastern Department did "not think that the question of the Assyrians affects the issue. That question will be dealt with on its own merits and is one for the League of Nations to decide. We therefore do not wish to interfere with the decision already reached and communicated to the League." Allen Leeper shared these views and on October 11 instructed that Ashley Clarke be so informed. Britain would not participate in the Inter-governmental Conference.

C. The Aftermath of the Conference

On December 4, 1933, a certified true copy of the now-completed 1933 Convention was forwarded to Sir John Simon, the Secretary of State for Foreign Affairs, by the League Secretariat's Acting Legal Adviser on behalf of the Secretary-General. Shortly thereafter, the Foreign Office's Treaty Department head, George Warner, and Second Legal Adviser William Beckett addressed some of the treaty's technical and policy implications. Warner, for example, remarked that the Convention "seem[ed] to contain the elements of juridical conundra." He wondered, for example, "what 'domicile' in Arts 4 & 5" meant. Beckett identified some "blemishes," too, noting that he had "no doubt that we could have had these [problems] put right" if Britain had been represented at the Geneva Conference. The Second Legal Adviser drew attention, as well, to the Convention's Article 23 provision that allowed "a signatory or acceding Party to make almost any reservations it likes."

Whether the United Kingdom would resort to such reservations, or even become a treaty party at all, was not immediately clear. Already on October 27, the Foreign Office Under Secretary had sent a memorandum to Sir John Gilmour regarding potential British acceptance of the refugee convention's obligations. In a December 21 letter to the Under Secretary of State, Sir Ernest Holderness offered the Home Secretary's reply. Sir John wished now to reaffirm a principle he had articulated in an August 3, 1933 memorandum: "His Majesty's Government must . . . reserve the right under the Aliens Order, 1920, to deal with all aliens who desire to obtain admission to this country, whether or not they come within the category of stateless refugees." Accordingly, "certain pro-

visions in Articles 1, 2 and 6 of the [draft] Convention could not be agreed to."
From the Home Office's standpoint, refugees were merely another group of foreigners seeking entrance into British territory, and Britain possessed the sovereign authority to limit legitimately their entry. Whether stateless or not, an alien
was an alien.

But this basic premise did not self-evidently dictate a course of action. On
December 30, 1933, the League Department's John Nicholls minuted: "The
H.O. object to articles 1, 2, & 6, but do not state definitely that H.M.G. of U.K.
should not sign or accede to it. Art 23. [of the final treaty] wd. allow us to make
any reservations we like in so doing, so that we could sign or accede without altering the Aliens Order." Second Legal Adviser Beckett agreed: "we must ask the
HO to state definitely if they think the UK can accede to this convention subject to reservations and if so ask them to draft the reservations which they think
necessary." In a letter drafted on January 17, 1934, the League of Nations Office's
Allen Leeper formally sought clarification from the Home Office.

Meanwhile, because the 1933 Convention figured on the agenda of the
forthcoming League Council session, the British government had to consider
which, if any, states non-members of the League might be sent the 1933 Convention for their signature or accession consideration. On January 1, 1934, Foreign Office First Secretary Ralph Stevenson offered this brief observation: "The
U.K. is not a party & was not represented at the conference which drew up the
Convention. It does not seem therefore to be a matter of any great moment to
us whether the convention is communicated to states non-members or not."
Here, again, the implicit premise seemed to be that Britain's interest in refugees
was engaged only once those aliens had actually entered British territorial jurisdiction.[20] Britain had no positive duty as sovereign to foster the acceptance by
other states of formal "refugee protection" obligations. Nor, apparently, did national groups forced to flee their homelands warrant the concerted legal protection of the international community.

During 1934 and 1935, the Home Office regularly resisted accession to the
1933 Convention because it judged that "once the Convention affording legal
protection to 'Nansen' refugees had been accepted, there would be pressures to
extend its benefits to German and perhaps unknown future classes of
refugees."[21] Britain's sovereign prerogatives to limit admission into its territory
might be unduly constrained.[22] A 1935 Foreign Office memorandum captured
well this concern: "it was felt that it might be difficult, under the growing pressure from societies interested in the German refugee problem, to resist a demand
for the extension of the terms of the Convention to all refugees and stateless persons, and the Home Office were particularly anxious to avoid any such commitment, which would appear to perpetuate the problem of German and other
refugees." The Home and Foreign Offices continued to cling to the fiction that
the "refugee problem" was merely transitory. Even so, His Majesty's Government

decided in 1936 that it would send its representatives to an intergovernmental conference in Geneva that would focus on refugees from Germany. Here, what Britain's Government had long feared would nevertheless be attempted, though unsuccessfully: the extension of the 1933 Convention's legal benefits to German refugees.

D. The 1936 Provisional Arrangement

On January 24, 1936, the League Council authorized the convocation of a conference to establish a system of international legal protection for German refugees. The lack of passports and juridical status, Council members seemed then to appreciate, had inflicted great hardships on these emigrants. A draft Arrangement "based on the previous work and, in particular, on the provisions of the [1933] Convention" was therefore prepared by High Commissioner Malcolm. Thereafter, on Thursday, July 2, 1936, Sir Neill convened in Geneva an inter-governmental conference attended by the representatives of fifteen states: Belgium, Czechoslovakia, Denmark, Ecuador, France, the Irish Free State, Latvia, the Netherlands, Norway, Poland, Roumania [sic], Sweden, Switzerland, Uruguay, and the United Kingdom, which had dispatched the Home Office's E.N. Cooper and Roger Makins of the Foreign Office. Also joining the three-day deliberations were observers sent by the United States and Finland governments.

Though the conferees decided to meet in private, the representatives of non-governmental organizations were nevertheless permitted to attend the proceedings—despite a protest by Britain's chief delegate, E.N. Cooper, and opposition by some French delegation officials. Indeed, the memorials of two private groups, the International Conference for the Right of Asylum and the International Conference of German Émigrés, were even issued during the conference's course to government delegates. In his post-conference report to Foreign Secretary Anthony Eden, Cooper noted that "certain delegates . . . [had] spoke[n] strongly in favour of admitting as observers the representatives of the voluntary organisations who had come to Geneva for the purpose of securing as far as possible that their views should be brought to the attention of the Conference." These advocates of PVO participation had included Nansen Office High Commissioner Michael Hansson and "Monsieur Jean Loquet and Monsieur L. de Brouckere, the principal French and Belgian delegates, both well known *left-wing progressive* figures in their respective countries and in League circles."[23] Roger Makins of the League Department agreed with Cooper, judging the decision to admit non-governmental representatives "a very bad precedent." In Makins' view, "these people should have been treated on the same footing as the press and other members of the public." Treaty-making was the proper domain of *sovereign state* governments.

During "the course of the [July 1936] Inter-Governmental Conference," Sir Neil would subsequently relate, "it was brought out that those countries which were prepared to take a share in the international settlement of the problem of refugees from Germany felt that the application of all the provisions of the 1933 Convention to those refugees would be premature. It [was] for this reason that the Provisional Arrangement differ[ed] from the 1933 Convention." Roger Makins proffered an alternate interpretation: "The Conference was not very well prepared by the Secretariat, and insufficient notice was given that the application of all the clauses of the 1933 Refugees [sic] Convention to German refugees would be discussed. There was an almost unanimous refusal on the part of the delegates to embark on this discussion, but this was inevitable in the circumstances." Cooper's account was similar to that submitted by Makins:

> At the end of the afternoon session on [Saturday,] the 4th [of] July, Sir Neill Malcolm asked the members of the Conference if they were prepared to consider the second item on the Agenda as to drafting a convention determining the status of refugees. Sir Neill Malcolm explained that what he had in mind was something similar to Chapter IV–X of the 1933 Convention covering such subjects as the right to work, public assistance, social insurance, education and the like. Several delegates pointed out that no indication had been given that these matters would be raised, no papers or draft text had been circulated to Governments and it was quite evident that no one was prepared to discuss the problem *in vacuo*.

In retrospect, it appears that Sir Neill's strategy may have been to press for state acceptance of a formal treaty immediately after state agreement on a Provisional Arrangement had been secured.

Despite Malcolm's failure to push delegates toward treaty deliberations *per se*, one "subject of prolonged discussion" proved the expulsion/*non-refoulement* Article of the proposed Arrangement. At the commencement of debate on the subject, E.N. Cooper articulated Britain's policy in accordance with his instructions: "His Majesty's Government was in full sympathy with the proposal that no genuine refugee should be reconducted to the frontier of the Reich." Nevertheless, "the same effect might be achieved without committing Governments to a provision of so far reaching a character as was contemplated in the draft text and which, if accepted, would almost certainly be hedged about with reservations—if indeed Governments did not contract out of the clause altogether—thereby rendering nugatory the intention of the Article." Cooper thus proposed a substitute clause for the second paragraph of draft Article II(2): "refugees who [had] left Germany for political, racial or religious reasons and who could not be permitted to prolong their stay indefinitely in the country in which they were living, should be given ample time and opportunity of making arrangements to leave the country." Such persons, moreover, "would not be reconducted to the frontiers of the Reich except as an extreme measure and only then if they [had] refused either to make arrangements or to take advantage of any arrangements made for their departure to another country."

Mr. Cooper subsequently reported to Eden that there was "no doubt that the liberal attitude of His Majesty's Government as expressed in the [proposed] substitute clause [had] created an excellent impression upon the delegates." Ultimately, however, the Article's final text proved a "compromise between the original draft text and the British amendment" offered by Cooper. Even so, Britain's chief delegate felt obliged to declare at the conference's final session "that, having regard to the manner in which the admission and control of aliens [was] carried out in the United Kingdom, it would be necessary for His Majesty's Government to contract out of clause 3 of [final] Article IV." Cooper's statement proved inaccurate, however, as Britain ultimately offered a reservation only to the second paragraph of article 4, which would "not be applicable to refugees who have been admitted to the United Kingdom for a temporary visit or purpose. The term 'public order,'" moreover, was "deemed to include matters relating to crime and morals." Cooper's *faux pas* might have been avoided had he heeded Makins' "warnings . . . to send for a Legal Adviser."

At first, the informal agreement of July 4, 1936 was signed by six states: Belgium, Denmark, France, Norway, Spain, and Switzerland. Great Britain would not sign until September 24, nearly three months after the Geneva Conference's conclusion. Roger Makins commented on July 21 that "the Home Office [was] still considering the formulation of the reservations which they [had found] it necessary to make to this arrangement." He had asked them "to treat the question as one of urgency, for it would create a bad impression if the United Kingdom's signature was long delayed."

E. Signature of the Provisional Arrangement
On September 25, 1936, E.N. Cooper of the Home Office signed the "Provisional Arrangement Concerning the Status of Refugees coming from Germany." This quasi-formal agreement provided for the issuance of identity certificates for refugees from Germany who lacked these papers and sought to protect such refugees from arbitrary expulsion and repatriation. As a consequence of Britain's acceptance of the Provisional Arrangement, the earlier Home Office objections to 1933 Convention accession could now be withdrawn. German refugees *per se* would now be afforded some protection—though not in a strictly *legal* sense and subject to the significant limitations imposed by British reservations to the Arrangement. With the German issue addressed, then, Britain could safely accede to a treaty protecting refugees of Russian, Armenian, Assyrian, Assyro-Chaldean, and Turkish nationality.

F. Accession to the 1933 Convention

Three weeks after its signature of the 1936 Provisional Agreement, on October 14, 1936, the British Government finally signed an Instrument of Accession to the 1933 Convention. It did so, however, only with significant reservations to five articles:

(1) *Ad* Article 1: His Majesty's Government in the United Kingdom regard the Convention as applicable only to Russian, Armenian and assimilated refugees who, at the date of the present accession, no longer enjoy the protection of their country of origin;

(2) *Ad* Article 3: The first paragraph will not be applicable to refugees who have been admitted to the United Kingdom for a temporary visit or purpose. The term 'public order' is deemed to include matters relating to crime and morals. Paragraph 2 of Article 3 is not accepted;

(3) *Ad* Article 7 will not be applicable to refugees who have been admitted to the United Kingdom for a temporary visit or purpose;

(4) *Ad* Article 12: Owing to the special position of schools and universities in the United Kingdom, this article is not accepted;

(5) Article 14 is not accepted.[24]

Three aspects of these reservations are especially notable. First, the British Government deliberately limited the category of protected refugees to those "no longer enjoy[ing] the protection of their country of origin." In this reservation to Article 1 of the Convention, Britain was supporting the "juridical" principle[25] that only "stateless" refugees merited protection. If a "refugee" continued to be linked formally to his or her sovereign state, then other sovereign states ought not, apparently, to intervene.

Secondly, of the eight states that eventually became parties to the Convention, *only* Britain explicitly rejected Article 3 (2), the treaty's provision for *non-refoulement* of refugees: "Elle s'engage, dans tous les cas, a` ne pas refouler les refugies sur les frontieres de leur pays d'origine."

Finally, and intriguingly, Britain's rejection of Article 3(2) may well have been based in part on a mistranslation of the French language text of the treaty. The 1933 Inter-governmental Conference had been conducted in French, and the only authoritative version of the 1933 Convention was likewise in French. Nevertheless, an unofficial English translation was communicated "for information" purposes to the Council and to League of Nations members, including Britain. That version's rendition of Article 3(2), apparently prepared on the basis of the Draft Convention, was flawed.[26] It misleadingly suggested that states parties undertook "not to *refuse entry* to refugees at the frontiers of their countries of origin." In fact, "the word '*refouler*' does not mean to 'refuse entry,' but to return or reconduct, in other words: to send back." Thus, as Grahl-Madsen has argued, "the provision [did] not refer to admission of refugees, but merely to the treatment of refugees who [were] already in the territory of the Contracting State."[27] Significantly, the Head of the Foreign Office's Treaty Department, George Warner, made notations on the English translation of the 1933 Convention, but *none* on the French original that had been transmitted from Geneva by Harold Patteson.[28]

III. Conclusion

Four themes emerge from a review of the evolution of Britain's policy-making toward the 1933 Convention and the relationship of "sovereignty" understandings to that policy-making. First, individuals and non-state actors played a prominent role in challenging the "state sovereignty" view to which His Majesty's Government stubbornly clung during the inter-war period. Among the more prominent individuals who might arguably be included in the refugee advocacy "epistemic community" of the inter-war period were Monsieur de Navailles, Jacques Rubinstein, and British nationals Lord Robert Cecil, Major Thomas Johnson, Sir Walter Napier, and Sir Neil Malcolm. Private Voluntary Organizations, too, played important roles at times. Perhaps the most conspicuous such PVO role, and the most controversial one, was that assumed during the July 1936 Inter-Governmental Conference, when PVOs were granted access to the proceedings and two private group memorials were issued to state government delegates. In the post-WWII period, of course, non-state actors have come to exert a significant influence on efforts to afford international legal protection to national groups, whether refugee or otherwise.

Second, the practice of "quasi-legal" agreements, the "Arrangements" of 1928 and 1936, was shrewdly introduced by the refugee advocacy community in the inter-war period, and to some effect. Informal formalities, these non-binding instruments became wedges to crack open the sovereignty door, if only slightly. In Britain's case, certainly, its signature of the 1936 Provisional Arrangement made possible its accession, days later, to the 1933 Convention. The use of explicitly non-binding agreements and declarations to promote the international protection of national and other groups would come to be employed fairly regularly in the Cold War period, and perhaps even more so, thereafter.[29] Among the more prominent examples of this advocacy strategy: the U.N. General Assembly's Resolutions 1514 "Declaration on Colonial Independence" (1960), 1541 (1960), and 2625 "Declaration on Friendly Relations" (1970); the "Conclusions on International Protection" adopted by the Executive Committee of the U.N. High Commissioner for Refugees (1975–present); the "Guiding Principles on Internal Displacement" (1998); and the Final Act of the Conference on Security and Co-Operation in Europe (the "CSCE Final Act" or "Helsinki Final Act" of 1975).

Third, the story of British policy-making related here illustrates the danger of imputing state government motives or understandings based solely on public rhetoric or behavior. The British Government rejected altogether the 1933 Convention's provision on *non-refoulement* but accepted with reservation a similar provision in the 1936 Arrangement. This action seems not to have reflected a changed British understanding of the sovereign state's duties, but rather British officials' too heavy reliance upon a faulty translation of the French treaty. Surely, public government discourse and practices can be strongly suggestive of motives and attitudes, but researchers relying exclusively upon them do so at their peril. International norms scholars working in the "nationality," "national self-determination," and "refugee protection" realms would do well to keep this in mind.

Finally, the 1933 Convention story underscores the pervasiveness and persistence among inter-war British foreign policy thinking of the "state sovereignty" notion. "National sovereignty" considerations were conspicuously absent, and one might persuasively argue, unhappily so. HMG's officials wished to exclude non-governmental organizations from deliberations associated with the creation of state duties; such discussions were exclusively a sovereign state province. British policy-makers defined then Britain's sovereign interests and duties in territorial terms. Britain had no interest in refugees beyond its borders. Nor had it any positive legal duty toward them, whether to protect them or to advocate their protection by other sovereign states. And when it finally agreed in 1936 formally to afford certain limited legal privileges to refugees representing such national groups as Armenian, Assyrian, and Assyro-Chaldean, Britain was willing to do so only if those refugees were no longer legally connected to their home states. Not until after World War II would such views come regularly to be challenged in Britain and beyond. Even so, "state sovereignty" notions and policies have proven remarkably durable.

NOTES

1. This essay first appeared in the *International Journal of Refugee Law* 11(1999): 597–624. The *IJRL* version includes extensive references to primary source documents from the British Public Record Office (PRO) and the League of Nations Archives. References to those documents, and to many secondary sources, are included in the *IJRL* article, but have been omitted here.
2. See, e.g., Gil Loescher, *Refugee Movements and International Security*, Adelphi Paper 268 (London: IISS, Summer 1992).
3. Claudena Skran, *Refugees in Inter-War Europe: The Emergence of a Regime* (Oxford: Oxford University Press, 1995), p. 3.
4. On British refugee policy-making in the inter-war period, see A.J. Sherman, *Island Refuge: Britain and Refugees from the Third Reich 1933–1939* (Berkeley: University of California Press, 1973); Joshua B. Stein, "Britain and the Jews of Danzig 1938–1939," *The Wiener Library Bulletin* 32 (1979): 29–33; Joshua B. Stein, "Great Britain and the Evian Conference," *The Wiener Library Bulletin* 29 (1976): 40–52; and John P. Fox, "Great Britain and the German Jews 1933," *The Wiener Library Bulletin* 26 (1972): 40–46. On Britain's wartime policy toward Jewish refugees *per se*, see Bernard Wasserstein, *Britain and the Jews of Europe 1939–1945* (Oxford: Clarendon Press, 1979).
5. The 1933 Convention was ratified by eight states: Belgium, Bulgaria, Czechoslovakia,

Denmark, France, Great Britain, Italy, and Norway. It was signed by not ratified by Egypt. Adherents of the treaty included: Estonia, Finland, Greece, Latvia, Sweden, Switzerland, the United States, and Iraq.

    The 1938 Convention was signed by eight states: Belgium, Denmark, France, Great Britain, the Netherlands, Norway, and Spain. Only three ratified it, however: Belgium (September 1, 1938), Great Britain (September 26, 1938), and France (March 23, 1945).

6. Stephen D. Krasner, "Westphalia and All That," in Judith Goldstein and Robert O. Keohane, eds., *Ideas and Foreign Policy: Beliefs, Institutions, and Political Change* (Ithaca, NY: Cornell University Press, 1993), p. 235. Other noteworthy works that address sovereignty and its relationship to nationalism include: Daniel Philpott, *Revolutions in Sovereignty: How Ideas Shaped Modern International Relations* (Princeton, NJ: Princeton University Press, forthcoming); and James Mayall, *Nationalism and International Society* (New York: Cambridge University Press, 1990).

7. J. Samuel Barkin and Bruce Cronin, "The State and the Nation: Changing Norms and the Rules of Sovereignty in International Relations," *International* Organization 48 (Winter 1994): 109, 110. On the influence of "legitimacy" on international rule-related state behavior, see Thomas M. Franck, *The Power of Legitimacy Among Nations* (Oxford: Oxford University Press, 1990).

8. Judith Goldstein and Robert O. Keohane, "Ideas and Foreign Policy: An Analytical Framework," in Goldstein and Keohane, eds., *Ideas and Foreign Policy*, pp. 21–22.

9. Skran, *Refugees in Inter-war Europe*, p. 269.

10. Janice E. Thomson, "State Practices, International Norms, and the Decline of Mercenarism," *International Studies Quarterly* 34 (March 1990): 45. Emphasis added. For her book-length study, see Janice E. Thomson, *Mercenaries, Pirates, and Sovereigns: State-building and Extraterritorial Violence in Early Modern Europe* (Princeton, NJ : Princeton University Press, 1994).

11. Two prominent works that significantly draw upon the documentary record are: Eric Ringmar, *Identity, Interest and Action: A Cultural Explanation of Sweden's Intervention in the Thirty Years' War* (Cambridge: Cambridge University Press, 1996); and Jeffrey Legro, *Cooperation Under Fire: Anglo-German Restraint During World War II* (Ithaca, NY: Cornell University Press, 1995).

12. The Convention, for example, "set the first universal standard on the treatment of refugees, a standard which accorded refugees better treatment than that which they generally received in host countries." Skran, *Refugees in Inter-War Europe*, p. 129. Skran cogently demonstrates the domestic political impact of the 1933 Convention. See her *Refugees in Inter-War Europe*, pp. 125–30, 136–7. For a contrary view, see Gunnel Stenberg, *Non-Expulsion and Non-Refoulement* (Uppsala, Sweden: Iustus Förlag, 1989), p. 44.

13. J.L. Rubinstein, "The Refugee Problem," *International Affairs* 15 (September–October 1936): 727.

14. In 1933, for example, delegates to the Commission came from Belgium, Germany, Bulgaria, China, Estonia, France, Great Britain, Greece, Italy, Latvia, Poland, Romania, Czechoslovakia and Yugoslavia.

15. The governments of thirteen states—Argentina, Australia, the United Kingdom, Colombia, Czechoslovakia, Estonia, Greece, Hungary, British India, Nicaragua, Switzerland, Venezuela, and Yugoslavia—offered no direct response to the recommended drafting of a Convention. The governments of three—Austria, Denmark, and the United States—referred only generally to their earlier observations reprinted in the 1931 Report of the Nansen Office's Governing Body.

16. Cecil was one of Britain's delegates to the League Assembly of 1932. On Cecil's life and background, see Viscount Cecil, *A Great Experiment* (New York: Oxford University Press, 1941) and *All the Way* (London, 1949).

17. An "epistemic community" has been defined as "a network of professionals with recognized expertise and competence in a particular domain and an authoritative claim to policy-relevant knowledge within that domain or issue area." Members of a given epistemic community have a shared set of normative and principled beliefs, shared causal

beliefs, shared notions of validity, and a common policy enterprise. Peter M. Haas, "Introduction: Epistemic Communities and International Policy Coordination," *International Organization* 46 (1992): 3.

Haas and others have argued that epistemic communities can assume significant roles in the international policy coordination process, and more specifically, in the development of international rules. These "networks of knowledge-based experts" play a part, for example, in "articulating the cause-and-effect relationships of complex problems, helping states identify their interests, framing the issues for collective debate, proposing specific policies, and identifying salient points for negotiation." Haas, "Introduction," p. 2.

It is difficult to argue convincingly that the refugee advocates of the inter-war period constituted an "epistemic community" because insufficient evidence exists of the specific beliefs of those prominent individuals involved in refugee rule development and advocacy.

18. Rubinstein, "The Refugee Problem," pp. 727, 728.
19. Sherman, *Island Refuge*, p. 35.
20. Prepared for "supplementaries" and "approved by the H.O.," the following note was drafted for Sir John Simon in response to a question by MP Rhys Davies. It reflected well the Foreign Office's thinking in December of 1933: "The problem of refugees from such countries as Russia & Armenia is not one of any substantial importance in the U. Kingdom & it therefore did not seem necessary for H.M.G. to be represented at the Conference or to be parties [sic] to the Convention. The Convention concerns the civil & social rights of such refugees in the countries which are parties to the Convention."
21. Sherman, *Island Refuge*, p. 71.
22. The fears expressed by the Home Office were not groundless. A high-profile report generated by a League "Committee of Experts" in January of 1936, for example, concluded: "Refugees coming from Germany have as yet no international juridical status. This situation should be remedied without delay." In his Appendix to that report, moreover, M. Michael Hansson specifically argued that "the benefits of the 1933 Convention should be extended to refugees coming from Germany by means of a special protocol or declarations on the part of Governments."
23. Emphasis added. France's principal delegate was, Makins commented, "a grandson of Karl Marx."
24. Such reservations were typical of those made by other 1933 Convention parties. Bulgaria, for example, made reservations to Articles 1, 2, 6, 7, 8, 10, 13, and 15; Czechoslovakia to Articles 3, 4, 5, 7, 8, 9, 10, 11, 14, and 15; Norway to Article 2 and 14; Denmark to Articles 7 and 14; Italy to Article 3; France to Articles 7 and 15, Belgium to Articles 2, 9, 10 and 14. Moreover, states parties generally rejected the treaty's applicability to their colonial territories.
25. On the "juridical perspective" to refugees, see James C. Hathaway, "The Evolution of Refugee Status in International Law, 1920–1950," *International and Comparative Law Quarterly* 33 (April 1984): 349, 350–61.
26. Atle Grahl-Madsen, *The Status of Refugees in International Law - Volume II, Asylum, Entry and Sojourn* (Leiden: A.W. Sijthoff, 1972), p. 99, note 47.
27. Grahl-Madsen, *The Status of Refugees in International Law*, pp. 98–99. Guy S. Goodwin-Gill argues, however, that *refoulement* understood as a practice in continental European immigration practice, already included rejection at the frontier. Guy S. Goodwin-Gill, *The Refugee in International Law* (Oxford, Clarendon Press, 2nd ed., 1996), pp. 117–19, 121–24.
28. Further support for the interpretation that Britain was not generally opposed in 1936 to a prohibition on refugee reconduction, if it was then to a prohibition on the refusal of entry to refugees, is provided by E.N. Cooper's July 1936 proposal. At the Inter-Governmental Conference in Geneva, Cooper suggested that reconduction of German refugees should be permitted only "as an extreme measure and only if they had refused either to make arrangements or to take advantage of any arrangements made for their departure to another country." Moreover, when Britain ultimately acceded to the 1936 Provisional Arrangement, it did not reject altogether that agreement's Article 4(2) reconduction proscription. It did, however, limit that provision's effect by a reservation: "Paragraph 2 of

article 4 will not be applicable to refugees who have been admitted to the United Kingdom for a temporary visit or purpose. The term 'public order' is deemed to include matters relating to crime and morals."

29. For excellent recent works addressing this subject, see Thomas Risse, Stephen Ropp, and Kathryn Sikkink, eds., *The Power of Human Rights: International Norms and Domestic Change* (Cambridge University Press, 1999); and Daniel C. Thomas, *The Helsinki Effect: International Norms, Human Rights and the Demise of Communism* (Princeton University Press, forthcoming).

The International Law of Nationalism: Group Identity and Legal History

Nathaniel Berman

> [It sometimes appears] as if there were fashions in international law just as in neckties. At the end of the first World War, "international protection of minorities" was the great fashion. . . . Recently this fashion has become nearly obsolete. Today the well-dressed international lawyer wears "human rights."
> —J. L. KUNZ, THE PRESENT STATUS OF THE INTERNATIONAL LAW FOR THE PROTECTION OF MINORITIES (1954)

> How could the self-determination granted to the Algerians in 1962 have been refused to the German population who in 1938 had been living in Czechoslovakia for [only] twenty years?
> —GEORGES BONNET, DANS LA TOURMENTE, 1938–1948 (1971)

> Although it has no national minorities on its territory, France [is] conscious of the importance of this question for many participating States. . . .
> —FRENCH CSCE DELEGATE (1991)

Reprinted from Nathaniel Berman, "The International Law of Nationalism," *International Law and Ethnic Conflict*, edited by David Wippman. Copyright © 1998 Cornell University. Used by permission of the publisher, Cornell University Press.

*The rules that govern intelligible identity . . . operate through repetition.
. . . [T]he subject is a consequence of certain rule-governed discourses that
govern the intelligible invocation of identity. . . . "[A]gency," then, is to be
located within the possibility of a variation on that repetition. . . . There
is no self prior . . . to its entrance into this conflicted cultural field.*
— JUDITH BUTLER, *GENDER TROUBLE: FEMINISM AND THE
SUBVERSION OF IDENTITY* (1990)

I. INTRODUCTION: DISCONTINUOUS HISTORY, SHIFTING IDENTITIES

A "VERITABLE INTERNATIONAL law of nationalism" is emerging in the
post-modern cold war period, a body of theory and practice that has an uneasy
relationship to its own deeply troubled history.[1] A vast amount of work has gone
into the reestablishment of this field of international law: theoretical clarification of legal terms designating the protagonists of nationalist conflicts (such as
"nations," "peoples," and "minorities"), doctrinal specification of rights like self-
determination and cultural autonomy, drafting of innovative general conventions, deployment of policy packages on particular conflicts, and philosophical
debate about nationalism's cultural meaning. At the same time, a sense of historical déjà-vu seems pervasive: the past few years have seen the striking resurgence of forgotten nationalist conflicts as well as legal notions that once seemed
relegated to subordinate status, such as international minority rights.

Nonetheless doctrinal and policy discussions often seem quite divorced
from historical reflection. This striking disjunction between the sense of un-
canny historical repetition and the concern for appalling current exigencies often leads to both the misinterpretation of history and the impoverishment of
current doctrine and policy. The conventional portrayal of past legal responses
to nationalism as piecemeal adumbrations that need to be developed into a coherent system is symptomatic; it ignores the fact that past efforts have themselves taken comprehensive and systematic form. Conventional accounts ignore
the discontinuities in the history of the international law of nationalism: rather
than a smooth process of customary law "ripening," this history has been one of
construction, denunciation, rupture, and resumption. These discontinuities
make history a rather embarrassing guest at the policy-proposing feast, while
making policy proposers seem like well-intentioned naifs at the table of historical wisdom.

In contrast to conventional, linear approaches, I define an international law
of nationalism as a *historically contingent* array of doctrinal and policy options for
development by a contingent embodiment of international authority on nationalist conflicts whose protagonists are designated by a contingent set of legal categories. The historical discontinuities between the various incarnations of the international law of nationalism may be tracked through the discontinuities in the

international projections of international and nationalist identity. In order to build an account of a particular nationalist conflict, international law projects onto the protagonists a set of historically contingent categories—states, nations, peoples, minorities, religions, races, indigenous peoples, individuals, and so forth—a set whose elements and valorizations have changed over time. In addition, legal analyses of nationalist conflict always identify a state, group of states, or institution as the "international legal organ," as embodying the authority of the international legal community. These projections identify the general roles that international law provides for the protagonists in its accounts of specific nationalist dramas; they may, accordingly, be referred to as "protagonist-positions" ready to be filled by particular groups, states, or institutions in particular contexts.

The determination of the set of protagonist-positions and the manner of their application are informed by cultural projections that have often been contested within given periods and have dramatically changed over time. Yet the study of the international law of nationalism demonstrates a more complex imbrication of doctrinal, policy, and cultural contingencies than does this elementary Legal Realist insight about the relative indeterminacy of formal categories. Rather, it shows the crucial role that the construction of separate domains of doctrine, policy, and culture has played in the history of this field. In particular, the understanding of some problems as "cultural" upon which "law" can be deployed is itself a contingent feature of international legal history that has played different roles in different periods.[2] Even the decision whether to call this field the "international law of nationalism" or "international law and ethnic conflict" requires one to take a position in international and local struggles with highly charged histories.

Moreover, nationalists often form their self-understanding, as well as their self-presentation, in response to their understanding of international legal categories. Nationalists everywhere have internalized, resisted, or denied the identities projected by international law because of those identities' cultural meanings, legal implications, or tactical consequences. In performing, transforming, and deforming these internationally projected identities, nationalists reshape their meaning and may even thereby redirect the general course of the international law of nationalism. Focusing on the contingency of the identity-constitutive elements of the international law of nationalism thus brings out its culturally constructive, as well as contentious, dimension.

Ignoring this dimension often gives rise to indeterminate arguments between those who would see a given international action as simply imposing the international community's interests or values and those who would see it as demonstrating deep empathy with the nationalist protagonists. For example, Western plans for Bosnia, all involving some form of partition, have been characterized as the ratification of Serb aggression by outside powers acting on cultural stereotypes, on the one hand, and as the compassionate striving for ethnic reconciliation through delicately balancing the protagonists' desires, on the other. In contrast to such dichotomies, an emphasis on law's culturally constructive dimension shows how the legal projection of internationalist and nationalist identity serves *simultaneously* to legitimate international power *and* to construct a possible field for principled humanitarian action. *No* formulation or deployment of a plan for a conflict like Bosnia is possible that does not project a contestable set of identity positions onto the conflict's protagonists; the worth and effectiveness of any particular plan will depend on the manner of the reappropriation and redeployment of these projections by those protagonists. These projections, such as those of coherent, unitary, and stable ethnic identities able to serve as the basis for a partition plan, may be resisted by some of the protagonists as a violent imposition, be embraced by others as conforming to their self-image, and impel still others to transform their meaning through political struggle.

International power and principle do not "belong to two different planes."[3] Rather, the power of international law to shape the identity of the protagonists of such conflicts cannot be separated from even its principled activities to remedy them. The tenacity of hackneyed oppositions in international debate—idealism and realism, law and politics—reflects a failure to understand this dynamic.

Relating legal discontinuities to contingent projections of identity highlights the significance of the different postures international law has taken in relation to nationalist conflict. Three of the most important of these postures may be called theoretical or doctrinal formalism, policy pragmatism, and cultural activism. The relationship among these postures may be schematized as follows:

(1) *Formalism*: When a group makes a claim against a sovereign state, international law first determines whether the claims transcend the state's domestic jurisdiction and then determines whether the group meets the criteria defining a people, minority group, collection of individuals, or another legal category; finally, balancing rights claims with other relevant legal factors, international law may provide the right to self-determination, minority rights, individual human rights, or other legal remedy.

(2) *Pragmatism*: Confronted with ethnic, nationalist, etc., tensions, international policymakers propose legal frameworks to international authority and local parties embodying policies able to satisfy as many of the competing interests as practicable; shedding formalist determinism for functionalist flexibility, the policymaker can explore how various legal techniques would work in particular situations.

(3) *Cultural activism*: International law plays a culturally constructive role in shaping nationalist identity and thus in altering the course of nationalist conflict; international law's culturally differential projections

also inform its own formalist and pragmatic analyses; at various times, international lawyers have overtly embraced, implicitly pursued, politically opposed, or tactically transformed such cultural activism.

Of course, I have intentionally simplified and exaggerated the differences among these three postures, for we are all formalists, pragmatists, and cultural activists. It would be more accurate to speak of formalist, pragmatic, and cultural aspirations that all international lawyers share: all seek to provide general normative criteria, to formulate workable policies to remedy particular problems, and to consider the effects of their cultural proclivities.

Yet the form and relative valorization of these postures have undergone dramatic historical transformations. Cultural activism, for example, was explicitly celebrated by most international lawyers in relation to Africa and Asia as recently as the interwar period in the guise of the "civilizing mission;" this activism overtly framed doctrinal and policy options. During the later phases of the Cold War, policy pragmatism predominated, with formalism seen as an outdated rigidity that pragmatism sought to transcend and cultural activism seen as an allegation of imperialism that pragmatism sought to disprove. Since 1989, cultural activism has resurfaced in both affirmative and critical forms: the former in the resurgence of explicit cultural projections by lawyers and policymakers, most notoriously in talk of a "clash of civilizations," and the latter in the effort to render explicit, and therefore contestable, the cultural functions of international law and policy.

This chapter considers the critical potential of an emphasis on the cultural dimension in discussing formalism and pragmatism. It rejects the way the formalist aspiration for doctrinal generalization implies that groups existed before the catagories that would subsequently be applied to them; similarly, it rejects the way the pragmatic aspiration for neutral policy implies that those categories can be deployed purely tactically to manage preexisting interests. Rather, I argue that groups' identities and tactics come to be defined by themselves and by international authorities in response to a cultural conjuncture partly constructed by those very categories. Yet I also explore the way the construction of a realm of "cultural" problems—a construction that has taken widely divergent historical forms—has shaped and legitimated different kinds of international power. The chapter thus contributes to showing how the international "construction of the cultural" enables us "to see the cultural not as the *source* of conflict—different cultures—but as the *effect of* discriminatory practices—the production of cultural *differentiation as* a sign of authority."[4]

Descriptions of the history of minority rights can illustrate the relationship between these postures. For example, the most recent edition of *Oppenheim* briefly notes pre–World War I efforts, reviews the interwar system in some detail, declares that minority protection was "subsumed" in the post–World War II concern with individual rights, and discusses the relevant postwar documents. It concludes by adding that "[i]n some instances minorities might be a sufficiently cohesive group to constitute a 'people' enjoying the right to self-determination now recognised in several international instruments."[5] A faultless performance in the genre of the treatise, *Oppenheim's* discussion could also be viewed as a typical product of the pragmatic posture. It frustrates our formalist aspirations, for its analytical modesty seems unacceptably question begging: what does *subsumed* assert about the state of customary law; how can *sufficiently cohesive* be . applied to particular cases? From a cultural perspective, *Oppenheim's* seamless chronological account elides the controversies that marked each period and the ruptures that lie between periods. Its recourse to phrases like *subsumed* and *sufficiently cohesive* smoothes over always conflictual processes both among and within the legal, political, and cultural domains.

Another recent commentator is rather closer to the cultural perspective when he writes that between World War II and 1989, the "problem of minorities was occulted: it was a practically taboo subject."[6] Yet he fails to explore the relationship between this description and the linear processes normally demanded of customary international law. For example, customary law concepts like *ripening* and *desuetude* do not evoke the phenomenon suggested by highly charged, and therefore more apt, terms like *occultation* and *taboo*. Nor does he reflect on how the link between nationalism and taboo might participate in the history of Western projections of fears and fantasies about "occult" cultures, projections that have played crucial roles in the international law of nationalism.

The rest of this chapter provides an overview of the structure and history of the international law of nationalism alternative to the kind of account exemplified by *Oppenheim.* Part II explores some illustrative ways in which international law has projected its own identity and that of nationalist protagonists in several historical periods. Part III examines the justification of change in the international law of nationalism through illustrative arguments about continuity and discontinuity with previous historical periods. Throughout I show how this field has been structured by discursive and practical movement between internationalism and nationalism, power and principle, "law" and "culture."

II. THE PROJECTION OF INTERNATIONAL AUTHORITY AND GROUP IDENTITY

> *. . . I cannot but express the conviction that the German Government . . . will never accept as satisfactory . . . any solution which does not comply with the principle of a State of nationalities as opposed to a national State in which the Sudeten will continue to be treated as a minority and not as a Staatsvolk ("State nation").*
>
> —SIR NEVILLE HENDERSON (1938)

[The presidency] considers it especially important that selective application of principles be avoided. The principle of self-determination e.g. cannot exclusively apply to the existing [Yugoslav] republics while being deemed inapplicable to national minorities within those republics.

—DUTCH E.C. PRESIDENCY (1991)

Comprehensive approaches to nationalist conflict have been embodied in a series of legal regimes over the last century and a half. One can distinguish at least five major incarnations of the international law of nationalism during this period: (1) pre-World War I management of the disintegrating Ottoman Empire, whose high point was the 1878 Treaty of Berlin; (2) post-World War I disposition of the defeated and dissolved empires, whose milestones include the 1919 Peace and Minority Protection Treaties, the 1923 Geneva Convention on Upper Silesia, and, in a kind of coda, the 1947 Palestine Partition Resolution; (3) the 1930s revision of the Versailles settlement, symbolized by the 1938 Four-Power Agreement on Czechoslovakia; (4) the decolonization decades, epitomized in the 1960 General Assembly Resolution 1514, the "colonial declaration of independence;" and (5) post-1989 efforts, such as the European Framework Convention for the Protection of National Minorities, the 1991 Draft Convention on Yugoslavia, and the 1994 Washington and 1995 Dayton agreements on Bosnia. These documents echo each other in remarkable ways: the proposals for former Yugoslavia, for example, employ every technique (self-determination, minority protection, regional autonomy, citizenship rights, international tribunals, and so on) developed in the preceding two centuries; in their encyclopedic range, they resemble the Upper Silesia and Palestine plans. This list is deliberately heterogeneous, selective, and, particularly with the inclusion of 1938, directed against seamless narratives of legal evolution and conventional distinctions between "legal" and "political" approaches.

The leading protagonist-positions that we use today to analyze nationalist conflicts—states, nations, peoples, minorities, individuals—have been part of the international law of nationalism at least since the nineteenth century. International law appears to have created a small set of stable protagonist-positions by which stunningly disparate conflicts have come to be framed over five continents for almost two centuries. Of course, one might bemoan the paucity of legal imagination, the forcing of the diversity of human conflict into a small set of categories. Yet for good or for ill, this power of international law to effectively frame the terms in which such disparate conflicts have been understood both internationally and locally seems quite astonishing.

Nevertheless, we should beware of taking this appearance at face value: a protagonist-position (for example, "minority group") that may be important in one period (such as 1878) may be subordinated or absent in a subsequent period (such as 1960) and may live again in a still later period (such as 1996). Indeed, we may distinguish different periods of the international law of nationalism by

their distinctive cast of protagonist-positions. As a result, a group that understood itself in one way at one may come to understand itself, or at least to present itself, in another way in a subsequent period because of the shifting value
given to the legal protagonist-positions. The Arab-Israeli conflict provides a rich
example of the ways in which groups shift their performance of their identities
due to changes in the international projection and valorization of protagonist-
positions: at various times, it may have been either culturally persuasive, legally
dispositive, or tactically useful to perform group identity as a "religion," a "minority," a territorial "people," a transfrontier "nation," a "people not yet able to
stand by themselves under the strenuous conditions of the modern world," a
"provisional government," and so forth.

Attempts to resolve uncertainties about group identity through definitional
formalism or policy pragmatism thus often appear arbitrary in the face of the
dynamics of nationalist conflict. Such conflicts always involve turbulent political and discursive processes in which the protagonists' identity and interests
change in their own or others' eyes. Such transformations can affect both the international and nationalist sides of the equation. An institution or group of
states may shift from being recognized as the representative of universal legal
principle to being perceived as a partisan powerbroker and vice versa; articular
groups may shift from the status of a "nation" to that of a "minority" or a mere
collection of "persons" and vice versa. In the first fifty years of the twentieth century, for example, the Sudeten Germans successively occupied the positions of a
part of the Hapsburg Staatsvolk prior to 1914, one of the legion of national
claimants at the Paris Peace Conference in 1919, an internationally protected minority in the 1920, a self-determination aspirant in the early 1930s, an agent of
a foreign power in the late 1930s, a part of a majority group in 1938–45, and a
group of expelled refugees after 1945; at each stage, the legitimacy and impartiality of international legal authority was also contested. Each of these transformations came about through both discursive and political-military conflict.
One could trace an equally complex transformation of the identity and tactics
of the Balkan national groups during the twentieth century.

In the next two sections, therefore, I explore arguments about the shifting
identity and status of international authority and of group identity.

A. International Authority

*The Treaty of Berlin must be presented . . . as a law of necessity, imposed
by the superior exigencies of European peace. . . . And you, for whom a
conciliation treaty is inadequate, who want a victory treaty, do you hear
the cannon and the hail of bullets carrying away the human victims over
there in Bosnia?*

—BENOIT BRUNSWIK, *LE TRAITÉ DE BERLIN,
ANNOTÉ ET COMMENTÉ* (1878)

Justifications of international authority involve the claim of an institution or group of states to embody general legal principles, transcending partisan power. Comprehensive international settlements almost always rest on an explicit assertion that the international community seeks to resolve nationalist conflicts in light of its responsibility for a general peace. The persuasiveness of such assertions rest on historically and culturally contingent projections about the identity of international authority rather than solely on their formal rigor or pragmatic feasibility; these projections construct the juxtaposition between the international "legal" community and the nationalist "cultural" Other that has played a decisive role in establishing international authority. While the surprisingly enduring general form of this juxtaposition highlights the structural continuities in the history of justifications of international authority, the shifts in its constitutive projections mark the historical discontinuities and the fierce debates about particular deployments of international power.

The preamble to the recent European Framework Convention for the Protection of National Minorities carefully balances the *supra*national interest in unity and continental peace, sovereign prerogatives, and minority rights.[7] This careful contemporary drafting seems designed to avoid the rather more piquant formulations found in the convention's predecessors, in which the tension among such elements is readily apparent to today's readers. Examples of such tension may be found in assertions of international authority in the late nineteenth century, the Versailles system, and the revisionist thirties.

The 1878 Treaty of Berlin was the most systematic nineteenth-century attempt to condition international recognition of new states (such as Serbia) on minority group protection as well as to impose such protections on an already existing state (such as the Ottoman Empire). The treaty thus embodied a forceful assertion of international authority; for example, it "finally broke with the diplomatic fiction" of portraying Ottoman concessions on minority rights as "emanating from the Sultans' initiative."[8] The treaty's distinctive assertion of international authority comes in the preamble's declaration that "les questions soulevées en Orient" are to be settled "dans une pensée d'ordre Européen." This Europe/"Orient" dichotomy, which the treaty clearly presents as equivalent to that between universal legal reason and particularistic cultural passion, shows the way in which the position of protagonists can shift over time. Today, of course, an overt identification of universal legal reason with Europe would be viewed by many as a dubious, or perhaps ironic, assertion. The transformation of "Europe" from a universal to a particularist protagonist-position is a familiar, if still contested, historical process; yet as we shall see, the Europe/"Orient" distinction still can provide a guiding thread through much of this topic.

The Permanent Court's declarations of international legal supremacy in the interwar minority protection system are less jarring than the 1878 Europe/"Orient" juxtaposition but no less assertive of international authority. In 1923, for example, the court asserted international authority to define both states and national minorities by focusing on the simultaneity of the rebirth of Poland and of its obligations under the Minority Protection Treaty—on the fact that the peace treaty, which recognized the Polish state, and the Minority Treaty were "signed on the same day."[9] The court concluded that Polish sovereign rights were on a legal as well as temporal par with its minority protection obligations. The definitions of "Poland" and its "minorities" were governed by a new international legal order that took priority over them both; no Polish law could "interfere" with these obligations. The court in this way rejected the Polish argument that minorities in Poland could only be defined and thus placed under international protection once Poland had decided who its citizens were; rather, international law would determine the composition of both the Polish citizenry and its minorities. And just as the 1878 identification of Europe with universal authority would be challenged today, so Poland had described the League of Nations in 1923 as a mere "contracting Power" without "universal competence" over minority rights. Moreover, Poland and other states that were to be bound to the minority protection system had objected to its implication that they were nations "of inferior civilization."

The 1938 Czechoslovak crisis provides a disturbing, and disturbingly consistent, variant of this pattern. The Note transmitting the Anglo-French proposals to the Czech government declared that the two Great Powers had decided that "the further maintenance within the boundaries of the Czechoslovak State of the districts mainly inhabited by the Sudeten Deutsch cannot, in fact, continue any longer without imperiling the interests of Czechoslovakia herself and of European peace. . . . [B]ecause th[e] cause [of peace] is common both to Europe in general and to Czechoslovakia herself they have felt it their duty jointly to set forth the conditions necessary to secure it."[10]

This statement follows in the pattern of the two earlier examples: the assertion of international authority to resolve nationalist conflict through imposing conditions on a sovereign to satisfy the national claims of a minority group in the interest of European, as well as local, peace. In this case, the disjunction between general and particular interest is glaring: the (highly contestable) claim of saving general European peace at the expense of a dispute in a "faraway country between people of whom we know nothing." Yet it is striking that the Note's rhetoric is not exceptional but is made available by an established pattern from which it is, *in form*, hard to distinguish. Of course, the 1938 Czechs were subjected to a wholly different order of coercion to come to terms than the 1919 Poles. Nevertheless, it should be remembered that some of the Polish Minority Treaty provisions were also simply to be "dictated to Poland."

In Part III I will discuss in greater depth the way in which the relationships between such instances have been historically portrayed. The point here is that neither formalist criteria nor pragmatist exigencies can fully account for the degree of persuasiveness of such assertions of international authority. Arguments about the identity and stature of that authority depend on variations on a repeating rhetorical structure that itself has enduring cultural power yet also shifts historically in tandem with shifts in its constitutive projections. This perspective does not deny that one can and perhaps should be persuaded by arguments that posit vast differences between the European Powers in 1878 Berlin, 1919 Paris, 1938 Munich, and 1995 Strasbourg. One can, for example, be persuaded that the 1919 Allies were a legitimate embodiment of international authority fit to intervene on behalf of Polish minorities, whereas the four Powers assembled at Munich to deal with the Czech minorities were unworthy powerbrokers. Such persuasion comes not at the level of the general structure but of its contingent cultural and political projections; more crucially, such persuasion depends on the projections that construct the contingent form of the juxtaposition of a legally supreme "international community," on the one hand, and battling particularist nationalisms, in the guise of an "Orient," a "civilizational inferior," or a "faraway people," on the other. Persuasion is made possible *both* by the structure's relative stability *and* by its contingency—its institution by, and ongoing reliance on, variable projections. The lack of international backing for three years to "impose a settlement" in Bosnia partly reflected the failure of such a settlement's proponents to make culturally persuasive arguments about the international community's stature rather than merely debate about formal legal competence or pragmatic tactical capacity.

B. Group Identity (or, What Is a Nation?)

The Plebiscite always seems to me to be the devil, and as likely to precipitate as to prevent.

—VISCOUNT HALIFAX (1938)

If we now turn to the dynamic role of international law in relation to groups, the transmutation of 'nations' into 'minorities' or 'persons', and vice versa, we find a multilayered imbrication of culturally and historically variable projections. I will focus on three contingent aspects of such projections: (1) the projection by international law of non-European peoples as "civilizationally" distinct from European peoples and as "developmentally" ranked among themselves; (2) the projection of distinctions among *European* peoples on the basis of cultural rank; and (3) the instability and mutability of the meaning of the legal categories—that is, their transformation through their reappropriation and redeployment by nationalists. While some may assert that the first two kinds of culturally differential projections could be eliminated through legal generalization, the cultural perspective contends that there are *no* distinctions between protagonist-positions like "nations" and "minorities" that are not produced through such contingent and contestable projections. Ostensibly neutral for-

malist or pragmatist approaches can only proceed either by provisionally holding steady, affirmatively acting to deny, or implicitly taking rigid partisan positions on contestable cultural projections.

1. The Europe/Non-Europe Dichotomy. In the twentieth century, the international legal version of the Europe/non-Europe dichotomy has taken a variety of
forms, from the violent to the subtle. Perhaps the most familiar overt example
of cultural projections framing the legal definition of groups was the Versailles
settlement's disparate treatment of the European and non-European possessions
of the war's defeated and collapsed empires. While the settlement provided self-
determination for many European peoples and minority protection for others,
it provided the Mandate system for non-European peoples—those peoples "not
yet able to stand by themselves" and who, therefore, needed to be entrusted to
the tutelage of "advanced nations" as a "sacred trust of civilisation." This distinction, which no internationalist would make so overtly today, was justified
with formal and pragmatic arguments made possible by the construction of a
realm of civilizational difference and the projection of particular cultural traits
on non-European peoples.[11]

Such distinctions remained entrenched throughout the interwar period,
though at times they were contested to a greater or lesser degree. For example,
the Italians sought to disarm criticism of their invasion of Ethiopia in 1935
through manipulating Ethiopia's anomalous position as both African and sovereign; by using the rhetoric of the Mandate system, the Italians responded to
League of Nations criticism in terms of Versailles' own distinctions between "civilized" and "uncivilized" peoples. A group of distinguished French intellectuals
published the "Manifesto for the Defense of the West," which asserted that defense of Western "culture" required supporting the invasion of Ethiopia. In response, another group attacked the invasion with the "Manifesto for the Respect
of International Law," protesting against the "abuse" of the idea of the "West"
and its "culture." Consider also that one expression of Western outrage at the
1939 German declaration of a protectorate over Bohemia and Moravia was that
it was an impermissible contamination of European by non-European protagonist-positions: Germany had turned the Czech lands into a "white protectorate,"
enacting the "first German colonial statute for a white and civilized nation."[12]

Article 22 of the League Covenant, the Mandate article, pursued the process
of cultural differentiation further, explicitly making legal distinctions *among*
non-European peoples depend on their cultural dignity. The status of Mandated
Territories ranged from "provisional recognitions of independence" with temporary Mandatory tutelage to indefinite administration by the Mandatory
Power as "an integral portion of its territory." The amount of control by the
Mandatory Power depended on a people's "stage of development" and "remote-
ness from the centres of civilisation."

International lawyers might contend hopefully that such embarrassments lie safely in the past: surely no contemporary document would make such invidious distinctions. And, indeed, decolonization brought with it attrition in the number of protagonist-positions. The categorical call of the 1960 General Assembly Resolution 1514 for self-determination for "all peoples" entailed a rejection of an entire range of protagonist-positions distinctive to colonialism and the Mandate system. These protagonist-positions had been used to evaluate the relative merit of nationalist claims. For example, at the 1900 meeting of the Institut de Droit International, international lawyers had discussed whether the permissibility of third-party intervention to support or oppose self-determination claims might depend on whether the claimants were Europeans seeking to "reconstitute a nationality" or were "savage countries or countries outside of Christendom." Resolution 1514's categorical language rejected the kind of protagonist-positions that had made such discussions possible. Similarly, the resolution explicitly rejected the protagonist-position of the Mandate system's "peoples not yet able to stand by themselves."

The purging of the colonial taint from the letter of international law through the generalized language of Resolution 1514 seemed to displace the onus of any differential treatment from law to residual political or cultural bias that could eventually be eliminated. Yet the evident hyperbole of Resolution 1514 and the persistence of differential projections in the "political" domain showed the untenability of this generalization and displacement. Resolution 1514's hyperbole should be seen not as a failed attempt at doctrinal generalization but as an effective intervention in a particular legal-historical conjuncture, that of decolonization. The resolution's exclusion of the kind of differential cultural projections embodied in the Mandate system was a condemnation of the way cultural discourse had functioned in international law prior to decolonization—specifically, the invidious effect of the projection of different kinds and degrees of "civilization." Yet anticolonialism's exclusion of an overt cultural discourse in law contributed to the persistence of this discourse, freed from critical legal scrutiny, in other institutions and disciplines. Since 1989, Resolution 1514's generalization and displacement have given way to a new willingness to make overt cultural judgments. For example, those seeking to reestablish activist international authority have proposed reviving some form of trusteeship, proposals that appeared in various guises in debates about Cambodia, Bosnia, Somalia, and Haiti.[13] At the same time, those critical of ostensibly neutral formalist and pragmatic discourses have sought to explicate the cultural functions of international action and inaction.

The purpose of this analysis of historical projections about non-European peoples is thus not simply to saddle international law with the guilt of its colonial past. Rather, it should teach us to examine the contingent and contestable projections deployed through today's putatively general doctrines and neutral policies, just as we have learned to discern the differential projections deployed through the legal practices of the past. More fundamentally, it should teach us that the function of cultural discourse is both protean and ambivalent. The projection of the civilizational Other in the Mandate system legitimated disparate application of legal principles, while providing some opening for legal criticism of colonialism. The explication of today's cultural projections can show how new configurations of international authority are constructed; it can also make available for discursive and political contestation the contingent projections framing the technocratic discourse still often used in debate about the deployment of international power.

2. Distinctions Among Europeans. Although subject to less critical analysis than the Europe/non-Europe dichotomy, the projection of cultural differences among *European* peoples has been of great historical importance and has reemerged today. I have elsewhere argued that this kind of distinction played an implicit role in legal justifications of the arms embargoes on Spain in the 1930s and Bosnia in the 1990s.[14] Other forms of intra-European distinctions have long concerned dichotomies between Eastern and Western Europe, often centering on the implications of the word *national* to describe the protagonist-position "minority group."

A telling example of such intra-European distinctions was provided by the opening statement of the French delegate to the CSCE Meeting of Experts on National Minorities: "Although it has no national minorities on its territory, France, conscious of the importance which this question has for many participating States and of many populations, is ready to participate in the elaboration of conclusions which would be inspired by these ideas and to give them its accord."[15] The dividing line lies between those states "which have been constructed, founded, assembled through a slow economic, social, cultural, and political process" and those "where the entanglement of peoples remains extreme and is the sometimes recent reminder of tumultuous upheavals."[16] In short, the French delegate projects the problem of minorities onto other states; or, more specifically in the European context, he projects it *eastward.* France will participate in the elaboration of norms, norms for *others.* To be sure, one could linger long over the complicated justifications that a French speaker would give for the statement that France has no "national minorities." At the end of this dalliance, one might even be persuaded that the superior magnetism of French culture has succeeded in assimilating those who might have become "national minorities" in lesser cultures. Or perhaps not. In either case, the French position shows how the affirmation or denial of an identity like "national minority" requires contentious cultural exclusions and inclusions.

Such controversies about the "nationalness" of minority group identity have long played a crucial role in European discussions. Indeed, a decisive moment in the 1919 debates over the legal projection of the European minorities concerned the use of the adjective *national* and the related question of collective rights. The early drafts of the Polish Minority Protection Treaty would have protected Poland's "several national minorities;" these minorities would also have been recognized as "distinct public corporations" and would, among other things, have had a right to proportional representation in all state elective bodies. The final version of the treaty, however, suppressed the word *national* from the definition of the protected minorities, replacing it with the phrase "persons who belong to racial, religious, or linguistic minorities;" collective rights were deleted except in certain provisions relating to education. The 1919 suppression of the term *national* and the focus on "persons who belong to" rather than the groups themselves include in their progeny the familiar formulation of Article 27 of the Covenant on Civil and Political Rights.

Significantly, the Permanent Court gave more extensive recognition to collective identity in the *Greco-Bulgarian "Communities" Case,* involving Balkan population exchange, than in other minority protection cases. The court attributed its evaluation of these "communities" to the importance of collective identity in "Eastern countries." This cultural "tradition" meant that the treaty at issue should not be interpreted in accordance with those who saw it primarily as safeguarding "individual rights." The court consequently declared that the existence of the protected Balkan "communities" was rooted in their members' "sentiment of solidarity" rather than in the law of the territorial sovereign. International supremacy over state law was thus grounded through the projection of a collectivist "Eastern tradition," which could only be safeguarded internationally.

The reappearance of the term *national* in recent documents like the U.N. Declaration on the Rights of Persons Belonging to National or Ethnic, Religious, and Linguistic Minorities and the European Framework Convention for the Protection of National Minorities may indicate a shift in international attitudes. Alternatively, it may indicate that the term *national minority* has lost the legal meaning, as well as some of the political and cultural charge, that accompanied it in the first decades of the century.[17] In any event, the controversies that attended the earlier use of the word *national* have certainly not been resolved. Moreover, recent documents differ among themselves. The U.N. declaration and the European Framework Convention stress individual rights. By contrast, the various proposals for former Yugoslavia, including the 1991 Draft Convention for Yugoslavia and the Washington and Dayton Agreements (documents for the "East"), formalize the role of nationalist identity in their institutional proposals.

3. Instability and Mutability. The competing cultural projections that produce conflict over the determination of the set of protagonist-positions persist in struggle over their interpretation and deployment, frustrating attempts at stabilization through formal definition or pragmatic functionalization. The 1919 debate about the "nationalness" of minorities, for example, was understood not only as opposing states to minorities generally but also as opposing two different cultural conceptions of group identity—those of Western and Eastern Europe. Yet the suppression of the word *national* in the Polish treaty was not necessarily viewed by all concerned as the end of the matter. Some Eastern European Jews who sought recognition as "national minorities" felt that the "demands of the Jews . . . 'may be called ethnic rights in the language of western Europe; the word 'national' was not essential as long as the thing was secured'."[18] For such interpreters, the treaty provision should be read ironically, at the expense of both the drafters and of other Jews who sought to use the treaty to promote their own, non-nationalist, definition of Jewish identity. These nationalist protagonists seemed to announce their intention to strategically play the formal, pragmatic, and cultural levels against each other: they would seek to advance their cultural self-understanding through a pragmatic retreat on the formal definition in order to secure their view in other forums. If this ironic reading had been generally known, it might have reinforced Polish trepidations about the treaty; Paderewski, for example, had objected that it would "transform the Jews into an autonomous nation."[19]

Paderewski had also warned of "the migratory capacities of the Jewish population, which so readily transports itself from one State to another."[20] He might have been more genteel had he pointed to the danger of their reading capacities, their ready "transportation" of textual meaning from literality to ironic reversal. Paderewski warned the Western Powers that they could not simply project the "national" problem eastward; the Jews' "migratory capacities" meant that they "will claim elsewhere the national principles which they would enjoy in Poland." Paderewski thus was paradoxically arguing against distinguishing Eastern and Western Europe in law by appealing to the Western Europeans' fear of contamination by Eastern European *cultures*. He hoped the Westerners would adopt legal generality precisely as a method of maintaining cultural separation: legal neutrality in the service of xenophobia and racism.

If Paderewski seemed concerned with the Jews' wily cosmopolitanism, the Yugoslavs worried more about their minorities' cultural primitivism. The Yugoslav representative argued that "[i]n view of the fact that owing to their intellectually and politically backward condition, a large proportion of the minorities in our state might be prompted to misinterpret these clauses, it is necessary for the Conference to declare that it is not at all a case of privilege but of the protection of rights."[21] In this argument, it was "intellectual backwardness" that posed the danger of the interpretive instability of the minority protection treaty. If cosmopolitans were feared due to their deliberate efforts to transmogrify their "minority" status, primitives were viewed as prone to naively exuberant exaggerations of its subtly restricted meaning.

Both the Polish and the Yugoslav arguments rested on the twin notions that the minorities' self-understanding would be transformed by the possibilities they discerned in the legal categories and that this understanding could in turn transform the international meaning of the categories. This instability seemed to be particularly dangerous in the case of the protagonist-position "minority," which has always stood between that of individual citizenship and "nationhood." The delegates of the two new states sought to prevent giving their "minorities" the sense that the shift from the status of "individuals" to that of "minorities" could continue even further along the spectrum, all the way to "nationhood."

Discussions like those described in this section indicate the complexity of attempting to provide definitive criteria for distinguishing among protagonist-positions. Discursive and political transformations often shift groups across a range of identities and back again. A full spectrum shift, which some groups have traversed in its entirety, could be described thus: "nations" or "peoples" arise to claim self-determination because their submersion in a non-national state excludes expression of their national identity; "national minorities" arise to claim collective minority protection because national states exclude their cultural identity; "persons who belong to ethnic, religious, or linguistic minorities" arise to assert individual rights because "national" cultures (majority or minority) exclude expression of their individuality. Or vice versa: "persons" may unite to form "national minorities" because the availability of that legal category may enable them to understand their own cultural or political alternatives in a new, more collective, way; "national minorities" may form "nations" or "peoples" because of the possibilities opened up by those categories; and, finally, "nations" or "peoples" may form states because sovereignty is the legal and cultural signifier of full participation in the international community. And there are many other variations, both directional and motivational, of such movements up and down the scale of identity. Attempts to stop the movement along the scale, such as the Polish or Yugoslav effort to give a restrictive meaning to the word *minority*, involve contentious cultural projections that cannot be definitively stabilized by doctrinal fiat or pragmatic management. Moreover, all such attempts depend on a contestable construction of a cultural realm, whose contingent form makes possible their efforts to restrain, facilitate, or transform identity.

III. HISTORY CONTINUOUS AND DISCONTINUOUS

As for the Palais des Nations, . . . there are excellent facilities for a
conference, with the capacity to expand quickly to absorb numerous
delegates and then contract down to a small secretariat. Yet, sometimes, as
I wandered at night through the deserted art deco halls, I felt haunted by
the 1930's and wondered whether Yugoslavia would do to the UN what
Abyssinia did to the League of Nations.

—LORD OWEN, *BALKAN ODYSSEY* (1995)

As I have noted, today's discussions of nationalist conflicts are marked by a radical disjunction between technocratic urgency and historical déjà-vu. This sense of both the inevitability and incongruity of analogies to past events itself partakes of a tradition. Past phases of this tradition, however, have involved thickly textured arguments about continuity and innovation rather than stark compartmentalization between historical precedent and current exigencies. It is a tradition in which past texts have been continually reread in a manner modifying, preserving, transforming, or reversing their earlier meaning. If today's disjunction between historical and programmatic discussions seems both theoretically and normatively inadequate, rereading these earlier discussions can teach us much about our own implicit fidelity to, and rupture with, the past. To illustrate this method, I will briefly examine texts from three transitional moments in the international law of nationalism: the Versailles period (1919), the revisionist late 1930s, and the pre-decolonization early 1950s. Debates about the relative propriety of different periods' assertions of legal competence over nationalist conflict always involve competing views about the proper configuration of elements such as power and principle, idealism and realism, law and politics. These arguments can only be studied by close examination of particular texts, showing both the elaboration of competing configurations and the way they construct a realm of cultural difference to justify or refute the "legality" of legal innovation.

A. 1919

The provisions of the World War I peace treaties for dealing with nationalist claims in Eastern and Central Europe remain the most systematic deployment on a vast region of the various legal techniques for dealing with nationalism. The system's place in international legal history is ambivalent: international policymakers have rejected it as outdated due to its ultimate collapse, yet they constantly seem to be struggling to imitate it, particularly in their most ostensibly updated, cutting-edge efforts. At its inception, the Versailles system was itself debated both in terms of its continuities with nineteenth-century precedents and of its creative legal innovations; given the similar current ambivalence toward the legal past, the 1919 debates, particularly those concerning the minority protection treaties, warrant close analysis.

"In the first place, I would point out that this Treaty does not constitute any fresh departure."[22] With these words, Clemenceau launched into his historical argument to overcome Paderewski's objections to the Polish Minority Protection Treaty. Clemenceau focused on arguing that the treaty embodied specifically legal norms, both because of its continuity with past practices and its distance from their "political" aspects. Thus, he asserted that "[i]t has long been the established procedure of the public law of Europe that when a state is created or even when large accessions of territory are made to an established state, the joint and formal recognition by the Great Powers should be accompanied by the requirement that such State should, in the form of a binding international convention, undertake to comply with certain principles of government." The precedents to which Clemenceau referred were all drawn from the nineteenth century minority protection guarantees that were made conditions of international recognition of the states detached from the Ottoman Empire; this "established procedure" was epitomized in the 1878 Treaty of Berlin.

On first reading, Clemenceau thus seemed to present legal history as a smooth evolutionary process. He treated the nineteenth-century agreements as worthy precedents, even though not wholly purified of the appearance of improper Great Power interest. The nineteenth-century agreements were "open to the criticism" that they could give the Great Powers a pretext to intervene impermissibly in the affairs of the states with minority obligations. The new treaties, therefore, "differ[ed] in form" from their predecessors, placing the guarantees in the hands of the League of Nations rather than the Great Powers. This change, coupled with judicial review, would complete the move from a "political" to a legal system. This continuity and discontinuity with the past seems no more problematic than the familiar riddles implicit in the "ripening" metaphor in the evolution oft customary law.

Clemenceau's ironic relationship to his precedents, however, begins to emerge when we read his argument in light of the letter from Paderewski to which he was responding. Paderewski had declared that "[t]he Polish nation has not forgotten that the dismemberment of Poland was the consequence of the intervention of foreign Powers in affairs concerning her religious minorities, and this painful memory makes Poland fear external interference in internal matters of state more than anything."[23] Paderewski cited this history to ground his protest against the minority protection system's infringement of Poland's "sovereign rights." He argued that this insult to the Polish state was "equivalent to regarding the Polish nation as a nation of inferior standard of civilization." Clemenceau's recourse to precedents drawn from the recognition of the Balkan states in the nineteenth century thus might have confirmed Paderewski's worst fears: that Poland was being treated as "Balkan" in the pejorative sense, its internal affairs associated with the perennial "questions soulevées en Orient." A comparison between the treatment of Polish and Czech minority issues by the peace conference would have confirmed this view. Beneš, unlike Paderewski, convinced the Commission of New States and Minorities that his new country should be viewed as a Western European society.

For Paderewski, both the continuities and discontinuities with the past worked to delegitimate the new treaty. The current representatives of international legal authority were potentially new versions of the ignoble protagonists of past Great Power interventions who used minority rights as a cover for political interest; conversely, the high dignity that Poland now merited was being wrongly downgraded to that of states who were viewed not as quite real, not quite up to the level of other European states. Paderewski presented the relation between the Minority Protection Treaty and earlier precedents as a mocking parody. The low figures of the past were being incongruously dressed in noble costume; the sainted martyr from the past was being unfairly cast as a reprobate sinner. Furthermore, it sought to simultaneously use the present and the past to legitimize each other: the current international authority would use its high legal dignity to ennoble that of the past retrospectively, while looking to the past for the source of its own legitimacy. For Paderewski, by contrast, linking the League with the Great Powers of the past only heightened the danger of the League's reenactment of the latter's unpalatable role; similarly, casting the newly sovereign Polish nation in the same subordinate role as the Poland so easily dismembered in the past offended its contemporary dignity.

Clemenceau's portrayal of the role of the Great Powers, like his portrayal of Poland, also involved a complex and ironic response to Paderewski's fears. For Paderewski, the only way to purge international authority of the taint of impermissible political bias was precisely by heightening that authority through generalizing minority protection duties, making them "obligatory for all states belonging to the League." In response, Clemenceau declared: "The Principal Allied and Associated Powers are of opinion that they would be false to the responsibility which rests upon them if on this occasion they departed from what has become an established tradition. In this connection I must also recall to your consideration the fact that it is to the endeavors and sacrifices of the Powers in whose name I am addressing you that the Polish nation owes the recovery of its independence." Clemenceau thus coupled his assertion of the Allied and Associated Powers' responsibility to the legal "tradition" with a reminder of Poland's material dependence on them: it is on the support of "these Powers" for the League that "Poland will to a large extent depend for the secure possession" of its territory. This assertion, that Polish sovereignty was an expression of a just claim to national self-determination, on the one hand, and attributable to the power of the Allies and therefore subject to their conditions, on the other, was enshrined in the first lines of the Polish Minority Protection Treaty ("[w]hereas the Allied and Associated Powers have by the success of their arms restored to the Polish nation the independence of which it has been unjustly deprived"). The repeated stress on this point was an ironic commentary on the disclaimer of the treaty's "political" dimension; according to the logic of Clemenceau's argument, if the move from the Great Power guarantee to that of the League was incomplete, so was the move from "politics" to "law." It suggests rather more continuity with precisely the purportedly negative features of the nineteenth-century system than the rest of Clemenceau's argument would allow.

A close reading thus shows how both statesmen presented complex claims about the new system's continuity and discontinuity with its predecessors.

Clemenceau's argument seemed on first reading to assert a gradual evolution from Great Power politics to international law, while Paderewski's argument seemed like a traditionalist clinging to sovereign political prerogatives. Yet more careful analysis shows how Clemenceau sought to preserve the political elements of the nineteenth century system in his emphasis on Allied power, while Paderewski insisted on a fuller evolution from politics to law. Similarly, in drawing parallels between the Paris and Berlin conferences and between the restoration of Polish sovereignty and the settlement of exotic Balkan matters, Clemenceau promoted the continued extension of international supremacy where Paderewski would have required rupture in deference to Polish nationalism; yet in refusing to extend international scrutiny to all League members, the Allies continued the deference to Western European sovereignty where Poland demanded an innovative generalization of international supremacy. Finally, Paderewski sought to use historical precedent to demonstrate the minority protection system's demeaning cultural activism and thus to debunk its impartial legal pretensions; Clemenceau, implicitly embracing the history of Western European cultural activism, asserted that the tradition of imposing special obligations on the Central and Eastern European states legitimated the legal dignity of the current treaty. The two statesmen's opposed configurations of nationalism and internationalism, power and principle, continuity and discontinuity thus hinged on the contestation of internationalist cultural activism and the projection of cultural difference among European nations.

B. 1938

If 1919 is remembered in conventional legal histories as the moment of transition from a political to a legal conception of the international law of nationalism, 1938 is remembered as the reverse. Just as the former narrative must be rethought, so must the latter. The haste, yet inexorability, with which the irredentism of the 1930s is mentioned in the opening passages of many writings on international minority rights indicates the unresolved, traumatic role of the events evoked by "Munich" in the international law of nationalism; while this irredentism is generally cited to explain the eclipse of minority rights, it is never clear how new proposals meet the problem.

To be sure, pragmatists may seek to reassure us that the 1938 Four-Power Agreement in Munich was merely a case of misjudgment, however grave. For such an interpretation, the non-fascist powers simply erred in the way they weighed the national claims of the Sudetendeutsche and German state interests against the national claims of ethnic Czechs, the multiethnic claims of many Czech citizens, and Czechoslovakia's state interests: excessively deferring to a powerful state, erroneously weighing competing ethnic claims. Yet the agreement and the period debate cannot be so easily dismissed as an aberration either doctrinally or pragmatically. Munich haunts the international imagination today because of its consistency with the enduring structural elements of the international law of nationalism. Although Cold War invocations of Munich have been thoroughly criticized, the lack of examination of its significance for minority rights (the purported substance of the dispute) has allowed its uncritical deployment in current debate about nationalist conflict. Munich has been cited vehemently during the wars in the Balkans.[24] The current resurgence of minority rights requires that we explicitly grapple with the 1930s events that contributed so decisively to their long occultation.[25]

It is often said that Munich was a "reverse Versailles," the final undoing of the interwar regime, the transformation of Europe from a "pluralist" to a "hegemonic" system.[26] By contrast, historian A. J. P. Taylor declared (ironically?) that Munich "was a triumph for all that was best and most enlightened in British life;" the "offence redressed at Munich" was the "subjection of three million Germans to Czech rule," a violation of the principle of "equal justice between peoples."[27] These conflicting views may be seen as a debate about the justice and practicality of the protagonist-position "protected minority," to which the Sudetens were "subjected." The buildup to Munich was replete with British and French statements critical of the "minority" protagonist-position, at least in the context of the Sudetens' dynamically shifting self-understanding. Thus, British mediator Lord Runciman described the transformation of Sudeten aspirations from "some degree of home rule" within Czechoslovakia to the demand for the "full right of self-determination."[28] He sympathetically declared that it "is a hard thing to be ruled by an alien race," particularly when many Sudetens considered the Czechs to be cultural inferiors. This transformation of Sudeten identity, which garnered decisive international support in 1938, illustrates the ambivalences toward the "minority" protagonist-position and the role of the construction of a realm of cultural identity and competing projections of cultural difference.

The Munich Agreement itself, *when read out of context*, is shocking precisely because of its familiarity, its consistency with its predecessor treaties. Indeed, read paragraph by paragraph, it seems to defer to earlier treaties rather than to "reverse" them. Its first three paragraphs recall the Treaty of Berlin in providing for the conditions under which an incumbent sovereign must evacuate territories under nationalist dispute. The fourth paragraph's provisions for the transfer of "predominantly German" areas evoke the thirteenth of Wilson's Fourteen Points, which called for the establishment of Poland on territories with "indisputably Polish populations." The fifth paragraph evokes provisions of the Versailles Treaty in its call for a plebiscite in territories to be determined by an international commission and occupied by "international bodies" until after the plebiscite. Indeed, it practically cites the Versailles Treaty in its declaration that the plebiscite will be held under the "conditions of the Saar plebiscite," a Versailles-ordained event. The sixth paragraph vests the final determination of frontiers in an international commission, in line with similar expert bodies under Versailles auspices. Its seventh paragraph echoes Versailles's Article 91 in its granting of the right of option "into and out of the transferred territories." Finally, two months after Munich, the Czechs and Germans concluded an agreement to protect their respective "national minorities." The agreement, envisioning a mixed German-Czech commission with possible direct representation of the minorities' themselves, echoed similar arrangements after the partition of Upper Silesia.

A reverse Versailles? For the Germans, we should speak, rather, of a parodic Versailles—a mocking imitation of international legal texts whose substance the Germans sought to destroy, a destruction achieved at Munich through a variation on those very texts. For the British and French, the situation is more complicated. Whatever the subjective intentions of Daladier and Chamberlain, the appeal of the agreement lay in part in the way it seemed to preserve and yet transform the cardinal Versailles principles. I have argued elsewhere that this desire to preserve-and-transform the Versailles principles produced a "parodic/realist" destabilization of international discourse.[29] Yet many contemporaries viewed the relationship of the Munich Agreement to Versailles as a "ripening," an implementation of principles imperfectly adhered to in 1919. Such an argument was made possible by the adherence to the form of the international law of nationalism: the assertion of international authority in the cause of peace, the impositions on sovereignty, the combination of "objective self-determination" (expert determination of ethnic borders) and "subjective" self-determination (the plebiscite principle), with their supplements of the rights of citizenship, option, and minority protection. The ultimate in legal discontinuity, the dismemberment of Versailles-created Czechoslovakia, could be justified by some as a reconfiguration, rather than a rejection, of the Versailles principles.

That this interpretation, *in context*, was horribly, murderously, wrong goes without saying. Yet Munich should neither be used to reject an international law of nationalism nor be dismissed as a now-irrelevant aberration. There is no history of the international law of nationalism without Munich: it endures both as one of the possible variants of the legal structure and as a crucial turning point in its history. Allegations of new "Munich sellouts" are made possible by the structural affinity of that settlement with legal tradition; in particular, they are made possible by the contingency of that structure, its institution through contingent projections of cultural difference that may legitimate or delegitimate particular assertions of legal authority. The persuasiveness of the claim of the "injustice" of "subjecting Germans to Czech rule" lies in complex projections of cultural identity, difference, and hierarchy in relation to the contending groups as well as the international authorities who did the "subjecting." If international law is serious about resurrecting minority rights, as in the EU's conditions on recognition of new states, it must be prepared to meet the objections to which they are vulnerable.[30] The powerful interference with sovereign prerogatives involved in the imposition of minority rights must be openly justified; the cultural objections raised against the limitation of certain peoples to minority status rather than full nationhood must be confronted; the technical ability of international law to enforce the protections must be assured. No assertions of international authority are innocent of power, culturally neutral, or safe from cooptation by abhorrent forces; they may, nonetheless, be required.

C. 1938 and Decolonization

Munich marked a rupture in the international law of nationalism, integrating the postwar "occultation" of minority rights and the general denigration of interwar legal conceptions. After World War II, "no one proposed to revive the dead letter of the minorities treaties."[31] Most observers assumed that something like the Czech experience would be the inevitable result of such a legal regime. The distinctive blend of international authority and nationalist desire epitomized in minority rights thus could not be resurrected after the war. Rather, they became disjoined from each other. On the one hand, the concern for nationalist desire came to take the form of a right to self-determination redefined as independence within the colonial borders of the non-European possessions of European powers. On the other hand, internationalist aspirations were channeled into doctrines and institutions to protect individual human rights; minority protection survived only in the pallid Article 27 of the Covenant on Civil and Political Rights. This disjuncture between deference to nationalism and assertion of internationalism was the fate of the international law of nationalism during the decolonization decades.

Yet conventional accounts of the post-World War II period often omit a transitional period during which some invoked the interwar period to justify a new international law of nationalism on the basis of a rejuvenated systematic vision. In 1953, for example, one distinguished commentator declared that the "superior interests of the international community" gave it the right to evaluate critically nationalist claims.[32] He asserted that "specialists of public law condemn the nationalist phraseology according to which every national claim should be accepted." The two main criteria for evaluating such claims would be whether granting them would advance "democracy" and "civilization." Thus, a people living in a democratic state would not be able to join a nondemocratic state, nor would a people living in a "State of a high degree of civilization" be allowed to join a "State of illiterates." The latter case would be condemnable "in the name of culture as much as that of democracy." The dismemberment of Czechoslovakia was used as a central argument for critical scrutiny of nationalist claims, particularly those of the colonized peoples. This proposal thus reasserted international competence to judge nationalist claims in light of superior values; it combined new ideas about human rights and democracy with interwar ideas about cultural difference and internationalist supremacy.

This kind of comprehensive approach to nationalism, in which international authority would have the competence to rank national claims according to cultural judgments, was not to win out during the decolonization decades. Rather, one particular element of the international law of nationalism, decolonization within colonial borders, was to prevail against such a revival of comprehensive deployments of the gamut of doctrinal and policy options. Another key element in the old international law of nationalism, minority protection, was delegitimized due to the anticolonial stress on unconditional sovereignty as well as to the "lessons of Munich." Nationalist claims were thus divided into two groups: claims that merited full self-determination, to which international law must defer (that is, decolonization), and those not meriting full self-determination, in relation to which international law would be largely irrelevant.

Thus, in the immediate postwar period, Munich had become the terrain of competing interpretations. This debate opposed those who used it as an argument to evaluate every self-determination claim in the name of internationalism to those who used it to turn self-determination into a formal right applied to formally defined cases. The gradually developing anticolonial consensus gave victory to this latter interpretation and, together with Cold War competition, gradually suppressed all explicit legal discussion of cultural status in the old sense. For many anticolonialists, a formalist approach to self-determination and sovereignty was the only way to bring an end to the imperial deployment of both flexible pragmatism and cultural activism. This emphasis on decolonization and its delegitimization of internationalist supremacy over nationalist claims made impossible a systematic approach in the manner of either the late nineteenth century or the interwar period.

IV. CONCLUSION: A NEW INTERNATIONAL LAW OF NATIONALISM?

Religious freedom does not only affect the Jews; in imposing it on Serbia as a condition of its independence, the Treaty equally provides it for the Muslims. The territories attributed by the Congress to Prince Milan give him a great number of Muslims who will have to become Serbian citizens, in law and in everyday life. This will be, in our view, the best way for Serbia to fulfill its destiny.
                              —BENOIT BRUNSWIK, *LE TRAITÉ DE BERLIN,*
                                   ANNOTÉ ET COMMENTE (1878)

In the first place, it is altogether remarkable to observe that the Arbitration Commission, established in the framework of the Peace Conference for Yugoslavia, . . . has not hesitated . . . to classify minority

rights in the superior category of peremptory norms of international law
(jus cogens).

—PIERRE-MARIE DUPUY, *DROIT INTERNATIONAL*
PUBLIC (1993)

During the early 1990s, a conventional metaphor to describe resurgence of nationalist tensions was "the thawing out of nationalism from the Communist freezer," yielding old antagonisms in particularly horrible and diseased form. Perhaps the end of the Cold War's freezing of the old international law of nationalism might similarly be said to have led to the reemergence of the categories and approaches of that law—although presumably in reformed, rather than diseased, shape. The analysis presented in this chapter suggests some explanations for today's "altogether remarkable" resurrection of minority rights other than such question-begging metaphors.

The end of the Cold War has facilitated the emergence of a new comprehensive international law of nationalism due to its revival of the central features of previous comprehensive approaches: a vigorous sense of international legal authority, the availability to that authority of the entire range of doctrinal and policy techniques, and the construction of a realm of cultural difference that both legitimates and informs the deployment of international power. The first feature follows from the rather familiar point that the end of the Cold War has transformed the structure of international authority. Although the exuberance of the immediate post-1989 period has evaporated, the notion of a relatively unified international authority has persisted. Thus far, the international legal community has not been divided along ideological lines like those of the 1930s or the Cold War. Such a relatively unified international authority has been an indispensable premise of all comprehensive approaches to nationalist conflict: some institution or group of states must be able to occupy the position of "international legal organ" in whose name power and principle can be asserted.

Second, the decline of the anti-imperialist stress on formal deference to a formal version of self-determination and sovereignty has made it possible for internationalists to consider systematically the array of techniques for settling nationalist conflict. The new reassertion of international authority thus makes possible options such as the imposition of minority rights. Minority rights, always a good barometer of the state of the international law of nationalism, are associated with the strong internationalist assertion of the right to impose conditions on new states formed in acts of national self-determination—and, therefore, such rights were relegated to the back burner during the heyday of anticolonialist suspicion of the principledness of international power.

Finally, explicit affirmations and contestations of cultural activism have reemerged in debates about the deployment of international power. Proponents and critics of international cultural activism have clashed in debates about new forms of trusteeship and "failed states," in the highly culturally charged debate about Bosnia and the "Sarajevo ideal," in the debate about cultural relativism and universal human rights. The legitimation of international authority through the construction of a realm of cultural difference has been contested in the critique of end-of-history liberal-triumphalism and its more ominous twin, the "clash of civilizations." The birth pangs of a new, systematic international law of nationalism may be heard in these debates in which cultural discourse plays a variety of shifting and politically ambivalent roles.

The comprehensive frameworks embodied in documents such as the 1995 Draft Convention on Yugoslavia and the 1995 Dayton Agreements are some of the most advanced expressions of the new international law of nationalism, made possible by the three developments I have discussed. This return to comprehensive frameworks does not mean that the deep ambivalences structuring this field—internationalism and nationalism, power and principle—have been resolved. Each of the new comprehensive documents is subject to competing interpretations; each interpretation involves contestable projections of cultural difference as well as contestations of the role of culture as a legitimator of international action.

As in the past, the new international law of nationalism is a terrain of discursive and political struggle, not a set of doctrinal definitions or neutral pragmatic solutions. As a commentator on the 1878 Treaty of Berlin wrote: "[The Treaty] represents all the solutions or purported solutions which the eastern crisis [la crise orientale] has provoked in people's spirits. The Treaty has an advantage over criticism: criticism seeks only the victory of one solution over the others . . . while the Treaty of Berlin, incorporating all opinions, . . . provides to each the means of peacefully working for its definitive victory."[33] This passage may be viewed as an early example of the approach pursued in this essay, that of understanding doctrinal and policy analyses in light of their projection of cultural fears and fantasies. Nationalism has always appeared to the international imagination as an exotic, frightening, and fascinating stimulus to legal creativity; the international law of nationalism has always furnished a terrain of conflict in which the construction of a realm of cultural difference and competing projections of international and nationalist identity have played a crucial role. Yet if we have learned to be wary of the Western- and Eurocentric version of this relationship, if we have abandoned expressions such as "la crise orientale," we should not delude ourselves into thinking that we have acceded to the rationalist utopia of pure doctrine and neutral pragmatics. Asserting such transcendence simply means that the cultural imagination will continue to operate implicitly, if not unconsciously. The refusal of cultural discourse may serve to reject the oppressive form it has taken, most egregiously in colonialism; it may also mask the cultural projections deployed through ostensibly neutral doctrine and policy.

The new international law of nationalism, like its predecessors, will not take the form of complete theoretical and doctrinal generalization or fully neutral technocratic policy but that of a new set of persuasive practices, implicating contestable and contingent projections. It will be a resumption of a tradition whose record embodies both the noblest and basest efforts of international community. The reemergence of an international law of nationalism makes possible both concrete humanitarian efforts and the necessity to scrutinize a whole range of cultural and political projections uncritically, or unconsciously, deployed by previous generations. It is not possible to decide *a priori* whether a new international law of nationalism should be embraced or resisted, whether today's conditions continue to demand anti-imperialist assertions of strict respect for sovereignty, make palatable the revival of cultural activism, or facilitate vigorous international action that can realize the noblest aspirations of both while avoiding their oppressive dimensions. Yet the history of the international law of nationalism demonstrates that it is simply not possible to construct a neutral approach innocent of differential cultural projections and unimplicated in the partisan imposition of power. Rather, the legacy of international law's troubling efforts to engage with nationalism should be the vigilant awareness of the possibilities and dangers implicit in all the approaches and the willingness to deploy them tactically to prevent the horrors that have, more often than not, followed even the noblest legal dreams.

NOTES

1. I paraphrase Judge Petren, who, in 1975, wrote of the crystallization of a "veritable international law of decolonization." Western Sahara Case, 1975 ICJ 12, 100 (Advisory Opinmodernion of October 16).

2. On the relationship between the construction of "culture" and the legitimation of Western dominance, *see, e.g.,* Samir Amin, *Imperialism and Culturalism Complement Each Other,* 48 MONTHLY REV. 1 (1996); Antony Anghie, *Francisco de Vitoria and the Colonial Origins of International Law,* 5 SOC. & LEGAL STUD. 321 (1996); Annelise Riles, *Aspiration and Control: International Legal Rhetoric and the Essentialization of Culture,* 106 HARV. L. REV. 723 (1993); Nathaniel Berman, *Modernism, Nationalism, and the Rhetoric of Reconstruction,* 4 YALE J. L. & HUMAN. 351 (1992); Lila Abu-Lughod, *Writing Against Culture,* in RECAPTURING ANTHROPOLOGY 137 (Richard Fox ed., 1991). *Cf.* James Clifford, THE PREDICAMENT OF CULTURE 10 (1988) ("Culture is a deeply compromised idea I cannot yet do without.").

3. E. H. Carr, THE TWENTY YEARS CRISIS 93 (1951).

4. Homi K. Bhabha, THE LOCATION OF CULTURE 114 (1994).

5. Robert Jennings & Authur Watts (eds.), OPPENHEIM'S INTERNATIONAL LAW 977 (9th ed. 1992).

6. Paul Tavernier, *A Propos de la Convention-Cadre du Conseil de l'Europe pour la Protection des Minorités Nationales,* 100 RGDIP 385 (1995). (All translations are Berman's unless otherwise noted.)

7. The preamble states: "Considering that the aim of the Council of Europe is to achieve greater unity between its members. . . . Bring resolved to ensure . . . the effective protection of national minorities . . . , respecting the territorial integrity and national sovereignty of state . . ."

8. Benoit Brunswik, LE TRAITÉ DE BERLIN, ANNOTÉ ET COMMENTÉ 34 (1878).

9. Polish Nationality Case (Advisory Op. No. 7), P.C.I.J. (Ser. B.) at 13–16 (1923).
10. The Anglo-French Proposals Presented to the Czechoslovak Government on September 19, 1938, in CORRESPONDENCE RESPECTING CZECHOSLOVAKIA, SEPTEMBER 1938 at 8, 9 (1938).
11. See, for example, this almost unreadable passage in the extremely influential preparatory memo by Jan Smuts, *The League of Nations: A Practical Proposal* (1918), in David Hunter Miller II, THE DRAFTING OF THE COVENANT 23, 28 (1928): "[T]he German colonies in the Pacific and Africa are inhabited by barbarians, who not only cannot possibly govern themselves, but to whom it would be impracticable to apply the idea of self-determination in the European sense."
12. Eugene V. Erdley, GERMANY'S FIRST EUROPEAN PROTECTORATE: THE FATE OF THE CZECHS AND SLOVAKS (1942), 15, 41.
13. See, *e.g.*, Gerald B. Helman and Stephen R. Ratner, *Saving Failed States*, 89 FOREIGN POL'Y 3 (1992).
14. Nathaniel Berman, *Between 'Alliance' and 'Localization': Nationalism and the New Oscillationism*, 26 N.Y.U. INT'L L. & Pol. 901 (1994).
15. Discours d'Ouverture de M. Bernard Dejean de la Batie, Chef de la Délégation Française, CSCE Meeting of Experts on National Minorities, July 2, 1991, at 10. France has always maintained that it has no minorities within the meaning of Article 27 of the Covenant on Civil and Political Rights. See, *e.g.*, Pierre-Marie Dupuy, DROIT INTERNATIONAL PUBLIC 157 n.2 (2d ed. 1993).
16. *Id.*, at 3.
17. Thus, one commentator on the European Convention declares that the term *national* in "national minority" refers not to the "nationalness" of the minority but to the fact that the group is a minority on the "national territory" of the state in which it resides. Heinrich Klebes, *The Council of Europe's Framework Convention for the Protection of National Minorities: Introduction*, 16 HUM. RTS. L.J. 92, 93 (1995). If Klebes is right, then the convention intends the phrase in the opposite sense from the interwar usage. The Explanatory Memorandum on the Convention notes that it was "impossible to arrive at a definition" of the phrase and, therefore, it "was decided to adopt a pragmatic approach." "Explanatory Memorandum on the Framework Convention," in *id.* at 101, 102. *Cf.* the "Report of the CSCE Meeting of Experts on National Minorities," reprinted in 30 I.L.M. (1991), 1692, 1696. ("[N]ot all ethnic cultural, linguistic, or religious differences lead to the creation of national minorities.")
18. Oscar Janowsky, THE JEWS AND MINORITY RIGHTS, 1898–1919 (1933), 300.
19. Memorandum of M. Paderewski, (June 15, 1919), in X LA PAIX DE VERSAILLES 129, 129, 132 (1932).Both proponents and critics of the minroites treaties discussed the "danger" that they would grant minorities, particularly the Jews, the status of a "State within the State." See, *e.g.*, Annex (B) to Eighth Meeting, Second Report (May 13, 1919) in *id.*, at 42, 45.
20. Memorandum of M. Paderewski, *supra* note 19, at 129, 133.
21. Letter of the Serb-Croat-Slovene Delegation (November 5, 1919), in X LA PAIX DE VERSAILLES, *supra* note 19, at 359, 362.
22. Letter Addressed to M. Paderewski by the Conference (Clemenceau Letter) (June 24, 1919, in X LA PAIX DE VERSAILLES, *supra* note 19, at 160 (161).
23. Memorandum of M. Paderewski, *supra* note 19, at 129.
24. Most strikingly, it was evoked in 1991 by the Yugoslav defense minister, who compared the secession of Slovenia to that of the Sudentenland (LE MONDE, July 20, 1991); by the Venezulan delegate during the 1993 Security Council debate on the arms embargo in an eloquent comparison of Izetbegovic with Edouard Beneš (U.N. Doc S/PV.3247, June 29, 1993, at 128–31), a comparison also evoked by Izetbegovic himself; and by Jacques Chirac in 1995, who compared the Western treatment of Bosnia with the treatment of Czechoslovakia by Chamberlain and Daladier (THE INDEPENDENT, July 17, 1995). David Owen's defense of the European role in Bosnia often seems obsessed with the "too many false analogies" drawn with "Europe in the 1930s and 1940's." David Owen, BALKAN ODYSSEY 366 (1995).

25. I explore the international legal and cultural implications of the Munich settlement in greater detail in *Beyond Colonialism and Nationalism? Ethiopia, Czechoslovakia and 'Peaceful Change'*, NORDIC J. INT'L L. 421 (1996).

26. Otto Feinstein, *Conflict at Munich: Pluralism vs. Hegemonism*, in APPEASING FASCISM 19 (Melvin Small and Otto Feinstein eds., 1991)

27. A. J. P. Taylor, THE ORIGINS OF THE SECOND WORLD WAR 189 (1961).

28. Letter of Lord Runciman to Neville Chamberlain, September 21, 1938, reprinted in CORRESPONDENCE RESPECTING CZECHOSLOVAKIA, SEPTEMBER 1938 at 3 (1938).

29. See *Beyond Colonialism and Nationalism?*, *supra* note 25.

30. European Community, Declaration on Yugoslavia and on the Guidelines on the Recognition of New States, reprinted in 31 I.L.M. 1485 (1992).

31. William E. Rappard, *Vues Rétrospectives sur la Société des Nations*, 71 RCADI 117, 187 (1947–II).

32. Boris Mirkine-Guétzch, *Quelques Problèmes de la Mise en Oeuvre de la Déclaration Universelle des Droits de l'Homme*, 83 RCADI 255, 347–48 (1953–II).

33. Brunswik, *supra* note 8, at ix.

The International Legal Challenges Posed by the Rise of Nations

Part II: Introduction

IN RECOUNTING THE "rise of nations" story, Part's 1's essays served to illumine the international system's ongoing transformation over the past two centuries. States can no longer lay exclusive claim to international legal personality. Nor can states be deemed the only politically salient actors in the international realm. A range of nonstate entities, including national groups or "peoples," have increasingly and conspicuously manifested their global significance. Such prominent developments have placed international law in a potentially problematic situation. If international law may accurately be characterized as a historically *state-constituted* system of rules regulating *state* conduct, what will become of that system in a period of relative decline in state prominence? In order to remain relevant and consequential during a period of political, economic, and social change, international law will likely be compelled to adapt to new circumstances. It will likely need, as well, to engage more regularly with a wider array of politically salient entities—to listen and to speak to them.

After the Second World War, the exponential proliferation of international organizations necessitated significant changes in the rules governing international legal personality. In 1949, for example, the International Court of Justice (I.C.J.) rendered its seminal Advisory Opinion on *U.N. Reparations*.[1] The Court had been asked to consider whether the United Nations might bring claims against states for injuries suffered by the United Nations itself or by those in its service. The I.C.J. observed then that the capacity to bring claims had traditionally belonged exclusively to states because those entities had been historically held as the only international legal persons. The Court noted, however, that "[t]hroughout its history, the development of international law has been influenced by the requirements of international life, and the progressive increase of action upon the international plane by certain entities which are not States." Accordingly, the I.C.J. found the United Nations legally competent to bring a claim because "the attribution of international personality" to that international organization was "indispensable" to the prosecution of its mission. In addition to the United Nations, some nongovernmental entities, including the International Committee of the Red Cross and transnational corporations, have come to be regarded as possessing a limited degree of international legal personality.[2] The continuing development of international humanitarian law and the *jus in bello* suggests that particular individuals may also constitute subjects of international law, possessing certain international rights and duties, albeit ones far less extensive than those of states. So, too, may certain national groups.[3]

What if "nations" were recognized, though, as international legal persons with rights and duties genuinely comparable to those now associated with states? What implications would such a change have for international politics and law? Almost certainly, it would alter fundamentally the existing international system and legal order, radically challenging state primacy and prerogatives. First, nonstate ethnic groups would secure far greater participation in those international bodies that have helped to develop the international law of nationalism. Increased participation by these national groups would surely undermine state efforts to perpetuate a legal system protecting state privileges. Even so, debates over which particular cultural groups merited international legal status would inevitable perpetuate. Second, nations would enjoy a status robustly commensurate to that of states. This hierarchical shift would necessarily have important consequences for the principles of self-determination, minority rights, and territorial integrity. Third, the granting to nations of state-like international legal status would likely render states vulnerable to a wide array of claims by nations for past and present wrongs. Such claims could probably not be satisfied in the context of current institutions given the claims' complexities and, in cases of conflicting claims, their incompatibilities.

Part II's essays do not advocate the formal recognition of nations as full-fledged international legal persons per se. Instead, they identify provocative legal issues that reflect the "rise of nations" phenomenon and suggest ways in which state-nation tension might or should be mitigated. Oscar Schachter's essay, for example, offers a general framework within which to analyze both the causes and effects of state decline. Here, Schachter includes the "resurgence of particularisms" (i.e., the "rise of nations") with global capital, civil society, and popular sovereignty as factors eroding state primacy in the international system. He concludes that states will not whither away, but that they will increasingly be compelled to share the international legal stage with nonstate actors.

The escalating prominence of nations enhances the ability of nations to press their claims. Benedict Kingsbury considers a number of "domains of discourse" in which ethnic groups hold interests: self-determination, minority rights, human rights, equality or nondiscrimination, and historical or indigenous claims. The international community's often ad hoc response within each of these domains, Kingsbury contends, has hampered the authority and effectiveness of international institutional efforts to address ethnic crises and to resolve national claims. Furthermore, the proper role of the nation in each of these domains remains ambiguous, with many states resisting the implications of politically active and powerful nations.

One way to mitigate this problem is proposed by Maivân Clech Lâm: establish some political and institutional room for ethnic groups within the international system. At a minimum, this would entail affording ethnic groups greater representation in international organizations and other fora, and increased opportunities to press their claims on the international plane. At a maximum, international institutions would be reconfigured to overturn a system that "elevate[s] states and suppress[es] peoples." Lâm remains ultimately pessimistic, however, about the willingness of states to relinquish their prerogatives.

Even if states were willing more generously to accommodate ethnic groups in the international system, Lea Brilmayer questions whether many claims raised by nations could satisfactorily be resolved. Such claims, she observes, tend to be framed largely in terms of "corrective justice"—that is, righting past wrongs. The mechanisms of international justice are ill suited to address claims of this type, Brilmayer submits. International institutions, for example, have little power to compel a state to accept a corrective viewed by that state as contrary to its interests. When corrective justice is dispensed, states often question its impartiality. Finally, she contends, corrective justice approaches often yield new injustices, thus perpetuating a pattern of retribution. Brilmayer's conclusions are surely sober ones. Nevertheless, her essay underscores, as do the others featured here, the growing challenge to the international community posed by the rise of nations.

NOTES

1. *International Court of Justice Reports* (1949), 174.
2. Jonathan I. Charney, "Transnational Corporations and Developing Public International Law," *Duke Law Journal* (1983): 748–88; Stephan Hobb, "Global Challenges to Statehood: The Increasingly Important Role of Nongovernmental Organizations," *Indiana Journal of Global Legal Studies* 5(1997): 191–209; Karsten Nowrot, "The Status of Non-governmental Organizations Under International Law," *Indiana Journal of Global Legal Studies* 6 (1999): 579–645.
3. Matthew Lippman, "Crimes Against Humanity," *Boston College Third World Law Journal* 17 (1997): 171–274. Louis B. Sohn, "The New International Law: Protection of the Rights of Individuals Rather than States," *American University Law Review* 32 (1982): 1–64.

FOR FURTHER READING

Brietzke, Paul H. "Self-Determination, or Jurisprudential Confusion: Exacerbating Political Conflict," *Wisconsin International Law Journal* 14 (1995): 69–131.
Brilmayer, Lea. "International Remedies," *Yale Journal of International Law* 14 (1989): 579–89.
Friedmann, Wolfgang G. *The Changing Structure of International Law.* New York, Columbia University Press, 1964.

Gottlieb, Gidon. *Nation Against State: A New Approach to Ethnic Conflicts and the Decline of Sovereignty*. New York: Council on Foreign Relations, 1993.

Grant, Thomas D. "Defining Statehood: The Montevideo Convention and its Discontents," *Columbia Journal of Transnational Law* 37 (1999): 403–56.

Hickey, James E. Jr., "The Source of International Legal Personality in the 21st Century," *Hofstra Law & Policy Symposium* 2 (1997): 1–18.

Krasner, Stephen D. "Pervasive Not Perverse: Semi-Sovereigns as the Global Norm," *Cornell International Law Journal* 30 (1997) 651–80.

Otto, Diane. "Nongovernmental Organizations in the United Nations System: The Emerging Role of International Civil Society," *Human Rights Quarterly* 16 (1996): 107–41.

Schreuer, Christoph. "The Waning of the Sovereign State: Towards a New Paradigm for International Law," *European Journal of International Law* 4 (1993): 447–71.

Spiro, Peter J. "New Players on the International Stage," *Hofstra Law & Policy Symposium* 2 (1997): 19–36.

Strange, Susan. *The Retreat of the State: The Diffusion of Power in the World Economy*. Cambridge: Cambridge University Press, 1996.

The Decline of the Nation-State and Its Implications for International Law

Oscar Schachter

MY SUBJECT, THE decline of the nation-state, goes to the heart of international law—its character as a system of discrete autonomous entities based on their defined territories, each exercising plenary authority over persons and things in that territory. That this juridical conception falls short of reality is well recognized. No state, not even the most powerful, is wholly autonomous, free of constraints and influences from outside its borders. Nor is its autonomy (or sovereignty) absolute in law.[1] It is limited by international law, which in the prevalent positivist conception is viewed as the collective expression of sovereign wills. States are equal in law, with the same rights and duties, but they of course vary widely in size, power, and values. There have always been weak and strong states.

The idea that the nation-state is generally declining in power and authority is a complex proposition based on a variety of factors. Economists, political scientists, journalists, and even businessmen have produced a spate of books and articles on various aspects of that theme.[2] The state, long seen as steadily amassing power, is now being viewed as increasingly vulnerable, even on its way out. The trends in that direction are attributed to a variety of developments: economic, technological, social, political, ideological, and psychological. Many observers see these developments as world-wide, affecting nearly all political com-

Reprinted from Oscar Schachter, "The Decline of the Nation-State and Its Implications for International Law," *Columbia Journal of Transnational Law* 36 (1997): 7–23.

munities. Their descriptive commentary is usually accompanied by indications of their preference. Weakened state power, as one would expect, is not only welcomed by free market supporters, but also from a different perspective, by political idealists who emphasize the values of popular participation and non-coercive rule. The state, in Nietzsche's words "the coldest of all cold monsters,"[3] does not inspire loyalty in the abstract. Many see it as an obstacle to achieving goals that are more important or "authentic" than allegiance to an authority based solely on a territorial nexus. I hope that my comments will throw some light on this large question and especially on its relation to the ideals and precepts of international law.

The discussion that follows will be presented under the following headings:

I. The Impact of Global Capitalism on State Authority,
II. The Enhanced Roles of Civil and Uncivil Society,
III. The Resurgence of Particularisms,
IV. Failed States, Illegal Regimes, and Popular Sovereignty, and
V. The Resilience of the State System.

I. THE IMPACT OF GLOBAL CAPITALISM ON STATE AUTHORITY

Global capitalism is not a new phenomenon, but its expansion in recent years has thrown a sharp light on the shrinking significance of national borders. The mobility of capital and technology—plus the global communications networks—is viewed as obliterating spatial lines, making nonsense of geographical demarcations. Some economists have been ready to conclude that "the nation-state is just about through as an economic unit."[4]

These economists often point to the size and mobility of finance capital. Capital transfers exceed a trillion dollars a day. Exchange controls have become almost impossible to apply. As one economist observed, "the sheer scale of profit-seeking finance capital that can be mobilized in currency markets far exceeds what any government, or even governments acting in concert can put against it."[5] States that are tempted to over-value their currency in foreign exchange quickly face large capital outflows which exchange controls cannot stop. It is true that governments may still fix interest rates and control the volume of currency; they may also run deficits in current accounts (as the United States has done for years). Yet they remain subject to the discipline of a global market that is largely unregulated. The International Monetary Fund and private credit rating agencies help to enforce that discipline.

The mobility of capital has also significantly altered the mercantilist ideas that emphasized trade restrictions. Although trade is still subject to political pressures of a populist or nationalist character, many governments are now more concerned with obtaining investment and finance capital. To encourage the flow of capital, governments tend to deregulate. The less developed countries are un-

der pressure to compete with each other by offering cheaper labor and lower
health and environmental standards in order to attract private investors. For
them, competition for capital may be a race to the bottom.

The role of the state has also been reduced by the explosive growth of direct
foreign investment by transnational corporations and portfolio investment by
pension and mutual funds. Much of such foreign investment takes place without
regard to the source state or its control. The old-style "imperialism" of capital-
exporting countries has no role in these cases and their state power is diminished.
Moreover, business firms, both large and small, increasingly seek profits in multinational markets, thus reducing their links to their national government.

On the ideological level, the superiority of markets over state control is almost universally accepted, even in countries like China and Vietnam that call
themselves communist. Today the market—anonymous, impersonal, pervasive—is viewed as the engine of development. The state steps back; its legal
power dwindles over currencies, interest rates, trade flows, rates of unemployment, and foreign investment. Non-state mechanisms develop; private rather
than public international rules prevail. A new international business class tends
to identify itself with the global aims of its transnational companies rather than
with the political objectives of its particular countries. The state no longer com-
mands the primary allegiance of this class though businessmen will still turn to
the state for intervention when it seems useful.

As a result, international law takes a new direction. Global capitalism and
more integrated investment and trade may bypass state control, but they require
international "public goods" that go beyond the province of the nation-state.
That includes the sets of rules, standards, dispute-settlement institutions, and
procedures that international lawyers consider their province. International markets require regimes for telecommunication and transportation, rules and procedures for financial stability and performance of contractual obligations, industrial and product standards, environmental protection rules, and much more.
The considerable *corpus juris* produced by United Nations bodies and the specialized agencies, composed of both hard and "soft" law, is an important part of
the international public goods required for transnational trade, investment,
communications, and other activities carried out mainly through non-state
channels. States play a major role in the creation and application of these legal
and quasi-legal regimes, but in doing so they transfer a large area of their internal authority to the international domain. Understandably, this has not been as
noticeable or controversial as the incursions into domestic jurisdiction in the human rights field. Viewed, however, from the standpoint of scope and depth, the
totality of such internationalization involves a large transfer of state power, and
in that respect, more transnational law.

A conspicuous transfer of authority from states to an international legal
regime has been the European Union, and to a lesser degree, the economic

integration institutions in other areas. The decline of state autonomy in the European Common Market, it will be recalled, began with the removal of customs barriers. It went on to include giving up national authority over exchange rates, opening financial markets, and adopting product standards, competition policies, and the numerous regulations that permit the free movement of peoples, goods, and services. The European Court of Justice has extended its authority so that it is not very far from a supreme court enforcing a federal constitution. It is premature, of course, to conclude that the European Union will become a federal union with states largely subordinate to central decisions. Resistance to that outcome remains strong. The conception of "subsidiarity" has won favor as a pragmatic principle under which the member states would retain the responsibilities that they can carry out more efficiently than the Union.

The law required by global capitalism extends beyond the law of state of state-controlled institutions. Much of the "lawyers' law" applicable to transnational business is created by business practices, private contracts, and organizational routines that, while they do not originate in legislation or judicial acts, nonetheless operate by characterizing private acts as legal or non-legal. The *lex mercatoria* is the historic example (even if some jurists see it as ultimately based in the state law). The increase in non-state arbitration for transnational business disputes is a factor in transforming private contract practices into authoritative law for the business community. Such law tends to reflect economic power and private interests and to escape scrutiny in the light of community values. Like other features of global capitalism, it raises the issue of the need for political restraints on private power.

II. THE ENHANCED ROLE OF CIVIL AND UNCIVIL SOCIETY

The decline of state authority is often associated with an increased political role for civil society, a less than precise term now commonly used for the non-governmental associations that seek to influence public policy.[6] The term came into wide use to describe the popular movements against communist rule in the 1980s. As currently used, it retains its favorable connotation as a more genuine expression of the peoples' will than government action. Moreover, many non-governmental associations see themselves as dedicated to "higher" community values and as less likely to be swayed by private interests or official bureaucracy. They fill the political space between the electoral process and the state administration in their chosen areas of interest. In that sense, they tend to reduce or check state power.

Civil society is not, of course, a new phenomenon. States have always faced competing non-state bodies: religious, ideological and economic. The importance of voluntary associations to democracy in the United States was emphasized by de Tocqueville in his mid-nineteenth century book *Democracy in America*. His enthusiastic comments have influenced the favorable assessment of nongovernmental organizations in comparison to governmental agencies. What is notable today is the phenomenal growth of organized nongovernmental movements and their diversity of interests. On the international level, they have become a force for political change in areas long seen as domestic—outside of international concern. They operate across national borders and frequently oppose entrenched government positions. A prime example is the movement for women's rights, which has spread widely and deeply and, in many ways, challenges the authority of the state. Other significant examples include the environmental movement, the human rights advocates, and the activist disarmament groups. In these and other areas, nongovernmental public interest bodies have developed techniques of advocacy and mobilization of opinion that ensure their impact on governments and international bodies. They have also fostered new social identities that cross national lines; people see themselves as environmentalists, feminists, human rights supporters, and the like. The phenomenal development of the computer networks has been a new factor, promising a much stronger role for interest groups acting on a world scale.

The influence of these developments on international law is substantial. The international conferences and organizations engaged in lawmaking have become increasingly open to the influence of the nongovernmental bodies, especially those mentioned above, devoted to advocacy of social goals.[7] A somewhat different role is played by the non-governmental scientific and technical bodies— now often referred to as "epistemic communities." Their findings and conclusions enter into governmental lawmaking in both national and international arenas. In many—and probably most—areas of contemporary international lawmaking, they have become an important factor adding a new dimension to international law. Civil society also embraces functional groups engaged in economic and professional activities, often across national lines. These associations and networks establish their own functional norms and procedures, creating effectively stateless law. The French commentator Guénhenno reminds us that these functional norms "are no longer the expression of a sovereignty but simply something that reduces uncertainties, a means of lowering the cost of transactions, of increasing transparence. It is as incongruous to pose the question of legitimacy as to question whether a computer program is just or unjust."[8] In this vision of borderless functional rationality, civil society creates its own law; the political realm of the state is largely irrelevant. This may seem somewhat naive, since issues of power and justice can arise even in rational functional networks and recourse to "higher" authority of sovereign or court is likely. Yet such recourse to state law may be relatively rare. It is not far-fetched to envisage a world of networked enterprises operating under their own functional norms with little or no role for the intervention of government law. The global information structure—"cyberspace"—is an obvious arena for such borderless law developed by networks communities.

The widespread approbation of civil society associations (especially in regard to international affairs) tends to obscure their diversity and conflicting ends. Most of them serve special and limited interests, not all of them benign. Patriotic movements can be racist; civic improvement societies may seek to exclude the poor or minorities; professional bodies often restrict access. Even the pure "do-gooders" may pursue ends that clash with other important objectives. True, a multiplicity of associations may provide checks and balances in some circumstances and even produce harmony in diversity. But to expect that the "common good" will usually emerge simply from the clash of competing interest groups is hardly realistic. In the real world, we have to look to the state in the final analysis to resolve such conflicts on the basis of public principles of justice and the common good.

Although the heading of this section refers to "uncivil society," a more descriptive term would be "criminal society." Criminal activity, of course, has always challenged state authority, but from the standpoint of international law a new dimension has been added. States and the international community are now threatened by transnational crime on an unprecedented scale. Some of the factors emphasized earlier as causes of globalization as well as the new communication networks have also increased the power of lawless groups. The scale of illegal drug traffic dwarfs the gross national product of many states and appears to be beyond the effective control of individual states or even the world community as a whole. The illegal arms trade also flourishes ostensibly beyond state control. International money laundering has expanded into a huge business. Terrorist activities, while mainly political in aim, also belong in the category of international criminal activity. All of these activities dramatically underscore the weakness of nation-states and of the international legal system. They are responsible for a substantial diversion of resources from useful development activities as well as for a far-reaching deterioration in the daily life of society. True, the problems are on the agenda of states and international bodies, but with states increasingly diminished in power they are even less likely to overcome organized crime and the social pathology linked to crime. Only the most unworldly optimist would look to the market economy for solutions.

III. THE RESURGENCE OF PARTICULARISMS

My third topic concerns the widespread assertion of substate identities that challenge the central authority of the juridical state. In the forefront are the claims made in the name of a "people" against alleged alien domination by a state. The political end sought may be independence, autonomy, or merger with another state. Though the international community has unanimously recognized these ends as "modes of implementing the right of self-determination by a people under alien domination," it also has expressed itself against action that would "dismember, totally or in part the territorial integrity or political unity of sovereign states possessing a government representing the whole people belonging to the territory without distinction as to race, creed or color."[9] Under this principle, separatist movements would not be legally justified by the international right of self-determination in those states where governments represent all peoples without discrimination as to race, creed, or color.

Even if this provision protecting the territorial integrity and "political unity" of existing states were accepted as the governing law, it would not meet the demands of "peoples" whose essential claim is that they are under "alien domination" and that the central government does not truly represent them. They see no good reason to differentiate their claims from those of peoples in overseas colonies.[10] Whether they are "a nation" or "a people" is seen as a matter of self-identification usually based on language, culture, and historic links to a particular territory. Memories of past glories, past injustices, and religious teachings often sustain their sense of a separate people. The fact that they may not appear very different from the other peoples in that state does not modify their sense of separateness. Freud's comment on the "narcissism of minor differences"[11] has been quoted by observers of internal conflicts where neighbors have slaughtered each other though they have lived side by side for generations and are not much different from each other.

Apart from arguments about self-determination, the international community's responses to separatist movements have been determined as a rule by whether the separatists succeed or fail to achieve power. The reality of effective control prevails, notwithstanding the maxim *ex injuria jus non oritur*. As long as a secessionist movement has not succeeded, it is usually regarded as a domestic matter except in some cases where the slaughter (when publicized) has evoked humanitarian responses. Suggestions have been made for an international quasi-judicial procedure based on agreed-upon standards for claims of secession, but such a procedure is far from realization.[12]

Other demands for regional and local self-government are less disruptive than separatist movements, but they too may be seen as challenges to the unity of national states. They are often asserted by minorities sharing language and cultural identities, especially when they constitute a majority in a particular region of the country.[13] To the extent they succeed in obtaining extensive self-government and economic rights, they reduce the role of the state's central authority and weaken national unity.

It is also noteworthy that the pressures for local rule and decentralization have proliferated quite apart from ethnic or other distinctive minorities. The demand for more local control is justified as giving people more direct control over matters close to them. Community, or neighborhood, responsibility is supported as participatory democracy. The fact that a trend toward localism has occurred when the world has become more interdependent and integrated has been regarded as paradoxical. However, it may be seen as a natural response to globalization, which leaves people with a sense that remote anonymous forces control their lives. The global market, the transnational firms, the world network of communications, supernational organizations, and the influx of foreigners all contribute to a perception of rapid change beyond the control of ordinary individuals. It is not strange that people then turn to the small community—the village, neighborhood, or ethnic group—where they can control their lives on the local level.

We must also note that this benign view of "localism" is not the whole picture. Our political and social world is too complex for that. Localism—whether based on federalism or ethnicity—may also be used to deprive vulnerable groups of benefits and protection that they receive from the central state. In the United States, for example, minorities and the poor often reasonably regard shifts in power to states and local governments as harmful to them. Similar attitudes probably exist elsewhere. It would take us beyond the scope of this paper to consider why this may be generally true, but there is ample historical evidence that relief from local tyranny and injustice may come from more distant central authority.

Thomas Franck has recently drawn attention to another reaction to globalization—namely a trend to "personal self-determination" through which a "growing part of humanity is seeking community with others based on commonalities that are neither genetic nor territorial."[14] He finds that more states now tend to accept multiple loyalties than previously and have modified their nationality laws to allow dual or multiple citizenship.

The modern type of cosmopolitanism can be seen as another indication of a decline in the authority of the state. Patriotism is diluted by multiple choices and traditional loyalties are blurred. Such developments are consistent with the global market ethos.

IV. FAILED STATES, ILLEGAL REGIMES, AND POPULAR SOVEREIGNTY

The most dramatic examples of the decline in state authority can be found in countries where government and civil order have virtually disappeared. Recent examples are Liberia, Somalia, and Afghanistan. The term "failed states" has come to be used for these cases and others like them. The United Nations has continued to treat them as member states, entitled in principle to "sovereign equality," but it has also recognized the necessity for international action that would go beyond relief and development aid in order to restore effective governmental functions. The most extensive action of this kind, taken in Cambodia, was an elaborate (and costly) rescue effort that involved U.N. oversight of an internal reconciliation process, elections, and the establishment of a constitutional government. Deference was paid in various ways to the principle of Cambodia's sovereignty, but for at least two years the Cambodian government (formed by a Supreme National Council) did not have full freedom to direct the

internal affairs of the country. The high cost of this effort and its uncertain outcome have left doubt that similar rescue efforts will be undertaken for other
failed states.

It is almost certain that internecine warfare will occur in other disintegrating states and result in the Hobbesian anarchy where lives are "nasty, brutish,
and short." Moral and humanitarian sentiment may call for international action,
but the experiences in Somalia, Liberia, Rwanda, and Bosnia have shown how
hard it is for outside forces to rebuild a shattered national order. Foreign governments in a position to give aid are deterred by the anarchy and above all by
the inability of the contending factions and their political leaders to achieve a
viable peace. The international community and the major powers are not prepared to impose order by brute force or to treat people as "wards" incapable of
self-rule. At the same time, they cannot ignore the desperate conditions and
their impact on other countries. The internal conditions that cause disintegration of a state have to be considered by the international agencies, however
daunting the problems appear. Aid is not always ineffective. There have been
fairly successful U.N. rescue actions in recent years—El Salvador, Mozambique,
Namibia. Economic assistance is a critical factor in reconstructing the failed
state. The international lending agencies, U.N. technical assistance, and the specialized agencies of the U.N. can play important roles, along with the non-
governmental organizations and the private business sector. But we must face
the sobering thought that the needs of distant strangers are not high on the lists
of national interests. The world may have become a "global neighborhood" in
some respects, but the distinction between "us" and "them" (whatever the lines)
remains a pervasive syndrome of humankind.

The spread of liberal democracy has also led to questioning a basic postu-
late of the state system. In its strong form, the argument contends that a government is not lawful unless it adheres in practice to democratic principles. Its
supporters point to the widespread expressions of popular sovereignty, as, for example, in article 21 of the Universal Declaration of Human Rights: "The will of
the people shall be the basis of authority of government." They maintain that
the will of the people can only be satisfactorily manifested through periodic and
genuine elections by equal and universal suffrage. The plain facts show that this
proposition has not been accepted in actual practice. Many, probably most,
states do not meet the standard; they are nonetheless recognized as having legitimate governments. To require electoral democracy as a condition of statehood can be regarded as profoundly subversive of the present state system that
embraces all forms of government. An international lawyer would have to conclude quite categorically that governments are not prohibited by international
law from recognizing states or governments that fail to practice democracy as
defined in the Universal Declaration. This proposition does not, however, fore-
close the case for popular sovereignty as a factor in determining the legitimacy

of governments. No bright line has been drawn, but international bodies have from time to time denied recognition to governments in effective control of a territory. They did so, for example, on the ground that the government in question lacked authenticity because of its tainted origin (i.e., foreign intervention) or because of its systematic racism and subordination to another state.[15] In a more controversial case, the U.N. Security Council demanded the ouster of a military regime in Haiti in 1993 and imposed mandatory sanctions to secure its implementation and the restoration of the elected government. Many governments expressed their reservations, however, and the Council resolution referred to the situation as "unique and exceptional." In particular, there was great doubt whether the military regime, however despotic, could be regarded as a threat to international peace.

A more interesting legal question is whether the state as a juridical concept should be linked in law to the will of its inhabitants. All governments today proclaim adherence to the will of their people, and in that sense popular sovereignty can be considered the prevailing myth. Governments that reject multiparty electoral democracy tend to point to its limitations as an expression of popular will. They claim legitimacy in the eyes of their people by virtue of tradition, religion, or simply acquiescence. It is also argued that, even if a government attained power by force, to deny it recognition would, in effect, deprive the people of representation and introduce an element of unreality into international relations. Views on these lines were expressed by many governments during the 1950s when the dispute over Chinese representation in the United Nations took place. A majority then considered that the test of effective control was more responsive to the wishes of the people than selecting a government in exile or denying any representation. In the case of Chinese representation, the U.N. General Assembly softened the effective control standard by declaring that its decisions would take account of the ability and willingness of the claimant government to carry out the principles and purposes of the U.N. Charter.

This position tends to give the benefit of the doubt to governments exercising actual control as against claimants who lack power. It does not require multiparty electoral democracy as a condition of recognition, but it leaves open political avenues to assert the relevance of the people's will as an important criterion when disputes arise over recognition of governments.

V. The Resilience of the State-System

A stateless society has long been a political ideal. In the nineteenth century, thinkers as diverse as William Godwin in England, Pierre Proudhon in France, Karl Marx and Nietzsche in Germany, Prince Kropotkin in Russia, and Thoreau in Concord, Massachusetts, looked forward to the disappearance of the state—an ideal in sharp contrast to the increasingly powerful state of the twentieth century. Today philosophical anarchism has few supporters, but antistatist sentiment is widespread and appears to be on the rise. It comprises two broad tendencies, as indicated in this discussion. One places emphasis on the free market; it calls for a minimal state, no more then necessary to provide the legal structure to maintain the capitalist economy and the core civil liberties. The other tendency stresses the values of participatory democracy in social and economic affairs as well as in the political realm. Its adherents look to nongovernmental associations and to local communities for authentic expressions of the people's will. The two tendencies (they can be labeled "right" and "left") often are on opposing sides in political controversy but in some circumstances they share similar antistatist positions. Both tendencies have had some influence in weakening the autonomy of the state and they are reflected in writings about the "end" of the nation-state. (The coming end of this millennium has also stimulated a fashion in "end-of" books.)

Despite these observed trends, it is most unlikely that the state will disappear in the foreseeable future. The resilience of the state system for the past three centuries signifies more than the strength of governing elites. The critical fact is that states alone have provided the structures of authority needed to cope with the incessant claims of competing societal groups and to provide public justice essential to social order and responsibility. The territorial nexus has a profound significance beyond natural resources. Territory, as Abi-Saab has written, is a primordial matrix, "le sanctuaire par excellence, dans la conscience collective des hommes. . . ."[16] We can foresee that in a new, even more globalized world, markets and "networks" based on functional rationality may partly take the place of state law. We may also foresee that local groups and enclaves will carry more of the burdens of governance, and that some transnational associations dedicated to higher values will be given public responsibility. All of these, as this article shows, have a growing role in the political and legal processes of contemporary society, but each is only partial, serving some interests, some groups. They do not ensure what the territorial state promises—an arena in which all in the defined territory have access to common institutions and the equal protection of law. It is not insignificant, from an international standpoint, that states provide individuals with a recognized legal identity and protection beyond their borders and that they also ensure protection of foreigners in their territories under rules of international responsibility. To be sure, inequalities among states and the dominance of major powers qualify the legal autonomy of many states. It still remains true that even the weaker states are equal in law and entitled to reciprocity in rights and obligations. It would be a mistake to consider that disparities in power render sovereignty insignificant. The recent emergence of a large part of the globe into statehood has conferred a dignity on millions whose identity was hitherto denied or obscured. Nor can we ignore the reality that the weak and vulnerable are, on the whole, more likely to obtain protection and benefits through their territorial state than through free markets or the nongovernmental associations that lack effective authority.

It would be foolish to attempt a definite normative assessment of so complicated and many-sided a phenomenon as that discussed in this paper. My own preferences move toward a middle road. Even if I do not regard the state as the "coldest of monsters," I find good reason to question concentrated state power. The enhanced role of civil society, the greater freedom of movement and communication, and the transnational networks of economic activity are all on the good side. At the same time, I consider the juridical state, with its territorial base, as a necessary structure of authority, capable of affording protection to all its people on the basis of equity and justice. I do not believe that its reduced autonomy portends its demise.

It is safe, in any case, to predict that the several trends discussed in this article will have a continuing impact on international law. Global enterprise and communication networks will continue to produce rules and procedures for transnational activities, many of which, like the *lex mercatoria*, will have only a limited link to national and international law. We can expect a greater mix and overlap of public and private international law with the line between them rather blurred. Movements towards democracy—liberal or populist—manifested through civil society will also influence international responses and add to human rights law and to principles of collective recognition. There will probably be new international "persons" and new conceptions of property and equity entering into international law. States may be declining in power, but the horizons of international law continue to expand.

NOTES

1. In deference to Professor Henkin, who regards sovereignty as a "bad word" which should be expunged, I will use "autonomy" in this paper. See Louis Henkin, *International Law: Politics, Values, Functions*, 216 RECUEIL. DES COURS 13, 24–25 (1990). See generally Oscar Schachter, *Sovereignty—Then and Now*, in ESSAYS IN HONOUR OF WANG TIEYA 671 (R. St. J. Macdonald ed., 1993) (providing an analysis of sovereignty).
2. See, e.g., Jean-Marie Guénhenno, THE END OF THE NATION-STATE (V. Elliot trans., 1995); Matthew Horsman & Andrew Marshall, AFTER THE NATION-STATE (1994); Kenichi Ohmae, THE END OF THE NATION STATE (1995); Walter Wriston, The Twilight of Sovereignty (1992). See generally, 124(2) DAEDALUS (Spring 1995) (special volume, *What Future for the State*); *cf.* Susan Strange, STATES AND MARKETS (2d ed. 1994); Benjamin Barber, JIHAD V. MCWORLD (1995) (deploring the erosion of state authority, especially in the economic sphere). International law is largely ignored in most of these writings.
3. F. W. Nietzsche, THUS SPOKE ZARATHUSTRA 48 (W. Kauffmann trans., 1978).
4. Charles Kindelberger, AMERICAN BUSINESS ABROAD 207 (1969).
5. Vincent Cable, *The Diminished Nation-State: A Study in the Loss of Economic Power*, 124(2) DAEDALUS (Spring 1995) at 27. See also Barber, *supra* note 2, at 241.
6. See generally CIVIL SOCIETY AND THE STATE (John Keane ed., 1988); M.J. Peterson, *Transnational Activity, International Society and World Politics*, 21 MILLENNIUM 371 (1992).
7. The Commission on Global Governance called for "more space in global governance for

people and their organizations—for civil society as distinct from governments." It also proposed a People's Assembly as part of the U.N. See Commission on Global Governance, OUR GLOBAL NEIGHBORHOOD 256-58 (1995).

8. Guénhenno, *supra* note 2, at 58. See generally GLOBAL LAW WITHOUT A STATE 3–108 (Gunther Teubner ed., 1996).

9. *Declaration on Principles of International Law concerning Friendly Relations and Co-operation among States in accordance with the Charter of the United Nations,* U.N. GAOR, G.A. Res. 2625, 25th Sess., Supp. No. 28, at 121, U.N. Doc. A/8082 (1970).

10. See Oscar Schachter, *Micronationalism and Secession,* in RECHT ZWISCHEN UMBRUCH UND BEWAHRUNG, FESTSCHRIFT FÜR RUDOLF BERNHARDT 179, 180–81 (Ulurich Beyerlin et al. eds. 1995); see generally A. Buchanan, SECESSION (1991); Daniel Turp, *Le droit de secession en droit international public,* 20 CAN. Y.B. INT'L L. 24, 24–78 (1982).

11. Sigmund Freud, CIVILIZATION AND ITS DISCONTENTS 72 (James Strachey trans., 1989).

12. See Schachter, *supra* note 10, at 185–86.

13. [See Kingsbury's article in this volume—eds.]; *cf.* Benedict Kingsbury, *Whose International Law? Sovereignty and Non-State Groups,* 88 PROC. AM. SOC'Y INT'L L. 1, 1–13 (1995).

14. [See Franck's piece in this volume—eds.]

15. See, e g , Security Council Res. 277, U.N. SCOR, U.N. Doc. S/RES/277 (1970) (denying representation to the Ian Smith regime in Rhodesia); G.A. Res. 3411 D, U.N. GAOR, U.N. Doc. A/10342 (1975) (denying recognition of the Bantustans set up by South Africa); Security Council Res. 541, U.N. SCOR, U.N. Doc. S/RES/541 (1983) (denying recognition to the "Turkish Republic of Northern Cypress"). See generally John Dugard, RECOGNITION AND THE UNITED NATIONS (1987).

16. Georges Abi-Saab, *Cours Général de Droit Internationale Public,* 207 REC. DES COURS 15, 69 (1987–VII).

Claims by Non-State Groups in International Law

Benedict Kingsbury

THE CAPACITY OF international society to deal with the challenges posed by the claims of non-state groups[1] is a matter of pressing concern. The adequacy of existing international structures is highly questionable. Fundamental conflicts exist between values of justice and the hitherto dominant values of order. While many of the issues are not primarily legal, public international law is necessarily involved. This article examines the norms developed in the international legal system to address issues arising in relations between states and non-state groups. This article argues that in international political debates, and in much (but by no means all) of the principal legal material, three distinct general domains of discourse have been employed to express and address claims by non-state groups.[2] The separate structure of each of these domains has obscured the overlap (if not the identity) of underlying justificatory purposes among these different domains.

Certain fundamental problems in the application of international legal norms to relations between states and non-state groups might be avoided by focusing attention on the commonality of justificatory purpose. In particular, such a unified analysis would help in resolving some of the problems of commensurability or reconciliation where the different domains appear to conflict, and ought to open the way to better balancing of competing rights and interests. More generally, this article argues that the international community has not done enough to develop either the normative framework, or the systems of monitoring and enforcement necessary to make the norms effective. The result is that in relations between states and non-state groups there is often no consensus among parties or non-parties concerning the nature or application of relevant norms. The response of the international community to particular conflicts or crises has often been ad hoc rather than a straightforward and predictable application of clear rules. Such a response diminishes the authority and effectiveness of international community action when it is finally attempted.

Many areas of international law, including state succession, state responsibility, the law of treaties, the law relating to title to territory, recognition, and the law of international organizations, are relevant to the legal analysis of claims by non-state groups. However, claims by non-state groups are characteristically expressed at the international level in five principal domains of discourse. Three of these are general: claims to self-determination; minority rights claims; and human rights claims, including those relying on principles of equality or non-discrimination. The other two, while important, by their nature have value only in a more limited and specialized range of circumstances. These are claims to sovereignty legitimized by historical arguments or other special circumstances, and claims to special rights by virtue of prior occupation.

Each of these five domains of discourse has its own bounded structure of legitimacy and justification, and thus shapes claims and responses made within it. It is common for claims by the same group, or arising out of the same situation, to be articulated simultaneously within different domains. The domain of discourse in which the claim is articulated and assessed will affect its political and legal nature, perceptions of its justification and merits, and the form of its legal expression and resolution, for both claimants and respondents.[3] There are both overlaps and conflicts between the different domains. The conflicts come sharply into focus where particular competing programs are in contention, as where conflicts appear between programs of group autonomy and gender equality. Often the rights and interests of one group are articulated and protected under one program, but this program does not itself take adequate account of the rights and interests of other groups or of affected individuals.[4] An important part of the international normative agenda is to address such conflicts between programs, to avoid the structure of irreconcilable clashes between competing universal norms.

Why is the development of a general international normative framework an objective worth pursuing? Law in this area has many functions, including that of mandating or guiding behavior of parties and non-parties, structuring coordinated responses, providing procedures for dispute or conflict resolution, and establishing the basis for an authoritative, perhaps even dispositive, decision.

Particularly important for present purposes is the compliance-pull exerted by legal norms. One useful account of compliance-pull in international law is Franck's discussion of legitimacy. In his terminology: "Legitimacy is a property of a rule or rule-making institution which itself exerts a pull toward compliance on those addressed normatively because those addressed believe that the rule or institution has come into being and operates in accordance with generally accepted principles of right process."[5] Expressed this way, legitimacy is a function of the norm-creating process and of fairness and efficacy in implementation. This interpretation of legitimacy resembles Fuller's inner morality of law in the emphasis on propriety of sources and of operation.[6] Certainly this form of procedural justice is important to international compliance-pull. Indeed, one of the concerns about international responses to the emergence of new states in the territory of Yugoslavia and the Soviet Union was that norms of minority protection, in particular, were being invented in the heat of the moment, applied on a case-by-case basis to new states by existing states which were not domestically committed to their internal application, and propounded without adequate systems of international monitoring and enforcement.

Franck, however, takes the further step of avoiding making legitimacy contingent on substantive justice, arguing that the secular international community must be distinguished from the moral community, and that in view of divergent perceptions of justice it is imperative for the global secular rule community to focus instead on legitimacy. He adheres to this view notwithstanding that "a legitimate rule may pull less powerfully toward compliance when it is seen to be unjust."[7] In relation to non-state claims which, to the state directly involved, have an acutely internal character, the compliance-pull arising from international legitimacy may well be insufficient to influence the behavior of the state unless there is also some perception that vindication of the claim does not involve profound injustice for the state and its major constituencies. The same is true, *mutatis mutandis*, to the extent that the behavior of non-state groups is directly affected by the compliance-pull of international norms: the more so because the direct involvement of these groups in the rule-making and supervision process has typically been very limited.

Does "legitimacy" have a definite meaning, and do the components of legitimacy have a significant impact on the effectiveness of international law? Koskenniemi argues that as used by Franck, "'[l]egitimacy', is an intermediate concept whose very imprecision makes it available to avoid the attacks routinely mounted against the formal (but too abstract) idea of legal validity and the substantive (but too controversial) notion of justness."[8] The "imprecision" referred to by Koskenniemi is a function of intermediacy between these poles: the concept of legitimacy is not itself incapable of concrete application. Doubtless the principal use of the concept of legitimacy as here articulated is by neo-liberal advocates of international cooperation in positing explanations of international behavior which go beyond those of classic realism. Nevertheless, the concept has a wider attraction, and does not involve discarding the insights of realism. Some variant of legitimacy is part of the explanation for rule-governed behavior, but the configurations of power and interest also remain central to any understanding of relations between states and non-state groups.

The configurations of power and interest have limited the effectiveness, and hence the scope of claims by non-state groups since 1945. New states emerging in Europe have accepted commitments to protect minority rights through their domestic legal orders, and to tolerate international supervision through such mechanisms as those established by the Conference on Security and Cooperation in Europe (CSCE). This is undoubtedly both a response to international pressure and a reflection of the overwhelming interest of the new states in providing any undertakings necessary to secure recognition of their statehood. However, acknowledgment that the acceptance and honoring by states of such commitments is influenced by perceptions of their interests does not itself call into question the significance of legitimacy as an independent variable. External forces encouraging and even coercing compliance with legitimate norms and institutions are themselves, in part, a product of the collective interest in maintaining legitimacy. In addition to the pressures from these external forces, the other factors of compliance-pull identified by Franck have played, and continue to play, a significant role.

The remainder of this article will be structured as follows. Section I will examine the five domains of discourse within which claims by non-state groups are typically expressed in international law. Section II will discuss the presently unsolved problem of how the principle of self-determination can be reconciled with the concern of states to maintain their territorial integrity and with the concern of the international community not to risk unlimited fragmentation of existing states. Section III will use a recent case study relating to the three general domains of discourse to illustrate the difficulties of developing ad hoc responses to acute issues raised by non-state claims where no adequate normative or procedural framework has been established in advance. This case study is of the views of the Arbitration Commission, established by the Conference on Yugoslavia, on questions as to whether and on what terms the European Community should recognize the new states which had formerly been republics of Yugoslavia. Faced with the imperative to accede to demands for recognition of self-determination by some units, the EC was not able to establish effective minority rights and human rights guarantees that might (conceivably) have limited the pressure for revisionist forms of self-determination. It will be argued that the compliance-pull or legitimacy of the norms and procedures prescribed ad hoc was thus, almost inevitably, very limited. Section IV will examine some of the implications for the normative development of international law of recent experience relating to claims by non-state groups, and will discuss problems arising from the separation of, and limitations of, the existing domains of discourse.

I. FIVE DOMAINS OF DISCOURSE FOR CLAIMS BY NON-STATE GROUPS

Each of the five international domains of discourse in which claims by non-state groups are expressed is of considerable contemporary importance. Three are very general in their range of potential application. The other two domains of discourse themselves incorporate conditions of eligibility which, however open-ended, limit the range of situations in which they may effectively be invoked, and they will be mentioned only briefly.

A. Self-Determination Claims

The charismatic principle of self-determination, and the nationalism to which it gives operational expression, has had a powerful normative appeal for more than a century. The political principle of nationalities had a significant pedigree before giving way to the more sweeping doctrines of self-determination espoused by Lenin and Wilson. In the United Nations period the principal normative formulations have been the principle of "equal rights and self-determination of peoples,"[9] contained in the UN Charter and elaborated in various subsequent non-treaty instruments, and the right of all peoples to self-determination, which is expressed in common Article 1 of the 1966 Covenants: "All peoples have the right of self-determination. By virtue of that right they freely determine their political status and freely pursue their economic, social and cultural development."[10]

Self-determination and its social-political analog, nationalism, are often associated, particularly in United States thinking, with liberalism. This tradition links self-determination with democratic choice, and especially with "free elections." Historically, however, nationalism has been variously associated with liberty and with the suppression of freedom, with democratization and with inequality for non-members of the nation. As Acton (who thought the theory of nationality retrogressive) wrote in 1862, nationalism "was appealed to in the name of the most contradictory principles of government, and served all parties in succession, because it was one in which all could unite."[11] Self-determination is not simply an end result or a legal process of choice: as Minogue points out, nationalism is "a spirit or style of politics."[12]

The rhetoric of self-determination is universal, and the range of possible claimants (peoples) supported by the rhetoric is very wide. The reality of international practice has been that self-determination has been available only to a limited range of units, each of which is, in principle, eligible for separate statehood if that is the choice of the unit. Having been interpreted as a right to form separate states, the international community has endeavored to limit the right to self-determination to a very narrow range of right holders.

Not surprisingly, the practical response of existing states to claims to separate statehood by new entities has been favorable only in a limited range of cases, which may be broken down into five principal categories:

(i) Mandated territories, trust territories, and territories treated as non self-governing under Chapter XI of the UN Charter;

(ii) Distinct political-geographical entities subject to carence de souveraineté (the only entity to have achieved statehood in accordance with this criterion thus far is Bangladesh, and even this case is not easy to interpret);

(iii) Other territories in respect of which self-determination is applied by the parties, as where a plebiscite it held to determine the fate of a territory;

(iv) Highest level constituent units of a federal state which has been (or is in the process of being) dissolved by agreement among all (or, in the case of Yugoslavia, most) of the constituent units; and possibly

(v) Formerly independent entities reasserting their independence with at least the tacit consent of the established state where incorporation into the other state was illegal or of dubious legality.

Thus most secessionist entities, such as the Turkish Republic of Northern Cyprus, have received minimal international recognition.[13] Irredentist claims on the basis of nationality, such as that espoused by Somalia before the civil war which began in 1991, have also received very little support. The general argument against accepting these claims has been that of territorial integrity and stability of frontiers. Where transitions have occurred, as in the case of decolonization, these principles are reinforced by the doctrine of *uti possidetis juris*.[14] The doctrine of *uti possidetis juris* has been invoked to limit the fragmentation of dissolved or disintegrated federations in the cases of the USSR and Yugoslavia, in what will represent, if generally accepted, a significant extension of the doctrine. Whereas in decolonization the boundaries set by one or more colonial powers are inherited by the new states without regard to ethnic or other considerations, here the internal boundaries of federal states were treated as establishing the international boundaries unless modified by agreement. In the case of Yugoslavia, this was treated by the EC as entailing that units within Republics, such as Kosovo, were not entitled to separate statehood. The Federal Constitution, under which Republics were the federating units and were alone entitled to secede, was cited as establishing the legal framework in respect of which the principle of *uti possidetis juris* would apply. While this is readily intelligible as an attempt to prevent virtually unlimited fragmentation, the logic of accepting statehood for Republics while denying any right to statehood to sub-Republic entities which enjoyed a considerable degree of autonomy within the federal state, and the exact status of which depended on particular political configurations and internal legal practices, is not itself compelling. Some of the difficulties with this approach are presently being confronted in the former Soviet Union. Within the 15 Union Republics of the USSR there were 20 Autonomous Republics, 8 Autonomous Regions *(oblast)*, *10* Autonomous Areas *(okrug)*, and many lower-level units, as well as numerous groups now seeking autonomy rights.

B. Minority Rights Claims

There is a sharp contrast between the sweeping entitlements associated in standard international practice with the right to self-determination and the very limited provisions applicable expressly to minorities since 1945. Minority protection provisions have long been included in bilateral treaties or in multilateral treaties involving particular territories or areas, and there were several 19th century examples of diplomatic representations or military intervention in response to oppression of minorities. A more general (although far from universal) institutional system of minority protection, involving the League of Nations and the Permanent Court of International Justice, was a particular feature of the public order of Europe, 1919-39. This model fell into disfavor during and after the Second World War. The focus shifted away from minority rights to universalization of individual human rights, although several local minority protection arrangements were adopted on a case-by-case basis, and the UN was required to face a number of contentious minority questions. Minority concerns are partially addressed through equality and non-discrimination provisions, and other human rights norms. However, the cautiously-worded Article 27 of the International Covenant on Civil and Political Rights (I.C.C.P.R.) remains for the time being the only express and legally binding minority rights provision of general application. Article 27 provides:

> In those States in which ethnic, religious or linguistic minorities exist, persons belonging to such minorities shall not be denied the right, in community with the other members of their group, to enjoy their own culture, to profess and practice their own religion, or to use their own language.

This provision is narrow in scope, and does not adequately address the range of minorities issues with which the international community is again being confronted.[15]

The subject of minorities is extremely sensitive for many states. Such concerns have been reflected to some extent in the Human Rights Committee, which has been divided over numerous issues concerning the application of Article 27, and has been unable even to adopt a General Comment on the article.

Article 27 is a limited provision. Several of the leading cases on it have in fact been brought by individual members of minority communities seeking what was in effect protection from policies of the minority community itself. As to the scope for protection of the interests of minority communities under Article 27, questions remain regarding the extent to which it places states under a duty to take positive measures, whether the right to enjoy "culture" extends to land and resource rights, and whether it effectively establishes rights for human groups as such. The case of *Ominayak v. Canada* was one of the most expansive decisions of the Human Rights Committee on the two latter questions. The case involved a claim brought by a group of Canadian indigenous people who had never received an adequate area of land and had suffered disastrous problems as a probable result. The Committee found that:

> Historical inequities, to which the State party refers, and certain more recent developments threaten the way of life and culture of the Lubicon Lake Band, and constitute a violation of Article 27 so long as they continue. The State party proposes to rectify the situation by a remedy that the Committee deems appropriate within the meaning of Article 2 of the Covenant.[16]

This implies that the right of members of a group to enjoy their culture may be violated where they are not allocated the land and control of resource development necessary to pursue economic activities of central importance to their culture, such as hunting or trapping. The right to enjoyment of culture also seems to extend to maintenance of the group's cohesiveness through, for instance, possession of a land base and pursuit of important cultural activities of an economic nature. While longstanding or "traditional" economic activities are more likely to fall within the ambit of "culture," this is a matter of appreciation; no such limitation is inherent in Article 27.

The dispositif in *Ominayak* is very brief and is not easy to interpret. Nevertheless, the finding that historical inequities which continued were a major component of the violation is potentially very significant. In *Ominayak,* historical inequities resulted especially from the failure of Canada (including, for responsibility purposes, the Province of Alberta) to honor the terms of a treaty with indigenous people . . . and possibly also the terms of certain legislation, by ensuring reasonable land rights for the Lubicon Lake Band. In particular, they were never allocated a suitable reservation despite a morally (and perhaps legally) compelling claim to one. The recent developments included rapid energy and other developments in the Band's traditional area from the early 1970s onward, with serious repercussions for the Band's hunting and trapping activities as well as for the life of the community. Thus Canada was responsible under the Covenant for the failure to rectify a continuing inequity, notwithstanding that the initial injustices predated the entry into force of the Covenant by many years.

It is also of interest that the Human Rights Committee's views in *Ominayak* address the position of the Band rather than the rights of Chief Ommayak, although he was the only individual author. This is an illustration of how Article 27 is likely to be regarded increasingly as a vehicle for direct recognition of collective rights.

It is clear that if some very serious conflicts are to be adequately addressed, more comprehensive and more detailed provisions for minority protection are needed, and that such provisions will only function effectively with adequate and dependable international supervision, monitoring, and national and international enforcement mechanisms. Two approaches to normative development are presently being pursued: particularized country-specific obligations, and general normative instruments.

1. Particularized Obligations. The first possible approach is to endeavor to secure the acceptance by specific states of particularized obligations with respect to minorities. Particularized obligations are naturally favored by representatives of non-target states, who are reluctant to assume potentially intrusive international obligations in this sensitive area. Policymakers from countries where potential ethnic fissures have not developed likewise do not wish to encourage latent tendencies to ethnic division within their own countries through promulgation of sweeping minority rights norms of general application, although there is debate about the risks and benefits of general normative commitments in such situations. A particularized approach was proposed by the EC in the November 1991 Draft Convention on Yugoslavia, but even if the obstacles are overcome and such an instrument is eventually adopted by the states of former Yugoslavia, it is unlikely that many other states will be induced to undertake such customized obligations in the absence of general agreement. There are also serious problems of supervision and of enforcement with respect to such instruments.

The experience of the League of Nations is an important reminder of the difficulties facing such a particularized approach. In total, some 25 treaties dealing with minorities in Europe were concluded and entered into force between 1919 and 1934.[17] The minorities treaties established that minority issues were, in certain circumstances, appropriate matters for international concern. Individuals and groups were provided with a forum of moderate effectiveness to which to address complaints, but they did not have direct rights to a hearing or a remedy.[18] Some cases were settled effectively, but non-state petitioners had no formal standing or right to representation, little access to information on the progress of their petition, no power to expedite it or to appeal against an adverse finding, and no certainty of their individual grievances being rectified. This was especially so if they lacked the backing of an influential state. The obligations concerning minorities were imposed on new states, defeated states, or states struggling to attain full international sovereignty. They did not apply to established victor states, and did relatively little in practice to protect any minorities outside Europe. They did not apply to any of the Great Powers except Germany, and then only in respect of Upper Silesia. The States bound by minorities obligations not unnaturally tended to resent the discrimination inherent in this selective minority protection, and compliance and supervision problems became increasingly acute throughout the latter part of the 1930s. Proposals for a general international treaty on minorities were made frequently, but once the particularized obligations were established it was not surprising that other states showed little interest in a universal instrument under which they would also assume obligations. This difficulty also confronts contemporary particularist efforts.

2. Development of General Norms on Rights of Minorities. Urgent efforts are now being directed to implementing the second approach: developing additional and more detailed normative standards, together with more effective and systematic procedures for implementation and enforcement. A Working Group of the United Nations Commission on Human Rights has, after many years of slow progress, been able to elaborate a draft Declaration on the Rights of Persons Belonging to National or Ethnic, Religious and Linguistic Minorities for consideration by the UN General Assembly. The Council of Europe is considering a European Charter for Regional or Minority Languages, and the European Commission for Democracy Through Law (the Venice Commission) in 1991 proposed that the Council of Europe adopt a European Convention for the Protection of Minorities, implementation of which would be supervised by a European Committee for the Protection of Minorities. The CSCE [now OSCE] included a cautious provision on minorities in the Helsinki Final Act of 1975, to the effect that:

> The Participating States on whose territory national minorities exist will respect the right of persons belonging to such minorities to equality before the law, will afford them the full opportunity for the actual enjoyment of human rights and fundamental freedoms and will, in this manner, protect their legitimate interests in this sphere.

The Document of the Copenhagen Meeting on the Human Dimension (1990) contains much more elaborate provisions, which have been reiterated and elaborated in subsequent CSCE documents. The CSCE has also begun to contribute significantly to monitoring and supervision. The Vienna Mechanism for monitoring of state compliance with CSCE commitments, and other Mechanisms in place or being developed, may help promote compliance in certain limited classes of situations where other states take a particular interest in the target state's treatment of minorities. The provision in the 1992 CSCE Helsinki Document for appointment of a High Commissioner on National Minorities with power to monitor national minority issues and to provide early warning to the Committee of Senior Officials is a step toward more general independent monitoring and supervision, although the effectiveness of this step will depend on the stature and resources of the High Commissioner as well as further supervision and sanctions initiatives. The High Commissioner's mandate relates to groups: the High Commissioner is expressly barred from considering "violations of CSCE commitments with regard to an individual person belonging to a national minority."[19]

C. Human Rights Claims

The principles of human rights are a major source of legitimation for claims by non-state groups. Such human rights claims have the greatest purchase when articulated as claims by aggregates of individuals who are seeking vindication only of the same rights as those enjoyed or espoused by other members of the ambient society. More difficult problems arise with this domain of discourse where the claim of the group is couched as something more than simply an aggregate of individual rights claims, or where the rights sought are not demonstrably identical with those enjoyed by the ambient population. In these and other situations the discourse of human rights and equality may lose its purchase for non-state groups, and they may find that their claims are opposed by others on human rights grounds. Equality rights, like other human rights, inure for the benefit of everyone, and may thus provide grounds for upholding or for rejecting a particular group claim.

The paucity of provisions for express minority rights has meant that many of the claims of non-dominant groups have been assessed only in the standard universalist discourse of human rights. Turpel,[20] rightly draws attention to the very cautious approach of the Human Rights Committee in its interpretation of the right to participate in public affairs (Article 25 of the I.C.C.P.R.) in the case brought by Mikmaq leaders with respect to the refusal of the Canadian Government to accept direct Mikmaq Grand Council participation in the First Ministers Conferences on matters concerning aboriginal peoples. The general right to political participation in constitutional deliberations was treated as being satisfied by the national system of representative government. The Human Rights Committee did not regard Article 25 as necessitating specific representation of particular groups, no matter that the agenda item may be of particular importance to them, and no matter that they may not be satisfied with their "representation" in the representative system. The concern of the Human Rights Committee to maintain a universalist interpretation of the Covenant, and thus not to set standards for political participation in one polity which it might feel unable to apply in another, is evident in the case law. The Committee's reticence is compounded by its unwillingness to adopt the concept of a margin of appreciation, so that its findings of no violation appear not simply as refusals to substitute its judgment for that of the state, but as legitimations of state policy. While the Committee has good reasons not to take an overly expansive view of its own role too quickly, and to emphasize universality, it has not done enough to elaborate the meaning of participation and representation in plural societies.

While the scope of existing norms is sometimes underestimated, there is a need for further normative development to deal with difficult problems in relating claims by non-state groups to human rights and equality norms. Non-state groups typically emphasize the need for greater sensitivity in accommodating their concerns within a human rights framework. It is also important that effective means be devised to hold non-state groups accountable, in appropriate circumstances, for their own violations of human rights. More generally, norms and procedures to resolve conflicts between group claims and rights of individual members of the group require further refinement, particularly where state power or other third party interests are involved.

D. Claims by Indigenous Peoples

Claims based on prior occupation or "indigeneity," which are discussed extensively in the articles by Lâm[21] and Turpel . . . , have the politically important characteristic of distinguishing and narrowing the range of potential claimants. Claims based on the special status of indigenous peoples are made by non-state groups in most parts of the world, and are aired internationally in the UN's Working Group on Indigenous Populations and many other fora. The term "indigenous people" is not yet well defined,[22] and the label "indigenous" has without doubt been arrogated on occasion to legitimize chauvinist assertions contrary to the human rights of others.[23] Nevertheless, the category of "indigenous peoples" is a circumscribed one; it may well come to influence discourse in the other three categories, but this process is only just beginning. At present indigenous peoples also utilize other domains of discourse in pursuing their claims. Cree in Quebec, for example, have argued that if the province proceeded to exercise the right to self-determination, the Cree would have a separate international legal right to self-determination; that historically Cree sovereignty was not surrendered to Quebec and could properly be (re)asserted; and that, international norms specifically applicable to indigenous peoples would also apply.

E. Historical Sovereignty Claims

Historically-based claims to sovereignty typically involve an assertion of territorial exclusivity. Although historical assertions are an important element in many claims to sovereignty (including some by "indigenous peoples"), claims of major international political significance directed toward a change of international sovereignty, in which historical revendication was the chief domain of discourse, had until recently largely been limited to: claims to retrocession of small colonial territories, such as Hong Kong, the Falklands/Malvinas, or Gibraltar; irredentist claims pursued without much immediate success, such as that of Venezuela in respect of part of Guyana and that of Guatemala in respect of Belize; certain boundary disputes; and possibly a small range of special situations where such historical assertions either accompanied or contradicted claims couched in terms of self-determination or rights of indigenous peoples. More recently, however, such assertions of historical sovereignty have been important in the dissolution or disintegration of federal states, and were crucial in legitimizing the claims to independence of Lithuania, Latvia and Estonia at a time when it seemed highly possible that decisionmakers in the Soviet Union would consider trying to use military force to prevent these claims from succeeding.

F. Impact of Legal Structure on Formulation of Claims

The structure of the law has had a strong shaping effect on international discourse; thus an inordinate amount of attention has been focused on the refusal of some states to describe indigenous groups internationally as indigenous peoples (even though these states use the term peoples freely in domestic political discourse). The equally fervent strategy on the part of some indigenous peoples is to secure recognition internationally as "peoples" so that they will win much of the battle with respect to all other claims. Legal structure—the preoccupation with "peoples" or "minorities"—interacts with social science and media classification to artificially reduce a great many claims to single categories. In particular, there is a clear preoccupation with "ethnic" claims and "ethnic" conflicts (taking ethnicity to include religious and linguistic elements). These classifications are often simplistic, and miss important parts of identities, and of the structure of claims and conflicts, including their territorial, historical, resource, and class aspects. The power of the lexicon shapes the way in which claims are formulated and groups define themselves: thus, for instance, the scramble to be considered one of the "backward classes" in India, or the rapid adoption among many non-state groups in Asia of the self-description "indigenous people" as it has become an empowering term internationally, even where the very same group may still have origin myths which recount their migration and subordination of another group still living in the same territory. Where a conflict may be largely about access to resources or about social stratification, the temptation for outsiders, and for participants, is often to define it as ethnic, thus clouding analysis and perhaps eventually altering its structure.

Persuasive arguments are made that in some situations attention ought to focus on the inadequacies of a system that does not secure fair access to positions in the civil administration and the military, rather than on ethnic tensions associated with marginalization. Powerful voices argue that normative acceptance of extensive claims couched in terms of ethnicity or other group identity provides a strong incentive for claims to be formulated this way, leads politics to become irretrievably dominated by ethnic demands and divisions, and impels the society and eventually the polity toward fracture. Many states deny that ethnic differences exist. Others assert that the differences that exist are not (and ought not to be) of any significance for the law, and in some states various peaceful forms of ethnic self-assertion are prohibited as threats to national unity. While some such denials and prohibitions are abusive, chauvinist ethnic claims have undoubtedly contributed to terrible ethnic conflicts, and there are proper concerns about deepening or causing divisions, and about fanning conflict.

Not every claim by a non-state group has equal (nor necessarily any) moral merit. Blanket moral relativism about such claims attracts a strong charge of moral irresponsibility. The International Covenant on Civil and Political Rights (ICCPR) addresses one aspect of this issue in providing that nothing in the Covenant "may be interpreted as implying for any State, group or person any right to engage in any activity or perform any act aimed at the destruction of any of the rights and freedoms recognized herein or at their limitation to a greater extent than is provided for. . . ." The further question of whether it is possible or desirable to prescribe general substantive norms in these areas is highly problematic. The circumspection of international tribunals in this area is to be noted: indeed, the scope for most non-state groups to bring claims remains very limited. On the other hand, it is clear that the claims of non-state groups, and the related problems of structuring relationships between states and non-state groups, are of central and enduring concern in contemporary international society. While they ought not to obscure other important questions from view, the dangers associated with abusive claims and demagoguery must be kept firmly in mind. The strategy of ignoring questions concerning the relations between states and non-state groups is neither viable nor internationally supported. . . .

II. SELF-DETERMINATION

[Kingsbury provides a detailed examination of self-determination, including: how to define those covered under the right of self-determination; its meaning; and the implementation of this right. This discussion is then applied to the case of the former Yugoslavia in section III. See the chapters by Hannum and Ratner in this volume on self-determination and *uti possidetis*—eds.]

III. A RECENT CASE STUDY:
THE EUROPEAN COMMUNITY AND YUGOSLAVIA

The international community has had particular difficulty in responding to post-Cold War claims by new entities, especially those established on the territories of the former Soviet Union and the former Yugoslavia. Here, considerations arising from the traditional law and practice of recognition of new states and governments have combined with political concerns about the nature and stability of new entities, and about controlling the rate and extent of state disintegration. European Community practice with regard to Yugoslavia exhibits an amalgam of often contradictory and unreconciled considerations about existing law, order, and justice. One of the Community's responses to issues arising in Yugoslavia was to establish the Conference on Yugoslavia. In addition to promoting European Political Cooperation, the EC hoped to use the Conference to control and condition the pace and nature of transition in Yugoslavia.

In two Declarations on December 16, 1991, the European Community and its member states set forth general guidelines concerning the recognition of new states in Eastern Europe and the Soviet Union. These declarations also set forth a policy and procedure whereby the Conference on Yugoslavia, with the advice of the Arbitration Commission,[24] would consider requests for recognition from Republics that had formed part of Yugoslavia. The stated general policy was that new states would be recognized only if they were democratic, had accepted the relevant international obligations, and committed themselves to proceed peacefully and by negotiation in good faith. More precisely, new states were required to respect the provisions of the UN Charter, the Helsinki Final Act, and the CSCE Charter of Paris for a New Europe, particularly concerning the rule of law, democracy, and human rights. They were expected to guarantee the rights of ethnic and national groups and of minorities, in conformity with engagements undertaken within the framework of the CSCE.

This formulation itself is revealing. Outside the declarations of the CSCE, which are not legally binding, there were no international treaties that set forth in detail the meaning of—let alone the means of realizing and ensuring—the rule of law, democracy, or rights of ethnic groups, national groups, or minorities. Indeed, these latter categories have not been fully defined. Furthermore, CSCE member states took very different views as to the meaning of relevant CSCE commitments when applied to themselves, such as the French position on the non-existence of minorities within the French Republic. In the case of Yugoslavia, these problems were partially addressed by the stopgap expedient of conditioning recognition on compliance with a draft Convention then under consideration by the Conference on Yugoslavia.[25] The other general requirements propounded by the EC related more closely to traditional interests of other states, although serious questions existed as to how even these requirements could be implemented. These requirements included respect for inviolability of frontiers and for the principle that frontiers can be changed only by peaceful means and on the basis of free agreement; respect for relevant commitments concerning disarmament, nuclear non-proliferation, security, and regional stability; and commitment to settle regional disputes and questions about state succession by agreement or, if necessary, by arbitration.

The opinions issued by the Arbitration Commission on November 29, 1991, and January 11, 1992, are an interesting blend of traditional and innovative international law.[26] They are propositions that would not be generally accepted by international lawyers but clearly appealed to constitutional law judges seeking to address unusual and difficult situations. The Commission declared on November 29, 1991, that the existence of a federal state, combining entities endowed with a degree of autonomy and with political power in relation to the federal institutions, implied that the Federal organs must represent the component units and must be effective; that, four of the six republics having made declarations of independence or sovereignty, the essential organs of the Federation no longer satisfied the requirements of participation and representativity; and that Yugoslavia ought thus to be regarded as a federation in the process of disintegration, rather than as a rump state from which certain units had seceded. Thus the rump state would not automatically succeed to the rights of Yugoslavia; questions of succession would have to be agreed upon by the Republics themselves, in conformity with international law. This view is broadly tenable under established international law, although some questions arise as to whether it is consistent with the treatment of state succession in relation to the former USSR.

The Commission also emphasized principles of order in response to a question, raised by Serbia, as to whether the internal boundaries between Serbia and Croatia, and Serbia and Bosnia-Herzegovina, were to be regarded as frontiers in international law. The Commission stated that the external borders of Yugoslavia must be respected; that the internal boundaries of Yugoslavia could only be modified by free agreement; that in the absence of such agreement the internal boundaries would take on the character of frontiers protected by international law by virtue of the general international legal principle of *uti possidetis juris*; and that any purported modification of external frontiers or internal boundaries effected by force would have no juridical effects. The last of these propositions was supported by reference to the U.N. General Assembly's 1970 Declaration on Friendly Relations, the Helsinki Final Act, and the draft Convention on Yugoslavia. Although the principle as to borders between independent states is well established,[27] it is interesting that none of the texts cited by the Commission is directly binding, and indeed the Commission's position as to modification of internal boundaries, an activity not infrequently attempted by various colonial powers, is not fully consistent with practice.

As to self-determination and minority rights, the Commission found more difficulty in simply basing itself on established international law. Serbia had posed the question whether the ethnic Serbs of Croatia and Bosnia-Herzego-vina had the right to self-determination. The Commission asserted that the principle of *uti possidetis juris* trumped irredentist claims based on the right to self-determination, holding that borders existing at the moment of independence were not subject to alteration to satisfy the requirements of self-determination except where the states involved so agreed. The Commission further held that in the present state of international law, not all the consequences of the right to self-determination are specified. The Commission pointedly refrained from saying that the ethnic Serbs in the two other Republics did not have the right to self-determination. Indeed, the Commission stated that Article I of the 1966 Covenants established that the right to self-determination was a principle protecting human rights, and that by virtue of this right each human being could properly claim to belong to the ethnic, religious or linguistic community of her or his choice.[28] The Commission drew from the principle of self-determination the operational consequence that, if the Republics so agreed, members of the Serbian communities in Bosnia-Herzegovina and Croatia could have the nationality of their choice, with all the rights and obligations following from that. Although the Commission is not explicit, it is presumed that choice of Serbian nationality would not entail loss of the right of residence in whichever state the individual lived. The Commission further found that imperative norms of international law (*i.e., jus cogens*) oblige states to ensure respect for minorities' rights. The Commission applied these obligations to the Republics in respect of all minorities within their territories. The Republics had to recognize the identity of ethnic, linguistic or religious communities. Beyond this, however, the Commission did not state what other rights international law conferred upon minorities, although it referred in general terms to international treaties in force, and to chapter II of the draft Convention on Yugoslavia of November 4, 1991. The Commission, however, in its unpublished Opinions concerning application for recognition by particular Republics, had necessarily to consider in detail the adequacy of particular legal provisions concerning use of minority languages, education, political representation or authority of minority communities, etc.

IV. IMPLICATIONS FOR THE DEVELOPMENT OF INTERNATIONAL LAW

Earlier sections pointed to the urgent need for development of more general international law principles, rules and structures suitable for dealing effectively with claims by non-state groups. The inability—or the failure—of the international community to develop sufficiently comprehensive and effective normative and procedural provisions for addressing claims by non-state groups has resulted in ad hoc attempts to develop these provisions in response to recent crises. These ad hoc provisions have come too late to effectively shape behavior, and they have lacked the legitimacy necessary to avoid or mitigate conflict. The lack of a generalized normative and procedural framework has also reinforced inevitable tendencies of major states to react in different ways to different claims, not for principled universal reasons but for particularist reasons reflecting the special interests of major states and decision makers.[29]

There are many explanations for the inadequate development of the norms of international law with respect to claims by non-state groups, In some respects this underdevelopment was deliberate; thus anxiety about the potentially harmful implications for state interests—and for individual rights—of conferring rights on non-state groups was a constant factor for most of the period from 1945 until about 1990. Normative development has also been impeded by well-known political obstacles, especially East-West and West-South divisions, associated with the structure of the post-1945 legal order. The absence of a focus on non-state groups was also an incidental byproduct of the preoccupation since 1945 with the development of norms and institutions for the protection of individual human rights, and with developing legal structures to facilitate specific and foreseen developments such as decolonization.

The political climate for normative development has become somewhat more propitious, although major differences continue. Perhaps equally important are the gradual changes in the structure of international order, including changes in the nature of state sovereignty. The changes in the nature of sovereignty are complex and uneven, but have been influenced by the proliferation of transnational non-state interactions; the transmission of ideas about such things as governance, markets, human rights, information, and environment; and increasing international accountability. The heightened level of self-assertion among national and other groups, and the increased willingness of the international community to consider some accommodation of the claims pressed by such groups, is sharpening the international focus on the nature of the state and of state sovereignty. An important report, issued by the United Nations Secretary-General in June 1992 and entitled "An Agenda For Peace," is evidence of changing views on state sovereignty, even within an inter-state organization. The Report examines the pressing need to enhance preventive diplomacy, peacemaking, peacekeeping, rebuilding peace after civil and international war, and amelioration of economic despair, social injustice, and political oppression, but adds:

> The foundation-stone of this work is and must remain the State. Respect for its fundamental sovereignty and integrity are crucial to any common international progress. The time of absolute and exclusive sovereignty, however, has passed; its theory was never matched by reality. It is the task of leaders of States today to understand this and to find a balance between the needs of good internal governance and the requirements of an ever more interdependent world. Commerce, communications and environmental matters transcend administrative borders; but inside these

borders is where individuals carry out the first order of their economic, political and social lives.

A major obstacle to further normative development is that posed by the real problems in formulating and agreeing upon norms of general application with sufficient specificity, and with the necessary hierarchical ordering and coherence, to be useful at the operational level. The universal substantive normative formulations in the field of self-determination are very broad and have in practice been hedged with exceptions and limitations. Furthermore, they are part of the same legal system as other potentially conflicting general normative propositions of apparently equal value. It has proved difficult to secure the level of agreement and acceptance necessary to adopt sweeping substantive prescriptions dealing specifically with minority rights. Detailed and workable norms of general application have been adopted in the field of human rights,[30] and this area may provide the best starting point for a substantive effort to unify the three general domains of discourse by reference to the underlying justificatory purposes of each. The ICCPR indeed, despite its limitations, provides a modest textual basis for such an enterprise, in that it does not itself formally separate the three general domains of discourse. It recognizes that self-determination is indispensable to the realization of other human rights, and interpreted literally it treats minority rights as essentially the same as human rights. In practice, however, the domains have been divided. Self-determination has been permitted to operate largely in a separate plane, and the efforts of the international community to relate self-determination to protection of minorities and human rights have been patchy and enjoyed only modest practical success. The powerful discourse of individual human rights has not been extended with sufficient sensitivity to particular problems relating to non-state groups. The regime of minority rights has been severely limited, in part because inadequate normative development in the three domains left room for anxiety that it might impair individual rights on the one hand, or shade threateningly into overdrawn self determination claims on the other.

Agreement is more easily secured on procedural rules. With respect to claims by non-state groups, however, procedural rules are not as well developed. Some of the procedural limitations are a result of the historically inter-state character of the international legal system. More effective procedural norms are beginning to appear, due to both the changing nature of the state and the increasing transnationalization of the international legal system. Nevertheless, with the monumental exception of decolonization, international bodies remain cautious when handling major claims by non-state groups. One reason for caution is the tendency of these bodies to maintain a universalist view of their practice, and thus to avoid setting workable precedents in one context which might, from their viewpoint, have disastrous political ramifications in another context.

The most ambitious practice is often particularist, frequently undertaken in ways designed to minimize precedential implications. The response of various countries to the claims and interests of Kurds in Northern Iraq in 1991 is one illustration.

The concentration on process, and the substantive neutrality of what Franck describes as the secular international rule community,[31] has important implications. It suggests that as a practical matter all eligible claims must be regarded as equally worthy. This is a politically impossible and morally uneasy position. A common response of international bodies has been to sidestep the problem by remaining circumspect. The normative response has been to try to restrict eligibility by narrow circumscription of the categories of rightholders. As this article has pointed out, however, definition of rightholders is only one aspect of the analysis of self-determination, minority rights, and equality provisions. The further questions of the meaning of the right, the justification of the right, and the consequences of the right, are at least as important.

Even if it is possible to articulate worthwhile general norms and to devise effective systems of international supervision, what is the proper role of the international community in relation to claims by non-state groups? Liberal internationalism tends to assume a moral obligation on the part of the international community to become involved, at least where basic rights are threatened or justice claims are denied. Foreign states and decision makers have generally been more circumspect, supporting significant involvement only where international security or other external interests are directly jeopardized, or in some extreme humanitarian emergencies, especially where domestic political circumstances are favorable to involvement. In the wake of the question, "who ought to act?" comes the question, "who ought to pay?" Public international law has been concerned with these questions mainly with regard to international organizations. More fundamentally, however, they are moral and political questions. There is a continuing tension between the universalism of liberal ethics, in which proximity and connection are irrelevant to moral worth, and the ordinary human instinct to attach greater importance to family, to community, and to what one is intimate or at least familiar with. Indeed, one of the ethical arguments for nationalism is precisely that it is instrumental in realizing these particularist individual goods.[32]

Would the existence of comprehensive and precise international normative provisions and supervisory machinery have made any difference to events in Yugoslavia, or Somalia, or anywhere else? Certainly the factors which caused states and other actors to be unwilling to engage in norm-creating and institution-building endeavors would also have militated against the effectiveness of any such norms or institutions, and little is to be gained from a counterfactual exercise in which normative and institutional issues are isolated from the political and ideological background. For present purposes it is more useful to address the further skeptical claim that even if developed in the future, international legal provisions and machinery are still unlikely to be effective. This claim fits poorly with the vigorous efforts of states and other international actors to develop such provisions and machinery with uncharacteristic speed. While a skeptic may discern traces of delusion, illusion, or even hypocrisy, the rapid innovations in the CSCE, for example, seem to manifest a strong belief that the normative provisions matter, although the provisions are formally political rather than "legal," and that the institutional mechanisms will work. More generally, reference may be made to studies of the effectiveness of various legal and other regimes.[33] While these studies provide some grounds for optimism about the potential effectiveness of international norms and institutions, few of them address human rights regimes, and fewer still address regimes dealing with claims by non-state groups. Problems of methodology, perspective, and data collection in these areas are formidable. Experience in other issue areas suggests that future regimes for relations between state and non-state groups might be workable, effective, and preferable to the alternatives. The importance of further work in this area has been widely recognized; the UN Sub-Commission on Prevention of Discrimination and Protection of Minorities has appointed a Special Rapporteur on "possible ways and means of facilitating the peaceful and constructive solution of problems involving minorities," and the CSCE has resolved to convene a seminar in 1993 on "Case Studies of National Minorities Issues: Positive Results."

Established international law principles, doctrines, and institutions for supervision and implementation may contribute significantly to the adjustment of relations between states and non-state groups. Even when the best possible interpretation is given to existing legal materials, however, it is clear that further normative and institutional development is urgently needed if adequate frameworks are to be established. It is also clear that part of the normative development involves more sophisticated reconciliation of the existing domains of discourse. The adequacy and effectiveness of such frameworks depends in part on their legitimacy, which itself has an impact on the willingness of those with the necessary power to apply or ignore them. Insofar as legitimacy is the compliance-pull felt by established states or entities emerging in accordance with well-established legal standards, legitimacy is likely to attach to principles of order, including principles for managed transition where necessary. Insofar as legitimacy is influenced by the perceptions of non-state groups with revisionist demands, it will depend both on the actual efficacy of the rules and on the extent to which they are consistent with claims of substantive and procedural justice. Given existing distributions of power, and the instrumental value of stability, considerations of order are likely to remain central to the international normative structure.

NOTES

1. The term "non-state groups" is used here in a non-technical way to denote encompassing groups important to the identity of individual members in which individual membership, while not necessarily resting on ascriptive identity, is not simply a matter of readily-reversed voluntary choice. It thus includes, but is not limited to, ethnic groups. The existence or absence of formal legal personality for the group under municipal or international law is not directly material.

2. The three general domains of discourse are: claims to self-determination, minority rights claims, and human rights claims.

3. For instance, there may well be political and legal differences depending on whether a particular indigenous land rights claim is: a claim to reassert an anterior sovereignty; a claim to special measures justified on grounds of the special historical circumstances of an indigenous people; a means obtaining a degree of self-determination; a general minority rights claim which should also be open to other minorities; simply a substantive equality claim. . . .

4. Some well-known examples of problems of this type are summarized in Douglas Sanders, *Collective Rights*, 13 HUM. RTS. Q. 368, 378–86 (1991). This theme is developed by Ian Brownlie, *The Rights of Peoples in Modern International Law*, in THE RIGHTS OF PEOPLES 1 (James Crawford ed., 1988)

5. Thomas M. Franck, THE POWER OF LEGITIMACY AMONG NATIONS (1990). Franck seeks to advance the voluntarist thesis that nations (coterminous with states in this usage) obey rules "[b]ecause they perceive the rule and its institutional penumbra to have a high degree of legitimacy." Quote in text and note at 25.

6. *Cf.* Lon L. Fuller, THE MORALITY OF LAW 33–94 (rev. ed. 1969). Franck's correlates of rule legitimacy include pedigree (meaning "the depth of the rule's roots in a historical process"), determinacy ("the rule's ability to communicate content"), coherence ("the rule's internal consistency and lateral connectedness to the principles underlying other rules"), and adherence ("the rule's vertical connectedness to a normative hierarchy, culminating in an ultimate rule of recognition, which embodies the principled purposes and values that define the community of states"). Thomas M. Franck, *The Emerging Right to Democratic Governance*, 86 AM. J. INT'L 46, 51 (1992).

7. Franck, *supra* 5, at 242.

8. Martti Koskenniemi, Book Review, 86 AM. J. INT'L L 175 (1992) (reviewing Thomas M. Franck, THE POWER OF LEGITIMACY AMONG NATIONS (1990)).

9. U.N. CHARTER, art. 1, ¶ 2.

10. International Covenant on Economic, Social and Cultural Rights, 993 U.N.T.S. 3, art. 1, ¶ 1 (1966).

11. John Emerich Edward Dalberg-Acton, *Nationality*, in ESSAYS ON FREEDOM AND POWER 166, 181 (Gertrude Himmelfarb ed., 1948).

12. Kenneth R. Minogue, NATIONALISM 135 (1968). He adds his assessment, based mainly on nineteenth century European examples, that as a style of politics nationalism is aimed at radical transformation, and "is hostile to long-established institutions and connections." *Id.* at 135.

13. The question of a "right to secede" raises different issues from the right to self-determination, and is not addressed in this article. For a recent discussion of some of the questions of political philosophy relating to a "right to secede," see Allen Buchanan, SECESSION: THE MORALITY OF POLITICAL DIVORCE FROM FORT SUMTER TO LITHUANIA AND QUEBEC (1991).

14. This doctrine states that parties should retain possession of that which they have acquired. [See Ratner's piece in this volume—eds.]

15. Probably the most influential current definition of "minority" is Capotorti's: "A group numerically inferior to the rest of the population of a State, in a non dominant position, whose members—being nationals of the State—possess ethnic, religious or linguistic characteristics differing from those of the rest of the population and show, if only implicitly, a sense of solidarity, directed toward preserving their culture, traditions, religion

or language." Francisco Capotorti, *Study on the Rights of Persons Belonging to Ethnic, Religious and Linguistic Minorities*, Special Rapporteur of the Sub-Commission on Prevention of Discrimination and Protection of Minorities, at 96, para. 568, U.N. Doc. E/CN.4/Sub.2/384/Rev.1 (1977).

16. Final Views, March 26, 1990, U.N. Doc. CCPR/C/38/D/167/1984 (1990) at 29.

17. These provisions have been treated, in general, as having ceased to have effect on account of the fundamental change of circumstances wrought by the Second World War and the ensuing reordering of the international system. . . . A number were clearly superseded by post-1944 instruments, including peace treaties and, possibly, the Helsinki Final Act. New questions may conceivably arise, however, as old states reemerge.

18. Jacob Robinson et al., WERE THE MINORITIES TREATIES A FAILURE? (1943); Pablo De Azcárate, LEAGUE OF NATIONS AND NATIONAL MINORITIES: AN EXPERIMENT (Eileen E. Brooke trans., 1945)—eds.

19. *The Challenges of Change*, CSCE Helsinki Document 1992, Helsinki Decisions, Chapter II (on file with author).

20. Mary Ellen Turpel, *Indigenous Peoples' Rights of Political Participation and Self-Determination: Recent International Legal Developments and the Continuing Struggle for Recognition*, 25 CORNELL INT'L L.J. 579 (1992).

21. [See Lâm's essay in this volume—eds.]

22. See generally Benedict Kingsbury, *"Indigenous Peoples" as an International Legal Concept*, in INDIGENOUS PEOPLES IN ASIA (R.H. Barnes et al. eds., [1995]).

23. Compare the argument made by Ved P. Nanda, *Ethnic Conflict in Fiji and International Human Rights Law*, 25 CORNELL INT'L L.J. 565 (1992).

24. The Arbitration Commission, established by the EC alongside the Conference on Yugoslavia, comprised presiding judges from constitutional courts of EC member-states under the Presidency of Robert Badinter, President of the French Council Constitutional. The Commission was not in fact empowered to arbitrate claims, but was expected to respond to requests for advice from the Conference. [See Ratner in this volume—eds.]

25. This draft was not transformed into an agreed treaty in the November 1991 negotiations, primarily because the adherence of the Milosevic regime in Belgrade could not be obtained. It continued to be discussed as a possible basis for future arrangements in the new phase of the peace process inaugurated in August 1992 by the enlarged London conference.

26. [For a more detailed examination, see Ratner's essay in this volume—eds.]

27. This was reaffirmed by the Security Council following Iraq's purported annexation of Kuwait. *See, e.g.*, U.N. SCOR Res. 661 (1990).

28. The assertion that Article I establishes an operational right to self-determination for individuals seems to be inconsistent with assumptions made by the UN Human Rights Committee in its case law denying that individuals are ever entitled to bring Optional Protocol claims in respect of Article 1.

29. The fragmentary response of the major actors in the international community to events in Somalia in 1991–92, and the difference in promptitude (and at least initially in scale) between these attempts and the contemporaneous undertakings in Bosnia-Herzegovina and Croatia, illustrates this point. There were, without doubt, serious obstacles to effective action in each case.

30. There continue to be important challenges to the validity of fundamental human rights norms, including challenges to the norms of equality and non-discrimination; the major general challenge, that posed by the international law principle of non-interference in domestic affairs, has gradually been eclipsed.

31. Franck, *supra* note 5.

32. See David Miller, *The Ethical Significance of Nationality*, 98 ETHICS 647 (1988); and Brian Barry, *Self-Government Revisited*, in THE NATURE OF POLITICAL THEORY 121–54 (David Miller and Larry Siedentop, eds., 1983).

33. A few of many examples of such studies are Jack Donnelly, *International Human Rights: A Regime Analysis*, 40 INT'L ORG. 599 (1986); Oran R. Young, INTERNATIONAL

COOPERATION: BUILDING REGIMES FOR NATURAL RESOURCES AND THE ENVIRONMENT (1989); INTERNATIONAL REGIMES IN EAST-WEST POLITICS (Volker Rittberger ed. 1990*); Ethan A. Nadelmann, *Global Prohibition Regimes: The Evolution of Norms in International Society,* 44 INT'L ORG. 479 (1990); Martin List & Volker Rittberger, *Regime Theory and International Environmental Management,* in THE INTERNATIONAL POLITICS OF THE ENVIRONMENT 85–109 (Andrew Huffell & Benedict Kingsbury eds. 1992).

Making Room for Peoples at the United Nations: Thoughts Provoked by Indigenous Claims to Self-Determination

Maivân Clech Lâm

> *The things which God Himself has made will pass away, how much sooner that which Romulus founded.*
>
> –St. Augustine[1]

> *But the international system itself is nothing other than a structure of ideas; and it has been made nowhere else than in the human mind. The international order forms the minds of those who make the international order. The masters of the world of tomorrow are the slaves of yesterday's ideas.*
>
> –Philip Allott[2]

IT HAS BEEN more than twenty years since I last saw Ithaca, New York. That was in the summer of 1970, when I arrived from New Haven to study Indonesian under a joint arrangement of the Cornell and Yale Southeast Asian programs. Relatively few Southeast Asians studied or lived in the United States

Reprinted with permission of the author from Maivân Clech Lâm, "Making Room for Peoples at the United Nations: Thought Provoked by Indigenous Claims to Self-Determination," *Cornell International Law Journal* 25 (1992): 603–22. The themes set out here are elaborated in the author's forthcoming *At the Edge of the State: Indigenous Peoples and Self-Determination* (Ardsley, NY: Transnational Publications, 2000).

then, and the Vietnam War was still raging. These factors, together with the natural gregariousness of our youth, made those of us at Cornell who had come from the Philippines, Indonesia, Malaysia, Thailand, Burma, Vietnam, Laos and Cambodia cling together in an unnamed but unmistakable community defined by rice, fish-sauce, ghost stories, and anti-imperialism. While few of us ever dared walk past the cemetery on Stewart Avenue alone at night, or even at twilight, many of us imagined that one day, U.S. degree in hand and middle-class parents properly placated, we would develop the courage necessary to join the revolutionary movements then energizing our respective countries. So indulgent were we of our socialist fantasies that one evening, only half in jest, we debated which of our countries should volunteer to retain capitalism so that there would remain, in our shared region, at least one place to which struggle-weary revolutionaries could repair for an occasional, good old-fashioned, capitalist fling. The person who volunteered his country for that task that night was the most capitalistically decadent and personally charming member of our group. As it turned out, he was also the only one of us to join a resistance movement upon returning home. I saw him a year ago; he was still delightful, still in the resistance.

I tell this story to mark my place in Cornell's lineage and simultaneously to place Cornell in a lineage that may be unknown to its current students. The story is also told to evoke the feeling of worlds within worlds and to suggest a sense of our century's crossing trajectories of momentary plans and enduring visions, all of which international law must now address. As I see it, international society today consists of, among other actors,[3] *states* that tend to pursue focused political plans, and *ethnic groups* or peoples who tend to entertain comprehensive visions of their identities and destinies.[4] The developments discussed in this [article], in which peoples challenge states, may thus be represented as a confrontation between plan and vision or, were it only so understood, a questioning of plan by vision.

In that confrontation, international law has traditionally privileged states and, by extension, their focused political goals. This privileging of states dates back to the 1648, Peace of Westphalia, which, it is generally agreed, formally established the interstate system in Europe. Today, three centuries later, the Westphalian-derived unidimensionality of international law encounters tremendous pressure, and approaches rupture, as other units in international society, among which ethnic groups may be the most potent, assert their presence and their visions.[5] Consequently, if international law is to continue to regulate international society, it may have to be reconceived, and its institutions restructured, so as to include peoples as well as states as its rightful subjects, entitled to engage in the mutual if differential construction, interpretation, and implementation of its norms.[6] This, in any event, is the conclusion I have come to after observing the decade-old campaign of indigenous peoples to have their right to self-determination recognized at the United Nations.

I shall support my conclusion in a two-step argument. First, I will discuss certain conceptual and institutional features of the present international legal system that I believe unduly, and detrimentally, elevate states and suppress peoples. Second, I will suggest revisions to these features that, in my view, would support a more productive tension between states and peoples, or plans and visions, than international law currently allows. . . .

I. THE INDIGENOUS CAMPAIGN FOR SELF-DETERMINATION

In 1982, in response to significant lobbying efforts mounted by indigenous peoples and their supporters in non-governmental organizations (NGOs), the U.N. Economic and Social Council created a Working Group on Indigenous Populations (Working Group), which it placed under its Sub-Commission on Prevention of Discrimination and Protection of Minorities. . . . Since its inception, the Working Group has met almost every summer in Geneva to receive the views of indigenous peoples, states, and NGOs on the twin subjects of "what is" and "what should be."

Indigenous peoples' conception of "what should be" is far from monolithic and further subdivides into immediate, intermediate, and long-term goals. Where a group's survival is imminently threatened, as in the Amazonian rainforest, indigenous peoples have urgently requested, and on occasion obtained, prompt and extraordinary Working Group intervention. In general, however, the Working Group prefers to direct its energies to the drafting of a Declaration of Indigenous Rights that could advance the intermediate indigenous goal of holding states accountable to international standards of respect and protection for indigenous peoples, lands, resources, and cultures.[7] Finally, the Working Group has moved slowest on the long-term foundational question of self-determination. This, notwithstanding that self-determination is "the most strident and persistently declared demand voiced before the Working Group."[8]

The classic U.N. statement on the right to self-determination reads: "All peoples have the right to self-determination; by virtue of that right they freely determine their political status and freely pursue their economic, social and cultural development."[9] As phrased, the right to self-determination amounts to a right to make decisions. The U.N. has specified that these decisions can legitimately produce a range of acceptable outcomes, from sovereign independence through free association with an independent state to incorporation with it. Furthermore, U.N. documents assert, the status of free association is reversible.

Indigenous [advocates] . . . have repeatedly asserted that their peoples intend to exercise the right to self-determination to effect a free association with surrounding states rather than independence. The association they envision, however, must include both a mutually satisfactory sharing of jurisdiction and the recognition that the indigenous share of that jurisdiction rests upon an inherent right, and not a revocable grant. These two demands, unadorned as they are, fundamentally challenge the principles of state sovereignty and exclusive jurisdiction that modern states have come to rely on. Their governments, consequently, vigorously resist the indigenous claim for self-determination that has launched this challenge. Preferring to ignore the call for free association, and the novel accommodations it requires, these governments instead raise the easy specter of secession, which they claim self-determination inevitably entails.

States and nations, lest we forget, have long endured the ebb and flow of their boundaries. In this respect, the modern doctrine of the territorial integrity of states represents but a vainglorious attempt to interdict history. In this century alone, several cumbersome empires crumbled under the weight of war in Central Europe and the Third World. Their constituent ethnic parts, in the meanwhile, survived. The spectacle of the making and unmaking of states continues today as both political fusion and fission unfold in Western Europe, the former Germanys, the Baltics, and the late USSR. These cataclysmic changes, furthermore, take place against a backdrop of remarkable interstate tolerance and calm which, however, turns into positive skittishness when confronted by indigenous claims to self-determination that, by comparison, generally would not, and probably could not, alter borders.[10]

States are not alone in assuming that the right to self-determination leads to a single predetermined end: secession.[11] The Working Group generally joins them in this assumption, which on its face is not farfetched since Third World peoples after World War II uniformly exercised their right to self-determination to achieve independence rather than association or incorporation with former colonial states. Nevertheless, the present extension of this assumption to a different issue, in a different world, illustrates the lag that has developed between legal theory or culture on the one hand (i.e., the settled expectation that self-determination is used to effect independence) and practice or history on the other (i.e., the actual indigenous preference for a self-determination that leads to equitable association). Or, to put it somewhat post-modernly, the persistence of the assumption demonstrates how the modernistically totalizing approach that "a rose is a rose is a rose" compels us to find a thorn even when the alchemical circumstances of the late, and interdependent, twentieth century have already transformed the defiant rose into an accommodating, if enigmatic, violet.

To prevent misunderstanding, let me assert unambiguously that indigenous peoples are asserting some kind of distance from their surrounding states. The following U.N. working definition of indigenous peoples recognizes as much:

Indigenous communities, peoples and nations are those which, having a historical continuity with pre-invasion and pre-colonial societies that have developed on their territories, consider themselves distinct from other sectors of the societies now prevailing in those territories, or parts of them. They form at present non-dominant sectors of society and are determined to preserve, develop and transmit to future generations their ancestral territories, and their ethnic identity, as the basis of their continued existence as peoples, in accordance with their own cultural patterns, social institutions and legal systems.

. . . [a]n indigenous person is one who belongs to these indigenous populations through self-identification as indigenous . . . and is recognized and accepted by these populations as one of its members. . . .[12]

Some 250 million people, inhabiting all major regions of the globe, currently fit this description, which affirms a distancing of indigenous peoples from their surrounding states on three counts: territory, institutions, and subjective identification.[13]

But the point I raise is this: even here, where territoriality is claimed (let alone in other ethnic/state conflicts, where territoriality is not), need self-determination trigger secession? The small size of many indigenous groups alone renders secession improbable. Secondly, as previously noted, representatives of indigenous peoples, even as they assert distance, regularly represent to the United Nations that they do not seek secession. Instead, what is being proposed here, and I suspect in other state/ethnic conflicts as well, are visions of simultaneously connected and distanced relationships between peoples and their surrounding states. Whether states have the material and ideological flexibility to respond to these visions or not remains to be seen. If they do, then these visions can become a matter for the two parties most concerned (an indigenous people and its surrounding state) to negotiate, preferably under the protection of the U.N., which can best assure that both equity and order will be respected in the process of change. The question that would then arise for international law in this scenario is this: Can peoples' multiple and evolving visions of connection to, and distance from, their surrounding states be juridically and institutionally accommodated? Given the pronounced indeterminacy of international law, I would suggest that the answer depends as much on will as on existing legal resources. But one must start with the resources: old, new, conceptual, and institutional.

II. EXISTING CONCEPTS

While states oppose indigenous claims to self-determination on ultimately economic and political grounds, they justify and perhaps even conceive of this opposition in terms of international legal concepts whose meanings have been not so much declared as historically filled in. The key concepts at issue here are sovereignty, statehood, peoples, and self-determination. A quick and highly interpretive review of the genealogy of these concepts offers some explanation for the present impasse between states and indigenous peoples.

A. The Religious Lineage

My point of departure is the Christian West, from whose cultural and political milieu present international law springs. Christendom's foundational document, the *New Testament,* tells us that an *agent provocateur* once asked Jesus what the Jews should do: serve Rome, or the Jewish theocracy? Like a good lawyer, Jesus replied: "Give to Caesar what is Caesar's, and to God what is God's." The point, confirmed in St. Augustine's *City of God,* is that at its origin the Christian West recognized that two different lineages simultaneously fixed the human position: the secular and the religious. Although the interests of these two lineages intertwined, they remained conceptually distinct. They shared personal and territorial jurisdiction, so to speak, but bifurcated on subject-matter jurisdiction, as this 494 A.D. letter from Pope Gelasius I to Emperor Anastasius I shows: "For if the bishops themselves . . . obey your laws so far as the sphere of public order is concerned lest they seem to obstruct your decrees in mundane matters, with what zeal, I ask you, ought you to obey those who have been charged with administering the sacred ceremonies?"[14]

The religious lineage marked all humans as the children of God, entitled to an irreducible dignity that secular power was bound to respect. Protecting this dignity, the Dominican Friar Antonio de Montesinos railed against the Spaniards for their barbarous treatment of early sixteenth century Hispaniola natives: "Are these not men? Have they not rational souls? Are you not bound to love them as you love yourselves?"[15] Another Spaniard, the jurist Franciscus de Vitoria, systematically elaborated on the rights of Indians. According to Vitoria, the natives of the New World were entitled not only to love but also to their own institutions. This, he reasoned, was not only because of their divine descent, but because of the inherent rationality and equal freedom accorded all men under the natural law that God has ordained. Robert A. Williams finds that Vitoria, generally innovative for his time, was planting, in that argument, the seeds of legal modernity, or secular universalism: "This singular innovation on Vitoria's part initiated the process by which the European state system's legal discourse was ultimately liberated from its stultifying, expressly theocentric, medievalized moorings and was adapted to the rationalizing demands of Renaissance Europe's secularized will to empire."[16] The rationalizing demands of empire in time collapsed the structural tension that had been maintained through medieval times between the secular and the religious. The collapse was signaled by the Thirty Years' War, which bitterly embroiled Pope, emperor, and princes; it was consummated in the 1648, Peace of Westphalia, which ended that struggle. Though the Peace of Westphalia is usually depicted as a landmark in the secularization of Europe, Antonio Cassese underlines the ongoing role

of religion after 1648, no longer as oppositional force, of course, but as forma-
tive ideology.

> All the States above-mentioned had a common religious matrix: they
> were Christian. . . . Another strong unifying factor was the pattern of
> internal economic and political development. All Western States were the
> outgrowth of capitalism and its matching phenomenon in the political
> field: absolutism (followed in subsequent years by parliamentary
> democracy).[17]

While the Peace of Westphalia extricated the Pope and the Holy Roman Emperor from the affairs of states then, it did not extricate Christianity itself, which
the new states could now use as their unmediated cultural tools in their quests
for absolutism. Thus, even though the peoples governed by the European dynasties of the 17th Century remained the theoretical kindred of God, they became once removed from Him and from the downward-flowing source of their
dignity by the new device of the unopposed and sovereign state. Of the two lineages that fixed the human condition in early Christendom then, only one, the
secular, remained in charge of men's earthly lives. The other, the religious, was
evicted from its secular premises, but not before being purloined of its magic.

B. The Secular Lineage

The French Revolution of 1789 secularized this magic and reversed the direction
of legitimacy.[18] Untrammeled either by the grace of God or the pleasure of the
King, the peoples of France now became sovereign in their own right and by
their own original consent empowered a republican government to act on their
behalf. I say peoples because, on the occasion of the creation of the modern
French state, a French people did not yet exist, as only Bretons, Basques, Gas-
cons, Auvergnats, etc., occupied France.[19] To the extent that the ethnic French
now exist, as they clearly do, it is as the later distillate of the common post-
revolutionary experiences of their heterogenous forebears who, by their shared
deeds, bit by bit transformed the culturally flat state of the 18th century into a
symbolically plausible nation of the 20th.

While the French state searched for and successfully fashioned a people, the
story of German unification is generally told as one of a people looking for a
state. A recent study rejecting this truism asserts that it was the Prussian government, and not the German people, that called forth the German State. Indeed, the peoples who inhabited the former lands of the 300 sovereign states that
constituted the Holy Roman Empire of the German Nation apparently strongly
opposed Bismarck's project of unification. The rebuke the Austrian poet Franz
Grillparzer administered to the Bismarck government is thought to reflect their

sentiment: "You claim that you have founded a Reich . . . but all you have done is to destroy a *Volk*."[20]

However different or controversial in genesis, the French and German entities eventually converged on the common goal of uniting a single cultural people with a single sovereign state. Once again, then, there was merger: of the cultural and the political dimensions this time. This German/French invention, denominated the nation-state, came not only to dominate Europe but was also the only European political model of ethnic/state relations exported to Asia, Africa, Oceania, and the Americas during the colonial period. Those whom the model convinced in these overseas territories, i.e., the elite, consequently developed the view that the non-state institutions that traditionally played a political role in their communities—such as the family, the ethnic group, the church, the mosque, and the village—represented but so many incidental, backward, and even illegitimate legacies that needed to be curtailed, if not discarded, on the road to modernity.

C. The Early Twentieth Century

Ironically, the political models that were not exported from Europe might have better suited the ethnically complex circumstances of the colonies. I think, for example, of Switzerland, where many ethnic groups continue to maintain a shared state; or even of the Ottoman, Austro-Hungarian and Czarist Empires, which came closer in function to the system of tributary relationships that crisscrossed Southeast Asia than the nation-state ever could. The second irony is that the nation state concept straight-jacketed even Europe, and may have hastened the outbreak of the First World War, which may have been the first war fought over nation-stateness as such: its presence, as well as its absence.

The League of Nations, certainly, gave itself the ambitious task after the war of rearranging the peoples and boundaries of Europe in such a way as to obtain a maximum fit between ethnicity and statehood. It fragmented the Ottoman and Austro-Hungarian empires into their ethnic parts as much as possible and, where ethnically or politically unfeasible, it created autonomous regimes for peoples enclosed within heterogeneous states. Both actions were justified on the principle of the self-determination of peoples, which Lenin had enunciated, and which Woodrow Wilson attempted to appropriate, if only eventually to redirect and constrict at the urging of Churchill, who rightly understood the concept's power to dismantle the British Empire. The League secured several autonomous regimes for ethnic minorities by first negotiating, and later supervising, minority treaties with target states. Significantly, the peoples protected by these treaties played no formal role in either their construction or implementation.

If Westphalia invented the modern state, and the French Revolution idealized its cultural unity, then the League invented the foil for the ideal: League wardship. Whether League wardship could have delivered order and justice to states and ethnic minorities will never be conclusively known, for the rise of fascism in Europe prematurely thwarted the experiment. A much older wardship system, however, i.e., U.S. federal Indian policy, has been tested, and proven legally untenable, as well as humanly unjustifiable in its impact on Native Americans. The major fault policy, as in the League system, in my opinion, is that ultimate decision-making powers affecting indigenous and minority peoples in the two circumstances rested exclusively with the surrounding state, or the League, and not the peoples themselves.

D. The Late Twentieth Century

The League, under pressure from the European colonial powers, wholly sidestepped the issue of the self-determination of non-European peoples after World War I. By the close of World War II, however, the Churchillian position on this question became wholly untenable. The war had loosened Western Europe's hold over its colonies, Third World nationalism was on the rise, and the victorious Soviet Union squarely supported decolonization. Recolonization became unthinkable to the Third World/Socialist majority voting block that coalesced at the United Nations after the War.

It was in this context that the U.N. included, in Article I of its 1945 Charter, the following reference to the principle of self-determination:

> [the Purposes of the United Nations are:] . . . 2. To develop friendly relations among nations based on respect for the principle of equal rights and self-determination of peoples, and to take other appropriate measures to strengthen universal peace.

Fifteen years later, the 1960 U.N. Declaration on the Granting of Independence to Colonial Countries and Peoples ("Declaration") called the principle a right, and defined it. The definition was reproduced in 1966 in the two U.N. human rights Covenants. Yet, neither the Charter, the Declaration, the Covenants, nor any other international law instrument defines the "peoples" who hold this right. As a result, the meanings of both "self-determination" and "peoples" remain contentious, and fluctuate with U.N. practice.

That practice was powerfully marked by three dominant concerns of the Third World/Socialist alliance of the post-war decades: termination of European rule in Asia, Africa, and Oceania; vigilance against its reappearance in a new form; and preservation of the territorial shells that the Europeans had left behind. The 1960 Declaration and its subsequent elaboration in various General Assembly resolutions record these concerns. For example, the 1960 Declaration begins: "The subjection of peoples to alien subjugation, domination and exploitation constitutes a denial of fundamental human rights, is contrary to the

Charter of the United Nations and is an impediment to the promotion of world peace and cooperation." Resolution 1541, passed the following day, specified that the term "colonial country" in the Declaration meant a non-self-governing territory which (note the alchemy) in turn referred to an entity geographically and ethnically separate from the administering state. The Resolution thus elliptically reproduced what speeches made in the General Assembly stated more directly: that only peoples separated by "blue-water" or "salt-water" from their subjugator, i.e., the distance from the Third World to Europe, could qualify for decolonization, or the reassertion of self-determination.[21] All other peoples subjugated by surrounding states, and this includes most of the world's indigenous and tribal peoples, would have their grievances individually addressed via the fast-developing body of human rights law or, collectively, via the wardship concept of self-government, self-rule, or autonomy, where they were available.

The debate on self-determination for indigenous peoples and other ethnic groups that neither aspire to statehood nor fit the classic "bluewater" model thus flounders on four obstacles: the Westphalian-derived theory that the nation-state is the perfected form of political organization towards which all political energy necessarily aspires; the League of Nations practice of treating peoples as wards of surrounding states or of the international community; the assumption that collective grievances are reducible to individual ones; and, finally, the conceit that, to paraphrase Orwell, some families of subjugation (blue-water) are more equal than others.

III. Existing Institutions
In addition to the conceptual rigidities discussed above, institutional rigidities exist as well. The U.N. today does not provide for ethnic groups not constituted as states to participate on a regular basis in U.N. deliberations, let alone U.N. lawmaking. The reason for this cannot be that there is an absolute theoretical bar against non-state participation since other non-state parties have been given votes and international legal personality in the U.N. system. I think, for example, of the employer and union representatives who voted at the [International Labor Organization] (ILO), and of present or former subjects of international law such is the U.N. and other international agencies, the Vatican, the former internationalized territories of Danzig, Trieste, and Memel, and of the various NGOs that have achieved active U.N. observer status for one purpose or another.

When indigenous representatives first attended sessions of the ILO and the Working Group, they "borrowed" the identity and voice of these non-state, non-ethnic groups. A Native American would thus sit and speak as a delegate of the International Commission of Jurists or other NGO, and a Maori would relay his people's concerns in his role as a New Zealand trade unionist. To its credit, the Working Group soon did away with the need for this formalistic contrivance and now invites all concerned parties to speak in their true representative capacity. But the Working Group remains the exceptional U.N. forum in this regard; moreover, it exists only by grace of the Economic and Social Council, which could terminate its work at any time. Ethnic group participation in the U.N.'s work thus remains uninstitutionalized and problematic.

Invitations to participate in the work of the United Nations depend perhaps less on a party's statist or non-statist position than on the nature of the discourse the party is expected to present. Today, the U.N. formally privileges three kinds of discourse: the politically hegemonic, the politically democratic, and the "apolitically" technical. The first takes place in the Security Council (which could as well be renamed the Hegemony Council), the second in the General Assembly, and the third in the several U.N. specialized agencies, ad hoc committees, and working groups. These discourses share one thing in common: being political, or utilitarian, or both, they focus on the narrow historical moment.

A fourth type of discourse, which I call visionary, and which Cornel West might call prophetic pragmatic, has insinuated itself at the U.N., but remains marginal.[22] It is a discourse that, to date, NGOs generally employ. It tends to juxtapose "what is" with "what should be," the gain of humans against the loss of nature, the power of states against the needs of peoples, historical expediency against cultural memory and vision. While I personally prefer the second member of each of these pairs, I am not privileging either; anthropologists know that it is the dialectic between the members of the pairs, between history and culture, so to speak, that serves as the key to creative human adaptation and survival. Lawyers need also to recognize this and, in the U.N.'s case, explicitly provide for the dialectic. I will now summarize where I think the dialectic has already insinuated itself, and where it can be taken.

IV. INSINUATED CONCEPTS

The concepts of sovereignty, statehood, peoples and self-determination retain ambiguities that may be developed to move us from one historical moment to the next. The right of self-determination formulated immediately after World War II to undo "blue-water" colonization has, in the 70s and 80s, been extended to support peoples' liberation from racist and alien domination by adjacent populations, as in the cases of South Africa and the West Bank. The Western Sahara case, decided by the International Court of Justice (I.C.J.) in 1975, opens up even greater space. In a display of admirable anthropological sensitivity to the specific cultural features of North African nomadic societies, the I.C.J. held that an ethnic people—defined by their sense of collective identity, mode of political self-regulation, and predictable territory of economic activity—could, absent traditional indices of formal government, stable population, and demarcated territory, still claim sovereignty and assert self-determination.

Then too, notwithstanding the official doctrine that the right of secession ended upon the liberation of all "blue-water" colonies, the earlier break-up of Pakistan, and now of the Soviet Union and Yugoslavia, unrolled, or is unrolling, in an atmosphere of great international anxiety but not prohibition. Indeed, if now Quebec, whose ethnic "depth" as Quebecois (as opposed to French) is chronologically shallower than that of any other cultural group presently claiming self-determination, also receives a hushed response from both Canada and the interstate system to its secession threat, what then remains of the prohibition against secession other than the selective and arbitrary exercise of raw power? Indigenous representatives from Canada attending . . . [a] Working Group session in Geneva passionately argued that a self-respecting international law cannot apply as lofty a principle as self determination in a racially discriminatory manner: "yes" for whites in Quebec, "no" for indigenous peoples throughout Canada.

Perhaps this impassioned plea, combined with the ongoing dissolution of states in nearby Eastern Europe and the former Soviet Union, prompted the Working Group at its 1991 session to include for the first time a provision, albeit ambiguous, recognizing a right of self-determination for indigenous peoples in its draft Declaration:

> Indigenous peoples have the right to self-determination in accordance with international law. By virtue of this right, they freely determine their relationship with the States in which they live in a spirit of co-existence with other citizens and freely pursue their economic, social and cultural and spiritual development in conditions of freedom and dignity.

V. INSINUATED PRACTICES

If the issues of self-determination and secession are again open to debate and extension, what of the institutions that could support the debate and extension? Here, too, a number of useful practices are insinuating themselves.

The Working Group on Indigenous Populations is doing on a small scale for indigenous and tribal peoples what the General Assembly once did for the Third World: which is to provide a forum for the world's powerless to voice their vision of identity and destiny in a setting of formal equality with others materially far more powerful than they. In the U.N.'s early years, many Third World representatives appearing in the General Assembly had little in the way of political plans, or even state structure, to present or represent. Western commentators frequently criticized their lack of positivist legal acumen and derided their aspirational speeches. But there was no backtracking: the U.N. had committed itself to the principle of political democracy in the General Assembly. Today, that principle permits a state such as Kiribati, with fewer than 100,000 inhabitants, to cast a vote of equal weight with China, a country of more than one billion. Incongruous as this result may seem, it reproduces in form, if no longer in spirit, the original purpose of the General Assembly, which was to be a one-vision-one-vote chamber, so to speak. I say form and not spirit because those early General Assembly visions as well as the generation that dreamt them have by now departed, exiting international history to enter international culture. The General Assembly's work currently rests with state technicians who appear content to confirm the Security Council's politics, which from the beginning were designed to be the politics of hegemony.

Outside, around, and beyond these two primary U.N. institutions are the untidy, relatively unsupervised, and often under-budgeted appendages of the U.N. where the inspired, the concerned, the wretched, or simply the unseated of the earth now congregate to relate their visions. At these margins, marginal people, whose role it is to tell us where international society's blockages are, and where breakthroughs might be, continue to gather as they once did at the General Assembly. The Working Group is a classic example of such a margin, where the interstate system interfaces with the network of indigenous peoples, and interested NGOs.

The interface occurs across several permeable surfaces. To begin with, Working Group members are official agents of the United Nations, and thus of its Member States. This means that they remain apprised of states' general perspectives on the tasks they have been assigned, including the task of drafting a Declaration of Indigenous Rights. On the other hand, because Working Group members are designated "independent experts" under contract, the U.N. must accord their professional freedom and competence a certain measure of respect. Furthermore, because members work for the entire U.N., and not for particular states, they remain relatively invulnerable to specific political pressure. The Working Group, in other words, is a creation of states, but not its creature.

In addition to states, the Working Group deals with NGOs and organizations of indigenous peoples. NGO representatives, like Working Group members, frequently issue from professional ranks. As such, the two groups share traditions of knowledge, of activities, and of knowing. NGOs supporting indigenous proposals perform a dual function vis-à-vis Working Group members. As independent agents, NGOs both entice the semi-independent Working Group members to tread new territory and professionally validate that treading in the eyes of states when it occurs.

The relationship between U.N. experts and indigenous peoples is a novel one that has evolved through mutual criticism, accommodation, and perhaps also appreciation. Culturally, socially, and professionally, Working Group members generally have far more in common with representatives of states and NGOS than they do with indigenous spokespersons. For example, not a single indigenous lawyer, and certainly there are many that the U.N. could have chosen, sits on the Working Group. Nevertheless, whether by chance, by the goodwill of the remarkable chair of the Working Group, Professor Erica Daes of

Greece, or by the insistence of indigenous representatives, the dialogue between indigenous representatives and members of the Working Group in Geneva has been surprisingly productive.

Discussions in the Working Group lack the formality and tokenism that marked the ILO deliberations on ILO Convention 169 Concerning Indigenous and Tribal Peoples in Independent Countries, where indigenous representatives spoke only at the whim of the chair of the session, and not by design or right. The Working Group, by contrast, actively promotes and eases, financially and otherwise, maximal access to its forum for indigenous peoples. Its sessions permit and encourage a supervised exchange of information between states, indigenous peoples, NGOs, and even individuals who speak simply because they ask to. Indigenous peoples in Geneva speak in their own voice, and states are obliged to respond to them as fellow negotiators, not wards. Year after year, the Working Group redrafts its Declaration in response to positions and counter-positions expressed at these sessions. Overall, the successive drafts have moved from the minimalist position of states, to the visionary one of indigenous peoples.

VI. Conclusions

In conclusion, I offer two concrete proposals, and a general justification, for making room for peoples at the United Nations. My minimalist proposal is that the U.N. make available, on a regular basis, and in the spirit of the Working Group, fora for indigenous peoples and other ethnic groups to question state decisions and arrangements that affect them. The time, place, and structure of such fora should be tailored to the particular needs that call them into existence. Beyond that, they should primarily provide a "level" field in which communities of peoples, under the observation of the U.N., may begin the process of negotiating and renegotiating their relationships with states.

My more ambitious proposal is that the U.N. formally acknowledge the right to self-determination of indigenous peoples so that they may become recognized subjects of international law competent to represent their interests in the international arena. I propose that this right be extended to indigenous peoples regardless of whether a particular people professes to exercise it to remain attached to its present state, to separate from it, or to form a compact of free association with it or another state. Indigenous peoples, more than other ethnic groups, rely on their connection to the territory of their ancestors to reproduce their place-specific cultures. As such they, more than other groups, require the protection of territory that the right to self-determination confers but that mere human rights, for example, would not. At the same time, the U.N. should set out criteria for, and be prepared to supervise, the fair and orderly negotiation of the exercise of these choices. The latter should not be irreversible, but can be constrained by reasonable notice and mutual compensation provisions.

As for justification, I offer the value of multiple inheritance. Anthropologically speaking, we all have but one task as a species: the creation of our survival with the materials inherited. The biological material we have inherited is the literally ambivalent double helix, and the creation is the manner in which its genes recombine and mutate through the generations. Biological determinism in this respect is a misnomer. It is rather culture, that other means of human survival, which has become ominously deterministic in the late twentieth century. The double helixes of the sacred and the secular collapsed at Westphalia, of culture and polity in the French Revolution, of the Security Council and the General Assembly during the Gulf War if not before. The demands of indigenous peoples for voice and self-determination deeply trouble the unidimensionally statist international society we have become precisely because they seek to reinstate ambivalence, recombination, and mutation. Yet that reinstatement could be vital to the reproduction of international society which, like any other, relies on sources of to difference for adaptation and survival.

At the U.N., the reinstatement could assume the form of a double helix consisting of the pragmatic strand of the system of states, and the prophetic strand of the network of peoples, engaged in dynamic genetic conversation, so to speak. These strands are by no means equal in power. Neither are they, nor should they be, coeval in function like two sets of chromosomes. The analogy ends at some point. What remains is that the perplexity as well as the safety in social life, whether domestic or international, lodge together in the space called indeterminacy. Not an "everything goes and nothing matters" indeterminacy, but one where existing hierarchies, generosities, promises, and abuses can be continually questioned, reviewed and restructured in the light of both present exigencies, past dreams, and future visions. States, I think, are generally structured to function best in the realm of expediency, but cultural communities remain the better guardians of the past and of the future. The United Nations— a pleasantly ambiguous term that covers both peoples and states—needs to bring them together in their separate but intertwining identities.

NOTES

1. Quoted in Norman H. Baynes, THE POLITICAL IDEAS OF ST. AUGUSTINE'S "DE CIVITATE DEI" 17 (1968).
2. Philip Allott, EUNOMIA: NEW ORDER FOR A NEW WORLD xv–xvi (1990).
3. To name the most obvious others: international organizations such as the United Nations and the International Monetary Fund, transnational corporations (TNCs) such as Dole and Phillip, and non-governmental organizations (NGOs) such as Amnesty International and the World Wildlife Fund. Philip Allott, in his recent work, similarly casts the net of international society widely: "(1)Society is the collective self-creating of human beings. (2)International society is the society of the whole human race and the society of all societies. (3)Law is the continuing structure system of human socializing. (4)International law is the law of international society." ALLOTT, *supra* note 2, at 3. He goes on to refute specifically the proposition that international society is nothing more than the society of nation-states.

4. The conceptual opposition I have set up here between states' plans and peoples' visions therefore highlights two different kinds of activities in international society, rather than two segregated categories of actors. I use the term "peoples" to mean an ethnic group or cultural community throughout this paper. Indigenous peoples, in turn, are ethnic groups who, the United Nations Working Group on Indigenous Populations suggests, are immemorially associated with a territory in which they wish to maintain a way of life that is different from the dominant culture of the surrounding state. See Julian Burger, REPORT FROM THE FRONTIER: THE STATE OF THE WORLD'S INDIGENOUS PEOPLES 6–7 (2d ed. 1987).

5. A list of today's most serious, ethnically charged challenges to states would include those in Canada, the Amazon region of South America, Eastern Europe, the former USSR, the Middle East, India, Sri Lanka, Myanmar, East Timor, and West Papua. The tension and atrocities that ethnic-related conflicts unleash in these places certainly call into question my positive use of the term "vision" to describe the goals of ethnic groups. . . . I assert here only that the ugly urgencies of history that have been largely generated by the destructive military and economic policies of the world's powerful states in the last five decades may have infected and distorted, but cannot negate, the memory and prescience encoded in the cultures of ethnic groups often far older than such states. To put it succinctly, cultures create Goethes; but it takes a culture *and a state* to create Hitlers.

6. For a range of views on whether peoples, as distinguished from states and individuals, detain international rights and, additionally, are, or should be, subjects of international law, see THE RIGHTS OF PEOPLES (James Crawford ed., 1988). A similar discussion that focuses exclusively on indigenous peoples is found in *Are Indigenous Peoples Entitled to International Juridical Personality?*, AM. SOC'Y INT'L L. PROC. 189 (1985) (panel discussion); and Russel Lawrence Barsh, *Indigenous Peoples: An Emerging Direct of International Law*, 80 AM. J. INT'L L. 369 (1986).

7. The seven parts of the 1991 draft Declaration address these topics: self-determination; culture; lands and resources; institutions; relations with surrounding states; conflict-resolution; and the Declaration as a statement of minimum standards.

8. Robert A. Williams, Jr., *Encounters on the Frontiers of International Human Rights Law: Redefining the Terms of Indigenous Peoples' Survival in the World*, 1990 DUKE L.J. 660, 693.

9. This paragraph first appeared in 1960 in the Declaration on the Granting of Independence to Colonial Countries and Peoples, G.A. Res. 1514, U.N. GAOR, 15th Sess., Supp. No. 16, at 66, U.N. Doc. A/4684 (1961). It reappeared as Articles I of both the International Covenant on Economic, Social, and Cultural Rights, G.A. Res. 2200, U.N. GAOR, 21st Sess., Supp. No. 16, at 49, U.N. Doc. A/6316 (1967); and the International Covenant on Civil and Political Rights, G.A. Res. 2200, U.N. GAOR, 21st Sess., Supp. No. 16, at 52, U.N. Doc. A/6316 (1967).

10. The "could not" follows from the relative material powerlessness of indigenous communities, many of which, in addition, are extremely small. . . .

11. For a brief but very thoughtful review of the issues packed in the concept of secession, see Note, *The Logic of Secession*, 89 YALE L.J. 89, 802 (1980). For specific views on when secession is or is not legitimate, see Ved Nanda, *Self-Determination Under International Law: Validity of Claims to Secede*, 13 CASE W. RES. J. INT'L L. 257 (1981); W. Michael Reisman, *Somali Self-Determination in the Horn*, in NATIONALISM AND SELF-DETERMINATION IN THE HORN OF AFRICA 151 (I. M. Lewis ed., 1983); Eisuke Suzuki, *Self-Determination and World Public Order: Community Response to Territorial Separation*, 16 VA. J. INT'L L. 779 (1976); Lee C. Buchheit, SECESSION: THE LEGITIMACY OF SELF-DETERMINATION (1978); Lea Brilmayer, *Secession and Self-Determination: A Territorial Interpretation*, 16 YALE J. INT'L L. 177 (1991); Allen Buchanan, SECESSION: THE MORALITY OF POLITICAL DIVORCE FROM FORT SUMTER TO LITHUANIA AND QUEBEC (1991).

12. 5 José Martinez Cobo, U.N. SUB-COMMISSION ON PREVENTION OF DISCRIMINATION AND PROTECTION OF MINORITIES, STUDY OF THE

PROBLEM OF DISCRIMINATION AGAINST INDIGENOUS POPULATIONS ¶¶ 379–81, U.N. Doc. E/CN.4/Sub.2/1986/7, U.N. Sales No. E.86.XIV.3 (1987).

13. Julian Burger, THE GAIA ATLAS OF FIRST PEOPLES 12 (1990).
14. Quoted in Robert A. Williams, THE AMERICAN INDIAN IN WESTERN LEGAL THOUGHT 16 (1990).
15. Quoted in *id.* at 86.
16. *Id.* at 96-97.
17. Antonio Cassese, INTERNATIONAL LAW IN A DIVIDED WORLD 38-39 (1986).
18. Ernest Gellner suggests that the magic, while secularized, remained relatively unavailable to states organized as constitutional monarchies. West European monarchs "by symbolizing the continuity of the state or the nation . . . prevent elective leaders, who are responsible for decision and policies, from acquiring too much magic. It is a way of helping ensure that real power is not sacred." Ernest Gellner, CULTURE, IDENTITY, AND POLITICS 163 (1987).
19. A work rich in data and theory on this subject is Eugen Weber, PEASANTS INTO FRENCHMEN: THE MODERNIZATION OF RURAL FRANCE 1870-1914 (1976). . . .
20. Quoted in James J. Sheehan, GERMAN HISTORY 1770–1866, 853–69 (1991) at 911.
21. For the debate See Van Langehove, THE QUESTION OF ABORIGINES BEFORE THE UNITED NATIONS: THE BELGIAN THESIS 83–84 (1954), cited in Patrick Thornberry, *Self-Determination, Minorities, Human Rights: A Review of International Instruments*, 38 INT'L & COMP. L.Q 867, 874 (1989).
22. See Cornel West, THE AMERICAN EVASION OF PHILOSOPHY (1989).

Groups, Histories, and International Law

Lea Brilmayer

READING THE INTERNATIONAL pages of the newspapers day after day, one sometimes gets the feeling that the stories never change. Many of the problems that we are concerned with today are almost the same as ten, twenty, or even more years ago. Some recurring problems—such as environmental degradation, epidemics of infectious diseases, drought, or famine—seem largely technological, and it is easy to understand why progress in resolving them might have to await scientific advances. But other problems—such as conflicts in South Africa, the Middle East, India, Armenia, or Ireland—are problems of human violence. As to these, the naive might think that progress ought to be more within human control.

The fact that problems of human violence persist demonstrates that this naive and optimistic view is sadly mistaken. Problems of human violence linger on, festering in a special way. Some of the most intractable problems in contemporary international politics concern the claims of non-state groups. The example that comes most readily to mind is the Palestinians' continuing claims against the state of Israel. This dispute not only endangers the lives and property of the immediate participants, but also seriously colors relations among other states in the vicinity, as when Saddam Hussein claimed solidarity with the Palestinian cause as a defense for his invasion of Kuwait. The claims of non-state

Reprinted from R. Lea Brilmayer, "Groups, Histories, and International Law," *Cornell International Law Journal* 25 (1992): 555–63. © Copyright 1992 by Cornell University. All rights reserved.

groups are not unique to the Middle East, of course. Other group conflicts add seriously to international instability. Certainly the civil wars in Yugoslavia, Somalia, and Ethiopia have elicited well-warranted international concern. The situation in Kashmir threatens to trigger a nuclear war between Pakistan and India. What all of these problems have in common is that they are not just traditional international disputes between state actors. One or more of the disputants are non-state groups.

It is no coincidence that many of our most pressing current problems concern the rights of non-state groups. This essay investigates the reasons that the international system has not been able to resolve such problems. Implicit in this analysis may be some prescriptions about how the international system would have to change to become better suited to dealing with problems of this sort. But I am actually fairly pessimistic. The changes necessary for my prognosis to improve are so substantial that it is unlikely that they will occur.

The main problem with resolving the claims of non-state groups is that many such claims are based on corrective justice: they are claims, in other words, to right past wrongs. International law is not good at providing corrective justice and thus is unlikely to resolve problems in a way that satisfies groups with historical grievances. Aggrieved groups must, of necessity, take things into their own hands. Hence the international instability. Furthermore, non-state groups are less able than traditional state actors to resolve disputes definitively because they lack a strong centralized command structure. Unless the group as a whole recognizes a proposed solution as a satisfying response to its felt grievances, a non-state actor may be unable to commit to the solution because of internal group dynamics.

There are two parts to this essay's claim: first, that international law is not adept at righting historical wrongs, and second, that many group claims are claims of this sort. International law is not well-suited to promoting corrective justice because it works primarily through incentives rather than sanctions. The fact that international law cannot provide corrective justice affects the claims of non-state groups because non-state groups are largely defined by their histories. The argument is not intended as a technical contribution to the international legal literature, but as a more jurisprudential observation about the international legal system. After making this two-step argument, this essay will conclude with a few remarks about its relevance to some current problems.

I. INTERNATIONAL LAW AND CORRECTIVE JUSTICE
It is sometimes said that international law is not really law at all because there are no international legal sanctions.[1] Because there is no centralized enforcement mechanism, it is said, states obey international law or not, as they please. This is something of an overstatement, for international sanction processes do exist. Some are formal, such as World Court proceedings or the United Nations Se-

curity Council's measures against Iraq after its invasion of Kuwait. More commonly, sanctions are informal and include economic boycotts, diplomatic pressure, and world public opinion.[2]

But even if an overstatement, the point nonetheless has some force. Although domestic legal sanctions are not perfect, in comparison international legal sanctions seem considerably less developed. Getting international legal sanctions to work requires political organization, persistence, and sometimes luck. The underdeveloped nature of the international sanctioning process is part of the reason that international law is ill-equipped to dispense corrective justice.

The relative lack of international sanctions means it is difficult to force a state to go along with something that is not in its self-interest. International law necessarily puts a premium on accommodation and conciliation; it is better at cajoling than compelling. For this reason, the most effective international remedies offer something to both sides of a dispute. When the status quo is unattractive to both sides, international law may help resolve a dispute because both sides have incentives to agree to the proposed international solution. However, when one side prefers the status quo to all other options, the international system is hard put to force that side to cooperate.

The remedy proposed by the international system must be, as the economists would put it, Pareto superior to the status quo. Both sides to the dispute must see some advantage to the proposed solution because it is difficult to force either side to comply. But corrective justice remedies are not Pareto superior; they are intrinsically zero sum. The object is to redress the injury to the complaining party by forcing the alleged wrongdoer to disgorge unjust benefits and to make the complainant whole.[3] The alleged wrongdoer is unlikely to view this prospect in a positive light because it gains no advantage. Thus, it will almost certainly prefer the status quo to a corrective justice remedy.

To the extent that international law cannot offer the victim a remedy, the victim is bound to be dissatisfied. With no legal remedies available, its only solution is self-help. Whether or not the alleged wrongdoer is in fact culpable, the complaining party feels aggrieved because it has no opportunity to make its case.[4] Hence the violence, which is designed to make the status quo unlivable for the wrongdoer. Through terrorism or open insurrection, the complaining party seeks to bring the alleged wrongdoer to the bargaining table. Extralegal means are used to achieve what legal means cannot.

Even if the victim succeeds in bringing its opponent to the bargaining table, there is still no guarantee of corrective justice. The wrongdoer will not necessarily agree to correct historical wrongs; it will not agree to a remedy that puts it in a worse position than where it currently stands. Tolerating the existing level of violence may be preferable to disgorging unjust advantages. The victim's ability to pressure the wrongdoer, rather than its historical entitlements, determines its remedy.

The international system works better with forward-looking solutions to problems than with remedies for historical wrongs. Unlike corrective justice, forward-looking solutions need not be zero sum and, in some situations, may make everyone better off. Treaty regimes typify such situations: states agree to cooperate in controlling environmental degradation or armaments because all expect to gain an advantage. Election monitoring represents another situation in which all parties may benefit. In Namibia and Cambodia, for example, all sides sought to gain from the increased stability and electoral opportunities that United Nations monitoring could provide. All sides of the dispute had incentives to abandon the status quo.

In contrast, the international system rarely has been able to provide corrective justice. Although two possible examples that come to mind are the Nuremburg trials and the Persian Gulf war, neither is a paradigm of corrective justice; both, to the contrary, are examples of "victors' justice." Although in both cases the outcomes were defensible in the sense that the guilty party was punished, a proceeding in which an interested party determines the scope of retribution is hardly impartial.[5] More to the point for present purposes, such examples are quite rare and depend upon a display of force that the international system typically does not or cannot provide.[6]

The inability of international law to provide corrective justice is self-perpetuating because the longer that corrective justice goes unenforced, the less possible it becomes to institute it at a later point. Once one starts to undo history, there is no stopping point. One group of individuals claims a piece of territory on the grounds that, at some point in the past, it was wrongfully taken away from them. But was their own possession of the territory legitimate? Very likely, there are arguments that it was not. Some earlier group may have its own claim of even earlier ownership. If we could simply trace back to the point where all possession was rightful, corrective justice would require returning matters to this original status quo. But there probably is no such point, and if there were, it would be too long ago to be useful because the injustice has gone uncorrected since time immemorial. The difficulty of choosing some arbitrary Archimedean point from which "justice" will be measured contributes to the continuing inability of international law to satisfy grievances based on perceptions of historical injustice.

And corrective justice, in some circumstances, creates new injustices of its own. The longer that a wrong has gone unremedied, the more likely it is that expectations have settled around the status quo. This is particularly true concerning territorial acquisitions. New residents may well be quite innocent of the original wrongdoing. They settle, make both economic and psychological investments in their new homes, and build new lives. When the time comes to correct the original wrong, the parties who now bear the costs of the remedy may not be those who were responsible. The longer that the status quo remains unchallenged, the less likely that corrective justice will be felt only by the individuals who wrongfully created it.

II. Groups, Histories, and Corrective Justice

What has all of this to do with non-state groups? First, many of the claims made by non-state groups demand corrective justice. The corrective justice claims of non-state groups contribute significantly to violence and instability in the contemporary world. Second, non-state groups find it relatively difficult to relinquish corrective justice claims and to settle for accommodation with opponents. Non-state groups' inability to compromise stems from intragroup dynamics, particularly their inability to force a compromise solution upon their members, and from the fact that non-state groups are often largely defined by their histories. Unlike state actors, abandonment of a group's historical claims threatens the group's very identity.

Let me start by mentioning some examples of group claims that rest on corrective justice. The first I addressed at some length in a previous article: the right of secession.[7] My argument was that secessionist demands necessarily involve a claimed right to territory. Secessionists must show a right to territory because they are claiming a right to some particular piece of land on which to establish a state of their own. In most instances, the claim to territory will be based upon some historical argument that the territory was once theirs but was wrongfully taken from them. This, of course, is a claim of corrective justice.

A second example is similar, although "secession" is not really the right word to describe it. The Palestinians claim a historical right to a particular piece of land, one to which the Israelis claim a competing historical entitlement. Because the occupied West Bank does not now lie clearly within the recognized borders of Israel, one cannot call the Palestinian argument "secessionist." The structure of the demand is similar, however, because it is based upon claims of historical entitlement to the West Bank or, indeed, to Israel itself.

A third example deals with the rights of native peoples. This sort of claim has not, by and large, given rise to as much instability as the claims discussed above—probably because many indigenous groups are geographically dispersed, economically disadvantaged, and otherwise not well-situated to fight for what they believe to be properly theirs. Native rights are, however, a good example of how group rights tend to be tied to historical claims. Whether one thinks of the claims of the Native Americans of North America, the aboriginal peoples of Australia, or the black inhabitants of South Africa, the historical grievances are palpable.

The fact of these historical grievances does not mean that corrective justice is always the best strategy for arguing Natives' rights claims. Indeed, it would be unwise to rely entirely on corrective justice; for in most of these cases, the probability of full reparations is next to zero, and the claimants appreciate that a full corrective justice claim stands no chance of success. Corrective justice claims may be coupled with demands for amelioration of ongoing conditions, however. Demands for wealth redistribution, for instance, may be based on historical occurrences, such as colonialism, and be inspired by the wish to obtain at least partial compensation for past harms and indignities. But these demands may also be founded on inequities that exist today and that will continue to exist tomorrow unless changes occur.

It seems worth asking, therefore, whether there is a reason that so many group claims are tied to group histories and historical group injuries. There is more involved than mere coincidence. Groups are defined, in part, by their histories. It should be no surprise that group demands are shaped by those histories and by the wrongs groups feel they have suffered. History is the glue that cements a collection of disassociated individuals into a group. True, a group is bound together by its present and its future as well as its past. A group's language, religion, and culture are part of its present and contribute to its cohesiveness; the future that the group envisions for itself contributes to the group's identity as well. But language, religion, and culture are a product of a group's past, and a group perceives a common future largely because it already possesses a common identity, an identity forged by the past. It is hard to imagine a fully committed group that does not share a common past. Solidarity comes from continuity over time, not from the chance coincidence of shared characteristics in the present and certainly not from the chance that common characteristics may exist in the future. One of the most unifying experiences that a group can share is a common and horrible injustice, especially if there is some possibility that working together might bring about redress.

It is precisely this sort of solidarity, coupled with a burning desire for corrective justice, that makes certain international problems so intractable—especially when historic injustice is perceived by both sides. How can the Serbs and the Croats solve their disputes given a history of mass extermination? How can the Palestinians and the Israelis make amends given what both groups have gone through? If collective amnesia were somehow possible (and if it were worth the costs—another matter, which we cannot go into here), the opposing groups would still find it difficult to sort things out. Issues such as the division of territory and resources, of providing for the rights of minorities, of making sure that horrible injustices cannot occur again in the future would remain. But things become much more difficult, however, given that most groups cannot, or will not, forget.

Forgetting would help, in part, because if groups were not saddled with the fear of history repeating itself, they might face their opponents with enough generosity and courage to induce a generous and courageous response. More importantly, perhaps, forgetting would help because groups would not have to feel that every concession to opponents would betray friends and family members who have already suffered. "Why should we make concessions that only reward their crimes?" ask the victims. Corrective justice becomes something owed to predecessors as well as something entitled to from adversaries. How can justice be traded for a chance to live more securely or comfortably in the future? To abandon the group's claim to corrective justice is to abandon the group, for part of what holds the group together—part of what distinguishes the member from the nonmember—is commitment to justice for the group.

This inability or unwillingness to forget applies to a certain degree to state as well as non-state actors. States also have a deeply felt need to hold on to the experience of unjust treatment and to do whatever possible to obtain retribution. As with non-state actors, the inability of international law to dispense corrective justice may be a hurdle preventing achievement of international stability and peaceful coexistence.

I would argue, though, that the abandonment of corrective justice claims threatens non-state groups more than traditional state actors because non-state groups lack international legal personality. Non-state group identities are more precarious, and such groups must be careful to conserve those resources that will keep them together, including a shared sense of injustice. Their cohesiveness, indeed, their existence depends on it.

Leaders of groups know that they put their authority at risk when they neglect the indicia of identity. Not only do they allow the disintegration of group boundaries, erasing the lines that differentiate their members from outsiders, but they leave themselves vulnerable to other would-be leaders who pay those boundaries greater attention.[8] The leader who neglects to emphasize the distinctiveness of the group or who is too willing to forget the past wrongs that the group has suffered loses his or her constituency. The more fractured the group, the greater the threat that other leaders will take advantage of a sense of historical injustice that the current leader has de-emphasized.

Again, the Israeli-Palestinian case provides examples. The Palestinian leadership obviously cannot afford to leave behind its claims of historical injustice. What would be the Palestinian reason for existence once the group sets history aside? The group is defined in part by its experience prior to and since Israeli independence. Israel, of course, is also defined by its sense of historical injustice. Most recently, the Holocaust and the Arab-Israeli violence have helped to pull the Israeli nation together although, of course, the Israelis share a much longer history that also figures into the sense of group identity. Today, it is not certain that a major Israeli party could consummate a peace agreement even if it wanted to, given the possibility that smaller parties are able to capitalize on any willingness to sell short Israel's perceived claims to historic justice. As a traditional state actor, however, Israel's ability to reach compromise is stronger than that of the Palestinians.

III. PROGNOSIS

So long as the Palestinian-Israeli dispute is perceived primarily in terms of corrective justice, there will be no solution. Each side would undoubtedly want an international solution framed in terms of corrective justice—but only so long as its own version of history was adopted. Each side would most prefer an authoritative declaration that it has been wronged and should now be entitled to full redress at the expense of the other. But if anything is clear in this dispute, it is that international involvement will not take the shape of corrective justice. The international community is unlikely to approach the problem in terms of historical fact: Who did what and lived where and at what time? Who received what promises and from whom and with what authority? Who was first responsible for the continuing round of violence? Did that party have a valid excuse? The problem is not so much that it is impossible, now, to determine those things—although certainly there is no denying the difficulties. The problem is that what matters now to most of the international community is fixing things for the future, not apportioning blame. And that is the form that an international remedy must assume. The solution must look to the future, not the past.

And yet it is hard to discount the human passion for corrective justice, the human tendency to see things in exactly these terms. The mere fact that both sides seem to agree that corrective justice matters—when they agree on almost nothing else—strongly suggests the inevitability of this perspective. And it is hard to say that the world would be better off if human beings did not care about such things. Certainly, the international community should care about doing justice. But if it should care about doing justice, then why should it not also care about *undoing injustice*? Perhaps what the international system most needs to learn is how to identify the point at which corrective justice must be left behind, to determine the point at which groups and states should start to continue on with life, looking forward to the future instead of back to the past.

Group claims persist and cause recurring violence because groups have a capacity for self-help that individuals rarely do. Few individuals have the material or spiritual capacity to mount a sustained campaign to right injustice in the international arena. Individuals, in particular, cannot carry on their fight beyond the range of a single lifetime. Unfortunately, groups have the need as well as the ability to carry on their claims because they cannot afford to set aside the very histories that give them their common existence. International law, however, does not have the luxury of focusing on symbolic or historic grievances of the sort that help to make such groups cohere. Except in the unlikely event that an international system should come into existence that would right collective wrongs, the inability of international law to deal with the rights of non-state actors seems likely to persist.

Notes

1. For a discussion of and challenge to this claim, see Anthony D'Amato, *Is International Law Really "Law"?*, 79 NW. U. L. REV. 1293 (1985). See generally Louis Henkin, How NATIONS BEHAVE 1-27 (2d ed. 1979). *Cf.* Thomas M. Franck, THE POWER OF LEGITIMACY AMONG NATIONS 3-26 (1990).

2. See generally Lea Brilmayer, *International Remedies*, 14 YALE J. INT'L L. 579 (1989).

3. It is possible, of course, that a remedy might be neither Pareto superior nor zero sum. A remedy might be negative sum, or it might be positive sum with the gain distributed in such a way as to make one party worse off. The point here is simply that a remedy that transfers utility from the wrongdoer to the victim, as corrective justice does, is zero sum and thus not Pareto superior.

4. Although I refer below to "victims" and "wrongdoers," it is of course possible that the complaining party may be mistaken about its right to corrective justice. What matters, however, is the fact that it *believes* that it has been wronged. Because there is no good process for achieving corrective justice, the self defined victim will continue to believe that it has been unfairly denied a remedy, resulting in the long running historical disputes that I describe.

5. In both cases, in other words, there was a genuine international crime that warranted a forceful response. However, control over enforcement was largely vested in the hands of parties with their own stakes in the dispute. In this sense, the process was not a paradigm of corrective justice.

6. Interestingly, even in the Persian Gulf war, where there was United Nations authorization for intervention, the Coalition forces did not attempt to right all the historical wrongs that they might have addressed. The Kurds sought regional autonomy, citing promises made to them earlier by Iraq as well as human rights abuses. The Coalition did not attempt to resolve this problem, preferring simply to maintain the status quo through establishment of safety zones with no independent international state status.

7. Lea Brilmayer, *Secession and Self-Determination: A Territorial Interpretation*, 16 YALE J. INT'L L. 177 (1991).

8. See generally Donald L. Horowitz, ETHNIC GROUPS IN CONFLICT 346 (1985) (discussing "outbidding" for ethnic support by emphasizing diligence).

International Legal Responses to the Rise of Nations

Part III: Introduction

EVER SINCE NATIONALISM'S emergence on the European stage during the Napoleonic Wars and the subsequent diffusion of nationalist ideology across the non-Western world, states have been compelled to address nations' growing political salience. As illustrated in Part II of this volume, nations have challenged state dominance of the global political system in a variety of ways and on a variety of levels. Just as states have attempted to defend their prerogatives against such nonstate actors as multinational corporations and international organizations,[1] states have guardedly responded to the "rise of nations" phenomenon. Much of the tension between states and nations reflects state leaders' wariness of policies that might erode the state's preeminent international legal status and weaken state legitimacy. States remain reluctant, as well, to relinquish power over their domestic affairs and to countenance external involvement in internal matters. Meanwhile, nations find themselves inevitably confronting states in their quest for political, economic, and social autonomy.

One paradox of this state-nation tension is that nations regularly decry international law's resistance to national demands for statehood. Nations, that is, often fight the state system in order to join it.[2] The articulation of national demands in territorial terms[3] especially threatens states: If nations come to be viewed as legitimately constituting their own statehoods, then the territorial integrity of nearly all states may be called into question. Even when nations do not demand independence per se—for example, when territorial autonomy within an existing state satisfies national demands—states prove resistant for fear that autonomy will lead to demands for independence.[4]

The notion of an international right to territorial autonomy has been rejected at virtually every turn by the international community of states. For example, a clause on territorial autonomy, contained in an earlier draft, was dropped from the final text of the European Framework Convention on the Protection of National Minorities (1995).[5] This concept may be judged consistent with, and proceeding logically from, the international right to internal self-determination. Nevertheless, "implementation of the principles in the [European] Framework Convention is to be achieved through 'national legislation and appropriate governmental policies.' . . . everything is at the discretion of the state with regard to its own particular circumstances and nothing is directly applicable."[6] Decisions about territorial autonomy are generally deemed internal affairs, not subject to international law.

Part III's essays both illustrate and analyze international law's responses to distinct rise of nations challenges. All frame the issue in self-determination terms. Such a focus is natural and appropriate: The post–World War II decolonization process transformed self-determination from a political principle to a legal right, thereby bringing the issue to international law's forefront. The crucial question posed today by self-determination is whether that right permits secession. Does self-determination, identified in the United Nations General Assembly's 1960 Declaration on the Granting of Independence to Colonial Countries and Peoples (Res. 1514), allow all "peoples"[7] to establish a state of their own, even if their action would detach territories from an existing state in order to establish a new state in which the "peoples" would reside?

To this question Hurst Hannum responds with an emphatic, no. Although Hannum's argument has been aggressively challenged,[8] his careful reading of the seminal documents informs his conclusion that, except in the most extreme cases, the right of self-determination does not automatically grant ethnic groups the right to independent statehood. Instead, the evolution of self-determination from decolonization and toward minority rights and autonomy (though not necessarily territorial autonomy), may establish a satisfactory mean between an overly statist outcome and one that recognizes national interests. "The norm of self-determination in the post-colonial era," Hannum contends, is "both a shield that protects a state (in most cases) from secession and a spear that pierces the governmental veil of sovereignty behind which undemocratic or discriminatory regimes attempt to hide."

Sometimes the independent statehood issue is thrust on the international community by the collapse of multiethnic states. Though external states may seek to thwart centrifugal pressures, the establishment of new states based on nationality criteria may often prove inevitable. In such cases, the crucial decision remaining is where to draw the borders between the successor states. Steven Ratner traces the development of *uti possidetis*: the practice of transforming a former colonial entity's internal boundaries, after that entity's decolonization, into state (i.e., "international") borders. Ratner acknowledges that one rationale for *uti possidetis* is to avoid conflicts between postimperial states. Nevertheless, he rejects the peremptory application of the principle to the modern, postcolonial period. Although the core cause of conflict between successor states is usually territorial, Ratner argues that "the assumption by states of [*uti possidetis's*] applicability from the outset [has] prevented any debate over the adjustment of boundaries and limited the universe of possible borders to one—leaving those people on the 'wrong' side of the border ripe for 'ethnic cleansing.' " Inspiring Ratner's critique of *uti possidetis* is the concept's statist underpinnings: National unity considerations are trumped by the goal of transforming entities into full-fledged states and, ideally, of maintaining the state system's stability. These value preferences reflect international law's continued state domination.

By its status quo orientation, one evinced by more than merely its *uti possidetis* practices, the international community has routinely permitted nations to remain divided by state borders. Even so, state leaders have at times sought to "retrieve" or to "redeem" their co-nationals in neighboring states. This is the phenomenon of "irredentism." Thomas Ambrosio takes the debate over self-determination and reverses its focus: Rather than exploring whether a group within a state may legally secede, he considers the international legality of forcible attempts by external states to unify nations. The irredentism issue lies at the nexus of self-determination, territorial integrity, and the use of force. Despite international law's solidly statist foundations, Ambrosio finds that the international community has proved inconsistent in its rhetorical defense of territorial integrity. Such variation in state practice has rather little to do, however, with a growing state cognizance of national interests. Rather, it reflects the political interests of external states that consistently inform international responses to irredentist conflicts. The perennial tension between law and politics often manifests itself in the tension between states and nations.

The states described in Eric Kolodner's essay take a very different approach to the state-nation problem: by "importing" their own nationals into regions populated by other ethnic groups, the states attempt to "solve" their minority problems by demographically overwhelming minority populations. The influx of settler populations—though a violation of the 1949 Geneva Conventions when it occurs in foreign-occupied territories—is often overlooked by the international community if it occurs within a state. In fact, Kolodner argues, "[t]his subtle form of invasion, which uses people as weapons, usually escapes international scrutiny, and is therefore rendered the most cost-effective and least controversial method of invading a territory and eliminating its inhabitants." When the international community forbids ethnic group secession and rejects border rectifications, it only encourages states to extend their demographic dominance over territories under their control, rendering moot the issues of secession and internal autonomy. The use of settler populations may effectively, though tragically, resolve the tension between state and nation by making the two nearly coterminous within the state's boundaries.[9]

Each of this part's essays examines attempts by the international legal order and individual states to address challenges posed by national demands. As the international law of nationalism evolves, it will continue to be compelled to confront the issues of secession, internal self-determination, territorial borders, the use of force, and demographic dominance. Drawing on existing legal rules and historic state practices, it may nevertheless move in unprecedented, perhaps at times initially ambiguous, directions.

NOTES

1. See, for example, the objections to the Multilateral Agreement on Investment. Robert Stumberg, "Direct Investment: Sovereignty by Subtraction: The Multilateral Agreement on Investment," *Cornell International Law Journal* 31 (1998): 492–598.

    States are particularly willing to defend aggressively their sovereignty against perceived encroachments by international organizations. Captain Davis Brown, "The Role of Regional Organizations in Stopping Civil Wars," *Air Force Law Review* 41 (1997): 255–82; Henry T. King and Theodore C. Theofrastous, "From Nuremberg to Rome: A Step Backward for U.S. Foreign Policy," *Case Western Reserve Journal of International Law* 31 (1999): 47–107; Jelena Pejic, "Creating a Permanent International Criminal Court: The Obstacles to Independence and Effectiveness," *Columbia Human Rights Law Review* 29 (1998): 291–354; Ibrahim J. Gassama, "Safeguarding the Democratic Entitlement: A Proposal for United Nations Involvement in National Politics," *Cornell International Law Journal* 30 (1997): 287–333; Kanishka Jayasuriya, "Globalization, Law, and the Transformation of Sovereignty: The Emergence of Global Regulatory Governance," *Indiana Journal of Global Legal Studies* 6 (1999): 425–455.

2. Berman's essay in part I of this volume aptly illustrates how circumstances shape the relevance of certain demands and self-classifications by cultural groups.

3. Lea Brilmayer, "Secession and Self-Determination: A Territorial Interpretation," *Yale Journal of International Law* 16 (1991): 177–202.

4. Andras B. Baka, "The European Convention on Human Rights and the Protection of Minorities Under International Law," *Connecticut Journal of International Law* 8 (1993): 227–42; Philip Chase, "Conflict in the Crimea: An Examination of Ethnic Conflict Under the Contemporary Model of Sovereignty," *Columbia Journal of Transnational Law* 31 (1996): 219–54; Geri L. Haight, "Unfulfilled Obligations: The Situation of the Ethnic Hungarian Minority in the Slovak Republic," *ILSA Journal of International & Comparative Law* 4 (1997): 27–120.

5. David Wippman, "Human Rights on the Eve of the Next Century: Aspects of Human Rights Implementation: The Evolution And Implementation of Minority Rights," *Fordham Law Review* 66 (1997): 597–626.

6. Geoff Gilbert, "The Council of Europe and Minority Rights," *Human Rights Quarterly* 18 (1996): 160–89.

7. What constitutes a "people" or "peoples" is not clearly defined by U.N.G.A. Resolution 1514.

8. Trent N. Tappe, "Chechnya and the State of Self-Determination in a Breakaway Region of the Former Soviet Union: Evaluating the Legitimacy of Secessionist Claims," *Columbia Journal of Transnational Law* 34 (1995): 255–96; Jennifer P. Harris, "An Application of the Principle of Self-Determination," *Human Rights Brief* 6 (1999): 28–30; Valerie Epps, "The New Dynamics of Self- Determination," *ILSA Journal of International & Comparative Law* 3 (1997): 433–42.

9. The mirror opposite of the "settler population" practice is that of "ethnic cleansing." Widespread use of the term, which derives from the Serbo-Croat word *čišćenje*, began during the early 1990s in the context of the wars of Yugoslav succession. Then, Serbs in Croatia and Bosnia "cleansed" ethnic Croats and Bosnian Muslims from territory they controlled. The forcible expulsion of a given ethnic group or groups, unfortunately, is as old as recorded history.

INTRODUCTION **213**

Ethnic cleansing is one means employed by states to resolve the tensions between state and nation. Nevertheless, the practice is typically construed as a issue for humanitarian law and the *jus in bello*, rather than for the international law of nationalism. Consequently, it was not included in this volume.

Alfred M. de Zayas, "International Law and Mass Population Transfers," *Harvard International Law Journal* 16 (1975): 207–58; Michael P. Roch, "Forced Displacement in the Former Yugoslavia: A Crime Under International Law?" *Dickinson Journal of International Law* 14 (1995) 1–30; Alfred de Zayas, "The Right to One's Homeland, Ethnic Cleansing, and the International Criminal Tribunal for the Former Yugoslavia," *Criminal Law Forum* 6 (1995): 257–314; John Quigley, "State Responsibility for Ethnic Cleansing," *U.C. Davis Law Review* 32 (1999): 341–87. Andrew Bell-Failkoff, *Ethnic Cleansing* (New York: St. Martin's Griffin, 1999); John Alego and Adele Algeo, "Among the New Words," *American Speech* 68 (1993): 411–12.

FOR FURTHER READING

Bookman, Milica Zarkovic. *The Demographic Struggle for Power: The Political Economy of Demographic Engineering in the Modern World.* Portland, OR: Frank Cass, 1997.

Cass, Deborah Z. "Re-Thinking Self-Determination: A Critical Analysis of Current International Law Theories," *Syracuse Journal of International Law and Commerce* 18 (1992)1 21–40.

Eastwood, Lawrence S. Jr. "Secession: State Practice and International Law After the Dissolution of the Soviet Union and Yugoslavia," *Duke Journal of Comparative & International Law* 3 (1993): 299–349.

Hannum, Hurst. "New Minority Rights for the Twenty-First Century," in *The Universal Declaration of Human Rights: Fifty Years and Beyond,* edited by Yael Danieli et al. Amityville, NY: Baywood Publishing Co., 1999.

Kirgis, Frederic L. Jr. "The Degrees of Self-Determination in The United Nations Era," *American Journal International Law* 88 (1994): 304–10.

Nanda, Ved P. "Revisiting Self-Determination as an International Law Concept," *ILSA Journal of International & Comparative Law* 3 (1997): 443–54.

Pomerance, Michla. "The Badinter Commission: The Use and Misuse of the International Court of Justice's Jurisprudence," *Michigan Journal of International Law* 20 (1998): 31–58.

Simpson, Gerry J. "The Diffusion of Sovereignty: Self-Determination in the Post-Colonial Age," *Stanford Journal of International Law* 32 (1996): 255–86.

Weller, Marc. "The International Response to the Dissolution of the Socialist Federal Republic of Yugoslavia," *American Journal of International Law* 86 (1992): 560–607.

Rethinking Self-Determination

Hurst Hannum

ONE METHOD OF resolving conflict suggested by a scholar of the Grand Academy of Lagado was to divide the brains of political opponents in half and then transpose the halves. The professor argued that

> the two half brains being left to debate the matter between themselves within the space of one skull, would soon come to a good understanding, and produce that moderation as well as regularity of thinking, so much to be wished for in the heads of those . . . who imagine they came into the world only to watch and govern its motion: and as to the difference of brains, in quantity or quality, among those who are directors in faction; the doctor assured us, from his own knowledge, that it was a perfect trifle.[1]

Although this solution, like others of similar modesty proposed by Swift, has not been widely adopted, the plethora of violent communal and ethnic conflicts in the modern world does occasionally lead one to search for radical responses. In contrast to the "compromise" suggested by the good doctor of Lagado, some have proposed separating warring factions through the "liberation" of oppressed peoples or, depending on one's perspective, through the "dismemberment" of states and empires. Of course, just what territory is being "liberated" is not always clear, as evidenced by the "ethnic cleansing" campaign pursued in the former Yugoslavia.

Reprinted with permission from Hurst Hannum, "Rethinking Self-Determination," *Virginia Journal of International Law* 34, no. 1 (1994): 1–69.

Separation is often justified by invoking the right of self-determination. Indeed, no contemporary norm of international law has been so vigorously promoted or widely accepted—at least in theory—as the right of all peoples to self-determination. Yet the meaning of that right remains as vague and imprecise as when it was enunciated by President Woodrow Wilson and others at Versailles.

Part I of this Article recounts the international norm of self-determination from Wilsonian formulations to the present. After a brief discussion of self-determination during the era of the League of Nations, the role of the United Nations in transforming a political principle into a rule of law is considered. Particular attention is given to the content of the right of self-determination as evinced by the lengthy debates leading to the adoption of the two international covenants on human rights in 1966.

In part II, the current meaning of the "right of self-determination" and its relationship to the process of decolonization are considered. Part III explores whether the right of self-determination includes the possibility of secession, and part IV discusses the link between human rights and the right of self-determination. The conclusion offers a new approach for dealing with self-determination in the post-colonial era.

I. HISTORICAL DEVELOPMENT

A. Nationalism, Woodrow Wilson, and the League of Nations

The principle of self-determination by "national" groups developed as a natural corollary to growing ethnic and linguistic political demands in the eighteenth and nineteenth centuries.[2] Although it is not inherently desirable that a nation be culturally or linguistically homogeneous, by the mid-nineteenth century the equation of a nation with a homogeneous populus had become common. John Stuart Mill's influential *Considerations on Representative Government* argued that "it is in general a necessary condition of free institutions that the boundaries of governments should coincide in the main with those of nationalities." "National self-determination" became the paradigm for political organization, raising expectations among various minority groups that were doomed to failure in light of the political and economic realities of the time.

"As an agency of destruction the theory of nationalism proved one of the most potent that even modern society has known."[3] Along with the physically destructive power of the machine gun, airplane, and other weapons used on a large scale for the first time, nationalist fervor hastened the disintegration of the Austro-Hungarian and Ottoman empires prior to and during World War I. The territory of the former empires required new sovereigns, and the principle of self-determination as a means of drawing new "nation-state" boundaries became the vehicle for legitimizing the victorious powers' re-division of Europe.

Although President Woodrow Wilson was the most public advocate of "self-determination" as a guiding principle in the post-war period, neither he nor the other Allied leaders believed that the principle was absolute or universal. Indeed, in Wilson's celebrated "Fourteen Points" speech to the United States Congress on January 8, 1918, the phrase "self-determination" is conspicuous by its absence,[4] even though the speech dealt with specific territorial settlements, including the creation of independent states out of the remnants of the Austro-Hungarian and Ottoman empires.[5]

A month later, Wilson addressed the question of self-determination directly:

> National aspirations must be respected; peoples may now be dominated and governed only by their own consent. "Self-determination" is not a mere phrase. It is an imperative principle of action, which statesmen will henceforth ignore at their peril.
>
> . . . Peoples and provinces are not to be bartered about from sovereignty to sovereignty as if they were mere chattels and pawns in a game. . . .
>
> . . . All well-defined national aspirations shall be accorded the utmost satisfaction that can be accorded them without introducing new or perpetuating old elements of discord and antagonism that would be likely in time to break the peace of Europe and consequently of the world.[6]

As the final sentence of this excerpt suggests, Wilson carefully balanced *realpolitik* concerns with the ideals of democracy and the "nation-state." Subsequent history reflected this limit on the principle of self-determination.

The success or failure of assertions of minority rights and self-determination in the early twentieth century depended to a great extent on support from one or more of the Great Powers, particularly during the Paris Peace Conference which re-divided post-war Europe . . . With a few exceptions in the less sensitive frontier regions, no plebiscites or referenda were held to determine the wishes of the people affected by the Versailles map-making.[7] . . . "Nevertheless, the treaties made at Paris gave the principle [of self-determination] far more attention than it had ever before enlisted."[8]

After the war, the principle of self-determination was addressed indirectly by the League of Nations through the system of mandates created pursuant to article 22 of the League Covenant. Accepting that the development of colonial peoples formerly under the sovereignty of the defeated powers was "a sacred trust of civilization," various members of the Allies agreed to administer fourteen territories under League supervision.

Some national groups not recognized as new states by the peace treaties or designated as mandates received protection under the "minorities treaties" adopted under the auspices of the victorious powers. . . . The minorities treaties were not intended to respond to the principle of self-determination, and they ultimately failed in many respects to protect vulnerable groups.[9] Consistent with previous attempts to address issues related to self-determination, the Allied Powers and the League of Nations imposed obligations only on defeated states or states otherwise beholden to the major powers.

Despite the apparently inconsistent manner in which self-determination claims were decided at the Peace Conference, Wilson proposed incorporating the principle of self-determination within the Covenant of the League of Nations. His draft provided:

> The Contracting Parties unite in guaranteeing to each other political independence and territorial integrity but it is understood between them that such territorial adjustments, if any, as may in future become necessary by reason of changes in present racial and political relationships, pursuant to the principle of self-determination, and also such territorial adjustments as may in the judgement of three-fourths of the delegates be demanded by the welfare and manifest interest of the people concerned, may be effected if agreeable to those peoples; and that territorial changes may in equity involve material compensation. The Contracting Powers accept without reservation the principle that the peace of the world is superior in importance to every question of political jurisdiction or boundary.

Even this modest formulation was dropped before adoption of the Covenant, but the final sentence's focus on peace accurately reflects the priorities of the Peace Conference, even in the mind of self-determination's most public proponent.

Modern commentators often forget the relative nature of Wilson's concept of self-determination. They also have neglected, until very recently, the "internal" aspect of self-determination promoted by Wilson and others: democracy. Indeed, this internal aspect, the conviction that the only legitimate basis for government is the consent of the governed, provided the ultimate justification for decolonization. . . .

While the equation of self-determination with democracy may have been the philosophical underpinning of Wilsonian principles, the states created in 1919 undertook no specific obligations to ensure a democratic form of government, despite the various minority guarantees that were given. These guarantees generally sought to protect culture and linguistic identity, but they did not offer many meaningful political rights or ensure participation in the processes of government. As discussed below, the principles of political autonomy and effective participation in government owe their legitimacy at least as much to post-1945 human rights norms as they do to the principle of national self-determination espoused in the preceding century.

The legal scope of the principle of self-determination at the end of the First

World War is perhaps best demonstrated by examining the case of the Aland Islands, one of the first controversies not directly related to the war to be addressed by the League of Nations. For centuries the Aland Islands, located in the Baltic Sea between Sweden and Finland, were considered by Sweden and Russia to have prime strategic importance. They were under Swedish control from 1157 to 1809 and retained their Swedish linguistic and cultural heritage thereafter. After Sweden's defeat by Russia in 1809, the Treaty of Frederiksham ceded Finland (including the Aland Islands) to Russia, and Finland became an autonomous Grand Duchy within the Russian empire. Following attempts at the Russification of Finland in the late nineteenth and early twentieth centuries, Finland declared its independence in December 1917, shortly after the March 1917 Russian Revolution. The question presented to the international community was whether the Aland Islands were a part of the new Finnish state or whether they should be permitted to reunite with their cultural motherland, Sweden.

The dispute continued for several years. The Alanders rejected initial Finnish offers of autonomy, and the Finnish government subsequently arrested two of the most prominent pro-Swedish Aland leaders. Finally, the League of Nations was called upon to determine the islands' status.[10]

The League appointed two bodies of experts to examine the Aland Islands question. The first, the Commission of Jurists, decided that the matter was indeed one of international concern, and therefore within the League's competence, because Finland had failed to acquire sovereignty over Aland both during the Russian empire's disintegration and prior to the Alanders' expressed wishes to be reunited with Sweden. The Committee's report went on to note:

> Although the principle of self-determination of peoples plays an important part in modern political thought, especially since the Great War, it must be pointed out that there is no mention of it in the Covenant of the League of Nations. The recognition of this principle in a certain number of international treaties cannot be considered as sufficient to put it upon the same footing as a positive rule of the Law of Nations.
> . . . Positive International Law does not recognise the right of national groups, as such, to separate themselves from the State of which they form part by the simple expression of a wish, any more than it recognises the right of other States to claim such a separation. Generally speaking, the grant or refusal of the right to a portion of its population of determining its own political fate by plebiscite or by some other method, is, exclusively, an attribute of the sovereignty of every State which is definitively constituted.[11]

The second body of experts, the Commission of Inquiry, considered how to resolve the dispute, after having first determined that Finland (including the

Aland Islands) became a fully constituted independent state following its declaration of independence from Russia in 1917. Despite its recognition that the vast majority of the Aland population would choose union with Sweden if a referendum were held, the Commission of Inquiry reached a similar conclusion as to the scope of self-determination, describing it as "a principle of justice and of liberty, expressed by a vague and general formula which has given rise to the most varied interpretations and differences of opinion."[12]

> To concede to minorities, either of language or religion, or to any
> fractions of a population the right of withdrawing from the community
> to which they belong, because it is their wish or their good pleasure,
> would be to destroy order and stability within States and to inaugurate
> anarchy in international life; it would be to uphold a theory
> incomparible with the very idea of the State as a territorial and political
> unity. . . .
> The separation of a minority from the State of which it forms a part
> and its incorporation in another State can only be considered as an
> altogether exceptional solution, a last resort when the State lacks either
> the will or the power to enact and apply just and effective guarantees.

Accordingly, the Commission recommended separation of the islands from Finland, pursuant to a plebescite in the islands, if Finland failed to offer the guarantees deemed necessary.

One may query whether the focus on self-determination and nationalism which characterized the inter-war era made a net contribution to peace in the world or to the protection of either individual or collective human rights. At the very least, subsequent history made it clear that self-determination provided no panacea for Europe's ills.

B. The United Nations and Decolonization

In part because of the inconsistent manner in which it was applied following the First World War, the principle of self-determination was not recognized initially as a fundamental right under the United Nations regime created in 1945. In addition, there was great reluctance to revive a concept used to justify Hitler's attempts to reunify the German "nation."

The "principle" of self-determination is mentioned only twice in the 1945 Charter of the United Nations, both times in the limiting context of developing "friendly relations among nations" and in conjunction with the principle of "equal rights . . . of peoples." The reference to "peoples" clearly encompasses a group beyond states and includes at least non-self-governing territories "whose peoples have not yet attained a full measure of self-government." Furthermore, the reference to friendly relations among "nations" carried no connotation of ethnicity or culture; it merely reflected the name of an organization, the "United Nations," composed of states. The equation of "nation" and "state" in the Charter is evidenced by paragraph 4 of article 1, which identifies as a purpose of the organization its serving as "a center for harmonizing the actions of nations in the attainment of these common ends."

Neither self-determination nor minority rights is mentioned in the 1948 Universal Declaration of Human Rights, although the Declaration does contain a preambular reference to developing amicable international relations. Whatever its political significance, the principle of self-determination had not attained the status of a rule of international law by the time of the drafting of the United Nations Charter or in the early United Nations era.

Under the moral and political imperatives of decolonization, however, the vague "principle" of self-determination soon evolved into the "right" to self-determination. This evolution was most clearly demonstrated by the General Assembly's 1960 Declaration on the Granting of Independence to Colonial Countries and Peoples ("Declaration on Colonial Independence").[13] Premised, *inter alia*, on the need for stability, peace, and respect for human rights, the Declaration on Colonial Independence "solemnly proclaims the necessity of bringing to a speedy and unconditional end colonialism in all its forms and manifestations." It declares that "all peoples have the right to self-determination; by virtue of that right they freely determine their political status and freely pursue their economic, social and cultural development." It also maintains that "inadequacy of political, economic, social or educational preparedness should never serve as a pretext for delaying independence." The final paragraph reaffirms "the sovereign rights of all peoples and their territorial integrity."

Paragraph 6 of the declaration sets forth a fundamental limiting principle, without which one almost never (at least in United Nations forums) finds a reference to self-determination: "Any attempt aimed at the partial or total disruption of the national unity and the territorial integrity of a country is incompatible with the purposes and principles of the Charter of the United Nations."

The thrust of the declaration is clear: all colonial territories have the right of independence. However, a closer reading reveals uncertainties arising from varying uses of the terms "peoples," "territories," and "countries." Although the title of the declaration refers only to "colonial" countries and peoples, operative paragraph 2 refers expansively to the right of "all peoples" to self-determination. Furthermore, operative paragraph 5 calls for the transfer of all sovereign powers to trust and non-self-governing territories "or all other territories which have not yet attained independence." Are peoples to be equated with territories, as suggested by the fifth paragraph and the final paragraph? Are there self-governing territories which are nonetheless entitled to independence? Is "alien" subjugation subjugation by non-citizens? foreigners? a group ethnically distinct from the group being "subjugated"? Is subjugation permissible so long as it is not by aliens?

Later United Nations texts offer answers to some of these questions. General Assembly Resolution 1541, adopted the day after the Declaration on Colonial Independence, sets forth a list of principles to guide states in determining whether they should transmit information on "non-self-governing" territories under article 73(e) of the Charter; it thus defines at least one of the categories of peoples entitled to self-determination. The resolution first notes that chapter XI of the Charter is applicable "to territories which were then [in 1945] known as the colonial type" and that the obligation to report continues until "a territory and its peoples attain a full measure of self-government." There is no mention of the right of self-determination, nor is there any reference to the Declaration on Colonial Independence adopted only a day before.

The remaining principles concern territories; the quotation immediately above clearly implies that a single territory can be home to many peoples. A territory is presumed to be non-self-governing if it is geographically separate and ethnically or culturally distinct. This presumption is reinforced if the territory is arbitrarily subordinated to the metropolitan state. Although these factors might be relevant to a common-sense definition of peoples entitled to self-determination, the requirement of geographical separateness[14] would eliminate most sub-state secessionist movements from consideration.

Resolution 1541 also defines "self-government." Self-government includes independence, "free association" with an independent state, or integration on a basis of equality with an independent state. The assumption is that independence will be the usual option, with the latter two possibilities subject to greater requirements of informed consent.

The questions raised by the Declaration on Colonial Independence were also addressed ten years later by the Declaration on Principles of International Law Concerning Friendly Relations and Co-operation Among States in Accordance with the Charter of the United Nations ("Declaration on Friendly Relations").[15] Adopted without a vote by the General Assembly after years of negotiation, the Declaration on Friendly Relations may be considered to state existing international law. Its provisions therefore possess unusual significance for a General Assembly resolution.

As its title suggests, the Declaration on Friendly Relations addresses a wide range of issues. The section concerned with equal rights and self-determination of peoples is worth quoting at length:

> By virtue of the principle of equal rights and self-determination of peoples enshrined in the Charter of the United Nations, all peoples have the right freely to determine, without external interference, their political status and to pursue their economic, social and cultural development, and every State has the duty to respect this right in accordance with the provisions of the Charter.

Every State has the duty to promote, through joint and separate action, realization of the principle of equal rights and self-determination of peoples, in accordance with the provisions of the Charter, and to render assistance to the United Nations in carrying out the responsibilities entrusted to it by the Charter regarding the implementation of the principle, in order:

(a) To promote friendly relations and co-operation among States; and
(b) To bring a speedy end to colonialism, having due regard to the freely expressed will of the peoples concerned; and bearing in mind that subjection of peoples to alien subjugation, domination and exploitation constitutes a violation of the principle, as well as a denial of fundamental human rights, and is contrary to the Charter.

Every State has the duty to promote through joint and separate action universal respect for and observance of human rights and fundamental freedoms in accordance with the Charter.

The establishment of a sovereign and independent State, the free association or integration with an independent State or the emergence into any other political status freely determined by a people constitute modes of implementing the right to self-determination by that people.

Every State has the duty to refrain from any forcible action which deprives peoples referred to above in the elaboration of the present principle of their right to self-determination and freedom and independence. In their actions against, and resistance to, such forcible action in pursuit of the exercise of their right to self-determination, such peoples are entitled to seek and to receive support in accordance with the purposes and principles of the Charter.

The territory of a colony or other Non-Self-Governing Territory has, under the Charter, a status separate and distinct from the territory of the State administering it; and such separate and distinct status under the Charter shall exist until the people of the colony or Non-Self-Governing Territory have exercised their right to self-determination in accordance with the Charter, and particularly its purposes and principles.

Nothing in the foregoing paragraphs shall be construed as authorizing or encouraging any action which would dismember or impair, totally or in part, the territorial integrity or political unity of sovereign and independent States conducting themselves in compliance with the principle of equal rights and self-determination of peoples as described above and thus possessed of a government representing the whole people belonging to the territory without distinction as to race, creed or colour.

> Every State shall refrain from any action aimed at the partial or total disruption of the national unity and territorial integrity of any other State or country.

The resolution also provides:

> All States enjoy sovereign equality. . . . In particular, sovereign equality includes the following elements:
>
> (d) The territorial integrity and political independence of the State are inviolable;
> (e) Each State has the right freely to choose and develop its political, social, economic and cultural systems.

The Legal Adviser to the United States Mission to the United Nations at the time the Declaration on Friendly Relations was drafted concluded that the section on self-determination "contains some tortured phraseology and . . . may not be set out in the most logical order, [but] a careful reading of it will show it to be a moderate and workable text."[16] Moderate, perhaps, but its workability in the post-colonial era is uncertain. First, the Declaration on Friendly Relations offers no definition of "peoples." Neither of the two purposes it sets forth suggests that self-determination is intended to provide every ethnically distinct people with its own state. In fact, the particular mention of the "distinct" status of "a colony or other Non-Self-Governing Territory" suggests a limited scope for the right of self-determination. Similarly, the use in the same paragraph of the singular "people" suggests that various minorities within a territory may not enjoy the same right of self-determination as that possessed by the people as a whole.

   Following previous United Nations formulations of the principle of self-determination, the Declaration on Friendly Relations places the goal of territorial integrity or political unity as a principle superior to that of self-determination: "Nothing in the foregoing paragraphs" shall be construed to authorize or encourage "any action" which would limit this principle. However, this restriction applies only to those states which conduct themselves "in compliance with the principle of equal rights and self-determination of peoples as described above and [are] *thus* possessed of a government representing the whole people belonging to the territory without distinction as to race, creed or colour." The requirement of representativeness suggests internal democracy. However, such a requirement does not imply that the only government that can be deemed "representative" is one that explicitly recognizes all of the various ethnic, religious, linguistic, and other communities within a state. Indeed, such a state might itself be considered to violate the requirement that it represent "the whole people . . . *without distinction* as to race, creed or colour."

A more persuasive interpretation, consistent with the concerns of most United Nations members when the declaration was adopted in 1970, is that a state will not be considered to be representative if it formally excludes a particular group from participation in the political process, based on that group's race, creed, or color (such as South Africa or Southern Rhodesia under the Smith regime). At the very least, a state with a democratic, non-discriminatory voting system whose political life is dominated by an ethnic majority would not be unrepresentative within the terms of the Declaration on Friendly Relations.

C. The International Covenants on Human Rights

The Declaration on Friendly Relations was adopted within a consciously political context, but it also reflects the promotion of self-determination as a "human right" in other United Nations forums. In 1948, on the same day that it adopted the Universal Declaration of Human Rights, the General Assembly requested that the Commission on Human Rights "continue to give priority in its work to the preparation of a draft Covenant on Human Rights and draft measures of implementation." This request eventually led to the 1966 adoption of the International Covenant on Economic, Social and Cultural Rights and the International Covenant on Civil and Political Rights (ICCPR), including its Optional Protocol, both of which entered into force in 1976.[17] Each has now been ratified by over 110 countries, and the covenants contain the most definitive legally binding statement of the contemporary right of self-determination.

The initial intention was to draft a single treaty, but disputes over the relative weight of civil-political and economic-social-cultural rights, as well as disagreements over the appropriate implementation procedures to be developed for each set of rights, led to a decision to draft two covenants. This decision, however, did not affect the provision on self-determination; the first article of both covenants is identical:

Article 1
1. All peoples have the right of self-determination. By virtue of that right they freely determine their political status and freely pursue their economic, social and cultural development.
2. All peoples may, for their own ends, freely dispose of their natural wealth and resources without prejudice to any obligations arising out of international economic co-operation, based upon the principle of mutual benefit, and international law. In no case may a people be deprived of its own means of subsistence.
3. The States Parties to the present Covenant, including those having responsibility for the administration of Non-Self-Governing and Trust Territories, shall promote the realization of the right of self-determination,

and shall respect that right, in conformity with the provisions of the Charter of the United Nations.

The relatively straightforward language of the first paragraph in particular is commonly cited as evidence of the universality of the right to self-determination, although its formulation does little to define the scope of the right. Nevertheless, the reference to "all" peoples and the fact that the article is found in human rights treaties intended to have universal applicability suggest a scope beyond that of decolonization.

As with previous articulations of the right of self-determination, one finds no definition of "peoples." Nothing suggests that "peoples" should be read as equivalent to "state." At the same time, however, substitution of "state" for "peoples" would neither render the article meaningless nor suggest an interpretation contrary to the recognized rights of states. For example, a state certainly has the right to determine freely its political status, pursue economic development, and dispose of its natural wealth and resources.

The covenants were discussed in the Commission on Human Rights from 1949 through 1955, when draft texts of each were forwarded to the Third Committee of the General Assembly. The Third Committee discussed the final wording for another eleven years before the covenants were adopted by the General Assembly and opened for signature and ratification in 1966. Unfortunately, these debates provide little clarification of the essential problem of defining a people and thus determining the scope of the right of self-determination.

[Hannum discusses in some detail here the U.N. General Assembly's role in the "self-determination article"—eds.]

The *travaux préparatoires* of any treaty are notoriously unreliable, because vague or imprecise treaty language is often adopted intentionally due to disagreement over the exact meaning of a particular provision. Interpretation is even more difficult in the context of multilateral treaties such as the covenants. Nevertheless, a careful examination of the legislative history of the covenants leads to the conclusion that a restrictive interpretation of the right of self-determination comports with the views of the majority of the states that supported the right.[18] This conclusion is supported by the Director of the United Nations Division of Human Rights at the time, who was intimately involved in the process of drafting the covenants. He observed that, despite the broad formulation of article 1 of the covenants, self-determination "would be understood in United Nations doctrine as a right belonging only to colonial peoples, which once it had been successfully exercised could not be invoked again, and it would not include a right of secession except for colonies."[19]

[Hannum details the varied interpretations of "self-determination" supported by delegations within the General Assembly's Third Committee.]

D. Subsequent Interpretation

Both covenants entered into force in 1976. States are required under article 40 of the Covenant on Civil and Political Rights to submit periodic reports to a body of experts, the Human Rights Committee, on the manner in which they have implemented the rights guaranteed in the Covenant. These reports and the subsequent discussions between Committee members and government representatives could provide evidence of the interpretation given by the Committee to both the internal and external aspects of self-determination.[20] Unfortunately, most countries have not specifically addressed article 1, or have done so in such general terms that little is added to an understanding of its content.

The Indian reservation to article 1 exemplifies the view of many countries that support a restricted interpretation of "self-determination":

> With reference to article 1 [of both covenants] . . . the Government of the Republic of India declares that the words "the right of self-determination" appearing in [those articles] apply only to the peoples under foreign domination and that these words do not apply to sovereign independent States or to a section of a people or nation—which is the essence of national integrity.

Three states, each a former colonial power, filed formal objections to the Indian reservation. The Netherlands stated that

> the right of self-determination as embodied in the Covenants is conferred upon all peoples. . . . Any attempt to limit the scope of this right or to attach conditions not provided for in the relevant instruments would undermine the concept of self-determination itself and would thereby seriously weaken its universally acceptable character.

France objected because the Indian reservation "attaches conditions not provided for by the Charter of the United Nations." The Federal Republic of Germany "strongly objected" to the Indian reservation, stating:

> The right of self-determination . . . applies to all peoples and not only to those under foreign domination. . . . The Federal Government cannot consider as valid any interpretation of the right of self-determination which is contrary to the clear language of the provisions in question. It moreover considers that any limitation of their applicability to all nations is incompatible with the object and purpose of the Covenants.

In a subsequent appearance before the Human Rights Committee, India reaffirmed the position it had adopted upon ratification and stated explicitly that the United Nations Charter as well as article 1 of the Covenant provide that "the right to self-determination in the international context applies only to dependent Territories and peoples."

The Human Rights Committee has also commented on the scope of the article 1 right of self-determination.[21] Under the Optional Protocol to the Covenant on Civil and Political Rights, individuals may address communications to the Human Rights Committee regarding the violation of rights guaranteed under the Covenant.[22] Several such individual applications have raised the issue of whether Indian bands in Canada enjoy a right of self-determination. However, the Committee has decided that although individuals who claim that their rights have been violated have standing to raise complaints under the Optional Protocol, article 1 confers a right of self-determination only upon "peoples, as such."[23] A similar attempt by residents of the Italian South Tyrol was rejected by the Committee in November 1990.[24] Although states can raise complaints regarding the violation of the right of a "people" to self determination under the optional provisions of article 41 of the Covenant,[25] no such complaint has been filed by any state.

Under paragraph 4 of article 40 of the ICCPR, the Human Rights Committee has the authority to make "general comments" on state reports submitted to it. Thus far, the Committee has commented on several provisions of the Covenant, considering both substantive questions and procedural issues related to reporting requirements. The Committee's general comment on article 1 was not adopted until 1984, and it does nothing to clarify the meaning of "self-determination" or the scope of state obligations under article 1. The Committee's chairman accurately noted that the right of self-determination is "one of the most awkward to define, since the abuse of that right could jeopardize international peace and security in giving States the impression that their territorial integrity was threatened."[26] Some Committee members have suggested that the right of self-determination extends beyond the colonial context, but the Committee as a whole has failed to provide any more precise delineation of the right.

E. The Conference on Security and Co-Operation in Europe

The Final Act of the Conference on Security and Co-Operation in Europe ("CSCE Final Act" or "Helsinki Final Act"), adopted in 1975 in Helsinki by 35 European states, is a regional, political document rather than a universal, legally binding agreement.[27] Nevertheless, it represents a significant understanding between the Western and Soviet blocs on a variety of issues. The CSCE Final Act addresses security, economic, and humanitarian concerns, and provides for a series of follow-up meetings which have offered an important forum for developing many of the themes in the CSCE Final Act.

Among the "Principles Guiding Relations between Participating States" agreed to in 1975 was respect for the "equal rights and self-determination of peoples." Principle VIII states:

> By virtue of the principle of equal rights and self-determination of
> peoples, all peoples always have the right, in full freedom, to determine,
> when and as they wish, their internal and external political status,
> without external interference, and to pursue as they wish their political,
> economic, social and cultural development.

Some commentators have found the Helsinki language much more expansive than previous international pronouncements regarding self-determination.[28] Indeed, the specific language, providing that "all" peoples "always" have the right to determine their internal and external political status, goes beyond the more terse formulation in the covenants on human rights. However, this formulation must be understood in the context of the principles of the inviolability of frontiers (principle III) and the territorial integrity of states (principle IV) also proclaimed in the Helsinki Final Act. Again, the proper interpretation of the right of self-determination turns on the definition of "peoples." There is no indication that sub-state groups are to determine their political status or pursue political and economic development without reference to the larger population of the state.

A more recent reference to the right of self-determination at a CSCE summit meeting would seem consciously to limit earlier formulations. The November 1990 Charter of Paris "reaffirms the equal rights of peoples and their right to self-determination in conformity with the Charter of the United Nations and with the relevant norms of international law, including those relating to territorial integrity of States."[29]

In the context of Soviet domination of Eastern Europe until the late 1980s, the 1975 Helsinki formulation may be seen merely as a Cold War reaffirmation of the right of the people of a state to be free from external influence in choosing its own form of government. There was no suggestion at Helsinki or in subsequent CSCE meetings that the right of self-determination could justify secession by an oppressed minority. "It seems that the right of self-determination cannot be realized on account of territorial integrity and secure borders, and so it does not imply the right to secession."[30]

F. The African Charter on Human and Peoples' Rights
Among other major human rights treaties, only the African Charter on Human and Peoples' Rights refers to self-determination.[31] The African Charter mentions the equality of peoples in article 19, including a statement that "nothing shall justify the domination of a people by another." Article 20 sets forth the right of self-determination.

Nearly all African states, which were among the leaders in developing the post-1945 "right" of self-determination in the context of decolonization, have adopted a very narrow interpretation of the right in the post-colonial context of independence.[32] Because of the extreme ethnic heterogeneity of most African states and the resulting difficulties in developing a sense of statehood in the post-independence period, the principles of territorial integrity and national unity have been widely felt to be more fundamental than that of self-determination.[33]

II. THE MEANING OF SELF-DETERMINATION

Although it is debatable whether the right of self-determination is *jus cogens*,[34] self-determination has undoubtedly attained the status of a "right" in international law. Formal statements by governments, the adoption by consensus of numerous United Nations resolutions, and the fact that more than half of the world's states have accepted the right of self-determination through their adherence to one or both of the United Nations covenants on human rights would seem to confirm the existence of self-determination as a norm of international law. Finally, governments and scholars from all regional and political perspectives accept the right of peoples to self-determination.[35] While it seems clear that self-determination has attained the status of a right, the scope of that right must be explored.

One controversial question regarding the right of self-determination is whether the right has been recognized outside the context of decolonization. As noted by a prominent British legal scholar, "the legal right of self-determination clearly applies to non-self-governing territories, trust territories and mandated territories. . . . Whether it also applies to other territories is uncertain."[36]

The various texts discussed above and the *travaux préparatoires* of the covenants do not establish that the right of self-determination, *defined as a unilateral right to independence*, was intended to apply outside the context of decolonization. As noted above, self-determination has meant at least decolonization since 1945. However, when addressing self-determination claims based on ethnicity or nationalist sentiment, one must recognize the shift from the territorially based *right* of self-determination developed by the United Nations in the context of decolonization to the ethnic-linguistic-national *principle* of self-determination advocated by Wilson and others in 1919. The difference is not only semantic. It reflects a fundamental limit on the definition that self-determination has acquired during the past four decades. The confusion created by these two often contradictory principles of territory and people was noted by the International Court of Justice in the Frontier Dispute case[37] and is also reflected in the EC position on Yugoslavia, discussed below.

Despite the apparently absolute formulation in various United Nations resolutions and the two international covenants on human rights, self-determination has never been considered an absolute right to be exercised irrespective of competing claims or rights, except in the limited context of "classic" colonialism. Only in situations where a European power dominated a non-contiguous territory, in which a majority of the population was indigenous or non-metropolitan, has a territory been considered to have an absolute right of self-determination— a right to independence, if that was what the population desired. In such circumstances, any claim by the colonial power that the exercise of self-determination would conflict with the right to territorial integrity has been rejected.

However, self-determination through independence has been rejected by the international community where this paradigm does not exist. Independence is not necessarily an option in situations in which (1) forcible incorporation of adjacent territory has led to absorption or displacement of the former population, and the resulting exercise of sovereignty has been generally accepted by the international community;[38] or (2) the colony in question is ethnically, historically, or culturally related to a large independent non-European neighbor.[39]

In such cases of "problematic" colonialism, where foreign domination has been blurred by the passage of time, demographic shifts, or historical claims, the international community has adopted a pragmatic, balancing approach to claims of a right of self-determination by the purported "colonial" people. Many of the charges of hypocrisy or inconsistency of United Nations practice are based on the false assumption that external self-determination was intended to be an absolute right extended to "all" peoples. A comparison to United States jurisprudence may be helpful. The First Amendment to the United States Constitution contains an absolute injunction: "Congress shall make no Law . . . abridging the freedom of speech." Nevertheless, the United States Supreme Court has long held that some speech, such as pornography, libel, and commercial speech, is subject to regulation. Similarly, the grammatically absolute grant of self-determination to all peoples has always been interpreted in a limited manner by the United Nations: all classic colonial peoples are entitled to immediate independence, while those falling outside that paradigm do not possess an absolute right to independence.

This does not mean that other aspects of the right of self-determination are also so limited. The covenants' description of the right of self-determination as a right of "all peoples" and the CSCE reference to "all" peoples "always" having the right of self-determination cannot be ignored. Both the right of a people organized as a state to freedom from external domination and the right of the people of a state to a government that reflects their wishes are essential components of the right of self-determination. These rights have universal applicability, and the statement that "no State has accepted the right of all peoples to self-determination"[40] is correct only if one equates self-determination exclusively with secession or independence.

States and their peoples have the right of independence from foreign domination. The General Assembly has expressed its concern "at the continuation of acts or threats of foreign military intervention and occupation that are threatening to suppress, or have already suppressed, the right to self-determination of an increasing number of sovereign peoples and nations."[41] Existing states that have been invaded or are otherwise controlled by a foreign power have a right of self-determination, a right to overthrow the invaders and re-establish true independence. The reference to "sovereign" peoples applies only to states or classic colonies subjected to military occupation, including Palestine, Western Sahara, and East Timor, but not to sub-state groups within recognized states.[42]

Self-determination is also relevant to the matrix of human rights law which has developed over the past four decades, including specific rights applicable to minorities and indigenous peoples.[43] Defining self-determination as self-government is consistent with early United Nations formulations, including the Charter, and its implications are only now being fully considered in the context of autonomous and other domestic constitutional arrangements. . . .

These observations do not dispose of two fundamental issues: defining the "peoples" entitled to self-determination and clarifying the scope of the right of self-determination. As discussed below, the reaction of states and international organizations to the disintegration of Yugoslavia and the Soviet Union has done little to advance our understanding. However, the political positions expressed do support the proposition that self-determination remains a viable principle of contemporary international law.

A. Defining the "Self"

Most discussions of "self-determination" begin with an attempt to break the term into its component parts: the definition of the relevant "self" and the manner in which its fate should be determined. Indeed, defining the "people" or the "self" that possesses the right of self-determination is the key issue in analyzing the scope of the right.

Defining the "self" normally includes subjective and objective components. At a minimum, it is necessary for members of the group concerned to think of themselves as a distinct group. It is also necessary for the group to have certain objectively determinable common characteristics, e.g., ethnicity, language, history, or religion. Of course, everyone belongs to many different groups at the same time. Defining which groups are relevant to the purposes of the right of self-determination is the challenge.

One critical observer of United Nations practice concludes that definitions of the relevant "self" have been hopelessly political and confused, yet surely one can arrive at a generally acceptable definition of "peoples" who possess the right of self-determination. One commentator provides a relatively straightforward set of criteria: "a people consists of a community of individuals bound together by mutual loyalties, an identifiable tradition, and a common cultural awareness, with historic ties to a given territory."[44] Other elements are suggested by General

Assembly Resolution 1541, which defines a non-self-governing territory as one which is geographically separate, ethnically or culturally distinct, and arbitrarily subordinated to the metropolitan state.

There are no doubt difficult or marginal cases, but in many instances it is rather easy to decide whether a given community is a "people" as long as one does not immediately attach legal consequences to the appellation. For example, there can be no doubt that Tibetans, Kurds, Tatars, Navajos, Basques, and Yanomami are "a body of persons composing a community, tribe, race, or nation." Conversely, it is difficult to identify the common characteristics—apart from citizenship—of Swiss, Indians, Nigerians, Guatemalans, and Americans, yet each of these groups is identified by the international community as a "people." Of course, there is no requirement that a state be composed of only a single people.

The impact of "settler" populations in a colonial territory presents even more complicated issues. Where the settlers constitute a dominant minority which practices systematic racial discrimination—as was formerly the situation in Rhodesia and South Africa—the United Nations has had no difficulty in upholding the right of (internal) self-determination of the indigenous majority. Other cases have been less clear: Indian settlers (initially brought by the British) in Fiji were considered to be part of the Fijian people. In contrast, the Ceylonese disenfranchisement of several hundred thousand Indian "estate Tamils"—brought to Ceylon in circumstances that are difficult to distinguish from Fiji—was unchallenged by all but India. Questions have been raised regarding status of British settler populations in Gibraltar and the Falkland (Malvinas) Islands, as well as the status of the ethnic Russian populations in the former Soviet republics. . . .

One critical commentator has concluded that

> [f]rom whichever angle the question of defining the "self" within the new "UN Law of Self-Determination" is approached . . . the Wilsonian dilemmas have persisted. Except for the most obvious cases of "decolonization", objective criteria have not been developed or applied for preferring one claim over another or for delimiting which population belongs to which territory.[45]

The recent attempt by the European Community (EC) to address these questions in Yugoslavia has been no more successful. If the former Yugoslav republics were exercising their right of self-determination, that right does not appear to have belonged to any objectively identifiable "people," unless "people" is defined simply as those who inhabit a particular administrative territory. As noted above, the population of Bosnia-Hercegovina is very heterogeneous. Similarly, it is difficult to identify the distinctive characteristics of the "people" of Macedonia.

Rather than defining people in an ethnic sense, the EC adopted a territorially based recognition policy, insisting that the internal administrative borders of Yugoslavia remain as the new international frontiers. While this is consistent with the post-1945 emphasis on territory in the context of decolonization, it is difficult to argue that Slovenia, Croatia, Bosnia-Hercegovina, and Macedonia were in a "neo-colonial" relationship with Yugoslavia/Serbia; certainly that argument was not made by the peoples concerned.

While the territorial approach has the advantage of simplicity, it fails utterly to deal with new minorities "trapped" by the creation of new states. In Bosnia-Hercegovina, for example, nearly two-thirds of the total eligible voters (99.7% of those who actually voted) approved independence in a referendum; however, the referendum was boycotted by the major Serb party. Thus, independence clearly did not enjoy the support of the second most important ethnic community in the territory. In such circumstances, which "people" should be granted the right of self-determination?

This neo-decolonization territorial approach can have troubling consequences if used to legitimize secession for groups possessing a distinct political status while denying the right of secession to territorially based ethnic communities not formally organized into political units. This seems to be the position taken by the Arbitration Commission established by the International Conference on Yugoslavia, which has implied that the right to secede varies according to the degree of autonomy recognized by the central government. In its first opinion, the Commission observed that "the existence of the State implies that federal organs represent the components of the Federation and wield effective power."[46] Since the composition and functioning of the essential organs of the Yugoslav Federation no longer satisfied "the requirements of participation and representativeness inherent in a federal State," the Commission concluded "that the Socialist Federal Republic of Yugoslavia is engaged in a process of dissolution."

Regrettably, this approach will encourage states to resist granting precisely those political and economic rights which might constitute the most realistic and effective response to claims for self-determination. In effect, a state would be penalized if it addressed ethnic or regional concerns by devolving power to autonomous regions. This is directly contrary to the message that should be sent by the international community to states faced with ethnic or regional conflicts.

B. What Status May the "Self" Determine?

Once the "self" has been identified, full independence is the most common result of the exercise of self-determination. However, while full independence has been the result in all but a handful of cases, there are several ways in which self-determination may be achieved. As noted above, General Assembly Resolution 1541 stated that a non-self-governing territory under chapter XI of the Charter can achieve "a full measure of self-government" through emergence as a sovereign independent state, free association with an independent state, or integration with an independent state. The 1970 Declaration on Friendly Relations expanded the available options to "any other political status freely determined by a people."

Resolution 1541 imposes detailed requirements on non-self-governing territories that opt for any status short of independence. Free association with another state requires a "free and voluntary choice . . . through informed and democratic processes," and must include the right of unilateral modification of the association by the peoples of the territory. Integration must be on the basis of "complete equality" between peoples of the territory and the country they are joining. Also, integration can only come about if the territory has attained "an advanced stage of self-government with free political institutions," and if integration is chosen with "full knowledge" and through democratic processes "impartially conducted and based on universal adult suffrage." By contrast, there are no procedural requirements for a non-self-governing territory to emerge as a sovereign independent state, perhaps because there is less danger that such an outcome will be inappropriately influenced by the former colonial power.

Assuming that the requisite consent has been demonstrated, there is a wide range of options by which a people may choose to exercise self-determination. Of course, any option short of full independence requires the consent of another state or people—confederation, federation, or autonomy implies the participation of at least two parties. In such a situation, one has to speak of "self"-determination exercised by both sides, because neither can compel the other to accept its preferred solution.

III. SECESSION

Where independence is the goal, acceptance of one group's claim to self-determination necessarily implies denial of another group's competing claim of territorial integrity. When a self-determination claim comes from only a portion of the entire population of a state—the latter having already been recognized by the international community as representing its "people"—denial of self-determination to the group can be seen as merely supporting the self-determination of the larger "people."

Secession is not presently recognized as a right under international law, nor does international law prohibit secession.

> The express acceptance in . . . [relevant United Nations resolutions] of the principles of the national unity and the territorial integrity of the State implies non-recognition of the right of secession. The right of peoples to self-determination, as it emerges from the United Nations, exists for peoples under colonial and alien domination, that is to say,

who are not living under the legal form of a State. The right to secession from an existing State Member of the United Nations does not exist as such in the instruments or in the practice followed by the Organization, since to seek to invoke it in order to disrupt the national unity and the territorial integrity of a State would be a misapplication of the principle of self-determination contrary to the purposes of the United Nations Charter.[47]

Several authors have argued for recognition of a "right to secession" as part of the right of self-determination,[48] but such a right does not yet exist. Professor Gros Espiell has observed that "if. . .beneath the guise of ostensible national unity, colonial and alien domination does in fact exist, whatever legal formula may be used in an attempt to conceal it, the right of the subject people concerned cannot be disregarded without international law being violated."[49] However, attempts to assert that a given nation, minority, or other group is under alien or colonial domination have only been universally accepted when the assertions relate to the internal self-determination of a recognized state under foreign occupation or control.

This conclusion does not answer the question of whether a norm legitimizing secession under certain circumstances should be created. There are at least four principal arguments in favor of the right to secede.

The first might be termed the liberal democratic theory.[50] This theory holds that, since the legitimacy of any government must rest upon the consent of the governed, the governed have the inalienable right to withdraw that consent whenever they wish. . . . While this approach has the appeal of consistency and simplicity, there are the immediately apparent problems of implementation: How is a decision to secede to be reached? Who draws the boundaries? What about enclaves? There are also more substantive questions: Should rich regions be permitted effectively to discard poorer parts of a country? Is a decision to secede irreversible? What are the implications for majority rule if a minority always retains the ability to opt out? These issues, along with the extreme unlikelihood that such a theory would ever be politically acceptable, suggest that the absolutist philosophical approach might at best serve as a starting point, despite its appealing simplicity and theoretical consistency.[51]

A second argument, which has attracted a great deal of attention since the 1970s, is founded on humanitarian or human rights concerns.

> The right of secession is seen as a variant of the right of self-defense—
> you defend yourself by seceding from an oppressive system. . . . There
> can be compelling reasons for secession such as if the physical survival or
> the cultural autonomy of a nation is threatened, or if a population would
> feel economically excluded and permanently deprived.[52]

. . . If a minority's physical existence is threatened, or if there is intense discrimination against a particular segment of society, some reaction against oppression is undoubtedly justified; even the Universal Declaration of Human Rights refers to "rebellion against tyranny and oppression" as a "last resort." However, secession may not be the most appropriate remedy. Overthrowing the oppressive government and restoring human rights would be as philosophically and politically sound as secession. And while secession may end the oppression, the norms of national unity and territorial integrity suggest that a less drastic alternative would be preferable. Finally, as demonstrated in some of the former republics of the Soviet Union and Yugoslavia, there is no guarantee that new states will be any more protective of human rights than those they replace. . . .

Unfortunately, asserting a right to secede in order to end discrimination becomes somewhat circular, unless one can agree on the scope of the rights allegedly being violated. Do minorities have the right not only to safeguard their own culture, language, and identity, but also to exercise political and economic authority over their own affairs? Is the fact that a political group finds itself permanently in the minority sufficient to give it the right to secede? . . .

A more persuasive position would hold that secession can be legally justified only when the very existence of a group is threatened. Genocide is illegal under customary international law; gross violations of human rights are also prohibited. However, no society or culture is static, and many groups find their traditional values under pressure from dominant, "modern" societies surrounding them. "Languages [and presumably cultures] are now dying at an alarming rate."[53] In the absence of active discrimination or human rights violations, is this sufficient to justify secession?

A more manageable approach would require a deliberate attack on a group before endowing it with a right to secede. The mere desire to insulate one's group from ill-defined pressures from a dominant society cannot suffice to engage international law and obligate the international community either to support the secession or to oppose forceful opposition to the secession. Justifying secession by a "nation" or "people" in response to anything less than the most serious human rights violations assumes a principle to which there has never been agreement. It assumes that each ethnic group or culture has the right to exercise power within its own "sovereign" state. International law should recognize a right to secession only in the rare circumstance when the physical existence of a territorially concentrated group is threatened by gross violations of fundamental human rights.

A third, more comprehensive theoretical justification of the right to secession has identified a list of criteria that might be used in specific cases to evaluate secessionist claims. Lee Buchheit's ambitious approach attempts to achieve a "calculation of legitimacy" through a balancing of the internal merits of the claimants' case [for secession] against the justifiable concerns of the international community expressed in its calculation of the disruptive consequences of the situation. By balancing these two aspects, the community will avoid being forced to articulate a single, immutable standard of legitimacy, to be applied with arithmetical remorselessness against each and every group in the same way. . . .

The pragmatic approach of Buchheit and others is welcome, but unfortunately the proposed criteria provide no readily manageable norm against which to judge the legitimacy of secessionist claims. The very flexibility that characterizes pragmatism leaves unanswered the fundamental question of whether ethnic homogeneity is a legitimate criterion for statehood. If ethnicity (or culture or religion) is not a determining factor, then we return to the philosophically absolutist approach of permitting any secession supported by a majority of the seceding people—however that people may be defined. Determining whether a particular secession would promote "general international harmony" or "human dignity" sounds much more like the relativist geopolitical calculations of the victors at Versailles than the absolutist anti-colonial advocacy of the United Nations General Assembly. . . .

Lea Brilmayer offers a fourth method for evaluating secessionist claims.[54] After persuasively criticizing theories of self-determination that rely on definitions of "people" or the principle of consent of the governed, Brilmayer proposes a territorially based test incorporating the following criteria: the immediacy and nature of the historical grievance of the secessionist group, the extent to which the group has kept its self-determination claim alive, and the extent to which the disputed territory has been settled by members of the dominant group. Brilmayer concedes that "the opponents of secession are probably correct as a matter of positive law," but offers little real guidance as to the weight to be given to her proposed criteria. The rather simplistic conclusion that "whatever conflict exists is not between principles, but over land," is of little help.

The fact that most theories concerned with the legitimacy of secession turn out to be geopolitical balancing acts is no surprise; the end result of secession is the recognition of the seceding entity as an independent state.[55] While the status of an entity as a state subject to international law may be independent of formal recognition, "recognition, as a public act of state, is an optional and political act and there is no legal duty in this regard."[56] Thus, the search for legal criteria for secession that can be counterposed against geopolitical or strategic concerns would seem to be illusory, as demonstrated only too clearly by the attitude of the European Community and others to Yugoslavia and the Soviet Union. Georgia and Macedonia went unrecognized for a considerable time, not because their "peoples" had no right of self-determination, but because their governments were thought to be either insufficiently democratic (Georgia) or to have chosen a name reflecting secret territorial ambitions (Macedonia).

A brief survey of attitudes towards several post-colonial secessionist attempts provides little support for any but the geopolitical non-theory of secession. The secession of Bangladesh, opposed initially by the vast majority of states, owes more to the Indian army and Soviet political support than to the principle of self-determination.

It has been suggested that there was no real African consensus opposing the attempted secession by Biafra from Nigeria, but only five states (Tanzania, Gabon, Ivory Coast, Zambia, and Haiti) formally recognized Biafra's independence. Katanga's attempted secession from the former Belgian Congo at the time of independence led to United Nations intervention in support of the central Congolese government. Other secessionist attempts, from Bougainville to Kurdistan, from Punjab to Quebec, have similarly failed to gain any significant international support. . . .

The dissolution of the Soviet Union and Czechoslovakia resulted from agreement and thus created no precedent for cases of contested secession. The voluntary division or dissolution of a state is certainly within that state's right of internal self-determination, unless the international community views the division as a fraudulent attempt to prevent real self-determination.

The contemporary European attitude towards secession as a component of self-determination is reflected in the response to the dissolution of Yugoslavia adopted by the twelve members of the European Community, an attitude generally followed by other CSCE members.[57] In the period immediately preceding and following the declarations of independence by the Yugoslav republics of Slovenia and Croatia in June 1991, the United States and the European Community supported Yugoslav unity, although they opposed the use of force by the federal authorities. A few days after the declarations, German and Austrian government officials began to suggest that the "right of self-determination" of Slovenia and Croatia should be recognized, but neither government recognized the two republics as independent states at that time.

While the initial opposition to recognition may have been grounded in fears of dangerous political instability inside and beyond Yugoslavia (fears which later proved to be fully justified), it was also consistent with restrictive legal formulations of the right of self-determination. The clear implication was that all of the parties considered acceptance of the newly declared independent status of the two republics to be a political rather than a legal question, not one whose response was mandated by international law.

Following armed clashes between federal Yugoslav forces and Slovenian forces, and the seizure of substantial Croatian territory by Croatian Serbs, the European Community adopted a "common position on the process of recognition" of new states in Eastern Europe and the Soviet Union. Notably missing in this declaration is any reference to a right of secession or even to the right of "peoples" to self-determination, although that terminology is used in the relevant CSCE documents. The EC declaration is tied to the inherently political issue of recognition, as amply evidenced by the requirements imposed on the potential new states with respect to democracy, human rights, minority rights, nuclear non-proliferation, and arbitration. "This extensive catalog of criteria, far in excess of traditional standards for recognition of statehood, confirms that the Community was not applying general international law in the determination of its position."[58] The reference to "normal standards of international practice and the political realities in each case" does not indicate that the former Yugoslav republics had an absolute right of self-determination under international law. The cases of Yugoslavia and the Soviet Union were formally considered both by the new states themselves (perhaps excluding Serbia and Montenegro) and by the international community to be instances of dissolution rather than secession. The question facing the European Community and others was what new sovereigns to recognize on former Yugoslav and Soviet territory.

[Hannum discusses here the Bosnia-Hercegovina case, and the role played by an EC Arbitration Commission—eds.]

Europe's approach to the Yugoslav conflict represents a one-time-only reaction to secessionist demands based on no discernable criteria other than the desire of some territorially based population to secede. The principle that borders should not be altered except by mutual agreement has been elevated to a hypocritical immutability and contradicted by the very act of recognizing secessionist states. New minorities have been trapped, not by any comprehensible legal principle, but by the historical accident of administrative borders drawn by an undemocratic government. Ethnic issues are ignored despite the fact that both Croatia and Bosnia-Hercegovina suffered greater violence than Slovenia precisely because Slovenia is much more ethnically homogeneous.

Support for secession should be grounded in the desires of a substantial majority of the population, and the opposition of a significant proportion of the population to independence should influence the international response to independence claims. If adherence to the principle of one-person, one-vote is deemed insufficient to validate a central government's maintenance of territorial integrity, then neither should merely winning a plebescite confer legitimacy on the numerical majority of a seceding entity.

It is also unreasonable to maintain the fiction of immutable borders under all circumstances, although the principle that frontiers cannot be changed by force need not be abandoned. Newly recognized states that base their self-determination claims on ethnic or religious concerns must recognize the legitimacy of similar claims made within the new state. Any border alterations must be based on the results of popular referenda, conducted with respect for human rights, although common-sense limitations of geographical contiguity may be imposed. However, the "price" for recognition of a new state based on ethnic self-determination or the accident of internal administrative borders should be acceptance of the possibility of peaceful changes in those borders: the new state must grant the same right of self-determination to its ethnic communities as it claimed for itself.

In light of the confusing precedents, many analysts have conceded defeat. "The complexity of the factors involved in claims for separation makes it impossible to recommend rules which would automatically determine the applicability of the right of self-determination."[59] "It would be uselessly pedantic . . . to draw up rules for when secession is right. It is enough to say that no minority is likely to attempt anything like this unless it or a substantial section of it has been driven desperate by events."[60] The latter observation may not be entirely accurate; many secessionist movements are driven by power-hungry elites. However, the quest for manageable criteria to evaluate secessionist claims, except where the physical existence of a group is threatened by gross violations of fundamental human rights, does seem to be misplaced.

Criteria are even more difficult to identify when there is no consensus on the fundamental issue of whether the homogeneous "nation-state" is the ideal form of government. British India, Rwanda-Urundi, Ethiopia, and the Trust Territory of the Pacific Islands were divided at least in part to achieve ethnically or religiously more homogeneous states. That objective remains the justification for the de facto division of Cyprus. Yet there is certainly as much moral rectitude in preferring a tolerant, multi-cultural state to a state founded on exclusionary ethnicity; this may in part explain the world's apparent preference for a pluralistic Bosnia-Hercegovina. Moreover, the right of the majority to unite deserves as much recognition as the right to separate.

Such fundamental issues cannot be properly addressed in the abstract. Outside the colonial context, however, "self-determination" has remained an abstraction for the past century.

IV. SELF-DETERMINATION AND HUMAN RIGHTS

[Hannum discusses at length the relationship between self-determination and human rights. Excerpts of his analysis follow—eds.]

Although the development of international human rights norms under the United Nations occurred at roughly the same time that decolonization was acquiring the status of a fundamental legal right, the drafting history of article 1 of the covenants demonstrates that the commitment to self-determination and decolonization preceded adoption of the broad panoply of human rights that exists today. Prior to states' widespread acceptance of the legitimacy of human rights norms, control over one's own government was seen as a necessary prerequisite to political participation and the protection of one's ethnic or national identity. There were no other internationally accepted means of securing such rights.

But if the content of self-determination is examined more closely, it is apparent that much of it has been subsumed by subsequent developments in human rights law. In particular, the two fundamental rights just mentioned—the right to participate effectively in the political and economic life of one's country and the right to protect one's identity—are likely to become an increasingly important focus of human rights activists and theorists in the future. . . .

Minority rights per se have occupied only a marginal place in international human rights law. . . .

Fortunately, recent initiatives by the United Nations and within Europe are expanding the substantive and procedural protections available to minorities.[61] . . . It is these rights, exercised by communities, that are essential to protect the identity of threatened peoples, whether they are classified as minorities, indigenous peoples, or regional or cultural communities. Protection of these rights, combined with the right of effective participation in the political and economic process, is the primary contemporary rationale for the exercise of the right of self-determination. . . .

V. Conclusion

The resurgence of ethnic conflicts in Europe in the late 1980s and the attempts to justify secession through assertion of the right of self-determination respond to at least two distinct issues. For both issues, "self-determination," often at least superficially based on ethnicity, religion, or language, is proclaimed as legitimizing resistance to central government authorities. However, the motivating concerns surrounding each issue are in fact quite different.

The first issue, perhaps the one most keenly felt in eastern Europe in the early 1990s, is lack of democracy—occurring most commonly under centralized authoritarian rule that denies real participation in the political process. Although the central authorities may be of a different ethnic or linguistic group, the primary complaint by ethnic or regional minorities is lack of political power, not discrimination. In Wilsonian terms, the primary need is for internal self-determination.

Such a situation results in human rights violations for all citizens of the state, not just minorities, although ethnic cohesion may provide the most convenient vehicle for organizing opposition to the central government. While there are exceptions, it is striking how few claims in such circumstances initially include a demand for full independence based on ethnic or linguistic criteria.

A second factor triggering ethnic conflict and moves toward secession is the existence of discrimination against or persecution of minorities by the state and its majority population. This persecution leads minorities to fear not only for their physical safety but also for the survival of their culture. Where the majority refuses even to recognize a substantial minority or ethnically distinct nation, and prevents it from sharing in the life of the state, external self-determination or secession may seem like the last hope for those who feel they are treated as aliens in their own country. Responding to authoritarian or discriminatory governments requires the establishment of democratic institutions, real guarantees of non-discrimination, and the assurance that people have a meaningful degree of control over their own affairs. "Self-determination may be understood as a right of cultural groupings to the political institutions necessary to allow them to exist and develop according to their distinctive characteristics. The institutions and degree of autonomy, necessarily, will vary as the circumstances of each case vary."[62]

It is not enough simply to invoke "self-determination" as a code word for ethnic supremacy or the assertion of increasingly vague "sovereignty." A slogan cannot by itself respond to the problems of political powerlessness and economic marginalization. As demonstrated too clearly in the former Yugoslavia and Soviet Union, ethnic self-determination is as likely to lead to new intolerance—intolerance by new majorities for new minorities—as it is to create stability and "naturally" pure ethnic states.

Accomplishing the goals of self-determination may, in some cases, require the creation of separate states. In the great majority of cases, however, creative intra-state solutions that recognize the value of diversity without mandating or encouraging division are more likely to achieve the desired results. No single constitutional structure can serve as a model for all situations, but there are many examples of relatively successful forms of decentralization, autonomy, or federalism adopted in the past twenty years by countries as diverse as Belgium, Nicaragua, and Spain.[63]

As self-determination is expressed in increasingly diverse relationships between central and sub-state entities, the relevance of international frontiers to the lives of most people will continue to diminish. The state is not about to disappear, but self-determination in the sense of independent statehood means little in the context of a Europe with a single European Community passport and a focus on regional rather than national concerns. The emphasis on relatively inconsequential borders may have been responsible in part for the slaughter in Bosnia-Hercegovina and Croatia. This is tragically ironic in light of the undoubted desire of the various components of the former Yugoslavia to join a Europe in which borders are becoming less relevant.

As the psychological and legal borders of the state become increasingly permeable, the international community is more willing to look beyond frontier posts and judge the legitimacy of states and governments. In the near future, formal diplomatic recognition of a state or government is unlikely to depend on a government's human rights record. But the existence of serious human rights violations will increasingly undermine the efforts of states to improve their international reputation or to conclude desired economic or security agreements. Where the denial of rights is wholesale and endemic to an undemocratic system, governments may even be equated with unrepresentative states and thus be deprived of international legitimacy. The humanitarian intervention in Somalia approved by the United Nations in December 1992 is an extreme measure unlikely to be repeated in the near future, but it represents a significant chink in the armor of "domestic jurisdiction" that may serve as a precedent for other, less intrusive, international actions.

The standard of legitimacy in the post-colonial era is not observance of the norm of self-determination, but rather adherence by the government of a state to widely accepted international human rights norms. As these norms expand to include rights of particular importance to ethnic, religious, linguistic, and cultural communities, self-determination loses some of its attraction as a means of protection. As human rights norms expand to include political participation and protection of identity (within a larger context of continuing protection for the individual members of both minorities and majorities), self-determination can be more meaningfully and readily exercised through options short of secession.

If self-determination is viewed as an end in itself reflecting a preference for homogeneous, independent, often small "nation-states," it is incapable of universal application without massive disruption. It runs counter to simultaneous trends towards greater regional economic and political cooperation and integration among states, and it will lead to intensified problems of minority rights and border-drawing.

However, if self-determination is viewed as a means to an end—that end being a democratic, participatory political and economic system in which the rights of individuals and the identity of minority communities are protected—its continuing validity is more easily perceived. In most instances, self-determination should come to mean not statehood or independence, but the exercise of what might be termed "functional sovereignty." This functional sovereignty will assign to sub-state groups the powers necessary to control political and economic matters of direct relevance to them, while bearing in mind the legitimate concerns of other segments of the population and the state itself. In some respects, functional sovereignty reflects the "principle of subsidiarity" developed within the European Community and the old injunction that "that government governs best which governs least."

The content of self-determination, like international law, is in constant evolution. This evolution is sometimes marked by the adoption of new terminology; at other times, definitions may change. For example, this author has suggested that a "right to autonomy" may now be developing "in the interstices of contemporary definitions of sovereignty, self-determination, and the human rights of individuals and groups."[64] While such new terminology might be clearer, redefining "self-determination" may be more politically acceptable than attempting to bury it.

The proposition that the internationally recognized right of self-determination does not now include the right of independent statehood or the right of secession, except in the most extreme circumstances, reflects the fact that we are entering a third stage in the evolution of the concept. The first, Wilsonian phase was avowedly political: while lip service was given to satisfying "national" aspirations and promoting democracy, there was no meaningful recognition of the "right" of all peoples to be free from external domination or to live in their own democratic "nation-state." The second, decolonization phase ultimately did come to express a relatively precise legal norm—the illegitimacy of colonialism and the right of territories colonized by distant Western powers to become independent states. The second phase did not address nationalism in the Wilsonian sense of that term.

The post-colonial era is the third stage, in which international law guarantees to individuals and non-colonial peoples a much broader range of human rights, including meaningful self-determination but generally excluding a right to independent statehood. Self-determination is no longer only a shield to be used against foreign forces and empires or to prevent the "bartering about" of peoples condemned by Wilson, nor is it the only vehicle through which the values of democracy and representative government can be promoted. Instead, self-determination should have wider application as it becomes infused with related human rights norms developed in the last half of the twentieth century.

The post-colonial norm of self-determination includes the right to be different and to enjoy a meaningful degree of control over one's own life, individually and collectively, as well as the right to participate in the affairs of the larger state. It operates in the context of an international order in which, paradoxically, the state's physical boundaries may be more secure than at any time in the last four centuries, while the actual power of the state is being substantially reduced. This reduced sovereignty results in part from the increasing interdependence of a world in which real political or economic independence is impossible. It also results from conscious choices made by states to link their fates through countless international agreements on trade, human rights, culture, the environment, health, telecommunications, and other matters.

Human rights norms do not yet encompass all of the values represented by self-determination, even if one excludes independent statehood from the latter concept. Thus, the "pull" of self-determination must be combined with the "push" of human rights and the rule of law to develop new rights that will protect minorities, indigenous peoples, and other groups often bypassed in the process of economic, social, and political modernization. At the same time, raising the floor of minority protections suggests a ceiling as well: secession will not be actively supported by the international community except in the most compelling circumstances.

Denial of the right to secede to minority or indigenous peoples may be seen as an overly statist position, but the reverse is true if such denial is accompanied by an affirmation of minority and human rights. The progressive development of rights to identity and effective participation certainly intrude on classic notions of a state's sovereign powers, even though they do not dictate any particular form of government. Thus, the norm of self-determination in the post-colonial era is both a shield that protects a state (in most cases) from secession and a spear that pierces the governmental veil of sovereignty behind which undemocratic or discriminatory regimes attempt to hide.

No state has an inherent right to continue to exist in its present form, but outside actors should neither encourage or discourage dissolution. Given the inability of the international community to agree that the paradigmatic "nation-state" is indeed desirable and the impossibility of ever equating every "nation" or "people" with its own state, external forces have no right to attempt to impose their own preferences as to the existence or non-existence of a particular state (unless the challenge to a state's existence is clearly due to external aggression).

Outside intervention may be appropriate to prevent massive violations of human rights or to provide humanitarian assistance where a government is either unable or unwilling to do so, but the legitimacy of the use of force in such situations does not depend on whether a civil war is secessionist or only revolutionary. In fact, clearer separation of the political issues of secession and the various proposals for the constitutional restructuring of Bosnia-Hercegovina, for example, from the humanitarian concern to prevent gross violations of human rights norms and the laws of war, might have made it easier for the international community to address the latter more effectively.

Desires for independence will not disappear, and they should not necessarily be opposed. Indeed, a state in which human rights are protected is much more likely to respond favorably to proposals for constitutional restructuring. Democratic governments in Belgium, Spain, Canada, and Czechoslovakia have been willing to devolve substantial powers to ethnic regions or communities and, in the last case, even to agree to peaceful dissolution. Undemocratic or weak regimes find it much more difficult to "lose" power to a regional or ethnic movement.

Organized communities concentrated within a certain territory have the right to develop their identity and may be gaining the right to influence or even control governmental acts of particular concern to them, but the "right" of an ethnically distinct community to acquire its own independent state remains as imaginary in the late twentieth century as it was in the nineteenth. Independence, as a purported expression of the right of self-determination, is only one among many political options that should be determined through democratic processes; it is not an absolute "right" the existence of which precludes rational debate or necessary compromise.

Once the rights to community identity and effective participation—along with other fundamental human rights—are guaranteed, the decision of political, ethnic, religious, or national communities to unite or to separate should not be dictated by international law. The state is merely a vehicle which will be retained by its citizens as long as it achieves progress towards substantive goals, such as preserving peace, ensuring the rule of law, and promoting economic and political development. The ultimate purpose served by the right of all peoples to self-determination is to ensure that progress towards those goals occurs.

NOTES

1. Jonathan Swift, Gulliver's Travels 202 (E.P. Dutton & Co., Inc. 1946) (1726).
2. Numerous scholars have described these developments, and the present work will not attempt to retrace their steps. See, e.g., Benedict Anderson, Imagined Communities (1983); John Breuilly, Nationalism and the State (1982); Alfred Cobban, The Nation State and National Self-Determination (rev. ed. 1969); Ernest Gellner, Nations and Nationalism (1983); E.J. Hobsbawm, Nations and Nationalism Since 1780 (2d ed. 1992); Oscar I. Janowsky, Nationalities and National Minorities (1945); Hans Kohn, Nationalism: Its Meaning and History (rev. ed. 1965); C.A. Macartney, National States and National Minorities (1934); Hugh Seton-Watson, Nations and States (1977).
3. Cobban, supra note 2, at 36.
4. Woodrow Wilson, The Fourteen Points Speech (Jan. 8, 1918), in 3 The Public Papers of Woodrow Wilson: War and Peace 155, 155–62 (Ray Stannard Baker & William E. Dodd eds., 1927) [collected work hereinafter Public Papers].
5. Id. at 160–61.
6. Woodrow Wilson, War Aims of Germany and Austria (Feb. 11, 1918), in Public Papers, supra note 4, at 177, 182–83 (emphasis added).
7. The classic works on plebiscites are Sarah Wambaugh, A Monograph on Plebiscites (1920), and Sarah Wambaugh, Plebiscites Since the World War, (1933) [hereinafter Wambaugh, Plebiscites Since the World War].
8. Wambaugh, Plebiscites Since the World War, supra note 7, at 41, 42.
9. See generally Inis L. Claude, Jr., National Minorities (1955); Janowsky, supra note 2; Macartney, supra note 2; Raymond Pearson, National Minorities in Eastern Europe 1848–1945 (1983); Louis B. Sohn & Thomas Buergenthal, International Protection of Human Rights 213–302 (1973). A convenient compilation of relevant texts is found in Treaties and International Instruments Concerning the Protection of Minorities 1919–1959, U.N. Doc. E/CN.4/Sub.2/133 (1951) [hereinafter Treaties Concerning the Protection of Minorities].
10. See generally James Barros, The Aland Islands Question: Its Settlement by the League of Nations (1968) (describing the history of the Aland Islands and the League of Nations' activities regarding their status).
11. Report of the International Committee of Jurists Entrusted by the Council of the League of Nations with the Task of Giving an Advisory Opinion upon the Legal Aspects of the Aaland Islands Question, League of Nations O.J. Spec. Supp. 3, at 5 (1920).
12. The Aaland Islands Question, at 27, League of Nations Doc. B7.21/68/106 (1921) (English version) (Report Submitted to the Council of the League of Nations by the Commission of Rapporteurs).
13. G.A. Res. 1514, U.N. GAOR, 15th Sess., Supp. No. 16, at 66, 67, U.N. Doc. A/L.323 and Add.1–6 (1960).
14. This is the so-called "salt water" test, which limited decolonization to territories administered by European states.
15. G.A. Res. 2625, U.N. GAOR, 25th Sess., Supp. No. 28, at 121, U.N. Doc. A/8028 (1970).
16. Robert Rosenstock, The Declaration on Principles of International Law Concerning Friendly Relations: A Survey, 65 Am. J. Int'l L. 713, 733 (1971).
17. International Covenant on Economic, Social and Cultural Rights, adopted Dec. 16, 1966, 993 U.N.T.S. 3 [hereinafter ICESCR]; International Covenant on Civil and Political Rights, adopted Dec. 19, 1966, 999 U.N.T.S. 171 [hereinafter ICCPR]; Optional Protocol to the International Covenant on Civil and Political Rights, opened for signature Dec. 19, 1966, 999 U.N.T.S. 302 [hereinafter Optional Protocol].
18. The most important documentation of this history includes the summary records of the debates in the Commission and Third Committee, supra note 88; Annotations on the Text

of the Draft International Covenants on Human Rights (Prepared by the Secretary-General), U.N. GAOR, 10th Sess., Annexes, Agenda Item 28, pt. 2, U.N. Doc. A/2929 (1955); Observations by Governments, U.N. GAOR, 10th Sess., Annexes, Agenda Item 28, pt. 1, at 3, U.N. Docs. A/2910 and A/2910/Adds.1–6 (1955); Report of the Third Committee, U.N. GAOR, 10th Sess., Annexes, Agenda Item 28, pt. 1, at 30, U.N. Doc. A/3077 (1955).

19. John P. Humphrey, Human Rights and the United Nations: A Great Adventure 129 (1984).

20. The external aspects of self-determination include the right of a nation to be free from external influence, and potentially the right to secession. The internal aspects of self-determination include the right to democracy, i.e., the right to participate in one's own government.

21. See generally Dominic McGoldrick, The Human Rights Committee 247–68 (1994).

22. Optional Protocol, supra note 17, art. 1.

23. See Report of the Human Rights Committee, U.N. GAOR, 42d Sess., Supp. No. 40, at 106, U.N. Doc. A/42/40 (1987).

24. Communication No. 413/1990, A.B. v. Italy, Report of the Human Rights Committee, U.N. GAOR, 46th Sess., Supp. No. 40, at 320, U.N. Doc. A/46/40 (1991) (decision on admissibility of Nov. 2, 1990).

25. ICCPR, supra note 17, art. 41.

26. Human Rights Committee, Summary Record of the 503d Meeting, U.N. GAOR, Hum. Rts. Comm., para. 32, U.N. Doc. CCPR/C/SR.503 (1984).

27. The parties included Canada and the United States but did not include Albania. Conference on Security and Co-Operation in Europe: Final Act, Aug. 1, 1975, 14 I.L.M. 1292.

28. See, e.g., Antonio Cassese, Political Self-Determination—Old Concepts and New Developments, in U.N. Law/Fundamental Rights: Two Topics in International Law 137, 152 (Antonio Cassese ed., 1979) (contending that "the Declaration gives a definition of self-determination that breaks new ground").

29. Conference for Security and Co-Operation in Europe: Charter of Paris for a New Europe, Nov. 21, 1990, 30 I.L.M. 190, 197 (adopted at the meeting of the heads of government of the participating States of the CSCE).

30. Vojislav Stanovcic, Legal Safeguards for Human and Political Rights, in The Helsinki Process and the Future of Europe 156, 167 (Samuel F. Wells, Jr. ed., 1990).

31. African Charter on Human and Peoples' Rights, adopted June 27, 1981, O.A.U. Doc. CAB/LEG/67/3 Rev. 5 [hereinafter African Charter]; cf. [European] Convention for Protection of Human Rights and Fundamental Freedoms, opened for signature Nov. 4, 1950, 213 U.N.T.S. 221; American Convention on Human Rights, opened for signature Nov. 22, 1969, 1144 U.N.T.S. 123.

32. Issa G. Shivji, The Concept of Human Rights in Africa 77 (1989).

33. See Hurst Hannum, Autonomy, Sovereignty, and Self-Determination: The Accommodation of Conflicting Rights 46–47 (1990) [hereinafter Hannum, Autonomy].

34. Among those who assert that self-determination has achieved the status of jus cogens, one might cite Ian Brownlie, Principles of Public International Law 515 (4th ed. 1990), and The Right to Self-Determination, Implementation of United Nations Resolutions, para. 50, U.N. Doc. E/CN.4/Sub.2/405/Rev.1 (1980) (Hector Gros Espiell, special rapporteur) [hereinafter Gros Espiell]. But compare the conflicting conclusion of another United Nations Rapporteur, The Right to Self-Determination, Historical and Current Developments on the Basis of United Nations Instruments, para. 154, U.N. Sales No. E.80.XIV.3 (1981) (Aurelieu Cristescu, special rapporteur) [hereinafter Cristescu] ("No United Nations instrument confers such an imperative character [as that of jus cogens] to the right of peoples to self-determination."); and 1 J.H.W. Verzijl, International Law in Historical Perspective 325 (1968) (Self-determination is even "unworthy of the appellation of a rule of law.").

35. Among the many sources which could be cited are Hanna Bokor-Szego, New States and International Law 11–30 (1970); Brownlie, supra note 34, at 515; James Crawford, The

Creation of States in International Law 101 (1979); Gros Espiell, supra note 34, at 13; Branimir M. Jankovic, Public International Law 220 (1984); 1 Oppenheim's International Law 285 (Sir Robert Jennings & Sir Arthur Watts eds., 9th ed. 1992); and Karl Josef Partsch, Fundamental Principles of Human Rights: Self-Determination, Equality and Non-Discrimination, in 1 Karel Vasak & Philip Alston, The International Dimensions of Human Rights 66 (1982).

36. Michael Akehurst, A Modern Introduction to International Law 296 (5th ed. 1984).
37. Frontier Dispute (Burkina Faso v. Mali), 1986 I.C.J. 554, 567 (Dec. 22).

> At first sight this principle [of uti possidetis juris] conflicts outright with another one, the right of peoples to self-determination. In fact, however, the maintenance of the territorial status quo in Africa is often seen as the wisest course, to preserve what has been achieved by peoples who have struggled for their independence, and to avoid a disruption which would deprive the continent of the gains achieved by much sacrifice. The essential requirement of stability in order to survive, to develop and gradually to consolidate their independence in all fields, has induced African States judiciously to consent to the respecting of colonial frontiers, and to take account of it in the interpretation of the principle of self-determination of peoples.

38. Examples of this situation include territorial settlements imposed at the end of the two world wars, Soviet expansionism during the creation of the Soviet Union in the 1920s, and the assumption of political control over indigenous peoples by states in the Western Hemisphere in the nineteenth century.
39. Examples include Goa-India and Hong Kong-China.
40. Michla Pomerance, Self-Determination in Law and Practice 68 (1982).
41. Universal Realization of the Right of Peoples to Self-Determination, G.A. Res. 44/80, U.N. GAOR, 44th Sess., Supp. No. 49, at 203, U.N. Doc. No. A/44/717 (1989).
42. Resolution 44/80 does nonetheless reaffirm in somewhat broader terms "the universal realization of the right of all peoples, including those under colonial, foreign and alien domination, to self-determination."
43. See Hannum, Autonomy, supra note 131, at 50–118 (discussing minority rights and human rights); see also infra part IV discussing the same.
44. Robert A. Friedlander, Proposed Criteria For Testing The Validity of Self-Determination As It Applies To Disaffected Minorities, 25 Chitty's L.J. 335, 336 (1977).
45. Pomerance, supra note 40, at 23.
46. Conference on Yugoslavia Arbitration Commission, Opinion No. 1, Dec. 7, 1991, reprinted in 31 I.L.M. 1494, 1495.
47. Gros Espiell, supra note 34, para. 90 (citation omitted). Cristescu, supra note 34, para. 279, arrives at a similar conclusion, citing G.A. Res. 2625.
48. The most comprehensive treatise is Lee C. Buchheit, Secession (1978).
49. Gros Espiell, supra note 34, para. 60 (citation omitted); see Oppenheim's International Law, supra note 35, at 290 n.31 ("The travaux preparatoires of the [United Nations] Charter and the subsequent practice of states suggest that the principle of self-determination is primarily applicable to colonial situations rather than to cases involving secession from a state (in which context, however, it may be noted that international law does not make civil war illegal).").
50. One of the most cogent and consistent exponents of this view is Harry Beran. See, e.g., Harry Beran, The Consent Theory of Political Obligation (1987) (arguing that political obligation and authority must rest on the actual personal consent of the citizens); Harry Beran, Self-Determination: A Philosophical Perspective, in Self-Determination in the Commonwealth (W.J. Allan Macartney ed., 1988) (arguing for the formulation of a normative theory of secession); Harry Beran, A Liberal Theory of Secession, 32 Pol. Stud. 21 (1984) (discussing a moral rather than legal right of self-determination).
51. A similar but more nuanced moral-philosophical case for secession is set forth in a recent book by Allen Buchanan. Allen Buchanan, Secession (1991).
52. Benyamin Neuberger, National Self-Determination in Postcolonial Africa 71 (1986).

53. Terence O'Brien, Economic Support for Minority Languages, in The Future of Cultural Minorities 82, 84 (Antony E. Alcock et al. eds., 1979).

54. Lea Brilmayer, Secession and Self-Determination: A Territorial Interpretation, 16 Yale J. Int'l L. 177 (1991).

55. Of course, a seceding entity could choose integration with a neighboring state or some other status instead of full independence, but the option of independence must logically be available when secession occurs.

56. Brownlie, supra note 34, at 92; see also Crawford, supra note 35, at 23 ("Recognition is increasingly intended and taken as an act, if not of political approval, at least of political accommodation.")

57. See generally Hurst Hannum, Self-Determination, Yugoslavia, and Europe: Old Wine in New Bottles?, 3 Transnat'l L. & Contemp. Probs. 57 (1993) (criticizing the European response to the Yugoslav crisis).

58. Marc Weller, The International Response to the Dissolution of the Socialist Federal Republic of Yugoslavia, 86 Am. J. Int'l L. 588.

59. Eisuke Suzuki, Self-Determination and World Public Order: Community Response to Territorial Separation, 16 Va. J. Int'l L. 779, 861 (1976).

60. Conor C. O'Brien, Preface to 1 World Minorities at xv (Georgina Ashworth ed., 1977).

61. See Hurst Hannum, Contemporary Developments in the International Protection of the Rights of Minorities, 66 Notre Dame L. Rev. 1431 (1991).

62. S. James Anaya, The Capacity of International Law to Advance Ethnic or Nationality Rights Claims, 75 Iowa L. Rev. 842 (1990).

63. See Hurst Hannum, Autonomy, Sovereignty, and Self-Determination: The Accommodation of Conflicting Rights 123–448 (1990) [hereinafter Hannum, Autonomy] (discussing a variety of autonomous arrangements).

64. Hannum, Autonomy, supra note 63, at 473.

Drawing a Better Line: *Uti Possidetis* and the Borders of New States

Steven R. Ratner

IT IS NOW conventional wisdom that the proliferation of ethnic-based violence constitutes the greatest threat to public order and human rights since the lifting of the Iron Curtain. The eruption of hatreds, whether suppressed or ignored for a half century or newly arisen, has unleashed centrifugal forces that are pulling states apart from Africa to Europe to South and Central Asia. To date, the response of the effective decision makers in the international community has been ambiguous and inconstant: the United Nations member states reiterate the importance of the unity of all states, but they accept accomplished breakups after the fact, all the while insisting on the protection of minorities within states. Political philosophers struggle with the circumstances under which secession and dissolution are desirable; international law declares the lack of either a blanket right to, or prohibition against, secession and seemingly relegates its achievement to a pure power calculus.

Secessions and breakups do not, however, solely concern ethnic groups seeking self-determination through political independence and statehood. They are fundamentally issues about control over land—what Georges Scelle called the

Reprinted from Steven R. Ratner, "Drawing a Better Line: Uti Possidetis and the Borders of New States," *American Journal of International Law* 90 (October 1996): 590–624. Reproduced with permission from 90 AJIL 590 (1996) © The American Society of International Law.

"obsession du territoire."[1] And the norms about the extent of that land when a new state emerges have traditionally been of less interest to international law than whether a new "subject" of international law has emerged. Should the map be drawn according to lines sketched out through processes now regarded as illegitimate and that may contribute to a worsening of human rights conditions in the new countries? Or must we resign ourselves to General Ratko Mladic's solution, where "borders are drawn with blood"[2] and remain extralegally ordained?

At the core of the legal debate over the territory of new states is the principle of *uti possidetis*. Stated simply, *uti possidetis* provides that states emerging from decolonization shall presumptively inherit the colonial administrative borders that they held at the time of independence. It largely governed the determination of the size and shape of the states of former Spanish Latin America beginning in the early 1800s, as well as former European Africa and Southeast Asia beginning in the 1950s. The relevance of *uti possidetis* today is evidenced by the practice of states during the dissolution of the former Soviet Union, Yugoslavia and Czechoslovakia, apparently sanctifying the former internal administrative lines as interstate frontiers.

Reliance on *uti possidetis* during the post-Cold War breakups has stemmed from three arguments or assumptions. First, *uti possidetis* reduces the prospects of armed conflict by providing the only clear outcome in such situations. Absent such a policy, all borders would be open to dispute, and new states would fall prey to irredentist neighbors or internal secessionist claimants. Second, because a cosmopolitan democratic state can function within any borders, the conversion of administrative borders to international borders is as sensible as any other approach and far simpler. Third, and buttressing the other two, *uti possidetis* is asserted as a default rule of international law mandating the conversion of all administrative boundaries into international borders. This rule emerged during the decolonization of Latin America and Africa but would apply by logical extension to the breakup of states today. The most significant elaboration of this extension came from the commission chaired by Judge Robert Badinter advising the European Community on legal questions associated with the breakup of Yugoslavia.[3]

These views seem compelling; yet the easy embrace by governments of *uti possidetis* and the suggestion that it is now a general rule of international law to govern the breakup of states lead to two distinct, yet opposite, spillover effects that endanger global order at this time of ethnic conflict. First, a policy or rule that transforms all administrative borders of modern states into international boundaries creates a significant hazard in the name of simplicity—namely, the temptation of ethnic separatists to divide the world further along administrative lines. If the Republic of Georgia's new borders must coincide with those of the former Georgian Soviet Socialist Republic, are not the future Republic of Abhazia's just as clearly those of the former Abhaz Autonomous Soviet Socialist

Republic? Would the Quebecois consider secession so readily if the new state had different borders from those established by Canada and the United Kingdom for the purpose of integrating Quebec into the Dominion?

Second, the extension of *uti possidetis* to modern breakups leads to genuine injustices and instability by leaving significant populations both unsatisfied with their status in new states and uncertain of political participation there. By hiding behind inflated notions of *uti possidetis*, state leaders avoid engaging the issue of territorial adjustments—even minor ones—which is central to the process of self-determination. In the case of Yugoslavia, for instance, although *uti possidetis* hardly caused the eruption of armed conflict, the assumption by states of its applicability from the outset prevented any debate over the adjustment of boundaries and limited the universe of possible borders to one—leaving those people on the "wrong" side of the border ripe for "ethnic cleansing." Elsewhere, whether with regard to left bank Dniestrians in the Republic of Moldova or Armenians in Nagorno-Karabakh, *uti possidetis* may prove a recipe for continued denial of human dignity to minorities.

It is thus time to reexamine this oft-invoked principle of international law and relations. For application of *uti possidetis* to the breakup of states today both ignores critical distinctions between internal lines and international boundaries and, more important, is profoundly at odds with current trends in international law and politics. Many internal borders do merit transformation into international boundaries based on historical and other characteristics; but the assumption that all such borders must be so transformed is unwarranted.

My argument proceeds in four parts. Part I reviews the genealogy and legal contours of the doctrine. Part II examines the relationship between internal and international borders to evaluate the functional rationale and consequences of *uti possidetis*. Part III discusses whether the political and legal factors that underlay the application of *uti possidetis* to colonial breakups justify its invocation today. And part IV ponders possible alternatives to *uti possidetis*, including their obvious hazards but less evident potential. My purpose is thus to marry the literature on frontiers and political geography with that of international law as a means of responding to the various claims to territory.

This article has a modest goal—to examine the propriety of *uti possidetis* to contemporary challenges related to state unity. It does not seek, or need, to posit a comprehensive theory of self-determination and secession, including the most vexing question of the appropriate unit of self-determination, which remains the goal of many legal scholars and political philosophers. Rather, I make several policy assumptions consistent with many views of self-determination without trying to examine all their ramifications.

First, I assume that the proliferation of states, each smaller and more ethnically based than that from which it emerged, is not desirable. A presumption in favor of such states accentuates arbitrary distinctions about human beings and undermines the cosmopolitan tenets on which all human rights law is based. Indeed, the proliferation of such states might make oppression of minorities within them particularly egregious. Smaller states may also prove economically handicapped or at least create economic inefficiencies as they replicate governmental functions on smaller scales and erect new barriers to trade.

Second, and notwithstanding the above, I assume that, in the process of the formation of new states, the cosmopolitan, multiethnic solution—democracy combined with respect for minority rights—may either prove impossible to construct or otherwise not satisfy the claims of certain minorities inhabiting distinct territories. Thus, when a state is breaking up, forced cohabitation within unchangeable administrative borders will not always maximize either public order or human rights. This does not equate with the assumption that there is or ought to be any broad, *ex ante* right to secession; I take the position that the international community should sanction attempted secessions particularly forcible ones—under the most limited circumstances, even if it may ultimately have to acknowledge a fait accompli. The question here, however, is whether a set of internal borders ought to survive this process.

I. A BRIEF HISTORY OF *UTI POSSIDETIS*

A. From Roman Law to the Law of Nations

Uti possidetis finds its origins in the Roman law of the republican era, as one of a series of edicts that the praetor, or administrator of justice, would issue upon application of some party during the initial stage of litigation. When two parties claimed ownership of real property, the edict would grant provisional possession to the possessor during the litigation, unless he had obtained the land clandestinely (*clam*), by violence (*vi*), or in a form revocable by the other party (*precario*).[4] *Uti possidetis* did not address the final disposition of the property but, rather, shifted the burden of proof during the proceedings to the party not holding the land. This represented an advantage for the possessor, who became the defendant in the case, even if he had wrongfully removed the plaintiff from the land. The edict came to be summarized in the phrase *uti possidetis, ita possideatis*: "As you possess, so may you possess."[5]

According to Moore, the early scholars of international law adopted the notion of *uti possidetis* but altered the doctrine in two critical ways: by changing the scope of application from private land claims to the state's territorial sovereignty; and, most critically, by transforming the provisional status into a permanent one.[6] This shift seems hardly surprising in an era when the use of force by states and any resulting acquisition of land were lawful: possession became ten-tenths of the law. This adaptation, of course, proved a complete reversal from the Roman law concept, which excluded even provisional possession to a party who accomplished it by violence, and which would have suggested a return to the *status quo ante bellum*.

B. Uti Possidetis *and Latin American Independence*

The juxtaposition of *uti possidetis* and self-determination began in Latin America, where the Creoles who wrested independence from their Spanish brethren beginning in the early nineteenth century seized upon the idea as a way of setting boundaries of the new countries. Scorned by the peninsulares, the new Americans in the Latin American bureaucracy had formed political allegiances to the administrative units in which they were raised and assigned for their jobs, rather than to Spanish America writ large. As a result, the three large groupings of Spanish territories that declared independence beginning in 1810 proved short-lived, splitting along their own internal lines into new states.

To the Creole leadership, adoption of a policy of *uti possidetis* served two purposes: to ensure that no land in South America remained *terra nullius* upon independence, open to possible claim by Spain or other non-American powers; and to prevent conflicts among the new states of the former empire by adopting a set of extant boundaries. Consistent with the law at the time, it incidentally ensured that all lands occupied only by indigenous peoples would be part of the new state.

The Latin American boundaries were derived from various sorts of Spanish governmental instruments setting up hierarchical and other units such as provinces, *alcaldías mayores, intendencias*, court (*audiencia*) districts, Captaincies-General, and Vice-Royalties. The meaning of these units changed over time, as did the frontiers of each through unilateral decisions of the Crown. The leaders of the new republics quickly began to codify *uti possidetis* in both treaties and domestic law. For example, when Venezuela split from Gran Colombia to resume a separate existence in 1830, the Constitution specified that its territory would comprise "all that which, previously to the political changes of 1810, was denominated the Captain-Generalship of Venezuela," an administrative unit within the larger former colonial division, the Vice-Royalty of New Granada.

Despite this general acceptance of the principle, the precise contours and effects of *uti possidetis* remained unclear. First, Latin states accepted the possibility that their final border might differ from the *uti possidetis* line, though they did not plan major revisions of the Spanish administrative borders. Second, and more important, the acceptance of *uti possidetis* in principle could not rectify confusions stemming from shifting territorial arrangements under the Crown, the absence of clearly demarcated boundaries due to ignorance of the local geography, or political tensions among the new Latin states. These factors led to warfare among them, as well as peaceful resolutions through boundary treaties or agreements to arbitrate.

Finally, states and scholars seemed to have different views on the meaning of *uti possidetis* as of a particular date, leading to the use of two new terms, *uti possidetis juris* and *uti possidetis facto*. The former view held that only the Spanish legal documents were dispositive for locating borders, effective possession being irrelevant; while the latter argued that the lands actually held by each state at independence would determine the border. In cases where the arbitration treaties did not specify an interpretation, arbitrators took different positions. Nevertheless, the *juris* addition became somewhat of a fixture alongside *uti possidetis*, signifying the primary importance of the legal instruments of the Spanish Crown, though not to the total exclusion of evidence of possession. *Uti possidetis facto* received its greatest acceptance in Brazil, which rejected the Spanish-American interpretation and thereby claimed, through possession alone, large stretches of land beyond the borders set in treaties by Spain and Portugal.

C. Decolonization in Africa

Before the arrival of the Europeans, the notion of frontiers as defined lines was hardly known in Africa. Instead, frontiers were zones through which one clan or tribe passed from one region to another; and any borders depended solely on who would be paid tribute. The European colonialists who arrived in large numbers in the eighteenth century did not draw lines immediately. Rather, each state made claims, leading to the recognition of spheres of influence, followed by more defined allocations, specific delimitations, and eventual alterations based on experience.[7] Drawing these borders with only slight knowledge of or regard for local inhabitants or geography, the European powers made territorial allocations to reduce armed conflict among themselves. In that sense alone were they rational.

The choice for Africa as decolonization approached was clear: either a wholesale restructuring of borders to rectify past injustices or acceptance of existing lines as the basis for new states. Pan-Africanists urged the former; but the European states and the indigenous elites opted for maintaining extant lines as the most feasible method for speedy decolonization. One year after the formation of the Organization of African Unity in 1963, with most of the continent decolonized but several territorial disputes already brewing, the OAU's heads of state and government pledged in the Cairo Declaration "to respect the frontiers existing on their achievement of independence."

Such a policy would serve an external and an internal purpose: externally, it would seek to prevent irredentist tendencies by neighbors from turning into territorial claims and the possible use of force. Internally, it would give clear notice to ethnic minorities that secession or adjustment of borders was not an option. African and European elites had struck a bargain to the benefit of both, permitting replacement of European rulers by indigenous ones. Although the OAU's stance was not without its critics in Africa, most leaders defended the policy. Border wars proved the exception, as African states either affirmatively settled their border disputes or simply did not push their claims. Internally, for a generation African leaders firmly rejected secession attempts on the continent.

As for *uti possidetis*, while the term does not appear in the OAU resolution, its meaning had been transformed again. No longer focused on retention of administrative boundaries of one colonial power as in Spanish America, the principle in common parlance now entailed notions of treaty succession to address boundaries between different colonial powers. Africa would inherit most of the internal and external lines of the European colonizers, yielding the most international frontiers of any continent relative to its area.

D. Dissolutions in Eastern Europe and the Soviet Union

The breakups of the former Yugoslavia, the Soviet Union and Czechoslovakia served as yet another opportunity to test the durability of *uti possidetis*. The internal structure of Yugoslavia, from its creation at Saint-Germain-en-Laye until its occupation during World War II, consisted at first of twenty-two regions, later reallocated into nine provinces whose borders followed physical and historical lines. After the war, Tito reorganized the polity into six republics that corresponded more closely to the pre-1918 political units—including units within Austria-Hungary (Slovenia, Bosnia-Herzegovina and Croatia) and the prewar Serbian state—and left significant ethnic minorities in each republic.

When Yugoslavia's republics began to declare their independence in 1991, the international community quickly adhered to the idea that the internal frontiers of the Socialist Federal Republic of Yugoslavia could not be altered by the use of force. The statements and resolutions to this effect by the European Community, the Conference on Security and Co-operation in Europe, and the UN Security Council also evinced their conclusion that, if Yugoslavia were indeed to dissolve, the only predictable way would be along the lines of the republics.[8] In January 1992, the newly created Arbitration Commission of the EC Conference on Yugoslavia endorsed this post-Cold War incarnation of *uti possidetis*.[9] These positions fell on deaf ears, in that the border claims only dissipated in the one area where both parties had simply decided not to fight, namely, the border between Slovenia and Croatia. For the borders among Serbia, Croatia and Bosnia, *uti possidetis* remained a mirage.

The administrative boundaries of the Soviet Union were far more complex, reflecting a history of redrawing by many Soviet leaders. In the 1920s, Soviet Russia absorbed new territories, including states independent only since the end of the world war (Ukraine, White Russia, Georgia, Armenia and Azerbaijan), as well as areas in Central Asia. By 1926, the USSR consisted of eight Union Republics whose dividing lines (including lines within republics) took into consideration ethnic factors, although not to the satisfaction of many groups. Stalin adjusted frontiers between and within the republics before World War II, dividing ethnic groups to strengthen his political hand and emasculate ethnonationalism in the hinterland. In 1939 and 1940, as contemplated in the Molotov-Ribbentrop Pact, the USSR invaded and annexed Estonia, Latvia, Lithuania and Romanian Bessarabia, creating four new Union Republics, and annexed parts of Poland. By the war's end, not only had the Soviet Union expanded externally through incorporation of areas of Eastern Europe, but its internal boundaries had been adjusted again, including through the transfer of parts of the former Baltic States to the older Union Republics. With a few notable exceptions, border changes leveled off after the war.[10]

The Soviet Union's dismemberment proved far more peaceful, initially at least. While the Baltic States rejected the conversion of the USSR's internal borders into interstate frontiers in light of the territory they had lost after their incorporation, the other states agreed to retain the administrative borders, a view codified in the 1993 Charter of the Commonwealth of Independent States. Nevertheless, the former republics still maintain claims against each other and do not appear to have yet achieved a consensus regarding the permissibility of secessions and territorial realignments.

The internal border within Czechoslovakia had a far longer pedigree. When the Allies created Czechoslovakia after World War I, they combined former areas of the Austro-Hungarian Empire—Bohemia, Moravia, Slovakia, part of Silesia, and Ruthenia. Bohemia and Moravia in the west had earlier been separate units within the Holy Roman Empire, and then part of the Austrian Empire, while Slovakia had been part of Hungary. The border between the Czech and Slovak parts of Czechoslovakia was thus the historical Moravian-Hungarian border. During World War II, the Germans used this line as an international frontier between the so-called protectorate of Bohemia and Moravia and the "independent" state of Slovakia. When Czechoslovakia was dissolving in 1993, the two sides readily agreed that this border would function as the international border, and neither has claims against the other.

E. Ascribing a Legal Valence

The employment by states of *uti possidetis* to respond to several bursts of state creation over the past two centuries appears to have endowed the principle with some normative status in the international legal order. Judging by the trends of decision over nearly two centuries, the contours of this principle in the decolonization context seem to evince four general characteristics.

First, state practice during the decolonization of Latin America, Africa and Asia lends support for regarding *uti possidetis* as a customary norm requiring states to presume the inheritance of their colonial borders unless, as occurred in some instances, the colonial power(s) or another decision maker (such as the United Nations) had determined otherwise. Most new states inherited their colonial borders without alteration. In cases of disputed boundaries, they have typically agreed to settle them through reference to *uti possidetis*. As noted, *uti possidetis* also appears in numerous constitutions in Latin America, and the 1964 Cairo resolution reflected the trends within Africa at that time. Finally, the Declaration on the Granting of Independence to Colonial Countries and Peoples indicates a preference, though hardly explicit, for the inheritance of borders.[11]

Nevertheless, expectations regarding lawfulness are not clear, with evidence lacking as to whether states regarded themselves as required to retain colonial borders absent other agreement. And the mere presence of *uti possidetis* in constitutions, bilateral treaties (including arbitration *compromis*) or Resolution 1514 does not demonstrate *opinio juris*. This gap suggests a less than rock-solid basis for a customary norm and at least the possibility that *uti possidetis* was no more than a policy decision adopted to avoid conflicts during decolonization.

The International Court of Justice has, of course, stated in dictum in *Frontier Dispute (Burkina Faso/Mali)* that *uti possidetis* is a "general principle" and a "rule of general scope" in the case of decolonization. It has never adjudicated whether *uti possidetis* is a norm of customary law, because, in these types of border disputes, both parties have stipulated by *compromis* or otherwise that their boundary would be determined according to the borders in effect at the time of independence. Nevertheless, the repeated assumption by the Court that *uti possidetis* is a norm of international law is probative. Without definitively opining on the issue, one may thus assume some support for regarding *uti possidetis* as a norm of regional customary law in Latin America and Africa, if not a general norm as well, in the context of decolonization.

Second, *uti possidetis* does not prevent the emergence of different borders during decolonization. In a significant number of situations, states emerged from colonial rule with other than their preindependence borders.[12] In addition, single colonies were split at independence through various processes.[13] *Uti possidetis* was not, then, a uniform practice by or obligation upon colonial powers— although the General Assembly has sought to limit those states' ability to divide a colonial territory unilaterally during the independence process. Some have cited these divergences to conclude that *uti possidetis* is devoid of legal content.[14]

Moreover, in resolving border disputes lingering from decolonization, states have agreed to accept deviations from *uti possidetis*. In the 1933 *Honduras Borders* case, the *compromis* authorized the tribunal to take account of "interests" of the parties that might go beyond the *uti possidetis* line of 1821, and indeed to modify that line as needed through an exchange of territory "which it may deem just." The panel determined a line different at points from the *uti possidetis* line, which often recognized territorial encroachments of each side on the other's territories. And the ICJ has refused to regard *uti possidetis* as a peremptory norm that would override a provision in *compromis* giving an arbitrator authority to take into account other historical and legal factors.

Third, *uti possidetis* does not bar postindependence changes in borders carried out by agreement. It is not a norm of *jus cogens*, and precludes states neither from altering their borders nor even from creating new states by mutual consent. Dissolutions may be found in the practice of Latin America, as well as elsewhere after World War II. More recently, the Helsinki Final Act did not rule out peaceful border adjustments in Europe (however unlikely they may be) but banned only changes through force.[15]

Fourth, *uti possidetis* does not override other legal claims arguing for borders different from those of the prior administrative units. Both the Vienna Convention on the Law of Treaties (1969) and the Vienna Convention on Succession of States in Respect of Treaties (1978) support this view with respect to boundaries originally determined by treaties—i.e., those separating colonies of different European powers—by specifically refraining from adopting the maintenance of such boundaries as a rule of conventional law. . . . Klabbers and Lefeber have built upon this limitation to create a negative version of *uti possidetis*, providing simply that the norm in the 1978 Vienna Convention concerning boundary treaties—that the attainment of independence is not per se a ground to invalidate existing boundaries—also applies with respect to internal colonial lines that become international borders.[16]

Thus, *uti possidetis* is agnostic on whether or not secessions or breakups should occur and is not simply the legal embodiment of a policy condemning them. It would not purport to render unlawful the changes in the borders of Pakistan and Ethiopia as a result of the creation of Bangladesh in 1971 and Eritrea in 1993—although it would seem to suggest that, in the absence of agreement, the borders of the new states should coincide with those of East Pakistan and the former Ethiopian province, respectively.

These traits of *uti possidetis* distinguish it from any idea of immutability and underline another important limitation of the principle: that it is not equivalent to the legal ban on the use of force—the norm of territorial integrity. That norm, clearly *jus cogens*,[17] prohibits changes in interstate borders through force, and is reflected in numerous treaties that do not forbid other types of changes in borders.[18] *Uti possidetis*, on the other hand, offers a presumption that the borders entitled to protection under Article 2(4) of the UN Charter should be those that correspond to colonial borders.

As for the extension of *uti possidetis* to today's situations, the actions of states in transforming existing borders in the cases of Yugoslavia, Czechoslovakia and the USSR may suggest some movement toward normative expectations, as endorsed by the Badinter Commission. But the history is brief and opinion remains divided. It is thus necessary to examine the propriety of this extension.

II. INTERNATIONAL BOUNDARIES AND INTERNAL ADMINISTRATIVE LINES

A full appraisal of the appropriateness of *uti possidetis* today requires a closer examination of the true target of the doctrine—borders themselves. International and internal borders serve highly different functions, and the rote application of *uti possidetis* also raises practical problems in the determination of boundaries.

A. Functional Distinctions

The core functional distinction between international borders and internal administrative boundaries lies in a critical antinomy: governments establish interstate boundaries to separate states and peoples, while they establish or recognize internal borders to unify and effectively govern a polity. The lines in each case promote control and efficiency, but for opposing purposes. As described by the geographer S. Whittemore Boggs, international boundaries "are in general negative rather than positive."[19] The historical basis for that separation was the physical preservation of the state. States used natural features, such as rivers, mountain ranges and lakes, or artificial lines to set up defenses, or at least warning tracks, against the ambitions of their neighbors. Today boundaries serve the more important function of limiting the territorial jurisdiction of states. A simple line determines which state, subject to international law, can prescribe and apply laws and policies relating to the full range of attributes of persons and property, whether citizenship, taxation or educational opportunities.

Inherent in the notion of jurisdictional separation is the state's authority, and exercise of it, to control movement across borders. Immigration standards, customs duties, export and import quotas, and other constraints on the movement of people, goods and intangibles all operate with respect to, and because of, international borders. States may facilitate free traffic through bilateral or multilateral arrangements, but the border enables the state to assert its own prerogative over transnational movements. If the state chose not to differentiate its policies from those of its neighbor or limit in some way transactions between them, it would presumably agree to a merger and disappearance of the border. Despite Oppenheim's depiction of boundaries as "imaginary lines,"[20] their reality is confronted every day.

When those governing a state look internally, their concern is not with protection from abroad, but with binding together or managing separate areas as a whole. Because a border by definition divides territories, and therefore has some separating function, it might appear that the ideal policy for a nation-state would be the absence of internal boundaries. The state without administrative divisions remains rare, however, because of the inability of most states to govern themselves without some sharing of authority with subnational levels. The pattern will range from a federal structure to greater concentration at the national level, but even the unitary state will likely have some administrative lines. These lines fragment the state in certain situations; e.g., in federal entities through different regimes of local laws, and actors within the state may push devolution at the expense of effective national governance. But the underlying assumption is that of a single state, with the goal of continued unity.

1. Varieties and Purposes of Internal Borders. The origins and logic of particular internal frontiers vary across states. Broadly speaking, states may either inherit such boundaries or establish them. Thus, the first category encompasses, in the terminology of the geographers Hartshorne and Boggs, antecedent boundaries, which predate the current cultural landscape. Examples include those corresponding to ancient lines of control, as with many English counties, or those traceable to old land grants of a colonial power, as with parts of the original thirteen U.S. states. They also include lines in empires or states defining administrative units that were formerly independent or quasi-independent states, such as some within Austria-Hungary and parts of modern Germany.

As for established boundaries, states expanding into territories without inhabitants of the governing nationality—the domestic equivalent, of sorts, of *terra nullius*—have drawn pioneer boundaries, determined before the arrival of settlers, as in much of the American and Canadian West and Australia. Like the borders in imperial Africa, these emphasize straight lines and usually pay little regard to demographic patterns of indigenous peoples. In the case of antecedent and pioneer boundaries, the state's policy toward unity tends to play a relatively small part in the location of administrative lines—they are either inherited or a product of a hasty decision undertaken for administrative convenience.

Just as possible is the prospect that the central government has drawn the borders or portions of them as part of the process of preserving the state's unity, including in response to centrifugal forces. Numerous states have created, abolished and redrawn internal boundaries in the course of the nation-building process. The drawing of such lines fosters unity in several ways based on the state's particular objectives. These goals are precisely those that drive the devolution of power to or its sharing with substate entities in the first place—political, administrative and economic.

Politically, the central and peripheral elites seek to forge a national identity, whether through obliteration of territorial units with competing sources of loyalty, or through compromise with those units on borders and other issues to ensure their respect for the unity of the greater polity. Thus, both the British and Canadian Governments adjusted the frontiers of Quebec and other provinces to integrate them into Canada. Sometimes Quebec has gained territory, while at others it has been lost to other provinces. The French revolutionary government eliminated the provinces of the ancien regime precisely to ensure tight control from Paris, and created departements that remain, with relatively small changes, to this day. And the Soviet Union determined the number and borders of the union and autonomous republics with the goal of national unification—at first, with some moderation and, under Stalin, in an extraordinarily cruel manner.

Administrative concerns demand lines that permit governmental agencies, at various levels, to divide up national responsibilities efficiently. (Expanding the borders of a metropolitan area to allow for better sharing of police, public utilities and welfare services is one obvious example.) Economic needs call for lines to ensure the efficient movement of peoples and goods within the state. These motives have also justified numerous border changes, as well as unrealized proposals for realignment that proved politically infeasible.

The extent to which the central government is willing and able to adjust internal borders turns significantly on the degree to which the state's structure of governance relies on devolution of power to these units. The classic federal states, such as the United States and Switzerland, evince a tradition of generally stable territorial units. Devolution may be reflected in constitutional provisions that restrict the central government's ability to alter administrative boundaries. In the United States, Canada, Australia, Germany and Switzerland, the central government can change the borders of subnational units only with their consent.

2. Popular Conceptions. Not only for the elites in nation-states do administrative borders serve different purposes from international borders. For the ordinary resident, the administrative border itself—even in the case of federal systems—generally has contrasting implications for daily life compared to interstate borders. While school systems, sales taxes, much private and public law, and even the official language may differ on either side of the administrative line, it stands apart from the international border by the ease with which it may be crossed. Traversing provincial lines to commute, take a vacation, accept new employment or visit relatives is routine, involving no passports or customs checks. This facility may prevail at the interstate level for states with a history of neighborly relations, but they typically retain the right to prevent entry of various undesirable persons.

Indeed, the integrative assumptions and purposes of internal borders can lead to their reification in terms of zones, more than particular lines. Zones straddling the line may develop their own distinct identity. In the United States, examples include the New York/New Jersey/Connecticut metropolitan area around New York City and the Maryland/Virginia region surrounding the District of Columbia; in Switzerland, one finds the multicantonal areas around Zurich and Geneva. These zones between internal units hark back to the classic international law notion of the frontier zone. According to this conception, the boundary line is only one element of an entire regime governing the area where one state ends and the other begins. It recognizes the need for the law to take into account the concerns for good-neighborliness and cross-border flows of people and goods. States have routinely concluded arrangements for international border areas.

Nevertheless, at the international level, the linear aspects of the boundary seem to overwhelm its zonal aspects. As made clear in the *Lac Lanoux* arbitration, modern international law has rejected the separate juridical status of the international frontier zone as a matter of customary law. It still treats the line as the only relevant legal construct for purposes of limiting the jurisdiction and activities of a state. It has done so, it seems, because the axiom that one state may not exercise its jurisdiction in the territory of another state operates most easily within the legal simplicity of the line, as compared to the intricate social construct of the zone. Moreover, the recognition of extraterritorial obligations has permitted the law to accept transboundary regimes without a formal assault on the sanctity of boundaries per se. At the internal level, however, with qualitatively different purposes and consequences for administrative units, the zonal characteristics of frontiers take on greater importance. International law seems to regard a state's choice of and regime for internal boundaries as well within the *domaine réservé.*

Of course, internal boundaries do matter, depending upon the degree of what Ronan Paddison calls national integration and nationalization prevailing in the state.[21] At one extreme, such lines can seem irrelevant in terms of economic integration, outcomes of national political races and other indicia of national unity. At the other, units with the strongest aversion to a national identity (such as Quebec) could come to regard them almost as if they were international ones. In the middle, one finds states whose internal borders reflect distinct identities and patterns of behavior, in particular, borders inherited from long ago, such as those of Scotland and Bavaria.

3. Shortcomings of *Uti Possidetis.* The *ipse dixit* transformation of all administrative borders into international ones suffers from two flaws inherent in the distinctions between these sets of lines. First, it seems reasonable to posit that when states are breaking up, the process of forging new national identities in the successor states will give the borders special significance. The very forces that propelled the creation of the new state are likely to cause it to erect barriers—to people, goods and even ideas—against its neighbors. The international border between Croatia and Serbia, or the Czech Republic and Slovakia, is not merely legally distinct from the previous interrepublican border; the change in its status has clear consequences for the people and governments of those states. These boundaries impart what Michael Walzer has called a "dimension" of "physical space" to the rights and common life on each side.[22]

When boundary lines assume this new significance, their location becomes even more critical. As noted, some internal lines, especially of the inherited variety, will functionally make optimal international borders because they define a truly distinct community whose unity and identity override other concerns. But other considerations and scenarios also abound. Groups separated by administrative lines within one state may well prove able to protect their interests through influence at the central level, but may not wish to tolerate separation into different states and the loss of that power. Families and other communities separated by administrative borders face special hurdles if they find themselves in two states. Economic efficiencies or codependence taken for granted in areas separated only by internal lines may disappear when the border becomes an international frontier. And military establishments integrated across administrative lines face constraints during dissolution.

In response to this functionalist critique, a defense of *uti possidetis* could assert that international borders now mean less than ever, and therefore that their precise location is increasingly irrelevant. No doubt in certain parts of the world—in particular, Europe—states are reducing the significance of international borders, with clear benefits. Yet for most of the world they remain one of the defining elements of the polity. Even in Europe, porosity does not equate with irrelevance. States breaking apart seem the least likely to regard the new border as irrelevant—even if secessionists claim that the new state will maintain close economic links with its neighbors.

Such a defense could also posit that any administrative line can effectively function as a suitable interstate boundary, as both law and political geography have rejected the doctrine of the natural borders of states. Borders themselves, wherever located, can indeed solidify differences between neighboring peoples and regions, and create new and separate national identities among similar groups on the opposite sides. It is thus unexceptionable that conversion of administrative borders to interstate boundaries is possible. But this proposition needs to be weighed against the competing concerns—particularly the evolving law of self-determination and human rights—which militate against forcing a people to live in a new state where they may face persecution, an issue explored in part III.

Second, conversion of administrative lines to international lines disregards the interconnection between the internal borders and the forging or maintenance of national unity. Politicians do not draw internal lines with the possibility of secession in mind. (If they foresaw the emergence of separate states, they might well draw the lines differently.) Thus, when the contract among the territorial units or between those units and the center, or the center's master plan for unity, collapses through disintegration, why assume that one of its core elements—the location of the internal borders—must remain unchanged? Rather, this scenario calls into question the parties' original bargain or scheme premised on the continuity of the whole state. In the case of Quebec, secessionists seemingly seek to have their cake and eat it, too—to secede and take with them land given to Quebec as part of its integration into Canada.

B. Practical Impediments to Uti Possidetis

Whether regarding the decolonization of empires or the dissolution of states, new governments or arbitrators attempting to rely on the location of administrative boundaries to determine international lines must begin with a set of clearly defined borders. If, as the World Court said in the Frontier Dispute case, *uti possidetis* turns on a " 'photograph' of the territorial situation,"[23] then those analyzing the image and "plugging it into" the *uti possidetis* equation must know two core things—what the photograph shows and when it was taken. In fact, the number of border disputes even where postcolonial states have applied *uti possidetis* demonstrates the absence of spatial and temporal clarity in many boundaries. These two ambiguities remain in applying *uti possidetis* in the modern context.

The first obstacle to applying *uti possidetis* is posed by the blurring of such lines during the governance of administrative units. The effective exercise of territorial jurisdiction by colonial authorities—or *effectivités*—has proved significant in numerous arbitrations as evidence of—and even substitution for—the line of *uti possidetis*.[24] The ICJ relied on *effectivités* in particular in *Land, Island and Maritime Frontier Dispute*, examining which areas near the disputed border were under the actual control of various Spanish colonial authorities, and even giving weight to *effectivités* exercised by the newly independent states after the departure of the Spaniards.

On the one hand, *effectivités* might raise few practical problems in extending *uti possidetis* to secessions and dissolutions, as the lines between administrative units might be especially clear within a state. The central and local officials might also be far more cognizant of the scope of their territorial authority than were the governors of colonial provinces and their masters in a distant European capital.

But today, even where those borders are clearly demarcated, the areas near them might just as possibly be under some type of joint legal control of the neighboring units, or conceivably under central control. Although the Frontier Dispute opinion suggests discounting *de facto* cross-border authority if it conflicts with a clear line of legal title, it does not make clear how to handle such *de jure* cross-border shared authority. Beyond boundary areas, title to land serving a national purpose—such as military bases and national parks—could rest with the central government. Central government enclaves make perfect sense in the context of one state but raise profound problems in the event of dissolution or secession, the absorption of enclaves during decolonization hardly serving as model precedents.

With regard to temporal clarity, states and arbitrators typically derive a set of boundaries through the use of a critical date—one that "designate[s] that point of time after which no acts of the parties can validly affect the legal situation in an international dispute."[25] The parties to a border dispute often specify that date in a treaty or *compromis*. It usually corresponds to the year of independence of the states involved, or a time when the independence process was sufficiently advanced that changes by the colonial authorities would be deemed irrelevant.

Although the doctrine is meant to help exclude from the decision-making process self-serving evidence created by a party after the dispute arose, the apparent simplicity of the critical date is misleading. Where the parties have not agreed on a critical date, arbitral tribunals have shown few clear patterns—employing a smorgasbord of formulas to determine the date, making their decisions without recourse to a critical date, and admitting evidence created after the date if it shed light on the earlier situation.

For states created from secessions and dissolutions, the critical date may also be difficult to determine, as parties may have strong incentives to adopt contrasting dates. The independence movement may have festered for many years, and the lines may have changed significantly over time, including during the process of dissolution. One could, of course, simply apply the rule stipulated in some arbitrations and assume that the date upon which secession or dissolution finally succeeds (possibly in terms of recognition of new entities) is the critical date, and that those administrative borders will prevail. But other positions are arguable. In the former Soviet Union, the Russian Federation could base a claim to Crimea upon the latter's long ties to Russia and seek a critical date before Khrushchev's 1956 "gift" to the Ukrainian SSR. Canada could claim that the critical date for determining the borders of an independent Quebec is not when it secedes, but a date before Canada accorded it new lands.

III. *Uti Possidetis* and Modern Developments in International Law

The functional distinction between internal and international boundaries that calls into question the simple conversion of one to the other does not suffice to demonstrate that *uti possidetis* should not become a rule of customary law for modern breakups and breakaways. For states indeed chose such a transformation during the decolonization of both Spanish America and European Africa. Does that trend of decision of the early nineteenth and middle twentieth centuries represent good law at the turn of the twenty-first? The answer demands scrutiny of the elements surrounding the prior use of *uti possidetis* and the circumstances in which it would operate today.

One response to the decolonization precedent turns on a critical factual distinction between earlier episodes and today. *Uti possidetis* in the decolonization context did not engender changing the kind of internal borders that it would in a state's breakup today because the boundaries between different parts of a colonial empire did not serve the same functions as typical internal boundaries. While the border between, for example, one French colony and another in French Africa was less of a dividing line than that between a French colony and a British colony, in several senses it was more of a dividing line than the border between one French department and another, or between American states.

In a colonial empire, the governors and other authorities of each territory generally enjoyed extensive internal authority and independence, far more than officials of internal units in the metropole. In the French African colonies, the governors-general of the two largest groups of colonies were independent of Paris, and the governors beneath them were given wide latitude within the individual colonies. Native civil servants also developed loyalties to their immediate colony. Indeed, neighboring colonies often had different legal status vis-à-vis the metropole, suggesting that the lines dividing them had assumed what one might term semi-international status. *Uti possidetis*, then, was less functionally illegitimate in the past than it would be today because the borders to be transformed more closely resembled international boundaries than do the administrative lines of states.

More significant than the lack of a functional parallel between today's internal borders and those between colonies of the same metropole is the intervening evolution of the legal landscape regarding self-determination. This shift suggests that the factors in the colonial context that presumably made *uti possidetis* acceptable law no longer prevail.

A. Self-Determination: From Decolonization Toward Democracy

1. Decolonization *Tout Court*. Despite the UN Charter's deliberately tepid mandate concerning decolonization, by 1945 the emergence of the United States and the Soviet Union as superpowers (both of them states without colonial empires in the formal sense) and the wartime humiliation of the leading colonial states had led to a growing sense that colonialism had run its course. The new organization seized on this agenda, propelling states toward accepting that the core UN principle of self-determination[26] demanded, at the least, the liberation of colonial peoples from metropolitan control. By 1960, this position had crystallized in General Assembly Resolution 1514, in which the Assembly declared, with no opposing votes, that "all peoples have the right to self-determination," and demanded that states cease any "repressive measures" that would impede their "right to complete independence." The Assembly would admit in Resolution 1541 that the self-government inherent in decolonization need not result only in independence, but that this decision would rest with the colonial peoples alone. Fundamentally, however, the community had determined to focus self-determination upon, if not simply equate it with, decolonization.

Decolonization did not have to entail adoption of *uti possidetis*. It could have involved the redrawing of borders along other lines, as expounded by the pan-Africanist movement. *Uti possidetis* became the preferred policy because it kept decolonization—a development regarded almost universally as imperative—orderly. It meant that colonial and local elites knew, more or less, what the map of Africa and Asia would look like before the process began. This agreement on the appropriate unit of self-determination eliminated that aspect of decolonization most likely to delay the process or lead to continental—or intercontinental—conflict. All that remained to achieve independence was working out the details through a transitional period (sometimes accompanied by a plebiscite) and selection of a government. This procedure rectified a major component of the injustices experienced by colonial peoples, putting most African and Asian peoples at least one step closer to representative government and self-determination. Decolonization through *uti possidetis* thus prevented the perfect from being the enemy of the good.

At the same time, the fate of peoples within these former colonial boundaries was of less concern to states, and thus international law offered little challenge to *uti possidetis*. Although the people's overall right to political participation remained the stated position of the international community, its degree of acceptance seemed less certain. Some postcolonial leaders would reveal themselves to be antidemocratic despots as bad as the European variety. And to those minorities within the new borders who could not advance their agenda for lack of sufficient ballots, states showed even less notice. Ideally, their grievances would be addressed through human rights protections; as a matter of state practice, their welfare was more or less irrelevant to the overall goal of new statehood.[27]

2. Recognition of Internal Self-Determination. As European empires gave way to new states, the preoccupation with decolonization as a form of self-determination began to ebb. International law came to regard self-determination as more than "the right of peoples of color not to be ruled by whites."[28] The decade after the adoption of Resolution 1514 was marked by two major developments. First, the 1966 International Covenant on Civil and Political Rights transformed the Universal Declaration's provisions on political participation into detailed, convention-based obligations. The inclusion at its front end of a right to self-determination not explicitly limited to decolonization offered a springboard for assertions of internal self-determination. And the provisions on nondiscrimination and minorities aimed at ensuring protections for groups within states.[29]

Second, the 1970 Friendly Relations Declaration extended the frontiers of self-determination with respect to the territorial aspect of states. Elaborating on the Charter principle of equal rights and self-determination of peoples, it suggested, in a now near mythic paragraph, that the borders of states may not be sacrosanct. Regardless of whether this passage recognizes any right to secede, it at least signals that the "national unity" of a state is earned by its government, and is not a *fait accompli*. This seemingly radical view in fact had an important precursor in the endorsement in 1921 of a limited right to separation by the second League of Nations commission considering Finland's sovereignty over the Aaland Islands.

In one sense, this shift may have no impact on *uti possidetis* as a principle to govern future breakups. By opening up the possibility of lawful breakups, the Friendly Relations Declaration might mean that the new entities ought to conform to the administrative units of the old. The need to avoid border disputes would thus matter as much as it had during the breakup of empires, justifying continued recourse to *uti possidetis*.

But the declaration, together with the Covenant, recognizes other important values. For example, it may suggest that new states ought to be delineated in a way that is conducive to their being led by a government "representing the whole people belonging to the territory without distinction as to race, creed or colour." This is not a recipe for ethnically determined lines; and the government of the former administrative unit, unchanged in size or shape, may meet that test in many situations. Yet it does open the door to drawing borders so that individuals will not simply be part of an oppressed minority in a new state.

Suppose a group representing the majority of an administrative unit of a state, but a minority within that state, intends to split off because the state refuses to accord it the representative government required under the Friendly Relations Declaration. The eventual new state is obligated under human rights law not to discriminate against its own minorities. But suppose that, during the disintegration or secession, the nascent state shows that it has no intention of adhering to that law. In this case, the areas controlled by those minorities might be far better off within the remnants of the old state (especially if one such minority was part of the majority in the old state). The Serb dominated parts of Croatia might be one example; parts of the former Soviet Union might be others.

Thus, in some circumstances, retention of the internal lines in unaltered form may detract from the norms inherent in the Friendly Relations Declaration and human rights law. To address the needs of a wider range of people, rather than the majority in the new state alone, a more flexible approach is required—one that would ideally rely on traditional human rights protections but would not preclude other remedies. When a new state is formed, its territory ought not to be irretrievably predetermined but should form an element in the goal of maximal internal self-determination. *Uti possidetis*, for its part, assumes that any benefits to internal self-determination from changes in borders are always outweighed by the risk of conflict.

3. Toward Democratic Participation. The years since 1970 have been characterized by further landmarks elaborating the scope of internal self-determination. In declaring that "all peoples always have the right, in full freedom, to determine, when and as they wish, their internal and external political status," the Helsinki Final Act contemplated a right of internal self-determination broader than that in the Friendly Relations Declaration. By the early 1990s, the end of the Soviet

Union had led more governments and international organizations explicitly to embrace the notion—always inherent in the Universal Declaration and the Covenant on Civil and Political Rights—that the only legitimate form of government is one selected by the people through free, fair and periodic elections.

The trends in state practice toward equating the right of internal self-determination with democracy do not categorically negate *uti possidetis* as the lawful response in the event of breakups. Presumably, new states based on prior internal borders could allow periodic and genuine elections, satisfying the basic element of the democratic entitlement. Just as *uti possidetis* proved a prerequisite to nation-building after decolonization by promoting stability and reducing the possibility of conflict, so could it also prove a condition for true internal self-determination.

Yet the recognition in international law of the primacy of political participation does exert some pull on the sanctity of *uti possidetis*. If the overriding purpose of a state is to permit its people to advance their values through a democratic process, then the formation of a new state ought to take that goal into account. One method of promoting this policy is to ensure that the inhabitants of the new state truly seek membership in it and adjust the frontiers so as to produce an acceptable degree of participation. Of course, if the administrative borders already serve to define a polity dedicated to democracy and supported by the populace, modification will be unnecessary.

The special nature of transitions to new statehood was recognized by the first League of Nations legal commission to examine the Aland Islands question, which acknowledged that the rights of unwilling participants cannot be readily discounted during the formation of new states. Thus, the inclusion of the islands within Finland when the latter formed part of Russia did not mean that they would lawfully be a part of an independent Finland if their people did not wish to be.[30] The claims of peoples caught in a transitional situation differ from those of peoples long present in a state offering them full civil rights: whatever the latter's origins, they would seem to have a weak claim to border adjustments that would put them in a neighboring state. The former group would seek the most democratic outcome in the already-fluid situation of new state formation; the other would appear to promote instability without regard to the costs of upsetting a democratic status quo.

This view is not without risks. To meet the needs of all dissatisfied groups trapped within a new state could lead to a perpetuation of secessions or a patchwork of enclaves of one state within another. Thus, democratic theory cannot be carried to this extreme, and other methods will be required to enable disaffected groups to participate in the political process. Nevertheless, under certain circumstances, such as those in the former Yugoslavia and parts of the former Soviet Union, an adjustment of the frontier may prove necessary for democracy building.

B. The Badinter Commission Revisited

With these normative sea changes now apparent, we return to the Badinter Commission's Opinion No. 3. There the commission stated that *uti possidetis* "is today recognized as a general principle" and that this "principle applies all the more readily" to the former Yugoslav republics.[31] The commission, however, erred in its comprehension of the nature and purpose of *uti possidetis. Uti possidetis* is not simply an abstract legal formula to be pulled out and applied automatically every time an entity seeks statehood. Rather, whatever normative force *uti possidetis* has enjoyed depended on two core considerations: the universally agreed policy goal it was serving—orderly decolonization—and the lack of any competing norms of internal self-determination. With decolonization now historically complete (more or less) and the law now cognizant of notions of internal self-determination and political participation, the foundations for *uti possidetis* are weak, and the validity of the principle for noncolonial breakups suspect.

The dissolution of Yugoslavia lacked either of these pillars of *uti possidetis*: first, it raised policy issues, equities and ramifications far more complex, and on which an international consensus was lacking, than those related to the removal of European control from Africa and Asia. These included the stability of the resulting units, the fate of minorities and the consequences for neighboring states. And second, it took place in a legal landscape far more cognizant of participatory rights than existed during the decolonization era.

The error of the Badinter Commission is highlighted by its misinterpretation of the key judicial precedent on which it relied—the 1986 Frontier Dispute case. The ICJ Chamber defined *uti possidetis* in that case as "a principle which upgraded former administrative delimitations, *established during the colonial period*, to international frontiers" and "therefore [as] a principle of a general kind which is logically connected with *this form of decolonization* wherever it occurs."[32] Both the italicized words and the context of the case—a dispute between two former French colonies—indicate that the Court limited its views on the normative status of *uti possidetis* to the emergence of nation-states from traditional self-identified European empires. By referring to decolonization, rather than self-determination, the Chamber properly avoided any suggestion that an upgrading of administrative boundaries would apply during the breakup of non-imperial states—even if the new states regarded themselves simply as subjugated peoples in an empire (e.g., the former Soviet republics). The commission's brief, broad opinion makes no reference to the limitations in the ICJ ruling; instead, its conclusions go well beyond accepted notions of *uti possidetis* without proffering a basis for its extension.

The commission seems to have assumed that, regardless of any differences between Yugoslavia and the decolonizations, or between the law in 1960 and in 1991, only *uti possidetis* would avoid anarchy by preventing attacks by one former Yugoslav republic on another. Thus, it concluded that only by recognizing the transformation of internal boundaries into international borders protected by Article 2(4) could it stop the war. This supposition seemed consistent with the European Community's September 1991 declaration rejecting territorial changes within Yugoslavia brought about by violence. But condemnation of force to change the status quo—clearly warranted in the context of Yugoslavia—does not coincide with a legal transformation of the status quo into a permanent solution by default.

C. Territorial Title and the Rejection of Terra Nullius

Alongside the postwar and post-Cold War developments regarding self-determination has been a change in the law governing the title of a state, or a people, to land. Under orthodox doctrine, title turned on classic forms of acquisition—occupation, accretion, cession, conquest and prescription. This law developed when only European states had standing as full subjects of international law, and their use of force against each other and indigenous peoples was regarded as lawful. A territory was open to acquisition through occupation if it was *terra nullius*—"belonging" to no one at the time. The law evolved to require effective occupation, not mere discovery, for a state to maintain territorial sovereignty over the land.[33] Indigenous peoples seemed to qualify as "no one," if not legally—which would open up their land to lawful occupation—then at least effectively—as Europeans acquired their land through pacts forced upon them.

Terra nullius, however, has no place in contemporary international law. In the most literal sense, it is anachronistic because nearly the entire global landmass is already under the accepted sovereignty of one state or another, in addition to a fair number of overlapping claims. Except for some oceanic rocks, a few disputed territories and Antarctica, today no land lies outside the territorial sovereignty of some state. But more important, the broader idea that the long-term inhabitants of land have no legally cognizable claim or title to it is profoundly at odds with international human rights law and thus legally obsolete. The ICJ belatedly recognized the inapplicability of the concept to organized indigenous peoples in the *Western Sahara* case, albeit through perhaps a somewhat rosy interpretation of colonial practice. The UN members have haltingly moved since then toward recognition of these rights, rejecting the analogy of these peoples to flora and fauna.

Instead, international law now accepts, at a minimum, that long-term inhabitants of a territory have rights that can override the claims of governments.[34] Those inhabitants have valid concerns as part of the general population. Indeed, by virtue of their unique attachment and historic claims to certain lands, they are entitled to a special voice in the strategy for internal self-determination. By implication, this would include a say on the size and shape of entities resulting from that process.

This welcome advance in the law, even if not solidified today in terms of conventions, custom or compliance mechanisms, calls into question the normativity of *uti possidetis* as applied to state breakups today. Just as one purpose of *uti possidetis* during decolonization was to eliminate the possibility of appropriation of lands that some states might regard as *terrae nullius*, so the rejection in law of that concept eliminates one of the purposes of the doctrine. If the land inhabited by indigenous peoples is not *terra nullius*, it seems highly questionable that a new state has the right to inherit that land at the expense of the indigenous peoples living there. Thus, although indigenous peoples appear to lack a unique right to secede from an existing state,[35] a new claimant state ought not to be able to "take its indigenous peoples with it" from the old state by assuming its size and shape are determined by prior internal borders. An example arises in the case of the lands in Quebec inhabited by the Cree Indians. Their rights under international law affect not only the underlying lawfulness of Quebec's attempts at secession, but the contours of an independent Quebec as well. To assume that Quebec must encompass all these lands, even if the indigenous peoples indicate another preference, would ignore their special claim to land and extend, to a new state, antiquated notions of territorial sovereignty.

IV. TOWARD RATIONAL LINE DRAWING

Once *uti possidetis* is examined functionally and legally, both its geographic and its normative underpinnings seem increasingly suspect. Yet its defenders can fall back on the two principal claims noted at the beginning of this article: (1) because liberal democratic states can function within any borders, the legal changes described above do not require abandonment of the principle; and (2) any alternative to *uti possidetis* is simply not feasible.[36] These arguments place a burden on proposals to move beyond *uti possidetis*.

The first is based on our cosmopolitan ideal—to build pluralist, democratic societies within whatever borders states have upon their birth. The West and most African elites saw this as the hope for Africa and its colonial-imposed borders. But democracy, even where it has sprouted in new states, does not guarantee the rights of minorities, or address those groups that do not wish to be part of the polity.[37] More important, in those states of the former Yugoslavia and Soviet Union where human rights have not taken root, the assumption that postindependence borders must coincide with preindependence lines has meant expulsions and refugee crises, "ethnic cleansing" within the state, and even genocide.

Thus, as much as liberal internationalists should cherish the idea of diverse peoples living together, we cannot always, as John Chipman points out, "impose a cosmopolitan diktat."[38] Instead, we must acknowledge that certain new states are not currently able or willing to guarantee the human rights of minorities in discrete territories, and must consider alternatives to leaving those groups at the mercy of new governments. Cosmopolitanism must remain the goal, not only because people can then identify themselves beyond real or imagined blood lines, but also because many minorities live within areas where border changes are not feasible. But in certain instances account may have to be taken of the need to avoid leaving peoples in new states where they do not wish to be or that will not treat them with dignity.

This strips the defense of *uti possidetis* and immutability to its negative core—the absence of any other solution. *Uti possidetis* thus represents the classic example of what Thomas Franck has called an "idiot rule"—a simple, clear norm that offers an acceptable outcome in most situations but whose very clarity undermines its legitimacy in others.[39] The rule may assume that no border is more rational than another, or that the issue of borders is simply so complex and emotional that states will always prove unable to reallocate territory peacefully. Either way, any solution other than acceptance of past injustices would be too complicated to be applied, would lead to chaos, and would therefore prove illegitimate. This argument also won the day during the African decolonizations, usually with good reason; and it seems to underlie certain creative proposals concerning intrastate conflict today.[40]

In the remainder of this article, I set out four guidelines for decision makers that suggest that the options are not so stark and lay the basis for a principled alternative to *uti possidetis*. These do not represent a comprehensive framework for decision, which extends beyond this article. Moreover, to move beyond the "idiot rule," it seems likely that states will need to develop some type of institutional mechanism, such as a mandatory or optional regional arbitration or conciliation commission, to help resolve the matter in the event negotiations bog down. They should also consider forestalling recognition of new states until borders are resolved, as well as lend their full support to a negotiated or arbitrated outcome. Whatever the application process, the possibilities must be shown so that the mechanisms can be created, or engaged.

A. A New Normative Starting Point

First, the functional and legal arguments against the automatic transformation of frontiers suggest a compelling need to respect the original Roman-law meaning of *uti possidetis*: to preserve the status quo only until states can resolve their competing claims, rather than apply the gloss from decolonization whereby states effectively presumed independence-day lines to be permanent. Reversion to the Latin notion, somewhat ironically, serves to update the principle from its decolonization form to take account of constitutive changes in the international order concerning human rights and self-determination. It further suggests endorsing the cautious and negative iteration of *uti possidetis* used by Klabbers and Lefeber to characterize the principle in its decolonization sense as a guide for the breakup of states: that the attainment of independence is not per se a ground to invalidate existing boundaries. If, during the creation of states, the new entities cannot agree on an appropriate division of territory, they should respect existing lines of control—likely to be designated by administrative lines—until an authoritative determination is reached on new boundaries.[41]

As a result, the provisional status will remain until the parties accept the costs and benefits of those borders or new ones. In many situations, states will and should retain the borders. But at least they will consider improving the welfare of individuals and long-term stability by revising frontiers. And, equally important, the prospect of border revisions may cause some secessionist groups to rethink their claims to statehood entirely.

This position differs critically from the Badinter Commission's view. The commission adopted a default rule that internal lines translate into international borders unless the parties agree otherwise, turning alteration of boundaries into the exception, rather than part of the policy. A provisional gloss accepts the utility of the status quo as a way to avoid conflict and suggests that these boundaries deserve consideration, and some deference, during the process of defining the size of a state attaining independence; but it falls short of sanctioning perpetuation of the status quo if new states are created.

The most immediate consequence of this starting point is an admittedly heavy burden on decision makers, whether national diplomats or international commissions or courts: to deal directly with the location of international borders, rather than retreat behind the simple, but anachronistic, decolonization form of *uti possidetis*. To date, states, courts and scholars have agreed on the unexceptionable proposition that there is no universal rule for arriving at an ideal line to divide territory—whether by adopting linguistic boundaries, natural frontiers or *uti possidetis*. But rather than looking for the ideal line, we must set more modest goals. Decision makers faced with potential or accomplished breakups must gauge if there is a significantly better line than that in place and draw the best line under the circumstances—significantly better because the displacement costs of adjusting borders cannot be ignored.

The community policies behind that better, more rational line are hardly obscure. The philosophers Margalit and Raz posited in their theory of self-determination that "the shape and boundaries of political units are to be determined by their service to individual well-being."[42] This notion reflects the essence of human rights as an undergirding concept in the implementation of self-determination. The human rights at stake are those not only of the populace of the claimant new state, but of its neighbors in the old state or other states as well. From a different discipline, political scientists have spoken of rational frontiers as those that reduce the risk of conflict by corresponding to some existing division of people. This reflects the basic policies of minimum public order.

Such a position in no way undermines the important norm of stability and finality of boundaries. That norm provides that if states have resolved a border dispute through a process meeting appropriate standards of lawfulness, then it should be presumed that their dispute is over and the border permanent. Of obvious merit in a semianarchical world, the norm embodies a decision by states to deny to their neighbors a continuously available process to challenge a boundary.[43] The norm does not, however, require that a provisional, *de facto*, or disputed, let alone illegitimate or illegal, border become permanent; and thus it does not mandate the status quo as a solution to unresolved or active claims. And a new interpretation of *uti possidetis* recognizes that once those borders are finally determined, they should remain stable.

B. Respect for the Peaceful Settlement of Disputes

Supplementing any proposal that states consider border changes is a requirement that the process take place through peaceful means alone. For states that have already split up, this requirement means nothing more or less than adherence to Article 2(4) of the Charter. If a state claims territory held by another state, it may not lawfully use force against that other state merely by asserting that, by dint of its territorial claim, it is not acting against the territorial integrity or political independence of that state.[44]

As for ongoing attempts at secession or dissolution, international law does not forbid the use of force in civil disputes, although aspects of *jus in bello* apply to internal wars.[45] A blanket prohibition on force would redound to the detriment of legitimate governments fighting unjustified secessionist or other insurgent movements, as well as of resistance forces attempting to overthrow tyranny. However, when the elites within the state have accepted the secession or dissolution, they should abstain from using force to adjust boundaries with which they are not satisfied, and begin negotiations. While new statehood need not hinge upon an agreement on borders, it seems prudent for decision makers to agree on them before independence. Prior negotiations provide the best opportunity for revisions to conciliate disaffected minorities, and offer a possible side benefit of preventing the dissolution altogether. This procedure, of course, is what various mediators urged on the Yugoslav parties in 1991, and the latter's readiness to ignore it highlights the risks facing all remedies—including *uti possidetis*—in this field.

C. Assessing the Relevance of Existing Internal Borders

With these basic policies in mind, diplomats, conciliators and arbitrators should scrutinize administrative boundaries for their suitability as international frontiers. This process is the critical prerequisite to determining whether a substantially better alternative is available and drawing a final line. Several factors merit consideration.

First, weight must be given to the age of the line. Borders centuries old count for more than those decades old, not only because of an aversion to opening closed issues, but also because of the likelihood that the populations will have adjusted to long-standing borders. They may also have developed a sufficient sense of community identity to justify retention of traditional borders. Recent borders, such as those created after Stalin's incorporation of the trans-Dniester region into the Moldavian SSR following Bessarabia's annexation in 1940, would have a poorer claim to transformation.

Moreover, the alteration of administrative borders during the process of self-determination would remain suspect in the event of a consummated secession or breakup. Such changes could occur if the central government drew new lines in a failed attempt to stave off division, analogous to Nigeria's reallocation of internal lines in 1967 as part of its (successful) effort to unite the country against the Biafran secession. This suggests that the critical date for determining the borders of new entities may in some cases precede their independence. In the 1989 Guinea-Bissau/Senegal maritime boundary arbitration, the panel recognized that a colony undergoing self-determination need not be bound by the agreements concluded by the imperial power once that process has begun, even if it precedes formal independence.

Second, the process by which the line was drawn will merit consideration. A constitutionally authorized line, for instance, ought to have a greater presumption of permanence than one determined solely at the command of a dictator. But as constitutions can be deceiving in many ways, the more fundamental question seems to be the equality of the participants in the process leading to the creation of the boundary. If a boundary is forced upon an area by a powerful central authority, or a powerful neighboring administrative unit, it would not reflect even the minimal wishes of the inhabitants, and their inability to change that border ought not to be probative. Nevertheless, despite the abstract appeal of lending more weight to lines freely arrived at than to those imposed on peoples, the former may still be inappropriate for international borders on the basis of an earlier critique of *uti possidetis*—that is, their location might well have been premised on the continued unity of the state, and separation breaks that bargain.

Last, because neither age nor origin directly addresses functional suitability as an international frontier, negotiators and arbitrators will have to take account of the viability of the entities that would emerge from secessions or breakups along existing lines. On the one hand, states have been unwilling to consider the size or shape of a claimant to statehood in the decision to accord recognition, especially territories emerging from colonial rule. But political geographers routinely study the effect of geography on national development; and theorists of self-determination have evaluated these issues in considering the propriety of secession. Even the ICJ has acknowledged the importance of economic issues by considering the efficient exploitation of resources in addressing disputed sea borders.

Thus, decision makers would be well-advised to consider whether the administrative lines would allow the new states—including the remnant of the prior state—to govern themselves adequately and develop economically. If the borders contain irrational elements for the governance and economy of separate states, as may well be the case given the distinct functions of internal and inter-state borders, the decision makers will have to consider alternatives. This question, too, is not without ambiguity; for example, a state need not be crippled if the existing lines render it landlocked (e.g., Belarus) or reliant on sources of energy from abroad (e.g., many of the former Soviet states). But some lines may be especially troublesome economically, such as those that deprive one state of access to other states and the sea, or divide a specific resource. In those cases, recognition of borders should be postponed until suitable arrangements are made—e.g., corridors to other states or the sea.

As for shape, administrative lines that create enclaves (one part of a unit that is separated from the bulk of the unit and surrounded by another unit) will be especially problematic as international frontiers. Although such areas have functioned in rare cases, they face tremendous obstacles to successful integration in the state. Similarly, a secession that leaves the old entity discontiguous, such as would arise in the case of Quebec, raises similar problems. In the abstract, administrative lines defining a compact territory, without unusual elongations and preferably without significant interior natural barriers, will make the state (whether the remnant of the old or the new) easier to govern administratively.

D. Self-Determination in Transitional Situations: Reexamining the Plebiscite Model

A provisional interpretation of *uti possidetis*, coupled with a prohibition on the use of force and scrutiny of existing administrative borders, still does not directly confront the core issue of human rights arguing against extension of the decolonization form of *uti possidetis*; namely, its failure to account for the harm to individual well-being that may result either from a lack of commitment by the new state (defined by the old borders) to protect certain groups or from their desire to locate elsewhere. That shortcoming necessitates a direct role for the affected populations in arriving at lines to replace the administrative borders. Thus, some form of consultation with the populace of a disputed territory on its future, though perhaps not a binding vote, is needed, if not already legally required. A policy to this end entails a renewed look at one of the successes of the Versailles Treaty, at times employed by the United Nations—the internationally supervised plebiscite.

Plebiscites provide a direct mechanism for peoples of a disputed territory to voice their preferences regarding their status. After World War I, the Allies used them to dispose of a small number of areas that had not been allocated by rewarding the victors with the spoils.[46] Since World War II, states have used the plebiscite almost exclusively in the decolonization context. Often under UN supervision, plebiscites confirmed the wishes of many colonial peoples for independence, and occasionally (as in the Northern Cameroons) boundaries were altered on the basis of those wishes. States have also not hesitated to undermine plebiscites—witness Indonesia's interference with the vote in West Irian in 1969—or to prevent them when they feared negative results—as with India's refusal to abide by the Security Council's 1947 demand for a plebiscite in Kashmir, and Morocco's continual frustration of the planned UN-supervised polling in the Western Sahara.

Seeking the voice of the people in contested areas seems a logical outflow of modern trends of self-determination, but plebiscites contain the seeds of their own frustration, engendering some opposition to them as optimal policies. These center on (1) the location and size of the plebiscite area; (2) the voting unit within the plebiscite area; and (3) the location of the line to be drawn as a result of the plebiscite. Each is likely to become the subject of intense political negotiations during self-determination disputes, as each party seeks to define the terms of the plebiscite so as to secure the most territory.

But the issue is not beyond imaginative solutions through diplomacy or third-party decision making. In certain areas, the population distribution may be so obvious, or the land so sparsely inhabited, as to warrant limiting the vote to a core area, e.g., only part of Kashmir. Evaluating the interwar period, Sarah Wambaugh offered a sensible approach to the size of the area when the parties cannot agree— one determined by the sides' furthest claims—and also noted the importance of historical and economic factors in determining the unit of voting.[47]

As for the line resulting from the plebiscite, almost any contiguous line will leave some voters where they do not wish to be, perhaps keeping alive the claims of irredentists or leading to migration of the disaffected. But state practice does not appear to demand that the line follow the plebiscite results exactly, whatever the consequences regarding the creation of enclaves or economically irrational configurations. In one significant internal plebiscite since decolonization, Switzerland managed to draw a line creating the new canton of Jura out of the canton of Bern in 1976. Although the Government followed the general results of the vote by placing the northern part of the contested area in the new canton and leaving the southern districts in the canton of Bern, several communes ended up with a status they had opposed. Decision makers could consider approaches that leave a minimum number of people disaffected or ensure that the losers on one side are balanced by those on the other. The plebiscite and new line can only make more people better off, not all people. Moreover, geographic factors will play a role and may dictate who will not end up in their preferred location.

Principles of equity used by international courts and states in border disputes could also have an important role in drawing a final line.[48] In the Frontier Dispute case, for example, Judge Abi-Saab pointed out that, when judges need to determine a border, their degrees of freedom to draw a line using equitable principles increase as the number of known border points decreases.[49]

While leaving much to the biases of arbitrators, equity offers some framework within which courts can take account of a variety of relevant factors.

V. Conclusion

If the hallmark of an effective legal system is some degree of predictability of outcome, an assault on extending the decolonization form of *uti possidetis* to the breakup of states would appear at first to undermine the cause. For that formulation is clearly the easiest short-run method for determining the borders of a new state. But law, of course, is about justice and legitimacy as well. And self-determination, by its nature, is an enormously complex and rich process in international law. If its goal is to enable individuals and groups to realize their human rights, then the complexity of the territorial element cannot be wished away through invocation of a hallowed formula.

This article has sought to demonstrate that the default rule requiring inheritance of prior boundaries suffers from functional and normative flaws when applied to administrative lines within states. In particular, the extension of *uti possidetis* to these situations is highly suspect because of (1) the difference between internal and international borders, as well as between internal state borders and the internal colonial lines to which the principle was formerly applied; (2) the supplanting of the policy imperative underlying *uti possidetis* (decolonization) with the uncertainty surrounding state breakups; and, most important, (3) the constitutive changes in international law, principally the emphasis on internal self-determination and participatory government and the demise of *terra nullius*. These factors all require recognition in the law and policies governing modern breakups or attempts at them. The results may be unsatisfying to some, and the questions raised (including the lack of centralized enforcement mechanisms) may lead many to conclude that *uti possidetis* should develop into a rule for these situations. Even under the approach suggested here, the scrutiny of existing borders may yield a determination that many should become the boundaries of new states, and perhaps the burden of proof should lie on those who seek to challenge them.

To adopt that course of action uniformly and automatically, however, perpetuates a subterfuge: a formalized self-determination that enables a new state to form along the administrative lines of the old territorial unit but neglects the underlying territorial issues that prompted the dissatisfaction in the first place, and perhaps lays the groundwork for a new round of interstate conflicts and attempted secessions. It rewards the leaders of secessionist movements by more readily granting them a new territory, but offers uncertain prospects for the human rights and political participation of the inhabitants or the public order of the region. Only by directly engaging the territorial question, with all its dimensions, is the international community likely to control the breakup of states in an orderly manner consistent with human dignity.

8

NOTES

1. Georges Scelle, *Obsession du Territoire*, in SYMBOLAE VERZIJL 347 (1958).
2. Warren Zimmermann, *The Choice in the Balkans*, N.Y. REV. BOOKS, Sept. 21, 1995, at 4, 4.
3. Conference on Yugoslavia, Arbitration Commission Opinion No. 3 (Jan. 11, 1992), 31 ILM 1499 (1992).
4. W. W. Buckland, A TEXT-BOOK OF ROMAN LAW FROM AUGUSTUS TO JUSTINIAN 734 (Peter Stein ed., 3d rev. ed. 1963); John Bassett Moore, COSTA RICA-PANAMA ARBITRATION: MEMORANDUM ON *UTI POSSIDETIS* 5–8 (1913). . . .
5. Moore, *supra* note 4, at 8.
6. *Id.* at 8–11 (citing works by Rivier, Bynkershoek, Oppenheim and Calvo); Eduardo Jimenez de Arechaga, *Boundaries in Latin America: Uti Possidetis Doctrine*, in 1 ENCYCLOPEDIA OF PUBLIC INTERNATIONAL LAW 449, 450 (Rudolf Bernhardt ed., 1992) [hereinafter ENCYCLOPEDIA].
7. Saadia Touval, THE BOUNDARY POLITICS OF INDEPENDENT AFRICA 16 (1972). See generally Thomas Pakenham, THE SCRAMBLE FOR AFRICA: WHITE MAN'S CONQUEST OF THE DARK CONTINENT FROM 1876 TO 1912 (1991).
8. See Marc Weller, *The International Response to the Dissolution of the Socialist Federal Republic of Yugoslavia*, 86 AJIL 569, 574–82 (1992).
9. See Opinion No. 3, *supra* note 3.
10. The most prominent were Nikita Khrushchev's so-called gift of Crimea from the RSFSR to the Ukrainian SSR in 1954 and the transfer of a large area in the Kazakh SSR to the Uzbek SSR in 1963.
11. GA Res. 1514 (XV), para. 4, UN GAOR, 15th Sess., Supp. No. 16, at 66, 67, UN Doc. A/4684 (1960) (requiring states to respect the "integrity of [the] national territory [of dependent peoples]"); id., para. 6 (prohibiting the "partial or total disruption of the national unity and territorial integrity of a country"). See also Rosalyn Higgins, PROBLEMS AND PROCESS: INTERNATIONAL LAW AND HOW WE USE IT 122 (1994).
12. To mention the most notable examples: Britain and France split the German colony of Togo after World War I, and the British area became part of Ghana, not Togo or a separate state. . . .These same powers split German Kamerun; the northern part of the British area voted for merger with Nigeria and the southern part for merger into the French area as Cameroun. . . . British and Italian Somalia became independent as one state and not two; Kuria Muria, an island in British-administered Aden (later South Yemen), became part of Muscat and Oman (now Oman) in 1967 after its people voted for separate status. . . .
13. See Michla Pomerance, SELF-DETERMINATION IN LAW AND PRACTICE: THE NEW DOCTRINE IN THE UNITED NATIONS 19–20 (1982) (plebiscites on reversion of Belgian Rwanda-Urundi to two countries and divisions of British Gilbert and Ellice Islands and of U.S. Trust Territories).
14. See Jacqueline Dutheil de la Rochère, *Les Procédures de règlement des différends frontaliers*, in LA FRONTIÈRE 125, 135 (Société Française pour le Droit International ed., 1980); Yehuda Z. Blum, HISTORIC TITLES IN INTERNATIONAL LAW 342 (1965).
15. Conference on Security and Co-operation in Europe, Final Act, Aug. 1, 1975, Principle III, 14 ILM 1292, 1294 (1975), 73 DEP'T ST. BULL. 323, 324–25 (1975) (parties regard frontiers as "inviolable" and will refrain from "assaulting these frontiers") [hereinafter Helsinki Final Act].
16. See Jan Klabbers & Rene Lefeber, *Africa: Lost between Self-Determination and uti possidetis*, in PEOPLES AND MINORITIES IN INTERNATIONAL LAW 37, 63 (Catherine Brolmann, Renee Lefeber & Marjoleine Zieck eds., 1993) [hereinafter PEOPLES AND MINORITIES].
17. See Military and Paramilitary Activities in and against Nicaragua (Nicar. v. U.S.), 1986 ICJ REP. 14, 100–01 (June 27).
18. See, e.g., ORGANIZATION OF AFRICAN UNITY, CHARTER Art. III(3), 479 UNTS

39, 74; Charter of Paris for a New Europe, Nov. 21, 1990, 30 ILM 190, 196 (1991) (repeating obligation under UN Charter Art. 2(4)).

19. S. Whittemore Boggs, INTERNATIONAL BOUNDARIES: A STUDY OF BOUNDARY FUNCTIONS AND PROBLEMS 10 (1940).

20. 1 OPPENHEIM'S INTERNATIONAL LAW 661 (Robert Jennings & Arthur Watts eds., 1992).

21. Ronan Paddison, THE FRAGMENTED STATE: THE POLITICAL GEOGRAPHY OF POWER 63–74, 108–15 (1983).

22. Michael Walzer, JUST AND UNJUST WARS 55, 57–58 (2d ed. 1992).

23. Frontier Dispute, 1986 ICJ REP. at 568.

24. See, e.g., Honduras Borders Case (Guat./Hond.), 2 R.I.A.A. 1309, 1324 (1933); Frontier Dispute, 1986 ICJ REP. at 587.

25. L. F. E. Goldie, *The Critical Date*, 12 INT'L & COMP. L.Q. 1251, 1267 (1963). . . .

26. [See Hannum's article in this volume–eds.]

27. See Hurst Hannum, AUTONOMY, SOVEREIGNTY, AND SELF-DETERMINATION: THE ACCOMMODATION OF CONFLICTING RIGHTS 71–72 (1990); Allan Rosas, *Internal Self-Determination*, in MODERN LAW OF SELF-DETERMINATION 225, 227–28 (Christian Tomuschat ed., 1993); Thomas M. Franck, *Postmodern Tribalism and the Right to Secession*, in PEOPLES AND MINORITIES, *supra* note 16, at.10.

28. *id.* See also Higgins, *supra* note 11, at 114–21.

29. See generally Patrick Thornberry, INTERNATIONAL LAW AND THE RIGHTS OF MINORITIES 141–247 (1991).

30. See Report of the International Commission of Jurists Entrusted by the Council of the League of Nations with the Task of Giving an Advisory Opinion upon the Legal Aspects of the Aaland Islands Question, LEAGUE OF NATIONS O.J. Spec. Supp. 3, at 10 (1920). . . . See also Nathaniel Berman, *"But the Alternative is Despair": European Nationalism and the Modernist Renewal of International Law*, 106 HARV. L. REV. 1792, 1862–68 (1993).

31. Opinion No. 3, *supra* note 3, 31 ILM at 1500 (citing Frontier Dispute, 1986 ICJ REP. at 565).

32. 1986 ICJ REP. at 566 (emphasis added).

33. Island of Palmas, 2 R.I.A.A. at 846; Legal Status of Eastern Greenland, 1933 PCIJ (ser. A/B) No. 53, at 45–46 (Apr. 5).

34. Western Sahara, 1975 ICJ REP. at 68 (absent ties of territorial sovereignty, people of disputed territory have right to self-determination under Resolution 1514). See also W. Michael Reisman, *Protecting Indigenous Rights in International Adjudication*, 89 AJIL 350, 354–57 (1995).

35. Riadza Torres, *The Rights of Indigenous Populations: The Emerging International Norm*, 16 YALE J. INT'L L. 203 (1991); Hannum, *supra* note 27, at 96 & n.339.

36. A third defense could note that some administrative borders mean something and should not be tampered with, a point acknowledged, but irrelevant to those many administrative borders that lack functional, historical or other justification.

37. See generally Renee de Nevers, *Democratization and Ethnic Conflict*, in ETHNIC CONFLICT AND INTERNATIONAL SECURITY 61 (Michael E. Brown ed., 1993).

38. John Chipman, *Managing the Politics of Parochialism*, in ETHNIC CONFLICT AND INTERNATIONAL SECURITY, *supra* note 37, at 237, 261.

39. Thomas M. Franck, THE POWER OF LEGITIMACY AMONG NATIONS 67–77 (1990). I appreciate this insight from Gregory Fox.

40. Compare Morton H. Halperin & David J. Scheffer, SELF-DETERMINATION IN THE NEW WORLD ORDER 86 (1992) (proposing residents of new states be able to choose citizenship of neighboring state); Ted Robert Gurr, MINORITIES AT RISK: A GLOBAL VIEW OF ETHNOPOLITICAL CONFLICTS 298–313 (1993) (proposing increased minorities' rights within existing states) with Gidon Gottlieb, NATION AGAINST STATE: A NEW APPROACH TO ETHNIC CONFLICTS AND THE DECLINE OF

SOVEREIGNTY 46–47, 75–76 (1993) (proposal for differing sets of borders for different purposes).

41. Such a view of *uti possidetis* applies only to the former internal boundaries, not the international boundaries. For example, the border between Italy and Yugoslavia does not become provisional when it becomes the border between Italy and Slovenia. Moreover, this proposal is limited to recent and future breakups, and does not suggest revising the post-independence borders in Africa, a policy that might run afoul of important norms of stability and finality of borders. But see Charles William Maynes, *The New Pessimism*, FOREIGN POL'Y, Fall 1995, at 33, 48 (proposing "incentives to redraw borders to obtain more viable states"); Makau wa Mutua, *Why Redraw the Map of Africa: A Moral and Legal Inquiry*, 16 MICH. J. INT'L L. 1113 (1995).

42. Avishai Margalit & Joseph Raz, *National Self-Determination*, 87 J. PHIL. 457 (1990).

43. Kaiyan Homi Kaikobad, *Some Observations on the Doctrine of Continuity and Finality of Boundaries*, 54 BRIT. Y.B. INT'L L. 119, 119 (1983). For the general principle behind the norm, see Grisbadarna Case (Nor./Swed.), Hague Ct. Rep. (Scott) 121, 130 (1909) (three-person panel) ("a state of things which actually exists and has existed for a long time should be changed as little as possible").

44. Friendly Relations Declaration, GA Res, 2625 (XXV), Annex, UN GAOR, 25th Sess., Supp. No. 28 at 121, 122, UN Doc. A/8028 (1970) (banning force to solve "territorial disputes and problems concerning frontiers of States" or to "violate international lines of demarcation"). See also SC Res. 502, UN SCOR, 37th Sess., Res. & Dec., at 15, UN Doc. S/INF/38 (1982) (Falkland Islands invasion); SC Res. 660, UN SCOR, 45th Sess., Res. & Dec., at 19, UN Doc. S/INF/46 (1990) (Iraqi invasion of Kuwait).

45. See, e.g., Geneva Convention Relative to the Protection of Civilian Persons in Time of War, Aug. 12, 1949, Art. 3, 6 UST 3516, 3518, 75 UNTS 287, 288–90; Protocol Additional to the Geneva Conventions of 12 August 1949, and Relating to the Protection of Victims of Non-International Armed Conflicts (Protocol II), Dec. 12, 1977, 1125 UNTS 609; Prosecutor v. Tadic, Appeal on Jurisdiction, UN Doc. IT-94-1-AR72, at 53–68, paras. 96–127 (1995), reprinted in 35 ILM 32, 62–70 (1996).

46. The Versailles Treaty called for plebiscites in Schleswig, the Saar, Allenstein, Upper Silesia, and Marienwalder. See 1 Sarah Wambaugh, PLEBISCITES SINCE THE WORLD WAR 3–45 (1933), which remains the authoritative account. . . .

47. *Id.*, 494, 503.

48. See Frontier Dispute, 1986 ICJ REP. at 567–68 (using equity to divide a pool equally); Land, Island, 1992 ICJ REP. at 514–15 (relying on equity to give effect to unratified treaty); MOORE, *supra* note 4, at 29.

49. Frontier Dispute, 1986 ICJ REP. at 662–63 (Abi-Saab, J., sep. op.).

Irredentism: Self-Determination and Interstate War

Thomas Ambrosio

Every divided country or partitioned people is unhappy.

—LEO TOLSTOY

INTERSTATE BOUNDARIES ARE often the result of arbitrary decisions that ignore demographic circumstances;[1] consequently, many nations are divided by interstate borders. If we accept Rogers Brubaker's assertion that nationalism is fundamentally "a form of remedial action . . . [that] addresses an allegedly deficient or 'pathological' condition and proposes to remedy it . . . [and] can be conceived as a set of variations on a single core lament: that the identity and interests of a putative nation are not properly expressed or realized,"[2] then for most divided or partitioned nations, a core component of nationalist mobilization is the belief that "the political and national unit should be congruent."[3] A policy of *irredentism*[4] is one in which a "national-state"[5] embarks on a program to annex (either *de jure* or *de facto*) territories of another state that their co-nationals inhabit in order to unify the nation under one political entity.[6] Though sometimes seen as similar to secession, irredentism is quite different: Secession can be defined as "an attempt by an ethnic group claiming a homeland to withdraw with its territory from the authority of a larger state of which it is a part";[7] or to paraphrase Donald Horowitz, irredentism refers to subtracting from one state and adding to another, while secession is subtracting alone. The two distinguishing features of irredentism are: (a) a pre-existing national-state, and (b) territorial claims against another state based upon national affinity.[8]

The literature on irredentism is not extensive in either the international law, international relations, or ethnic conflict fields. This is due to three factors. First, most works on ethnic conflicts tend to focus on domestic-level politics and processes. Ethnic conflicts are often seen as a problem *within* countries and not *between* them.[9] Second, when attention is given to the impact of ethnic conflicts on the international system, irredentism is almost always overlooked in favor of secessionist movements.[10] This makes sense since secession is first and foremost a domestic issue. Also, the number of secessionist crises tend to overwhelm the comparatively fewer irredentist problems; this is quite evident in the international law literature.[11] Finally, irredentism is perched between ethnic conflict and international relations studies and often falls in the cracks. In international relations theory, the dominant realist, neorealist, and neoliberal paradigms have significant problems allowing for domestic variables to explain state behavior— no less emotive variables such as ethnicity and nationalism.[12]

Because irredentism, unlike secession, is by definition an interstate conflict, there is no question that it falls into the realm of international law, which has traditionally focused on relations between states.[13] In addition, the issue of irredentism is important because it involves the central theme of this volume: the tension between self-determination and territorial integrity; that is, between nations and states. Nearly all irredentist projects are couched in terms of self-determination. In most cases, the aim of annexation is downplayed or disingenuously denied. Instead, an irredentist national-state contends that it is merely supporting the right of its co-nationals to exercise their *own* right of self-determination (through secession), rather than seeking territorial aggrandizement. The reality is quite different. The leaders of an irredentist state believe that the current interstate borders are illegitimate because they divide the nation and prevent it from constituting a unified political entity. They wish to overturn the status quo in order to achieve national goals. In many cases, the irredentist project becomes an obsession for the body politic and states will go to extraordinary lengths to achieve unity.[14]

Not all irredentist conflicts are alike, however. It is possible to distinguish between three types of irredenta: state-state, decolonization, and state collapse. In those cases that I denote as *state-state*, the irredentist and the target state (which contains the population and territory to be acquired) are both established states in the international system. The borders between them are relatively long-standing (even if just a few years), but may be diplomatically contested. The definitive example of state-state irredentism since the end of the Second World War is the Somali invasion of Ethiopia. However, a situation in which one nation has constituted two separate national-states—for example, North and South Korea, East and West Germany, the two Yemens, Romania and Moldova—would also fall under this category. Irredentist conflicts of the *decolonization* type include those in which states (either former colonies or not) attempt to reverse the legacies of colonialism by acquiring territories still retained by colonial powers; the continued possession of these territories by the colonial power, it is asserted, stands in opposition to the national and territorial integrity of the irredentist state. India's invasion of Portuguese-controlled Goa and Indonesia's annexation of East Timor fit into this category. In cases of *state collapse*, an overarching political structure has disintegrated and the successor states are attempting to forge new borders between them on the basis of ethnic criteria. With the collapse of socialist Yugoslavia and the Soviet Union, Croatia, Serbia,[15] and Armenia disregarded the administrative borders defined by the former central governments and sought territories from other successor states where their co-nationals resided.

This categorization of three types of irredenta reflects the distinction made within international law and the practice of third-party states toward irredentist conflicts. International law generally rejects irredentist claims in favor of the preservation of state boundaries. In cases of state-state irredentism, the actions of the irredentists have been consistently deemed illegitimate by the international community. On the other hand, the international community has largely taken a passive stance toward those irredentist conflicts arising out of the legacies of colonization. Outside of the colonial context, there has not been a case in which a forceful irredentist territorial gain has been formally recognized by the majority of the international community in the postwar period. In the conflict between state and nation, international law generally sides with states. However, there is more ambiguity when it comes to situations of state collapse: The practice of third-party states and international organizations has been mixed, with some irredentist states paying a large price for their policies and others allowed to *de facto* fulfill their goals.

This essay examines the place of irredentism in international law and the application of international legal rules to actual cases. I will proceed as follows. I first provide a brief overview of territorial acquisition and the development of the norm of territorial integrity. I then look at how this norm is affected by the principle of self-determination. While most other examinations of the relationship between territorial integrity and self-determination debate the issue of secession, this essay takes an external perspective—that is, whether the principle of self-determination allows for the subordination of territorial integrity to the goals of national-states. Next, I provide a number of brief accounts of irredentist conflicts within the three categories delineated above: state-state (Somali invasion of Ethiopia and the invasion of South Korea by North Korea); decolonization (India-Goa and Indonesia-East Timor); and lastly, state collapse (Serbia, Croatia, Armenia). Finally, I summarize the findings of this essay and posit some causes for the inconsistent application of international law in cases of irredentism.

Before I begin, a point of clarification is needed. Irredentist claims need not be pursued through military or forcible means. National states can seek territorial revisions through political or diplomatic channels. International law does not preclude changes of borders if such changes are done peacefully and with the consent of the parties involved;[16] though there is probably a preference that borders not be altered.[17] In this discussion of irredentism, I am specifically referring to *forcible* irredentism, which can be taken to mean the threat or use of force to fulfill the national goal of political unity.

I. TERRITORIAL AGGRANDIZEMENT AND SELF-DETERMINATION

Since irredentism is, by definition, an attempt to acquire territory under the sovereignty of another state, it is necessary to begin with the history of territorial acquisition in international law.[18] Until the early part of the twentieth century, a right of conquest was widely recognized among international law scholars and through state practice. While there are certainly those who disputed the existence of this 'right' and argued that it was contrary to the very idea of international law,[19] the Permanent Court of Arbitration at The Hague, in the *Islands of Palmas* case (1928), explicitly recognized that conquest had been an accepted manner of acquiring territory.[20] However, with the 1917 revolutions in Russia and the elucidation of the war aims of the United States during the First World War, there was a fundamental shift in the perceived legitimacy of this principle. The Russian Provisional Government, the Bolsheviks, and U.S. President Woodrow Wilson all rejected the notion of postwar annexations.[21] Despite having constructed secret deals prior to the outbreak of war for the distribution of the territories of the Central Powers, the victorious Allies, through much prodding by the Wilson administration, eventually acquiesced to a renunciation of the right of conquest (albeit with some exceptions[22]).[23]

Wilson's belief in the immorality of conquest and the need to preserve the territorial integrity of states was intimately tied to his support for the principle of self-determination.[24] If it was illegitimate, as Wilson stated, "to hand peoples about from sovereignty to sovereignty as if they were property," then it was equally illegitimate to annex peoples against their will. These two principles, territorial integrity and self-determination, raise an interesting question for irredentism when taken together: If territory cannot be acquired without the consent of the resident population, because this would violate the principle of self-determination, should these annexations be permitted if the population actually *wants* to be annexed by an irredentist state? With some exceptions,[25] it is probably safe to assume that the object of an irredentist project (i.e., the diaspora) rejects its current minority status and would prefer to live within the same state as its ethnic kin. Should the principle of territorial integrity be circumscribed by the will of the people being acquired? The answers to these questions were found in the postwar territorial settlement.

Many scholars have observed that the Allies' adherence to the universality of the principle of self-determination was limited by their geopolitical concerns.[26] It was quite clear that self-determination applied only to the disadvantage of the vanquished and not the victors.[27] Appeals to the Allies for border changes on behalf of these newly created diasporas were generally rejected because full national unity for these groups would upset the veneer of stability of the postwar European order.[28] If the Allies would not allow the defeated powers to unify their nations through peaceful means, the collective security arrangements found in the League of Nations precluded forcible changes to the status quo. Article 10 of the League Covenant (1919) stated: "The members of the League undertake to respect and preserve as against external aggression the territorial integrity and existing political independence of all Members of the League." Self-determination was not included in the League Covenant; instead it remained a political principle, rather than a right.[29] Thus, the League's support of state territorial integrity seemed to prohibit irredentist policies, despite the rhetorical commitment to self-determination on the part of the Allies. Because the emphasis of the postwar settlement was on peace, the national interests of the defeated powers were subordinated to the state interests of the Allies and the new states of Eastern Europe, both legally and politically.

As Barkin and Cronin have shown in this volume, the post–WWII settlement actively promoted the interests of states in light of Nazi Germany's effective use of self-determination to emasculate Czechoslovakia and to justify its stance toward Poland. From the end of the Second World War onward, states would be extremely wary of self-determination claims based on the desire for national unity.[30]

Although the post–Second World War international system transformed self-determination from a political concept to a legal right,[31] most international legal scholars see this right severely circumscribed by explicit statements supporting the territorial integrity of states.[32] Although self-determination is listed among the purposes of the United Nations, Article 2(4) of its Charter, "which prohibits member states from undertaking the threat or use of force against the territorial integrity or political independence of any state, or in any other manner inconsistent with the Purposes of the United Nations," would most certainly prohibit irredentism. Unlike cases of secession, in which there may be some ambiguity about whether article 2(4) applies to secessionist groups,[33] none seems to exist within the U.N. Charter itself when it comes to unilateral irredentism.[34]

Attempts to further define the relationship between territorial integrity and self-determination are found in a number of U.N. General Assembly resolutions. Much of the debate over the nature and scope of self-determination is whether this principle exists outside of the colonial context; i.e., whether non-colonial peoples possess the right to self-determination as found in the General Assembly resolutions. Although mostly seen in light of secession, these resolutions also have implications for irredentism. The General Assembly's 1960 Declaration on the Granting of Independence to Colonial Countries and Peoples (Resolution 1514) states: "Any attempt aimed at the partial or total disruption of the national unity and the territorial integrity of a country is incompatible with the purposes and principles of the Charter of the United Nations."[35] Although a number of U.N. resolutions allow for colonial peoples to use force to gain independence[36] or urge other states to help colonial peoples cast off colonial powers,[37] this would likely not apply to cases of irredentism. It does not matter how one interprets Resolution 1514—either allowing for postcolonial self-determination through secession or not—the outcome is the same. If self-determination is limited to the colonial context, then Resolution 1514 can be interpreted as prohibiting states from partitioning colonies or forcibly changing their borders. A broader approach to self-determination, which allows for secession from pre-existing states, would have a similar outcome: In both cases, states are prohibited from taking actions aimed at annexing the territory of another colony or state, even if its purpose is to achieve national unity through self-determination.

The General Assembly's 1970 "Declaration on Principles of International Law Concerning Friendly Relations and Co-operation Among States in Accordance with the Charter of the United Nations" (Resolution 2625) is crucial for understanding the relationship between territorial integrity and self-determination for two reasons. First, it was adopted by a consensus vote and therefore incorporated the views of the West, the Soviet bloc, and the decolonized world. Second, decolonization had largely been accomplished when it was adopted and therefore the resolution could be interpreted as setting a new standard, especially since Resolution 1514 was not referenced in its preamble. The "Declaration on Friendly Relations," like the U.N. Charter and Resolution 1514, is explicit in its defense of territorial integrity: "Every state shall refrain from any action aimed at the partial or total disruption of the national unity and territorial integrity of any other State or country." No exceptions to this principle are listed. It is interesting to note that this prohibition is found in several locations throughout the resolution in an almost identical form and without any qualifiers. The following is also included in Resolution 2625: "Every State has the duty to refrain from the threat or use of force to violate the existing international boundaries of another State or as a means of solving international disputes, including territorial disputes and problems concerning frontiers of States." Again, irredentist claims would seemingly be rejected despite its link with self-determination.

The situation is potentially less clear, however, when the U.N. General Assembly's 1974 "Definition of Aggression" is taken into account.[38] Article 7 of that resolution states:

> Nothing in this Definition, and in particular article 3 [which lists acts considered to be aggression], could, in any way prejudice the right to self-determination, freedom and independence, as derived from the Charter, of peoples forcibly deprived of the right referred to in the Declaration on Principles of International Law concerning Friendly

Relations and Cooperation among States in accordance with the Charter of the United Nations, particularly peoples under colonial and racist regimes or other forms of alien domination; *nor the right of these people to struggle to that end and to seek and receive support,* in accordance with the principles of the Charter and in conformity with the above-mentioned Declaration. [emphasis added]

While seemingly permitting states to aid peoples struggling for self-determination, and therefore may allow some room for irredentism, the resolution contains two restrictions. First, external support must be in accordance with the principles of the U.N. Charter. As cited above, article 2(4) of the Charter prohibits the use of force to violate the territorial integrity of states. Second, support must be given in conformity with the "Declaration on Friendly Relations." Again, the right to territorial integrity is affirmed in that resolution.

A. The Application of International Law to Irredentism

The U.N. Charter and subsequent resolutions, though often unclear or inconsistent on the details of self-determination, leave little ambiguity when it comes to irredentism. State policies of territorial annexation, even if shrouded in the cloak of self-determination, too closely resemble the aggressive wars that modern international law was designed to prevent;[39] this is reflected in the consistent expectation in the United Nations Charter that interstate disputes will be resolved through peaceful means.[40] Consequently, the international law of irredentism should lack the ambiguity (possibly) evident in the international law of secession. However, this is unfortunately not the case.

There are two potential problems when applying international law to cases of irredentism. First, state decision makers appear to understand that the unilateral use of force, no less launching wars of annexation, is deemed illegitimate by the vast majority of the states in the international system.[41] Consequently, states find alternative rationales for their actions, such as protection of nationals, self-defense, invitation, supporting self-determination, etc.[42] In cases of irredentism, it is more likely that the irredentist state will attempt to hide its actions. In other words, an overt use of force by a state will be rejected in favor of covert support to its diaspora; the irredentist then claims that its diaspora is involved in a secessionist campaign. Nevertheless, the final aim of the so-called secessionist struggle is really the merger of the anticipated break-away state with the national homeland, thus making a thinly veiled secession an act of irredentism. For example, the Kosovo Liberation Army and other Kosovar leaders officially claim that they are seeking independence for Kosovo and not a Greater Albania, but their real motives are often poorly hidden.[43] Therefore, the application of the international law of irredentism to any specific case will often get bogged down in the definition of the conflict at hand. For example, was the war in Bosnia-Herzegovina properly defined as an international conflict (i.e., an act of Serbian irredentism), or a case of secession (and hence an internal conflict), or a mixed conflict?[44] If it is not clear what law applies to a given conflict, then the application of international law will be hampered by this ambiguity.

The second problem is more fundamental to the nature of international law. For international law to have any substantive meaning in interstate relations, there must be some correspondence between the law and state practice. Although the purpose of this point is not to replicate the debate over when and how international law is truly law,[45] it does seem legitimate and necessary to view the provisions of international law in light of actual events. While violations of international law by individual states do not necessarily diminish or supplant the rules of the U.N. Charter or customary law, state actions and the reaction to those actions by other states do have an impact on both the vitality and interpretations of international law because the international system lacks hierarchy; that is, its subjects and enforcers are also its creators. International law becomes vacuous when verbal condemnation or official nonrecognition of illegal acts are substitutes for a more effective attempt either to punish or reverse these actions. Furthermore, inconsistent approaches to a question of international legality indicate ambiguity in the law and therefore reduce its robustness.[46] Therefore, in order to fully explore the legitimacy and effectiveness of international rules, it is necessary to examine both state practice and the enforcement of international law; a good indication of the latter is whether an irredentist state paid significant international costs for its policies. Since a number of irredentist campaigns have been launched since the founding of the United Nations, any analysis of the international law of irredentism would be woefully inadequate without reflecting on at least some of these cases.

II. POST–WORLD WAR TWO IRREDENTISM

Although the number of attempted secessions overwhelms the number of irredenta since 1945, irredentist crises have been quite significant. Below, I examine the international reaction to several cases of irredentism drawn from the three categories of irredenta identified above. I begin with two state-state irredenta: Somalia-Ethiopia; North and South Korea. Then, I examine India's invasion of Goa and Indonesia's invasion of East Timor, both of which were tied to decolonization. Finally, I contrast the three cases arising out of state collapse—Serbia, Croatia, and Armenia—in order to illustrate the differences in the costs paid by irredentist states in the post–Cold War period.

A. State-State Irredentism

1. Somalia-Ethiopia. For the past decade, Somalia has been seen as the prototype of the failed state with some scholars suggesting that the legal fiction of Somalian state sovereignty should be replaced with an international trusteeship.[47] It is difficult, given the country's total collapse in the early 1990s, to believe that Somalia launched an invasion of Ethiopia and, but for a timely counterattack by Soviet and Cuban troops, nearly annexed a huge swath of the Ethiopia's Ogaden region.[48] Although the United Nations did not act, it was clear that, with the exception of some Arab states, the international community held Somalia's actions to be illegitimate.

The Republic of Somalia was the most homogeneous state to emerge from African decolonization. However, because of the cession of the Ogaden region by Great Britain to King Menelik of Ethiopia in 1897, some two million ethnic Somalis resided in eastern Ethiopia. Somalian leaders consistently rejected the legitimacy of their western border and entered a reservation to the Organization of African Unity's "Resolution on Border Disputes," which called for African states to respect their postcolonial borders.[49] Taking advantage of Ethiopia's chronic political instability and a series of victories by the Western Somali Liberation Front (WSLF), which the Somalian government provided with weapons and logistical support, Somalia invaded Ethiopia in late July 1977.[50] Although Somalia officially denied any involvement, evidence to the contrary revealed the widespread use of Somalian troops, tanks, and weapons.[51] Somalia eventually admitted that its forces were in Ethiopia, but claimed that it had a right to intervene in order to prevent the WSLF's "legitimate" quest for self-determination from getting crushed by "foreign" (i.e., Soviet) involvement.[52]

By September 1977, Somalia controlled some ninety percent of the Ogaden region and was pressing into non-Somali-inhabited territories. The Soviet Union, which had previously supplied Somalia was weapons and foreign aid, had switched its support to Ethiopia just prior to the Somali invasion. The collapse of the Ethiopia's military situation prompted the Soviet Union to flood the Ethiopian government with massive quantities of military aid and to direct Cuban, Soviet, and North Korean troops to the region.[53] The Eastern Bloc-backed Ethiopian army launched a massive counterattack, which forced Somalia's army across the Ethiopia-Somalia border by mid-March 1978.[54] Although the WSLF continued its secessionist activities for another decade, a peace treaty between Somali and Ethiopia signed in April 1988 officially brought an end to hostilities between the two states.

The international reaction to Somalia's invasion of Ethiopia was complex because of Cold War politics. A Marxist coup in Ethiopia ended the United States' close relationship with that country and the Soviet Union was actively angling to replace U.S. influence with its own.[55] Consequently, Somalia, which had been closely allied with the USSR, was quite vocal in its criticism of this shift in Soviet policy and attempted to seek Western aid to substitute for its Soviet ties.[56] The Carter administration seemed quite eager to increase its influence in the strategic Horn of Africa, with the President reportedly telling Vice President Mondale, "I want you to tell Cy [Secretary of State Cyrus Vance] and Zbig [National Security Advisor Zbigniew Brzezinski] that I want them to move in every possible way to get Somalia to be our friend."[57] The United States was initially receptive to Somalia's call for military aid and sought to arrange similar aid packages from European and Arab countries.[58] However, the West's position changed once the Somalian army crossed the border into Ethiopia.[59] The United States, France, and Great Britain stated that they would only send Somalia "defensive" arms and later withdrew even this offer in order "to disassociate itself completely from Somalia's attempt to annex about one-third of Ethiopia."[60] The United States went so far as to block delivery of American arms to Somalia by its Middle East allies.[61] Even when Somalia renounced its Treaty of Friendship with the Soviet Union and expelled thousands of Soviet military and technical advisors, the United States still refused to change its position, despite the obvious geopolitical gain that would be associated by filling the vacuum left by the Soviets in Somalia. The United States was willing to consider defensive aid to Somalia only after its irredentist campaign had ended; and only then if it gave "a renewed commitment not to dishonor the international boundaries of either Ethiopia and Kenya."[62] Somalia scorned these "conditions," but was eventually forced to relent.

The position of the Eastern Bloc was made clear by its material support for Ethiopia. The Soviet Union criticized Somalia's "armed intervention in Ethiopia's domestic affairs, even on the specious pretext of implementation of the principle of self-determination."[63] Although both Ethiopia and the USSR demanded that the OAU and the United Nations take an active role in stopping Somalia, the OAU was ineffective; and, as one scholar noted, "it is both puzzling and noteworthy that the mechanism of the United Nations was completely ignored as a vehicle for addressing this war."[64] Nevertheless, other than a few Arab states that aided Somalia, most states refused to support Somali irredentism.[65]

2. The Korean War. The Korean War may, at first, appear to be less an irredentist conflict and more a Cold War ideological conflict. Certainly, there is no denying the ideological component of North Korea's decision to invade South Korea. However, the division of the Korean peninsula along the 38th parallel in 1945 by the United States and the Soviet Union was an aberration for the Korean people who possessed a deeply held and cohesive national identity.[66] Although neither of the Korean states were members of the United Nations,[67] nor were they intended to be permanent political entities, the division of the peninsula was some five years old and the Republic of Korea (ROK) had existed for two years prior to its invasion. Therefore, it is legitimate to place this conflict in the *state-state* category.

When the army of the Democratic People's Republic of Korea (DPRK) invaded the ROK on 25 June 1950, the United States immediately brought the matter before the U.N. Security Council. Because of the opportune absence of the Soviet representative, who was protesting the refusal of that body to seat the representative of the People's Republic of China, the Security Council adopted Resolution 82, which called on "all members to render every assistance to the United Nations in the execution of this resolution and to refrain from giving assistance to the North Koreans authorities." Two days later, the U.N. Security Council passed Resolution 83, which labeled the North Korean invasion a "breach of the peace" and "*[r]ecommend[ed]* that the Members of the United Nations furnish such assistance to the Republic of Korea as may be necessary to repel the armed attack and to restore international peace and security in the area." A little over a week later, the Council adopted resolution 84, which established a Unified Military Command under the leadership of the United States. All further Security Council resolutions on the Korean War were blocked by the return of the Soviet representative on 1 August. Consequently, the United States used the "Uniting for Peace" resolution, passed by the General Assembly on 3 November 1950, to bypass the Security Council.

These resolutions had the effect of declaring North Korea's actions an illegitimate use of force and an act of aggression (though that actual term was not used). It *recommended*, but not *demanded*, that the international community come to the aid of the ROK. Sixteen states contributed combat troops and four others sent medical units; U.N. forces, including U.S. soldiers, suffered some 160,000 casualties.[68] On the other hand, the Soviet Union and its Communist allies supported North Korea's invasion rhetorically and through differing levels of military assistance. They claimed, falsely, that the ROK had attacked first and that the DPRK was merely acting in self-defense. However, Kim Il Sung, the leader of North Korea at the time, was, according to Peter Lowe, "intensely nationalistic, proud, possessed of a mission to unify his country and contemptuous of opposition."[69] As another author put it: "National unification has always been the supreme and overriding goal of the Pyongyang regime. Internal and external circumstances change, but the drive toward the country's reunification continues unabated. . . ."[70] Kim believed that a window of opportunity existed for North Korea to unify the peninsula because the United States made the mistake of declaring that the ROK was outside of its "defense perimeter" in the Pacific.[71] Thus, the DPRK's actions were not an act of self-defense but an irredentist project resisted politically and militarily by the United States and its allies.

Although the two ideological camps were divided on their perceptions of the Korean War, with each side considering the other's actions illegitimate, the Security Council and General Assembly actions identified the North Korean invasion as illegitimate and one that required a commitment by the international community to reverse. The legitimacy of the U.N.'s stance, however, was weakened by a number of factors: the obvious role of the United States as the head of the anti-DPRK coalition implied that the United Nations was less of a neutral enforcer of international law and more a vehicle for U.S. policy; the absence of the Soviet Union from the Security Council votes; and the support given to the North Koreans by the Communist states.

B. Decolonization

The illegitimacy of colonialism is a central pillar of the world order established after the Second World War. As Steven Ratner has shown in his essay, the application of the principle of *uti possidetis* to decolonization entailed the transformation of the arbitrary borders drawn by the colonial powers into interstate borders. However, lingering colonialism, mostly by the Portugese, meant that certain states maintained irredentist claims against territories still controlled by colonial powers.

1. India's Invasion of Goa. On 18 December 1961, Indian troops invaded the Portuguese-controlled colonial enclave of Goa, easily pushing aside the token Portuguese resistance.[72] In response, Portugal sought help from the U.N. Security Council in order "to put a stop to the condemnable act of aggression of the Indian Union."[73] But, because Goa was deemed by the international community to be a colonial possession and New Delhi's actions were seen as furthering decolonization, India was not punished.

India's defense was multifaceted but essentially rested on the claim that its actions were justified because Goa's inhabitants were ethnically Indian and that the enclave's very existence represented a centuries-old legacy of colonialism that violated India's historical and national territorial integrity. According to the Indian delegate during the Security Council debate on the Goa situation: the territories were "integral parts of India" and "there can be no question of aggression against your own frontier, against your own people."[74] It was argued that India's actions were in line with General Assembly Resolution 1514 (XV), which condemned colonialism and demanded decolonization. Furthermore, India claimed (falsely) that the Portuguese were reinforcing its military contingent in Goa and intensifying its repressive actions there.[75]

The reaction by the U.N. Security Council was mixed. The Soviet Union and three anticolonial nonpermanent members of the Council supported India's actions, while the rest "deplored" India's use of force. Neither side was able to pass a resolution. The large contingent of former colonial states in the General Assembly agreed with India's assertion that the use of force was acceptable because furthered the cause of decolonization: "many of the new states, and also the Soviet Union, felt that colonialism was such an evil that the use of force to eliminate it should be tolerated."[76] It is interesting to note that this invasion, purported to further decolonization, was, in fact, not an action that promoted the self-determination of the people of Goa, since they were not asked whether they wanted to join India. Instead, *their* right to self-determination was seemingly qualified by Resolution 1514: according to James Crawford, the right of self-determination for colonial enclaves is trumped by the right of the surrounding state to national unity and territorial integrity.[77]

Ultimately, India paid no international price for its invasion of Goa. Neither the Security Council nor General Assembly took action against India, not even an official rebuke.

3. Indonesia-East Timor.[78] The Portugese revolution of 1974 ushered in a new government willing to decolonize its overseas possessions. The people of East Timor were given a choice between remaining with Portugal, independence, and union with Indonesia. Three main political factions emerged in the region, each supporting one of the options. Violent clashes between the three sides led the Portugese to withdraw. Consequently, FRETILIN, the acronym[79] of the leftist faction supporting independence, seized control of East Timor and declared independence on 28 November 1975. Ostensibly responding to a call for union with Indonesia from the other two factions, Indonesia launched a full-scale invasion on 7 December 1975 and a provisional government was formed in the East Timorese capital of Dili later that month. On 31 May 1976, the Indonesian government announced that the provisional assembly had passed a petition calling for integration with Indonesia. Jakarta adopted a "bill of integration" on 17 July 1976, thus formally annexing the territory. Despite this venere of legitimacy, the reality was quite different: Indonesia's military occupation was accomplished without the consent of the East Timorese.[80]

The Indonesians claimed "close ethnic ties with the people of the territory, historic title, and the need to protect the population from terrorist acts by FRETILIN."[81] In addition, the annexation of East Timor was promoted as an act of self-determination by the East Timorese, as President Sudharto's address to the Provisional Government of East Timor made clear: "You have come here to carry out the task of the whole people of East Timor, namely to submit the firm determination . . . to reintegrate [the East Timorese] with their half-brothers in . . . Indonesia. . . ."[82] This position was reiterated throughout the early period of occupation.

The overall international reaction to Indonesia's invasion was muted. On 12 December 1975, after a contentious debate, the U.N. General Assembly passed resolution 3485 (XXX) which "[s]trongly deplore[d] the military intervention of the armed forces of Indonesia in Portuguese Timor" and called on Indonesia "to desist from further violation of the territorial integrity of Portuguese Timor and to withdraw without delay its armed forces from the territory in order to enable the people of the Territory freely to exercise their right to self-determination and independence." The issue was also addressed by the Security Council, which unanimously adopted Resolution 384 on 22 December. This resolution recognized "the inalienable right of the people of East Timor to self-determination and independence," called on all states to respect East Timor's territorial integrity and for Indonesia to withdraw "without delay," and asked the Secretary-General to send a special representative to the region.

After this initial flurry of U.N. resolutions, the international community settled into a quiet acquiescence of Indonesia's territorial gains. Although the Security Council passed resolution 389 on 22 April 1976, which generally reiterated the points made in Resolution 384, and thus illustrated continued interest in the conflict, the Council neither declared the Indonesian invasion a breach of the peace nor an act of aggression, nor did it apply any of its enforcement mechanisms under Chapter VII of the U.N. Charter. Most interesting was the fact that neither Security Council resolution explicitly referred to Article 2(4) of the Charter.[83] As Korman observed: "The United States . . . had no intention of supporting any further United Nations action on East Timor and had been urging other powers to come to terms with Indonesia's 'irreversible' action, while Britain, France, and to a lesser extent the Soviet Union adopted a passive attitude on the question."[84]

General Assembly involvement was rather longer, but similarly hollow: Subsequent General Assembly resolutions on East Timor were watered down, with less states supporting East Timor each year. By 1979 (resolution 34/40), neither a direct nor indirect call for Indonesian troops to leave the region was included. In 1983 General Assembly failed to adopt a resolution and consideration of the issue was perennially postponed.[85]

Recognition of effective Indonesian sovereignty over East Timor was provided by several important states. On 19 July 1977, the State Department's Deputy Legal Advisor recognized "the validity of the sovereign authority of Indonesia in East Timor."[86] Australia, too, formally recognized Indonesia's annexation of East Timor and concluded a treaty with Indonesia on 11 December 1989, providing for joint oil exploration in the sea between East Timor and Australia. Consequently, Portugal, which considered itself the administering power in East Timor, brought suit against Australia in the International Court of Justice claiming that the treaty infringed on East Timor's right to self-determination and territorial integrity. The Court responded on 30 June 1995 by stating that it could not rule on the case because such a ruling would affect a nonconsenting third party, Indonesia.[87] This, in effect, preserved the status quo and did not overtly delegitimize Indonesia's actions.

C. State Collapse

Armenia, Serbia, and Croatia launched comparable irredentist projects out of the remnants of the Soviet Union and Yugoslavia: Each sought to detach territories from their neighbors once the overarching federal state dissolved. Although the international community did not respond militarily, in any substantive sense, until 1995, Serbia was placed under draconian sanctions by the United Nations Security Council. With its economy in shambles, Serbia was forced to relent and recognize the territorial integrity of Croatia and Bosnia-Herzegovina. Croatia, both a victim and perpetrator of irredentism, attempted to create a Greater Croatia at Bosnia's expense. While sanctions were not imposed, Croatia's chances of integrating into the West—by gaining entry into Western political, military, and economic institutions—were threatened by its actions. Armenia has not paid any significant cost for its involvement in the Nagorno-Karabakh conflict with Azerbaijan. In fact, Armenia received aid from both Russia and the United States; the latter even imposed sanctions against Azerbaijan.

1. Serbian Irredentism. The involvement of the international community in the wars of Yugoslav succession, which included both Serbian and Croatian irredentism, was the deepest and most complex engagement by international organizations and third-party states in an ethnic conflict this century, and indeed ever. The wars have had a fundamental impact on nearly all aspects of international law and will be felt well into the next century.[88] It is impossible to do justice to the events in the Balkans during the 1990s within the scope of this essay. Therefore my comments here will be, by necessity, limited.[89]

The Serbian irredentist campaigns in Croatia and Bosnia-Herzegovina were the product of the arbitrary borders drawn by the postwar Communist government; the rise of Slobodan Milosevic to power in Serbia; and the collapse of central authority within Yugoslavia.[90] Serbia's deep involvement in Croatia and Bosnia is beyond a doubt.[91] However, there was enough ambiguity surrounding the conflicts to complicate any immediate international resistence to Serbian aggression.[92] Nevertheless, the international community imposed severe penalties against Serbia for its actions; ultimately leading to Serbia's disengagement from Bosnia and Croatia and its official recognition of the borders between them.

The European Union's "Guidelines on the Recognition of New States in Eastern Europe and in the Soviet Union" (issued on 16 December 1991), the Badinter Commission's Opinion No. 3 of 11 January 1992, and the admission of Croatia and Bosnia-Herzegovina into the United Nations in 1992, were indicative of the international community's rejection of the forcible alteration of borders and the transformation of the former republic boundaries into interstate borders.[93] Serbia's actions in Croatia resulted a mandatory arms embargo imposed on Yugoslavia in September 1991,[94] economic sanctions from the European Union and United States in November 1991,[95] and the imposition of U.N. peacekeepers. The bloodletting in Bosnia brought mandatory economic sanctions by the U.N. Security Council on 30 May 1992,[96] which were strengthened less than a year later.[97] Acting under the Charter's Chapter VII enforcement powers, the Council demanded that all states break-off trade relations with the FRY. The sanctions regime also attempted to isolate the FRY diplomatically (all states were to reduce their diplomatic missions to Belgrade), culturally (no cultural exchanges or participation in sporting events), and scientifically. The publicly stated purpose behind these sanctions was twofold: (1) punish Serbia for its actions in Bosnia, and (2) weaken its resolve to continue the war by inflicting economic hardship against the country. Their effect was devastating on the Serbian economy and the welfare of its population.[98]

The international community, however, lacked any willingness to use force to counter Serb irredentism.[99] Military resources were used in the enforcement of the sanctions and the implementation of the no-fly-zone (NFZ),[100] but both measures were perceived as low-cost, low-risk actions that did not require the placement of ground forces in Bosnia and would likely not lead to an escalation of involvement.[101]

As the war dragged on, the international community seemed willing to discuss the possibility of partitioning Bosnia-Herzegovina, as evidenced by the Vance-Owen, Owen-Stoltenberg, and Contact Group plans.[102] Although Bosnia would remain within its internationally recognized boundaries, each of these plans seemed to be designed as temporary measures before the eventual partition of Bosnia. However, events such as the 5 February 1994 Sarajevo marketplace massacre, in which a mortar shell killed some seventy people in full view of the international media, galvanized the international community to take more direct action, including threats and the limited use of military force.

The economic sanctions eventually took their toll on Serbia, and its leaders were willing to relinquish their irredentist program for sanctions relief. When the Bosnian Serbs refused to comply, they were blockaded by Yugoslavia, leading to a number of military defeats for the Bosnian Serbs. A second marketplace shelling in 1995 brought massive airstrikes by NATO planes and the near collapse of the Bosnian Serb military. At Dayton, Ohio, under the direction of the United States, Slobodan Milosevic signed an accord recognizing Bosnia's existence and borders.[103]

2. Croatian Irredentism. Croatian President Tudjman hypocritically defended the territorial integrity of Croatia's republican borders while actively working to undermine Bosnia's territorial integrity. Although it might have appeared that the Croats and Bosnian Muslims should have been natural allies against the Serbs, since a Greater Serbia would come at the expense of these two groups, this was not to be. In a work published in English in 1981, Tudjman made his claims against Bosnia-Herzegovina clear: If he could not have all of Bosnia, Tudjman would settle for a Greater Croatia roughly based on the 1939 Cvetkovic-Macek Agreement, which partitioned Bosnia during the Royal Yugoslav period.[104] To this end, Tudjman secretly met with Serbian President Slobodan Milosevic in March 1991 in an effort to come to an agreement to divide Bosnia.[105]

Sporadic fighting between Muslims and Croats erupted throughout the fall of 1992 and the winter of 1993. With the introduction of the Vance-Owen Peace Plan in January 1993—which called for the cantonization of Bosnia into ten provinces with a weak central government—Croatian and Muslim forces began scrambling to consolidate control over territories assigned to them under the plan. Sustained fighting erupted in spring 1993 and, according to U.N. officials and Western analysts, the level of "savagery . . . rival[ed] anything seen so far in the republic's three-sided factional war."[106]

It is clear that one of Tudjman's principal goals was the eventual annexation of Croatian portions of Bosnia-Herzegovina into Croatia-proper. Equally important, if not more so, was the desire to have Croatia firmly integrated into Western Europe. According to Croatian Foreign Minister Mate Granic:

> [Croatia is] a Central European and Mediterranean country which wishes to pursue its integration into Central European and Euro-Atlantic associations—political, economic and security associations.
> It is in our interests to be part of . . . [these] processes as soon as possible. This means we want to be part of Partnership for Peace, later NATO, and we also want to sign agreements on trade and cooperation, and later gain associate membership and finally become members of the EU.[107]

The Tudjman regime possessed a two-part vision for the Croat nation: integration with the West and the establishment of a Greater Croatia. These two goals proved to be incompatible.

Despite some stunning victories in the early part of the war, the Bosnian Croats' military position rapidly deteriorated during the winter of 1993–94. In late January 1994, thousands of Croatian soldiers invaded Bosnia in order to prop up their ethnic kin in Bosnia. The subsequent reaction by the international community was swift and harsh. In response to a letter from Secretary General Boutros Boutros-Ghali, which confirmed Croatia's involvement in Bosnia,[108] the Security Council issued a statement that asserted that the Council was "deeply concerned" about the Croatian intervention and that it "strongly condemn[ed] [Croatia] for this serious hostile act . . . which constitutes a violation of international law, the Charter of the United Nations and relevant Security Council resolutions." Furthermore, the Security Council demanded that Croatia withdraw immediately or it would consider other "serious measures."[109] Although the final text did not include an explicit threat of economic sanctions, there was a clear implication that the Security Council was leaning that way.

The members of the European Union independently considered the topic of sanctions. Spanish and Danish foreign ministers indicated on 3 February that a decision by the European Union on sanctions against Croatia was "imminent" and that "the international community will have to seriously examine the issue."[110] Later, Danish Foreign Minister Niels Helveg Patersen stated that the European

Union "still envisages introducing sanctions against Croatia," which may have included "either trade sanctions or, alternatively, the possibility of withdrawing the preferential status Croatia enjoys in its trade with the Community."[111]

One factor holding up E.U. sanctions was the continued support for Croatia by the largest E.U. member: Germany. Although Germany was considered an ally of Croatia, its position began to shift during February 1994. At a meeting of high-ranking Western officials and security experts in Munich, German Chancellor Helmut Kohl blasted Croatia and threatened to suspend all economic aid to Zagreb: "Whoever changes borders through the use of force cannot count on the support of Germany," nor will anyone "who oversteps the limits of normal, acceptable behaviour under international law" receive Germany's backing.[112] He further called the Croatian troop deployment a "scandal" that must be countered by a serious response by the Europeans.[113] The writing was clearly on the wall: Sanctions would be put into place and Croatia would be isolated from the West if it did not change their policies.

The United States was the most determined to paint a bleak picture of Croatia's future if it did not withdraw from Bosnia. Early in the process, Charles Redman, U.S. special envoy to the region, and Peter Galbraith, U.S. Ambassador to Croatia, stressed the link between Croatia's Bosnia policy and U.S. support for Croatia. According to one account, Redman and Galbraith presented Tudjman with a clear choice and "limited-time offer": "isolation and sanctions if he pursues his irredentist claims on Croat lands in Bosnia, or U.S. backing for Croatia's integration into the political, economic and security institutions of the West."[114] If they failed, the Croats were told that "the door to the West will be shut on them forever."[115] In a speech in early March 1994, Tudjman admitted that "he was under enormous pressure from the United States and the European Union," but also that he had been "explicitly promised" the West's help on a number of issues, including integration into Western Europe.[116]

Ultimately the Croatian government acquiesced to Western pressure. Thus, Zagreb officially ended its irredentist project in Bosnia in an effort to avoid paying a significant price—exile from the West—for its national goals.[117]

3. Armenia-Azerbaijan. Although the conflict between the Turkic-speaking Shi'a Azeris and the Orthodox Christian Armenians has its roots in the treatment of the Armenians by the Turkish Ottomans, the territorial conflict between Armenia and Azerbaijan began with Josef Stalin's 1923 decision to attach the mostly Armenian region of Nagorno-Karabakh to the Azerbaijan Soviet Socialist Republic. In the waning years of the Soviet Union, an open conflict erupted between the two groups, with the Karabakh-Armenians declaring independence from Azerbaijan and attaching itself to Armenia. Upon the collapse of the Soviet Union, the inter-republic conflict was transformed into an interstate conflict.[118] By the time a ceasefire took hold in the region in May 1994, Armenia had emerged victorious, controlling not only Nagorno-Karabakh, but also Azerbaijani territory between the enclave and Armenia; in all, some 20 percent of Azerbaijan's territory was under occupation. While the costs of the war itself were quite high, the Republic of Armenia has largely avoided international censure or punishment on account of its alliance with Russia and its lobbying efforts in the United States.

Officially, Armenia has renounced all claims to Azerbaijani territory and only supports the self-determination of the Karabakh-Armenians. However, this was merely for international consumption and public relations purposes; in reality, Armenia has been heavily involved in the Karabakh conflict.[119] Instead of supporting Azerbaijan's territorial integrity, both the United States and Russia have supported Armenia's efforts either directly or indirectly: Russia has supplied arms and equipment to Armenia and the Karabakh-Armenians, and the United States has restricted all foreign aid to Azerbaijan (in response to Azerbaijan's blockade of Armenia) and provided Armenia with substantial direct foreign aid.[120]

Russia's interests in Nagorno-Karabakh are a reflection of its historic and cultural ties with the Christian Armenians[121] and its geopolitical interests, both to keep external powers out of its sphere of influence in the Transcaucasus and to ensure compliant regimes on its southern flank.[122] To this end, Russia concluded a military alliance with Armenia in November 1992[123] and a basing agreement in mid-1994.[124] According to Russian reports, the Russia has supplied Armenia with substantial military equipment, supplies, and spare parts free of charge between 1994 and 1996.[125]

U.S. support for Armenia was based, not on *realpolitik*, but rather the effective lobbying efforts of Armenian-Americans and the Republic of Armenia. The principal Armenian lobby, the Armenian Assembly of America, was founded in 1972 and has "command[ed] attention in Washington out of proportion to their numbers."[126] According to one report: "For years, Armenia has enjoyed political advantages in Washington that have made it the envy of its neighbors on Russia's southern border."[127] Their biggest successes have been the following: the inclusion of section 907 of the 1992 Freedom Support Act, which barred direct U.S. assistance to Azerbaijan; restricting the U.S. Congressional debate over Armenia's role in Nagorno-Karabakh; and ensuring a steady supply of U.S. foreign aid.[128]

Action within the United Nations has likewise been beneficial for Armenia. Despite its involvement in Nagorno-Karabakh, none of the Security Council resolutions on the Karabakh situation directly identified Armenia as an aggressor, as a Turkish draft resolution would have. Instead, the Council has called on all sides to cease hostilities.[129] Although the European Community issued a statement that "condemn[ed] these aggressive actions," no penalties or sanctions were imposed on Armenia.[130] Thus, Armenian irredentism was not resisted by the international community.

III. Conclusion

Although international law nominally rejects arguments of self-determination when dealing with issues of territorial aggrandizement and the use of force, the policies of the international community have been inconsistent. In this essay, I have identified three categories of irredenta—state-state, decolonization, and state collapse—and examined a number of case studies under each. I have found divergent reactions by the international community to irredentist projects corresponding to the three categories. Somalia and North Korea met with general and widespread disapproval of their actions. The invasion of another state, even if not a member of the United Nations (like the Republic of Korea), has consistently been deemed illegitimate by the majority of states in the international system. However, irredentism went unopposed within the context of decolonization: Neither India nor Indonesia paid any significant international costs for their policies. Eliminating the legacies of colonization was seen by many to be a greater evil than the use of force. The three cases of state collapse irredenta are more ambiguous because of the differing international reactions: Serbia paid a high cost for its actions, Croatia risked isolation from the West, and Armenia was largely unhindered in its Nagorno-Karabakh campaign. What can account for these divergent outcomes?

In his brief analysis of the legitimacy of self-determination in international law, Frederic Kirgis identifies two variables—the degree to which the self-determination claim is destabilizing and the degree to which the host government is representative—which impact the international community's acceptance of secessionist claims.[131] The first variable, in particular, can be seen as having an influence on the reaction to irredentist projects as well. That cases of state-state irredentism are the most disruptive to the international system can hardly be disputed. Crossing established interstate boundaries in an effort to acquire territory, regardless of motive or justification, undercuts the very foundations of the modern international system and community by challenging the premises of the peaceful resolution of disputes and territorial integrity. This disruption, however, appears to be palatable if connected to eliminating colonial control over territories.

The disintegration of multiethnic states is, in most cases, significantly disruptive to the international system. As Ratner has shown, the need to establish clearly defined borders between the successor states has led international bodies to adopt a dubious interpretation of *uti possidetis*. However, despite the formal acceptance *uti possidetis*, violations of this principle have not met with a consistent response by the international community. In a situation that can already be described as significant disruption (i.e., the collapse of a sovereign state), other factors—such as historical and cultural ties, domestic politics, and media perceptions—appear to play an increasingly significant role. For right or wrong, Serbia was clearly portrayed as the aggressor in wars of Yugoslav succession and international reaction to Serbia's actions were harshly resisted.[132] Croatia had significant advantages over Serbia in the realm of public relations, though Croatia's overt intervention into Bosnia in January 1994 called into question its relationship to the West. Armenia, through a mixture of lobbying, historic ties, and a location on the periphery of Europe, has not had to pay a significant price for its policies, despite being the most successful of the three.

These inconsistencies and contradictions illustrated in this brief examination of irredentism raise important problems. The acceptance of exceptions to the prohibition on the use of force, the importance of successful lobbying techniques,[133] and the persistence of ambiguity regarding the nature and scope of self-determination make the development of a coherent and universal international law of nationalism precarious. The divergence between law and policy in the practice of the major powers—seen most clearly in the international diplomacy toward the collapse of Yugoslavia and the Nagorno-Karabakh region—does not bode well for the international system.

NOTES

1. See Ratner's article in this volume.
2. Rogers Brubaker, *Nationalism Reframed* (Cambridge: Cambridge University Press, 1996), 79.
3. Ernest Gellner, *Nations and Nationalism* (Ithaca, NY: Cornell University Press, 1983), 1.
4. The term *irredentism* derives from the Italian *irredenta* (unredeemed) and originally referred to the political movement during the latter half of the nineteenth century and early twentieth century to detach Italian speakers from Swiss and Austro-Hungarian control and bring them into the newly formed Italian state.
5. I define 'national-state' as a state dominated by a particular nation which, in essence, owns the state; usually indicated by an eponymous relationship between state and nation. For example, Japan and the Japanese, France and the French, Croatia and the Croats, etc. The distinction between national-state and nation-state is that the former does not necessarily assume a match between nation and state: i.e., a national-state can contain significant minorities (Romania) or a significant diaspora (Armenia).
6. Thomas Ambrosio, "Irredentism: Ethnic Conflict and International Politics" (Ph.D. diss., University of Virginia, 1999).
7. Donald L. Horowitz, "Irredentas and Secession: Adjacent Phenomena, Neglected Connections," in *Irredentism and International Politics*, ed. Naomi Chazan (Boulder, CO: Lynne Reiner, 1991), 9–10.
8. This second requirement, some national tie between the irredentist state and the population being acquired, significantly narrows the definition of irredentism used in this essay. For example, Naomi Chazan defines irredentism as the attempt "to acquire or retrieve territories in the name of the nation they seek to represent." This is far more expansive than my definition because it would allow for cases of historical title to territory, even when the population residing on that territory lacks ethnic ties to the irredentist state; e.g., Argentina's invasion of the Falkland Islands. Chazan, "Conclusion," *Irredentism and International Politics*, supra note 7, at 141.
9. There are some notable exceptions: Michael E. Brown, ed., *Ethnic Conflict and International Security* (Princeton, NJ: Princeton University Press, 1993); Michael E. Brown, ed., *The International Dimensions of Internal Conflict* (MIT Press, 1996); David A. Lake

and Donald Rothchild, eds., *The International Spread of Ethnic Conflict* (Princeton, NJ: Princeton University Press, 1998).

10. In his seminal work, *Ethnic Groups in Conflict* (Berkeley: University of California Press, 1985), Donald Horowitz gives irredentism only meager attention [pp. 281–88] while reserving the bulk of his analysis for secession [pp. 229–81].

11. For example, there have been a plethora of articles and books that look specifically at the issue of secession in reference to self-determination, but none which look exclusively at irredentism. For a sampling, see Allen E. Buchanan, *Secession: The Morality of Political Divorce from Fort Sumter to Lithuania and Quebec* (Boulder, CO: Westview, 1991); Lea Brilmayer, "Secession and Self-Determination: A Territorial Interpretation," *Yale Journal of International Law* 16 (1991): 177–202; Deborah Z. Cass, "Re-Thinking Self-Determination: A Critical Analysis of Current International Law Theories," *Syracuse Journal of International Law and Commerce* 18 (spring 1992): 21–40; Lawrence S. Eastwood Jr., "Secession: State Practice and International Law After the Dissolution of the Soviet Union and Yugoslavia," *Duke Journal of Comparative and International Law* 3 (spring 1993): 299–349; also, Hannum's article in this volume.

12. Jack S. Levy, "Domestic Politics and War," *Journal of Interdisciplinary History* 18 (no. 4, spring 1988): 653–73; Fareed Zakaria, "Realism and Domestic Politics," *International Security* 17 (no. 1, summer 1992): 177–98. Especially, John F. Stack, Jr., "The Ethnic Challenge to International Relations Theory," in *Wars in the Midst of Peace*, eds. David Carment and Patrick James (Pittsburgh: University of Pittsburgh Press, 1997), 11–25.

13. See Fowler and Bunck's article in this volume.

14. Myron Weiner, "The Macedonian Syndrome: A Historical Model of International Relations and Political Development," *World Politics* 23 (July 1971): 665–83.

15. On 27 April 1992 the former Yugoslav republics of Serbia and Montenegro created a new federal state, the Federal Republic of Yugoslavia (FRY). This new entity has largely had its foreign policy and domestic political system defined by Slobodan Milosevic, the former president of Serbia and now president of the FRY, in the name of the Serb people. Milosevic's leading role in the new Yugoslavia has been recognized by the international community, as his presence at the Dayton talks of November 1995 clearly illustrated. Despite the fact that Serbia and the new Yugoslavia are two distinct entities, I will refer to that entity as Serbia when referring to its irredentist policies.

16. Island of Palmas Case (*United States v. The Netherlands*), Permanent Court of Arbitration (1928), *Reports of International Arbitral Awards* 2, 829; Case Concerning the Frontier Dispute (*Burkina Faso v. Republic of Mali*), *ICJ Reports* (1986), 554.

17. Jeffrey Herbst, "The Creation and Maintenance of National Boundaries in Africa," *International Organization* 43 (no. 4, autumn 1989): 673–92.

18. Sharon Korman traces the evolution of the right of conquest in *The Right to Conquest: The Acquisition of Territory by Force in International Law and Practice* (Oxford: Clarendon Press, 1996).

19. Ibid., 94–95.

20. "Title of acquisition of territorial sovereignty in present-day international law are either based on an act of effective apprehension, *such as occupation or conquest*, or, like, cession, presuppose that the ceding and the cessionary Power or at least one of them, have the faculty of effectively disposing of the ceded territory." Island of Palmas Case, *supra* note 16.

21. In his 2 April 1917 address to Congress requesting a declaration of war, Wilson stated: "We desire no conquest, no dominion. We seek no indemnities for ourselves."

22. The Allies did make territorial gains: the French annexed Alsece-Lorraine, there were some border adjustments for Italy (though, in their mind, not enough), and the Allies seized the colonial possessions of the vanquished and held them as mandates.

23. This was formalized a decade after the war's end in the General Treaty for the Renunciation of War (1928), also known as the Kellogg-Briand Pact.

24. Hurst Hannum has traced the development of this notion earlier in this volume and therefore my comments here will be brief.

25. Horowitz, *supra* note 10, at 285–86.

26. See Thomas D. Musgrave, *Self-Determination and National Minorities* (Oxford: Oxford University Press, 1997), 26–30.

27. Germany lost parts of its eastern frontier and Alscese-Lorraine, both of which were populated by Germans; Germans in the new state of Czechoslovakia were relegated to minority status; Austria was not permitted to become part of Germany; and Hungary lost nearly one third of its prewar Hungarian population to annexation by its neighbors.

28. In its place, the Allies instituted a series of minorities treaties, though innovative, were generally regarded as failures. Nathaniel Berman, "But the Alternative Is Despair": European Nationalism and the Modernist Renewal of International Law," *Harvard Law Review* 106 (June 1993): 1792–903.

29. See Hurst Hannum in this volume.

30. This is illustrated by the general rejection of national rights and the support of individual rights after the Second World War. Inis L. Claude Jr., *National Minorities* (Greenwood Press, 1955), 53, 69–78; Louis B. Soh, "The New International Law: Protection of the Rights of Individuals Rather than States," *American University* 32 (fall 1982): 1–64 (5–6).

31. The principle of self-determination is explicitly mentioned in the U.N. Charter Articles 1 and 55, and indirectly in 2 and 56. Chapters XI, XII, and XIII of the Charter deal with non-self-governing territories. U.N. General Assembly Resolution 637 (VII) and, more importantly, 1514 (XV) refer to the "right of self-determination." Also see common Article 1 in the International Covenant on Economic, Social and Cultural Rights and the International Covenant on Civil and Political Rights (adopted in 1966 and entered into force in 1976), and the International Court of Justice's Advisory Opinions on Namibia (South West Africa, *ICJ Reports* 1971, 16) and Western Sahara (Western Sahara Case, *ICJ Reports* 1975, 12).

32. The literature on self-determination has been extensive in the last several decades. For a sampling, see Gerry J. Simpson, "The Diffusion of Sovereignty: Self-Determination in the Post-Colonial Age," *Stanford Journal of International Law* 32 (summer 1996): 255–86; Ved P. Nanda, "Revisiting Self-Determination as an International Law Concept," *ILSA Journal of International and Comparative Law* 3 (winter 1997): 443; Frederic L. Kirgis Jr., "The Degrees of Self-Determination in the United Nations Era," *American Journal of International Law* 88 (April 1994): 304; and Hannum in this volume.

33. See Musgrave's chapter on secession, *supra* note 26, at 180–210. Hannum disagrees with Musgrave; Hurst Hannum, review of *Self-Determination and National Minorities*, by Thomas Musgrave, *American Journal of International Law* 93 (January 1999): 274.

34. There may be some ambiguity regarding whether territorial acquisition is lawful if undertaken in accordance with articles 51 (self-defense) or 24(2) (enforcement by the Security Council) of the U.N. Charter. Although Korman rejects such an exception, this debate is outside the scope of this essay since its focus is on unilateral, state-based irredentist projects. *Supra* note 18, at 200–201.

35. GA Res. 1514 (XV).

36. GA Res. 2105 (XX); GA Res. 2621 (XXV); GA Res. 33/24 (1978).

37. GA Res. 2131 (XXV); GA Res. 2160 (XXI).

38. Benjamin B. Rerencz, *Defining International Aggression* vol. 2 (New York: Oceana Publications, 1975).

39. See Anthony Clark Arend, "The United Nations and the World Order," *Georgetown Law Journal* 81 (March 1993): 491–533; idem., "International Law and the Recourse for Force: A Shift in Paradigms," *Stanford Journal of International Law*, 127 (1990): 1.

40. It is therefore not surprising that the first purpose of the United Nations, Article 1(1) reflects this aim: "To maintain international peace and security, and to that end: to take effective collective measures for the prevention and removal of threats to the peace, and for the suppression of acts of aggression or other breaches of the peace, and to bring about by peaceful means, an in conformity with the principles of justice and international law, adjustment or settlement of international disputes or situations with might lead to a breach of the peace."

Article 2(2) states: "All Members shall settle their international disputes by peaceful means in such a manner that international peace and security, and justice, are not endangered."

41. Anthony Arend and Robert Beck, *International Law and the Use of Force: Beyond the UN Charter Paradigm* (Routledge, 1993).

42. After listing a number of justifications made by states for the use of force, Oscar Schachter provides the following conclusion: "Not surprisingly, most outsiders view many of these legal contentions skeptically, primarily because states, in substantiating their claims, frequently seem to cite carefully chosen, if not fabricated, sets of facts. Thus, the legal justifications offered by states are often perceived as rationalizations contrived after the decision to intervene had been made." Oscar Schachter, "In Defense of International Rules on the Use of Force," *University of Chicago Law Review* 53 (winter 1986): 113–46.

43. *Corriere della Sera* (Milan), 9 July 1999, reproduced as "Independence Only Way to Settle Relations with Neighbours—Ethnic Albanian Leader," in *BBC Summary of World Broadcasts* 13 (July 1999), EE/D3585/A; Robert Scheer, "Kosovo Will Never be One with Serbia: The KLA Dreams of a Greater Albania, But the Serbs Continue to Dream of the Past," *Los Angeles Times*, 15 June 1999, B7; "Albanian Prime Minister Not Against 'Greater Albania,'" *Deutsche Presse-Agentur*, 10 April 1999, 08:48 Central European Time.

44. The International Criminal Tribunal for the former Yugoslavia was forced to deal with this issue before it could apply *jus in bello*. Sean D. Murphy, "Progress and Jurisprudence of the International Criminal Tribunal for the Former Yugoslavia," *American Journal of International Law* 93 (January 1999): 57–97; Theodor Meron, "Classification of Armed Conflict in the Former Yugoslavia: Nicaragua's Fallout," *American Journal of International Law* 92 (April 1998): 236–42; Robert M. Hayden, "Bosnia's Internal War and the International Criminal Court," *Fletcher Forum of World Affairs Journal* 22 (winter/spring 1998): 45–61.

45. For some insights into this debate specifically dealing with Article 2(4) of the U.N. Charter, see: Oscar Schachter, *supra* note 42; A. Mark Weisburd, *Use of Force* (University Park: Pennsylvania State University Press, 1997); W. Michael Reisman, "Coercion and Self-Determination: Construing Charter Article 2(4)," *American Journal of International Law* 78 (July 1984): 642–45; Franck, "Who Killed Article 2(4)?" *American Journal of International Law* 64 (1970): 809–37; Louis Henkin, "The Reports of the Death of Article 2(4) Are Greatly Exaggerated," *American Journal of International Law* 65 (1971): 544–48; and Arend and Beck, *supra* note 41.

46. Thomas M. Franck, *The Power of Legitimacy Among Nations* (Oxford: Oxford University Press, 1990). For article-length treatments of this subject, see idem. "Legitimacy in the International System," *American Journal of International Law* 82 (October 1988): 705–59; idem. "Is Justice Relevant to the International Legal System?" *Notre Dame Law Review* 64 (1989): 945–63.

47. Ruth Gordon, "Saving Failed States: Sometimes a Neocolonialist Notion," *American University Journal of International Law and Policy* 12 (1997): 903–74.

48. For an overview, see Robert F. Gorman, *Political Conflict on the Horn of Africa* (New York: Praeger, 1981).

49. Wiesburd, *supra* note 45 at 37; (Pennsylvania State University Press, 1997), 37; Makau wa Mutua, "Why Redraw the Map of Africa: A Moral and Legal Inquiry," *Michigan Journal of International Law* 16 (summer 1995): 1113 (1162–63).

50. "Ethiopia Says Somalians Control Most of Ogaden," *Washington Post*, 25 July 1977, A14.

51. Roger Mann, "Ethiopia Displays Somali Prisoners," *Washington Post*, 15 August 1977, A1; "Tour of Somali Ogaden Shows Popular Backing for Invaders," *Washington Post*, 25 August 1977, A12; Jim Hoagland, "US, France Spurn Somalia's Plea for Urgent Arms Aid," *Washington Post*, 1 September 1977, A25.

52. "Somalia Warns Cuba Against Intervention in Ethiopia Fighting," *Washington Post*, 17 August 1977, A28; Thomas Lippman, "Somalia to Order Mobilization, Cites Ethiopian Threat," *Washington Post*, 10 February 1978, A1.

53. Harold G. Marcus, *A History of Ethiopia* (Berkeley: University of California Press, 1994),

198; Jay Ross, "Ethiopia Pushes Drive to Recapture Ogaden Area," *Washington Post*, 9 February 1978, A15.

54. Thomas W. Lippman, "Somalia to Order Mobilization, Cites Ethiopian Threat," *Washington Post*, 10 February 1978, A1; John M. Goshko and Jay Ross, "US Issues a Warning to Ethiopia," *Washington Post*, 11 February 1978, A1; "Ethiopia's Ogaden War Reportedly Over," *Washington Post*, 15 March 1978, A24.

55. David Ottaway, "Soviet Wooing of Ethiopia May Push Somalia Toward US," *Washington Post*, 28 February 1977, A20; Murrey Marder, "Reversal of Once-Close Ties to Ethiopia Stirs Regret Here," *Washington Post*, 26 April 1977, A8.

56. David Ottaway, "Somali Leader Calls Soviet Arms for Ethiopia a 'Danger,' " *Washington Post*, 17 May 1977, A13.

57. Quoted in Murrey Marder, "Reversal of Once-Close Ties to Ethiopia Stirs Regret Here," *Washington Post*, 26 April 1977, A8.

58. Don Oberdorfer, "US Offers Military Aid to Somalia," *Washington Post*, 26 July 1977, A14.

59. Somalia apparently believed that the US would support its Ogaden campaign and claimed that the US misled it. "Somalia is Said to Charge US Misled It on Arms Aid," *Washington Post*, 19 September 1977, A15.

60. David Ottaway, "US Wary of Somali-Ethiopian War," *Washington Post*, 18 November 1977, A23.

61. David Ottaway, "US Wary of Somali-Ethiopian War," *Washington Post*, 18 November 1977, A23.

62. President Jimmy Carter quoted in "Carter, Congress Weigh US Arms Aid to Somalia," *Washington Post*, 16 March 1978, A25. Also see "Lengthy US-Somali Talks," *Washington Post*, 21 March 1978, A13; Don Oberdorfer, "US Revives Plan to Sell Defensive Arms to Somalia," *Washington Post*, 2 June 1978, A1.

63. *Izvestia* quoted in "Somalia Warns Cuba Against Intervention in Ethiopia Fighting," *Washington Post*, 17 August 1977, A28.

64. Weisburd, *supra* note 45, at 40.

65. Jim Hoagland, "US, France Spurn Somalia's Plea for Urgent Arms Aid," *Washington Post*, 1 September 1997, A25; Jay Ross and David Ottaway, "Egypt, Sudan Pledging Military Help to Somalia," *Washington Post*, 27 January 1978, A30.

66. Diane D. Pikcunas, *Nations at the Crossroads: Unification Policies for Germany, Korea, and China* (Washington, DC: Council for Social and Economic Studies, 1993), 20–21; Chong-Sik Lee, *The Politics of Korean Nationalism* (Berkeley: University of California Press, 1963).

67. The Republic of Korea, formed as the result of elections held on 9 May 1948, was recognized by the U.N. General Assembly as the only legitimate government on the Korean peninsula on 12 December 1948, but the ROK's application for U.N. membership was vetoed by the Soviet Union in the Security Council. Lester H. Brune, "The United Nations and Korea," in *The Korean War*, eds. Lester H. Brune, et al. (Westport, CT: Greenwood Press, 1996), 85–92 (86).

68. The United States suffered the overwhelming proportion of casualties. Peter Lowe, *The Origins of the Korean War* (London: Longman, 1986), 217–18.

69. Ibid., 119.

70. Loszek Cyrzyk, "Pyongyang's Reunification Policy," in *North Korea: Ideology, Politics, Economy*, ed. Han S. Park (Englewood Cliffs, NJ: Prentice Hall, 1996), 205–19 (206).

71. Henry Kissinger, *Diplomacy* (New York: Simon & Schuster, 1994), 475–76.

72. For a monograph-length examination of the events leading up to India's invasion of Goa, see P.D. Gaitonde, *The Liberation of Goa* (New York: St. Martin's Press, 1987).

73. Quoted in ibid., 170.

74. Quoted in Quincy Wright, "The Goa Incident," *American Journal of International Law* 56 (1962): 617–32 (619).

75. Weisburd, *supra* note 45, at 36.

76. Wright, *supra* note 74, at 629.

77. ". . . minute territories which approximate, in the geographical sense, to 'enclaves' of the claimant State, which are ethnically and economically parasitic upon or derivative of that

State . . . cannot be said in any legitimate sense to constitute separate territorial units." James Crawford, *The Creation of States in International Law* (Oxford: Clarendon Press, 1979), 384.

78. Indonesia's oppressive involvement in East Timor has increasingly come to be seen as illegitimate. The region was plunged into crisis in the fall of 1999 after an independence referendum was held. This section looks at the initial international reaction to Indonesia's invasion only.

79. FRETILIN stands for the Frente Revolucionária de Timor Leste Independente.

80. For an edited volume that looks at the situation in East Timor from a number of different perspectives, see Peter Carey and G. Carter Bently, eds., *East Timor at the Crossroads* (University of Hawai'i Press, 1995).

81. Korman, *supra* note 18, at 282.

82. Quoted in *East Timor and the International Community: Basic Documents*, ed. Heike Krieger (Cambridge University Press, 1997), 47.

83. This was not the case with the General Assembly resolutions. See GA Resolutions 3485 (XXX), 12 December 1975; 31/53, 1 December 1976; 32/34, 28 November 1977; 33/39, 13 December 1978.

84. Korman, *supra* note 18, at 284.

85. See the voting records in the General Assembly from 1975–1982 in *East Timor and the International Community,supra* note 82, at 129–33.

86. Quoted in Korman, *supra* note 18, at 286.

87. East Timor (Portugal v. Australia), 1995, Judgment , *ICJ Reports 1995*, 90. Also see Peter H. F. Bekker, "Decision: Treaty of 1989 . . .," *American Journal of International Law* 90 (January 1996): 94–98; Brian F. Fitzerald, "Portugal v. Australia," *Harvard International Law Journal* 37 (winter 1996): 260–71; Manooher Mofidi, "Prudential Timorousness in the Case Concerning East Timor (Portugal v. Australia)," *Detroit College of Law Journal of International Law and Practice* 7 (spring 1998): 35; Brandi J. Pummell, "The Timor Gap: Who Decides Who is in Control?" *Denver Journal of International Law and Policy* 26 (summer 1998): 655.

88. One of the earliest applications of international law to the collapse of Yugoslavia is Marc Weller's "The International Response to the Dissolution of the Socialist Federal Republic of Yugoslavia," *American Journal of International Law* 86 (July 1992): 569–607.

89. A more extensive examination can be found in Ambrosio, *supra* note 6, chapters 3–5.

90. See Laura Silber and Allan Little, *Yugoslavia: Death of a Nation* (New York: Penguin Books, 1997); Misha Glenny, *The Fall of Yugoslavia*, 3rd. ed. (New York: Penguin Books, 1996); and Lenard J. Cohen, *Broken Bonds*, 2nd. ed. (Boulder, CO: Westview, 1995); Susan L. Woodward, *Balkan Tragedy* (Washington, DC: Brookings Institution, 1995); Steven L. Burg and Paul S. Shoup, *The War in Bosnia-Herzegovina* (New York: M.E. Sharpe, 1998).

91. "Serbian Military Strategy," *International Defense Review* 25 (no. 1, 1 January 1992); David C. Isby, "Yugoslavia 1991-Armed Forces in Conflict," *Jane's Intelligence Review* 3 (no. 9, 1 September 1991): 394; Milan Vego, "Federal Army Deployments in Bosnia and Herzegovina," *Jane's Intelligence Review* 4 (no. 10, 1 October 1992): 445; "The Serbian Army in Bosnia and Herzegovina," *Jane's Intelligence Review—Pointer* (1 May 1994): 7.

92. A contrast is often made between Kuwait and Bosnia in the sense that the international community's response to the invasion of the former was more forceful because of its oil supplies. While this may certainly have been true, the differences between one state invading another and an attempt to alter administrative boundaries during a period of state collapse must also be considered and were likely the most consequential. See Anthony Parsons, "The UN Speaks Softly but Where's the Big Stick?" *The Daily Telegraph*, 15 June 1993, 20.

93. See Ratner's article in this volume.

94. S/RES/713, September 1991.

95. Jean-Pierre Pussochet, "The Court of Justice and International Action by the European Community: The Example of the Embargo Against the former Yugoslavia," *Fordham International Law Journal* 20 (June 1997): 1557–76.

96. S/RES/757, 30 May 1992.

97. S/RES/820, 17 April 1993.

98. Lt. Col. Susan S. Gibson, "International Economic Sanctions: The Importance of Government Structures," *Emory International Law Review* 13 (spring 1999): 161–245; Joy K. Fausey, "Does the United Nations' Use of Collective Sanctions to Protect Human Rights Violate Its Own Human Rights Standards?" *Connecticut Journal of International Law* 10 (fall 1994): 193–218.

99. James Gow, *Triumph of the Lack of Will* (New York: Columbia University Pres, 1997); Wayne Bert, *The Reluctant Superpower* (New York: St. Martin's Press, 1997).

100. The no-fly-zone (NFZ) was established pursuant to Security Council resolution 781 (9 October 1992). This was not fully enforced until April 1993 after the Council passed resolution 816 (31 March 1993) authorizing states to militarily enforce the flight ban.

101. The economic embargo against Serbia, however, was not enforced until July 1992 when the West European Union and NATO began operations in the Adriatic and Danube regions. Enforcement of the NFZ took over six months to authorize and came only after Serb airplanes were used to bomb villages in eastern Bosnia in March 1993.

102. Burg and Shoup, *supra* note 90, at 189–316.

103. Richard Holbrooke, *To End a War* (New York: Random House, 1998).

104. Franjo Tudjman praised the Cvetkovic-Macek agreement in *Nationalism in Contemporary Europe*, East European Monographs, no. 76 (New York: Columbia University Press, 1981), 113.

105. Silber and Little, *supra* note 90, at 131–32.

106. Jonathan C. Randal, "Croat-Muslim Combat in Bosnia Reaches New Ferocity," *Washington Post*, April 21, 1993, A21.

107. *Croatian TV* (Zagreb), October 29, 1996, 21:22 GMT, reproduced as "Foreign Minister Stresses Croatia's Wish to Be Part of Europe," in *BBC Summary of World Broadcasts*, October 31, 1996, EE/D2757/A.

108. Boutros Boutros-Ghali, "Letter Dated 1 February 1994 from the Secretary-General Addressed to the President of the Security Council," United Nations Security Council, February 2, 1994, S/1994/109. Boutros-Ghali stated: "As the offensives of the Bosnia and Herzegovina Government forces against the HVO have become successful, the numbers of Croatian soldiers appear to have increased."

109. "Provisional Verbatim Record of the Three Thousand Three Hundred and Thirty-Third Meeting," United Nations Security Council, February 3, 1994, S/PV.3333.

110. *Agence France Presse* (Paris), February 3, 1994, 15:59 GMT, reproduced as "Spain, Denmark Say Decision on Sanctions 'Imminent,' " in *FBIS-EEU*, February 7, 1994, 2.

111. *Agence France Presse* (Paris), February 10, 1994, 00:52 GMT, reproduced as "EC Considering Sanctions Against Croatia," in *FBIS-WEU*, February 10, 1994, 7.

112. *TANJUG* (Belgrade), February 5, 1994, 18:02 GMT, reproduced as "TANJUG: Kohl Says Tudjman Violating Law," in *FBIS-EEU*, February 7, 1994, 2.

113. "Kohl Threatens to Withdraw Croatian Aid, as Pressure Mounts," *Agence France Presse*, February 5, 1994.

114. David B. Ottaway, "U.S. Prevails on Croatia," *Washington Post*, February 26, 1994, A14.

115. Quoted in Samuel Huntington, *The Clash of Civilizations and the Remaking of World Order* (New York: Simon & Schuster, 1996), 296.

116. David B. Ottaway, "U.S. Prevails on Croatia," *Washington Post*, February 26, 1994, A14; Stephen Kinzer, "Croatian Leaders Backs Pact by Bosnia's Muslims and Croats," *New York Times*, March 5, 1994, sec. 1, p. 5.

117. Under Tudjman, however, Croatia-proper remained in *de facto* control of the Bosnian Croat "statelet" of Herceg-Bosna. See Thomas Ambrosio, "The Federation of Bosnia-Herzegovina: A Failure of Implementation," in *State and Nation Building in East Central Europe: Contemporary Perspectives*, John S. Micgiel, ed. (New York: Institute on East Central Europe, Columbia University, 1996), 225–41.

118. Both Armenia and Azerbaijan were admitted to the United Nations in 1992; A/RES/46/227 and A/RES/46/230, respectively.

119. Human Rights Watch/Helsinki, *Azerbaijan: Seven Years of Conflict in Nagorno Karabakh* (New York: Human Rights Watch, 1994), 67–73.

The official claims that the interests of Armenia and Nagorno-Karabakh were differenct became quite farcical when the president of the self-styled Nagorno-Karabakh Republic, Robert Kocharyan, became prime minister of Armenia on 20 March 1997; and on 30 March 1998 he was elected president of Armenia.

120. Armenia has consistently received nearly $100 million per year from the United States. Making it the fourth-largest recipient of US aid on a per capita basis. "Albright's Push for Foreign Aid Gets Mixed Receptions," *Congressional Quarterly Weekly Report*, 28 June 1997, 1538.

121. Felix O. Mamikoyan, the Armenian ambassador to Russia called Russia "Armenia's ally and protector 'from times immemorial.' " Quoted in Michael Parks, "Armenia Seeks Alliance's Help Against Azerbaijan," *Los Angeles Times*, 17 June 1992, A9.

122. Pavel Baev, *Russia's Policies in the Caucasus* (London: Royal Institute of International Affairs, 1997).

123. Yevgeny Krutikov and Guga Lolishvili, "Russia Concludes Military Alliance with Armenia and Georgia to Guard Against External Aggression," *Kuranty*, 4 November 1992, 3, reproduced in *Russian Press Digest*, 4 November 1992.

124. This agreement also set up a joint air-defense system. Yelena Visens, "Russia to Establish Military Base in Armenia," *Segodnya*, 10 June 1994, 1, reproduced in *Russian Press Digest*, 10 June 1994.

125. This included: 86 T72 tanks, 50 Armor Personnel Carriers, 32 Scud-B missiles. Michael P. Croissant, *The Armenian-Azerbaijan Conflict* (New York: Praeger, 1998), 120. Also see *Interfax* (Moscow), 28 February 1997, 12:17 GMT, reproduced as "President of Azerbaijan Says Russia-Armenia Military Ties Breach CIS Accord," in *BBCSWB*, 4 March 1997, SU/D2858/F.

126. Rochelle L. Stanfield, "Ethnic Politicking," *The National Journal* 21 (no. 52, 30 December 1989): 3096.

127. Carroll J. Doherty, "Armenia's Special Relationship with US is Showing Strain," *Congressional Quarterly Weekly Report*, 31 May 1997, 1270.

128. Starting from 1996, however, the Armenian lobby has seen its influence slip considerably on account of "a highly unusual coalition of oil companies, administration officials, Jewish-Americans and pro-Turkey lawmakers." A bit of explanation might be necessary. U.S. oil companies have been lobbying hard to end Azerbaijan's isolation in hopes that they would benefit from Azerbaijani oil reserves. Clinton administration officials have taken a renewed interest in the strategic value of the Caspian basin and hopes to build an alliance with Azerbaijan; in addition, the Administration wants to keep Azerbaijani oil out of Russian control. Furthermore, the Jewish-American and pro-Turkish lobbies are working close together in order to lift Baku's isolation: Israel's search for secular allies within the Muslim world have led it to form a *de facto* alliance with Turkey; since Azerbaijan is Turkey's ally, Israel hopes to widen its circle of friends within the Muslim world through its support for Azerbaijan. Supporters of Azerbaijan have been pushing for the "Silk Road Strategy Act," which will offer a framework for a broad U.S. engagement in the Caspian region and Central Asia and would end the ban on U.S. aid to Azerbaijan. If this act passes and the Armenian lobby continues to weaken, it is possible that Congress might take a harsher view of Armenian control over Nagorno-Karabakh.

Quote in footnote from "Petro-Politics Greases the Way for a Different US Approach to Nagorno-Karabakh Dispute," *Congressional Quarterly Weekly Report*, 27 June 1998, 1783. Also see Paul Starobin, "The New Great Game," *The National Journal* 31 (no. 11, 13 March 1999): 666; "Stoked by Farm Interests, Anti-Sanctions Movement Builds in Both Chambers," *Congressional Quarterly Weekly Report*, 27 March 1999, 767.

129. There seemed to be a flurry of Security Council resolutions in 1993: 822, 30 April 1993; 853, 29 July 1993; 874, 14 October 3; 884, 12 November 1993. Also see Weisburd, 112.

130. Konstantin Eggert, "European Community Accuses Armenia of Aggression Against Azerbaijan," *Izvestia*, 20 May 1992, 1, reproduced in *Current Digest of the Post-Soviet Press* 44 (no. 20, 17 June 1992): 12.

131. Kirgis, *supra* note 32.

132. James J. Sandkovich, *The U.S. Media and Yugoslavia, 1991–1995* (Praeger, 1998).

133. On the growing importance of ethnic groups on United States foreign policy, see Yossi Shain, "Multicultural Foreign Policy," *Foreign Policy* 100, 69–87; idem., "Ethnic Diasporas and U.S. Foreign Policy," *Political Science Quarterly* 109 (no. 5, 1994–95): 811–41.

Population Transfer: The Effects of Settler Infusion Policies on a Host Population's Right to Self-Determination

Eric Kolodner

THROUGHOUT HISTORY, GOVERNMENTS have used population transfer policies to subjugate, conquer, and colonize peoples worldwide. These policies have assumed two primary forms defined here as "forced relocation" and "settler infusion." Under the former, a government expels individuals from an area and forces them to relocate to a different territory. This more common form of population transfer occurs under a variety of circumstances, producing vastly different effects. Historical examples include the United States' forced removal and enslavement of Africans, the Nazis' mass transfer of Jews and Gypsies into World War II concentration camps, and Saddam Hussein's forced relocation of Kurds from Northern Iraq to Southern Iraq.

Settler infusion occurs when governments systematically transfer their own citizens into territories primarily inhabited by a different and distinct group of individuals. This is less commonly practiced, but its effects can be equally devastating. Under settler infusion policies, governments usually do not require their citizens to relocate, but give them financial incentives to do so. While gov-

Reprinted with permission from Eric Kolodner, "Population Transfer: The Effects of Settler Infusion Policies on a Host Population's Right to Self-Determination," *New York University Journal of International Law and Politics* 27, no. 1 (fall 1994): 159–226.

ernments tend to use forced relocation policies to conquer those being transferred, settler infusion policies are used to conquer and subjugate residents of
the territory receiving the new settlers. Historical examples of settler infusion include the United States' policy of transferring citizens into territories occupied
by the Native Americans, the Ottoman emperors' practice of relocating Turkish
citizens into Ottoman-conquered lands, and the Israeli government's current
policy of transferring Jews into the Occupied Territories.

This essay primarily examines settler infusion policies. In some instances,
settler infusion can present the gravest threat to a group's legal identity, cultural
integrity, and physical survival. This subtle form of invasion, which uses people
as weapons, usually escapes international scrutiny, and is therefore rendered the
most cost-effective and least controversial method of invading a territory and
eliminating its inhabitants. As one United States Congressman has noted:

> [P]opulation transfer, . . . the most dangerous and most insidious form of
> suppression, may be the most difficult to deal with, because there is
> clearly no basis for involving ourselves in population movements in other
> countries. Perhaps even more importantly, the outrage . . . [Americans]
> feel when they are confronted with what we call human rights violations,
> torture, suppression of religious liberties, etc., is not present when the
> issue is population movements. Population movements are not viewed as
> violent acts.[1]

Settler infusion policies may infringe upon the fundamental human rights of
both the settlers and the host population. This paper focuses on the impact that
settler infusion policies have upon host populations, and concentrates particularly
on the interrelationship between settler infusion policies and the host population's right to self-determination. The right to self-determination contains both
external and internal aspects. While the exercise of these two facets of self-determination carry significantly different ramifications, both involve issues of control.
Whereas the external right to self-determination entitles a people to control their
international political status, the internal right entitles them to have control over
their domestic political system and authority over the economic, social, and cultural conditions under which they live. Implementation of the right to self-determination involves "not only the completion of the process of achieving independence or other appropriate legal status . . . but also recognition of [a people's]
right to maintain, assure and perfect their full legal, political, economic, social
and cultural sovereignty."[2] Two current examples will provide perspectives on
these issues: the Israeli government's transfer of Jews into the Occupied Territories and the Chinese government's relocation of citizens into Tibet.

Part I concentrates first on forced relocation as a form of population transfer, and second on the general effects of settler infusion policies on a host pop-

ulation. Part II examines the right to self-determination. It briefly addresses the history of the right, its components, and its current status. Part III examines the interrelationship between settler infusion policies and a host population's right to self-determination. It discusses the discrimination and exploitation often underlying such policies, and argues that they violate both the internal and external aspects of a host population's right to self-determination.

I. Population Transfer

Because of the variety of circumstances under which population transfer has occurred, the international community has not yet formulated a sophisticated definition of this practice. In general terms, the "objective" elements of population transfer have been defined to include the "movement of large numbers of people, either into or away from a certain territory, with state involvement or acquiescence of government and without the free and informed consent of the people being moved or the people into whose territory they are being moved."[3] The "subjective" elements involve a government's intent behind its population transfer policy, a policy often undertaken to facilitate the subjugation, oppression, or destruction of a distinct group of individuals. A recent U.N. resolution addressed these "subjective" components:

> Population transfer may constitute part of a larger policy towards distinct ethnic, racial or religious groups and may be motivated by strategic, military, and political aims of imposing effective control over and assimilation of nations and peoples and at changing the demographic composition of the territories concerned.[4]

Only recently has the international community begun to address the complexities and subtleties of population transfer policies. In the past three years, for example, the U.N. Subcommission on Prevention of Discrimination and Protection of Minorities has passed resolutions on the "human rights dimensions of population transfer, including the implantation of settlers and settlements."[5] In 1991, the Subcommission completed a working paper on the human rights dimensions of population transfer. A 1992 Subcommission resolution recommended that the Commission on Human Rights appoint a Special Rapporteur to further study the issue. Other international organizations that have begun to address the damaging effects of population transfer include the World Bank, the U.N. Educational, Scientific and Cultural Organization (UNESCO), and the Unrepresented Nations and Peoples Organization.

A. Forced Relocation as a Form of Population Transfer

Forced relocation as a form of population transfer has roots stretching as far back as the first or second millennium, B.C. when the Assyrian, Egyptian, Mesopotamian, and Anatolian empires instituted such policies as a "tool to weaken, dismember, and eliminate the national dimensions of subject peoples."[6]

The European peoples, who colonized the Americas thousands of years later, inherited this form of population transfer from the ancient world and systematically employed it to subjugate indigenous peoples.

> The Spanish and English have left the world with a heritage of
> population transfer that has now become integrated into the dominant
> colonial-settler societies in the states of the Americas and Oceania, where
> a literary, religious, military and legal culture converged to denude the
> new-found lands of their indigenous human societies.[7]

Of all "New World" nations, the United States has distinguished itself as the most ambitious practitioner of forced resettlement. In fact, the United States was founded upon a dual policy of population transfer. On one hand, the U.S. government engaged in a dehumanizing policy of population transfer of Africans. By 1800, ten to fifteen million such individuals had been transplanted from their homelands to serve as labor for the fields of the South. Simultaneously, the government expelled Native Americans and infused settlers into the newly conquered lands.

The twentieth century has also witnessed numerous devastating examples of forced relocation. Following World War I, newly created nation-states engaged in "population exchanges" in which hundreds of thousands of individuals were uprooted. For example, as a result of the 1923 Treaty of Lausanne, 1.5 million Greeks of Turkish nationality were forced to leave Asia Minor and relocate in "the mother country," and "400,000 Turks of Greek nationality were required to leave Greece."[8] The most infamous example of recent population transfer occurred during World War II when Nazis killed millions through their policy of transferring Jews, Gypsies, and other minorities from their homes throughout Europe into concentration camps. The Iraqi and Turkish governments' forced removal of Kurds are more recent examples.

Recently, this type of population transfer has arisen in the context of large development projects, which are motivated not by political subjugation of the conquered but rather economic betterment of the impoverished. In India, for example, construction on the much-needed Narmada Dam precipitated the relocation of 70,000 Indian citizens, and, in Egypt the Aswan Dam project displaced over 100,000 Egyptians. Although the underlying justification for such involuntary resettlement might be benevolent, their effects can still be devastating. As one World Bank expert explained:

> [D]isplacement is always an extraordinarily disruptive and painful
> process, economically and culturally: it dismantles production systems, it

disorganizes entire human communities and it breaks up long established social networks. By destroying productive assets and disorganizing production systems, it creates a high risk of chronic impoverishment and pushes groups of people into a condition of transitory or permanent food insecurity.[9]

B. Settler Infusion as a Form of Population Transfer

The aforementioned examples have all involved the expulsion and forced relocation of a people from their home territory. That form of population transfer, often founded upon open aggression, produces immediate, visceral, and, at times, cataclysmic results. By contrast, settler infusion is often more elusive, and its effects are more gradual, although no less damaging. Under this form of population transfer, a government resettles its citizens in a territory primarily inhabited by a distinct ethnic, racial, religious, or linguistic group of individuals.

1. Historical and Current Examples of Settler Infusion. The Ottoman rulers of the fifteenth through nineteenth centuries were the first to perfect and systematize this type of population transfer. Following military victory, the Ottoman government encouraged Turks and other Muslims to colonize the conquered land in an effort to eliminate local opposition by altering the region's original demographic composition. These policies "have left behind a recipe for conflict which still challenges states of the former Ottoman empire."[10] Some contemporary examples of this type of population transfer include the Soviet government's infusion of settlers into the Baltic States, the Chinese government's infusion into Tibet, the Indonesian government's settler infusion into East Timor, the Moroccan government's settler infusion into the Western Sahara, the Ethiopian government's infusion into Eritrea, and the Israeli government's settler infusion into the Occupied Territories.

2. General Effects of Settler Infusion Policies. Settler infusion policies have different impacts upon each of the three distinct categories of individuals: the implanted settlers who relocate, the host populations who receive the new settlers, and the surrounding communities, which often confront the spillover effects from these policies. The ramifications upon implanted settlers depend on the extent of government involvement.[11] This essay discusses primarily the effects upon host populations, in particular the consequences of Chinese settler infusion policies upon the Tibetans and Israeli policies upon the Palestinians.

Settler infusion takes one or two generations to accomplish what a military invasion against the host population could accomplish in weeks or months. It modifies a territory's demographic composition, transforming an ethnic/cultural/religious majority into a minority whose voice of opposition is silenced. It is often a "significant factor in ethnic conflicts and unrest which contribute to further social, economic, political, and cultural instability."[12] Past settler implantation policies form the basis of many current conflicts.

Settler infusion inherently violates several internationally recognized human rights. The specific rights violated depend upon the context in which settler infusion occurs. For example, the nature of the specific violations will depend upon whether the resettlement is voluntary or involuntary;[13] whether the transfer occurs across international boundaries or within one country; whether it occurs in peacetime, belligerent occupation, or during war; and whether valid justifications exist for such a policy, for example, genuine development projects.[14]

The International Commission of Jurists has concluded that settler infusion during wartime and belligerent occupation violates the most fundamental principles of international law:

> [After] the Charter of the United Nations . . . with the right to conquest, the right to create settlements has also disappeared, and what is left is the bare right of temporary military occupation where necessary in lawful self-defense. This does not include a right to establish settlements of a civilian nature or settlements of a permanent character.[15]

Settler infusion may violate not only the U.N. Charter, but also Article 49 of the Fourth Geneva Convention which explicitly forbids an occupying power "to deport or transfer parts of its own civilian population into the territory it occupies."

Settler infusion may also violate the International Covenant on the Elimination of All Forms of Racial Discrimination, as well as the Convention on the Prevention and Punishment of the Crime of Genocide, which defines genocide to include acts "deliberately inflicting on the group conditions of life calculated to bring about its physical destruction in whole or in part." Finally, settler implantation often violates individual rights codified in numerous other international instruments, including the Universal Declaration on Human Rights, the International Covenant on Civil and Political Rights, and the International Covenant on Economic, Social and Cultural Rights. As the U.N. Subcommission on Prevention of Discrimination and Protection of Minorities affirmed in 1992, population transfer may violate the right to "freedom of movement, to choose one's residence . . . the right to be free from arbitrary interference with one's privacy, family or home, the right to an adequate standard of living, the inherent right to life, the right to liberty and security of person. . . ."[16]

II. SELF-DETERMINATION

While settler infusion may violate the aforementioned rights and international instruments, it may also violate a people's right to self-determination. With roots stretching back to the seventeenth century, the concept of self-determination has become ensconced within international law. "Perhaps no contemporary norm of international law has been so vigorously promoted or widely accepted as the right of all peoples to self-determination."[17] In the most general terms, self-determination is "an expression, in succinct form, of the aspiration to rule one's self and to not be ruled by others."[18] Promoted within a myriad of international instruments, self-determination buttresses the regime of international human rights law and constitutes a necessary element in the protection of other fundamental human rights.[19]

. . . Since the end of World War I, when the right to self-determination first assumed international importance, observers have argued over its parameters, requirements, and ramifications. Generally speaking, the debate has focused on two interrelated questions: who constitutes the "self-," and what does this "self" determine? To answer these questions, one must first decide whether the right to self-determination is an individual right, a collective right, or both. Most commentators today agree that self-determination should be conceptualized as a right *sui generis*, containing both individual and collective elements.

[Kolodner examines here self-determination's history and recent developments, the groups are entitled to self-determination, and the parameters of "determination." See Hannum's essay on self-determination featured in this volume.]

III. POPULATION TRANSFER AND SELF-DETERMINATION

The remainder of this essay will demonstrate that settler infusion as a means of population transfer infringes on a people's right to self-determination. This is true no matter how broadly or narrowly one defines the right to self-determination—whether it is viewed as an individual right, a collective right, or both; whether it applies only to "peoples," or to "minorities" and "indigenous peoples" under some circumstances; whether it applies only to traditional instances of colonialism, or to all situations in which people live under despotic governments; and whether it applies only to secessionary claims, or also to assertions of control over the economic, political, social, and cultural conditions under which a group of individuals live. For the purposes of this essay self-determination will be conceptualized generally as the extent to which a people possesses control over the various current and future conditions of their existence.

Although benign policies of settler infusion may not violate the right to self-determination, such instances of population transfer are extremely rare. Instead, policies of settler infusion are almost always implemented against a particular group of individuals in a discriminatory manner and are targeted to control or colonize them. Furthermore, settler infusion policies engender additional future discrimination against the host population in a variety of areas. The intent to discriminate and to subjugate, which forms a policy of settler infusion and the subsequent discrimination which inevitably emanates from the implementation of the policy, virtually guarantees the infringement of the host population's right to self-determination.

The relationship between settler infusion and self-determination will be viewed through the lens of two current situations in which the occupying nations are transferring their citizens into the territories that they occupy. Following is a brief review of these two situations: (1) the Chinese government's infusion of Chinese settlers into Tibet; and (2) the Israeli government's transferal of Jews into the Occupied Territories.

A. China and Tibet

On October 7, 1950, the Chinese invaded Tibet and within months had overrun the weaker Tibetan forces to effectuate the "glorious task of liberating Tibet."[20] The Chinese then coerced representatives of the Tibetan government into signing a "Seventeen Point Agreement" in which Tibet sacrificed its sovereignty to the Chinese. Tibet remains the largest territory to be stripped of its sovereignty since the end of World War II. China additionally lanced off territories of traditional Tibet and incorporated them into Chinese provinces, leaving a significantly smaller Tibetan Autonomous Region (TAR). In return, China promised to maintain Tibet's current political system, guarantee freedom of religion, ensure the development of the Tibetan culture and education system, promote the use of the Tibetan language, and improve Tibet's economic condition. The Tibetan government immediately repudiated the agreement as a document signed under duress without government approval.

Over the next nine years, the Chinese broke every promise in the Seventeen Point Agreement, prompting numerous Tibetan uprisings. Entire villages were razed and public executions became commonplace. Monks were forced to copulate publicly with nuns before being dispatched to one of the numerous labor camps the Chinese established along the Tibetan plateau. Ancient religious books and articles were burned. In 1959, events erupted in a huge Tibetan rebellion, which the Chinese crushed. The Dalai Lama, the Tibetan spiritual and temporal leader, fled the country and established his government-in-exile in India, where it remains today.

By the late 1960's, China had completely overrun Tibet. Over 1.2 million of Tibet's original six million inhabitants had been killed. Famine swept through the country for the first time in history. In 1976, only thirteen of Tibet's 6,254 monasteries remained standing. China had finally achieved its goals: it could freely exploit Tibet's vast natural resources, use Tibet's inhospitable terrain as a buffer against India, and begin transferring Chinese civilians into the newly occupied territory.

A unanimous international community has repeatedly condemned this Chinese invasion and occupation, although geopolitical concerns have tempered support for the Tibetans. In 1960, the International Commission of Jurists censured the Chinese for their systematic policy of genocide. The United Nations General Assembly has passed three resolutions criticizing Chinese policies in Tibet, and in 1961, it affirmed the Tibetans' right to self-determination. Most recently, in 1991, the U.N. Subcommission on the Prevention of Discrimination and Protection of Minorities passed a resolution which criticized the human rights situation in Tibet. Also in 1991, the Australian Parliament reaffirmed its support for the Tibetan right to self-determination. The United States Congress in its 1992–1993 Foreign Relations Act declared Tibet, including the regions which China subsequently annexed, "an occupied country under the established principles of international law." As one observer has summarized:

> In many respects, the legal debate about the status of Tibet is over self-determination in the classic sense rather than minority (or indigenous) rights. Certainly, the Tibetans' claim to self-determination and independence is at least as strong as that of any other recognized national group, although Tibet is unfortunately not alone in having been denied this right by a more powerful neighbor.[21]

Before 1950, Tibetans were the only inhabitants within their country. As Mao Tse Dong said following the Chinese invasion, "while several hundred thousand Han Chinese live in Sinkiang [the Northwest region of China which used to be East Turkestan], there are hardly any in Tibet, where our army finds itself in a totally different minority nationality area."[22] In the mid-1950's, Mao commenced the Chinese policy of settler infusion when he began sending Chinese farmers into parts of Eastern Tibet. By the late 1980's, China had sent millions of civilians into Tibet in addition to the 400,000 troops permanently housed there. The Chinese policy of settler infusion is certain to continue into the future. A Chinese publication announced in 1991 that 300,000 new settlers would be brought into Tibet to work on development projects. Furthermore, more recent reports indicate that large tracts of farmland are being prepared in Southern Tibet to resettle another 300,000 Chinese displaced by a development project in the Yarlung Valley. Although population statistics are difficult to ascertain, estimates suggest that there are approximately six million Tibetans and seven and one-half million Chinese living in traditional Tibet.

B. Israel and the Occupied Territories

The public is more familiar with the extensive history of the conflict between the Israeli government and the Palestinians in the Occupied Territories. The modern phase of this conflict began in the early 20th century as the Zionist movement convinced thousands of Jews to migrate back to Palestine, a region predominately occupied by Arabs.[23] After World War I, Great Britain was granted the territory of Palestine, which they divided into two political entities in 1921. The eastern portion eventually became Jordan, while in the western half, Jews and Palestinian Arabs continued to fight for ascendency. Following World War II, Britain relinquished control over this geographical region and, in 1947, the United Nations divided this territory into the new States of Palestine and Israel. Jerusalem, a city sacred to both Jews and Muslims, was to become an international enclave.

While the Jews accepted the partition plan, the Arabs did not. In 1948, various Arab nations simultaneously invaded Israel, but were unable to defeat this new state. Hostilities continued to mount, and pan-Arabism sentiment culminated in 1967 when Egypt, Syria, and Jordan amassed soldiers along the Israeli borders, blockaded a key Israeli port, and vowed to annihilate Israel. Israel, however, launched a preemptive strike and within six days had surprisingly defeated the Arabs, occupying Syria's Golan Heights, Egypt's Sinai Peninsula and Gaza Strip, Jordan's West Bank, and East Jerusalem.

Israel eventually returned the Sinai Peninsula to Egypt, but for the past twenty-six years has occupied and dominated the other four territories. The Palestinian uprising (intifada), which began in Gaza and the West Bank in 1987, stands witness to the continued hostilities and Israeli oppression of the Palestinians. The Israelis continue to detain illegally and torture Palestinians, deport them from the Occupied Territories, and confiscate their land and possessions. Mutual killings persist.

As in the Tibetan situation, the international community has repeatedly condemned Israel for its human rights abuses against the Palestinians and its prolonged occupation. The United States has also criticized the Israeli government for its treatment of Palestinians and has declared that Israel is an "occupying power" and therefore subject to the Fourth Geneva Convention. The international community has also asserted that the Palestinians are a "people" entitled to the right to self-determination. As one commentator remarked, "[d]espite the many problems associated with them, the diplomatic and political moves since the occupation began together have reinforced the view of the West Bank and Gaza as territories that jointly are a candidate for self-determination, and have weakened alternative views."[24]

Israel, however, continues to deny the illegality of its acts. While it acknowledges its obligations under a variety of legal instruments, Israel denies the legal applicability of the Fourth Geneva Convention. Israel asserts that, because prior to 1967 the West Bank and Gaza Strip were not legally parts of Jordan and Egypt respectively, Israel cannot be considered a "belligerently occupying" power. Instead, it is merely "administering" the territories until a true sovereign can be found. Many international observers find Israel's position unconvincing. Since 1977, the Israeli government has consistently infused Israeli citizens into the Occupied Territories.[25] As of November 1992, approximately 1,958,000 Palestinians and 101,000 Jews lived in the Occupied Territories. There were an estimated 398 Palestinian settlements and 144 Israeli settlements within these regions. Thus, although Jewish settlements comprise 27 percent of the total number of settlements in the Occupied Territories, Jews comprise less than 6 percent of the total population. By the year 2000, it is estimated that Jewish settlers will comprise 7.6 percent of the population of the Occupied Territories.

C. The Subjective Intent Behind Settler Infusion: Discrimination and Subjugation

Settler countries offer what appear to be benign reasons to justify their settler infusion practices. Modern governments that engage in these policies have the foresight to publicly enunciate palatable justifications, understanding that the international community, historically hesitant to infringe on state sovereignty, rarely will investigate further.

Generally, governments justify their settler infusion policies on the basis of allegedly historic claims to particular tracts of land. Some governments additionally assert that they infuse settlers into a territory to remedy their own overpopulation problems or to defend national security. Sometimes governments offer economic arguments such as the need to alleviate landlessness, redress an imbalance in socio-economic conditions, or increase agricultural production. Others assert that they actually infuse settlers into the territory for the host population's benefit, for example, to help a "backwards" people develop culturally and socially.

Although a government might present a charitable veneer or justify its policies through necessity, a closer examination of the situation often evinces an underlying racism. One observer, in comparing examples of population transfer throughout history, noted that "[a]ll [have] involve[d] racist or ethnocentric state ideologies."[26] A U.N. Subcommission on the Prevention of Discrimination and Protection of Minorities resolution recently asserted that population transfer often derives from discriminatory intent and inevitably exacerbates discrimination.[27]

As will be described below, settler infusion constitutes one prong of a broad discriminatory policy aimed at controlling a distinct group of individuals. It can be a sophisticated and effective tool of aggression and destruction. An aggressor or occupying government will be involved to varying degrees in implementing this policy by either coercing or encouraging its citizens to relocate. A government might offer financial support, provide logistical or transportation assistance, clear land, or build infrastructure; it might also implement its policy through strategic omissions, for example, by failing to address problems of overcrowding or unemployment.[28]

Discrimination and domination pervade the policies of settler infusion in the Occupied Territories and Tibet. Such intent is manifested both explicitly in the speeches of government officials, and more subtly by the occupying countries' policies. The population transfers in Tibet and the Occupied Territories aptly demonstrate such motivations. For example, although the Chinese have publicly justified their settler infusion policy as efforts to relieve overpopulation and economic problems in China, they have simultaneously announced their intentions to develop a "backward" society. Although Chinese government officials intermittently deny offering benefits to Chinese who relocate in Tibet, the government's own newspapers admit the existence of such incentives. Chinese are offered better wages and pensions and longer vacation periods for settling in Tibet. Chinese who stay longer than eight years receive further pay raises, and those who work for more than twenty years and retire in Tibet enjoy an additional ten percent increase in their pensions. "Whereas under Mao, the westward population transfer was forced, today the westward movement is both centrally and locally induced by development, subsidies and incentives."[29] Such preferential treatment further exacerbates the disparity in standards of living between the Chinese and Tibetans.

In a recently published book, two Chinese government economists aptly summarized the Chinese attitude towards the Tibetans: "The personnel . . . brought in from developed regions cannot be expected to live on the local fare. . . . They need good housing, hospitals, cinemas and schools for their children. . . ."[30]

Moreover, they will need jobs for their children, who themselves will have children necessitating higher quality housing, education, and employment which would otherwise not be necessary for the Tibetans.

Although less explicitly discriminatory, the Israeli government also offers incentives to its citizens who settle in the territories Israel occupies. As one observer noted, "the ambitious settlements program of the 1980's . . . was planned, encouraged and financed at the governmental level."[31] For example, the Israeli government grants Soviet Jews generous housing allowances to settle in Israel. As the demand for apartments within Israel increases, many established Israeli citizens find it difficult to afford to live there. These Israeli citizens are thus subtly induced to move into the Occupied Territories where housing is more affordable. Other Israeli government policies offer more explicit incentives for citizens to settle in the Occupied Territories. For example, the government absorbs approximately two-thirds of the housing and moving costs for families who relocate there; settlers' income tax is reduced by seven percent; settlers purchase land at five percent of its true value; settlers receive interest-free or low interest mortgages; and settlers are entitled to a $19,000 housing grant (for a family of four). One expert estimates that the incentives and assistance for Israelis living in the Occupied Territories are fifty percent greater than the support offered Israelis who live within the pre-1967 borders. Furthermore, per capita, Israeli settlers in the occupied territories receive fifty times more financial assistance than Palestinians living there.

D. Population Transfer Violates the "External" Right to Self-Determination

Most current commentators who debate the utility and extent of the right to self-determination focus upon the external aspect of this right. One observer defined the external right to self-determination as the right "to be free from foreign interference which affects the international status of that state."[32] Substantial opposition to current assertions of the right to self-determination has been advanced by commentators who render this right virtually conterminous with the right to secession.[33] One observer has criticized current movements for self-determination as "contentious incantation[s] of a purported 'people's' right . . . with [its] implied endorsement of secession in at least some circumstances."[34]

Justified concerns exist that granting a right to secede in today's world would effectuate an incessant cycle of demands for external self-determination where alleged "peoples" within "peoples" within "peoples" would petition for their right to independence from a multi-ethnic state. The ensuing international system would be highly fragmented, politically unstable, incapable of addressing global problems, and economically unfit to provide the necessities of life to many of the world's inhabitants.

Some commentators assert that there does not exist a right to secession. One observer has noted that "with the exception of Bangladesh, whose independence was due more to the Indian army than to the precepts of international law, no secessionist claim has been accepted by the international community since 1945."[35] Another commentator has argued that the right to secede from an existing U.N. member does not exist within U.N. instruments; however, a qualified right to secede exists if "the national unity claimed [by the U.N. member] and the territorial integrity invoked are merely legal fictions which cloak real colonialist and alien domination."[36]

The external right to self-determination, however, does not necessarily implicate secession. In fact, different peoples will "determine" a variety of different international identities. Although most peoples choose secession and independence, they can also choose to become loosely federated with another independent state, to run their own domestic affairs while relinquishing control of their foreign relations to another state, or to merge entirely with an existing nation. In 1965, for example, the territory of Ifnii chose to incorporate with Morocco; and in 1975, the Mariana Islands chose to become freely associated with the United States.

The implementation of the external right to self-determination focuses not upon the outcome of a people's choice, but rather upon the process by which they determine their international status. A legitimate exercise of the external right to self-determination necessitates a genuine and free expression of the will of the people involved. A policy of settler infusion precisely targets, dilutes, and potentially destroys this will; therefore, as a result of a population transfer policy, the host population's external right to self-determination is often violated, and its ability to exercise this right can be permanently destroyed.

Not only can a policy of settler infusion destroy the will and culture of a people; ironically, it can also dissuade the international community from accepting the validity of this people's claim to the right of self-determination. A settler infusion policy can significantly affect a number of the criteria by which the international community will judge the legitimacy of a people's struggle for external self-determination. These criteria include: the historical legitimacy and territorial integrity of the geographical area claimed by a people; the degree to which the demanding group can form a viable political entity; the consequences of self-determination upon the non-group members in the territory; and the effects upon the region as a whole. By "negatively" influencing these four factors, a policy of settler infusion, rather than buttressing the legitimacy of a people's claim to self-determination, will likely reduce the host population's chances for self-determination.

A people struggling for their external right to self-determination will simultaneously assert a right to control a particular territory to which they claim an historic link. Without a persuasive claim over a geographical area, a people's assertion of their external right to self-determination is severely undermined, especially if they are seeking independence. A group sparsely distributed throughout a large, multi-ethnic country is less likely to obtain the requisite status of "a people" than a group whose population is concentrated within a specific territory and whose history has revolved around this geographical area. "The mere fact that the secessionist group constitutes a distinct people does not by itself establish a right to secede. To be persuasive, a separatist argument must also present a territorial claim."[37]

A policy of settler infusion undermines a people's claim for external self-determination because it splinters and disintegrates the integrity of the territory to which they assert a right. Policies of settler infusion are often specifically designed to fragment and disconnect a people living within a territory. For example, in both Tibet and the Occupied Territories, settler communities have been established primarily next to villages and cities of the host population. The location of these settlements allows China and Israel not only to divide and conquer, but also to undermine the integrity of the host populations' territories. In the Occupied Territories, for instance, Israeli policies demonstrate that the "Palestinian population is destined to be squeezed into three small 'Bantustans' around major urban centers . . . thereby isolating the remaining populations from each other and eliminating the landed national dimension of the Palestinian people."[38] As newly arrived Chinese and Israelis establish roots alongside the Tibetans and Palestinians, and as infrastructure further separates the host populations' communities, the original inhabitants' exclusive claims to sovereignty over distinct territories become less convincing.

In the early stages of settler infusion, strategic settlements and infrastructure undermine the host population's claim to a distinct geographical region; over time, sheer numbers can permanently destroy this claim. As waves of new settlers pour into Tibet, for example, Tibet appears more Chinese than Tibetan. As one journalist wrote in 1985:

> Tibet's two largest cities . . . look thoroughly Chinese with residential districts and administrative buildings indistinguishable from their Beijing counterparts. Colorfully clad Tibetans are hard to spot among the Chinese who crowd the streets and make up more than half the population of Tibet's capital, Lhasa.[39]

Settler infusion also undermines the second prong of the aforementioned test, the potential viability of a host population's self-governance. As the number of settlers increase, the host population becomes increasingly marginalized by its gradually diminished capacity to exercise control over the economic, political, social, and cultural aspects of the territory. Not surprisingly, a people who have been reduced to an impoverished and uneducated existence will have difficulties asserting their ability to establish a viable system of self-government. The harmful effects of systematic settler infusion policies can be clearly seen in the Palestinian and Tibetan cases.

Settler infusion also exacerbates the impact self-determination has upon a territory's inhabitants who are not members of the demanding group. As more settlers enter a territory, establish roots, and become economically, socially, and culturally dependent upon events within the territory, a host population's exercise of self-determination becomes increasingly detrimental to the settlers. If it were to choose independence, the host population would be relatively free to promulgate conditions which would severely harm the settlers. The new government, for example, might strip the settlers of their possessions, disenfranchise them, or refuse to grant them citizenship.

A policy of settler infusion inherently produces tensions between the settlers and the host population.[40] Tibetan revolts over the past decade and the continued intifada in the Occupied Territories reflect such tensions. As one human rights group wrote about the Palestinian situation, "violence [between settlers and the Palestinians] is an inevitable result of the inherent conflict that occurs when Palestinian land and resources are seized and then illegally settled by Israeli Jews with their government's legal, financial, and military support."[41] There is little doubt that if the Tibetans or Palestinians were granted the external right to self-determination, some level of harmful behavior would be visited upon the Chinese and Israeli settlers who chose to remain.

Finally, settler infusion reduces the possibility that a people will be granted external self-determination by exacerbating the potential that the exercise of this right will adversely affect regional or global interests. As tensions, and possibly violence, escalate within a given territory, a substantial possibility always exists that hostilities will spill over into neighboring countries, threatening to spread military conflict. The current situation in the former Yugoslavia presents a salient example of this spillover effect. While the threat of regional or global involvement in a dispute between the Chinese and Tibetans in a newly liberated Tibet is probably minimal, such would not be the case in an independent Palestine. The animosity between Jews and Arabs runs deep; Arab groups which vow to eliminate the Jewish state continue to exist. A conflict between Jews and Palestinians in a newly-independent Palestine carries a significant threat of implicating regional and global actors.

Despite the outcome of the Tibetan and Palestinian struggles for self-determination, settler infusion has significantly hampered the ability of these peoples to freely choose their international status. Following a policy of settler implantation, the exercise of a host population's external right to self-determination raises especially difficult issues regarding the rights and privileges of the settlers, especially if they have lived within the territory for extended periods of time.

Questions that arise when settlers comprise the minority in a newly-created state include: the extent to which the settlers should enjoy cultural rights if their culture conflicts with the norms of the host population; the extent to which the settler population is protected from discrimination if its wealth is derived from previous policies of discrimination and exploitation against the host population; whether the new government can deprive the settlers of their property to compensate for past harms suffered by the host population; the composition of a judicial entity that decides such issues; whether the public school system can refuse to teach the settlers' language and history; and, under these circumstances whose "will" should be "determined" and the extent to which the settlers should be consulted or polled.

On the one hand, settlers who have lived in a territory for an extended period of time arguably have acquired some rights of their own. "There must, on humanitarian grounds, be a time when settlers and their descendants are not liable to deportation, even if their initial immigration was facilitated by an unlawful occupation."[42] Under these circumstances, it seems both unfair and unwarranted to institute a reverse population transfer whereby the distant descendants of the original settlers must return to their ancestors' homeland. As one commentator has summarized:

> No one would doubt the legitimacy of a State, once colonized, to require the ex-colonizer to remove from sovereign territory its organs of power-police, military, security and control personnel. . . . No one would deny the entitlement of a State, seeking to redress the consequences of

colonialization and the disruption it causes, to require or permit voluntary repatriation of the colonizers and their families: offering various inducements to "return" to a land many of them will never have known. . . . But forcing retransfer of peoples who were the hapless remnants of an empire to leave would not appear to be permitted by international law.[43]

On the other hand, not "returning" a number of settlers creates an incentive for future governments to institute further policies of settler infusion. Although the legitimate rulers of the relevant territory might eventually regain power, the aggressor nation would know that there would be no way to restore the previous political and demographic balance because its settlers would not be returned. Furthermore, an occupying government would have an incentive to institute its policy both broadly and immediately so as to infuse as many of its citizens as possible before the international community institutes actions to compel the restoration of the legitimate government.

A people's external right to self-determination must involve effective control over the process of choosing their international status. A free election or a referendum is generally considered the legitimate means to gauge a people's will for the purposes of external self-determination. However, in Tibet, for example, it is estimated that there are 7.5 million Chinese and only six million Tibetans. In addition, there are two million Chinese to only 1.8 million Tibetans in the Tibetan Autonomous Region, and the Chinese outnumber the Tibetans in Tibet's capital by three to one. If a plebiscite were held in Tibet today and the Chinese were entitled to participate, they would either dilute or completely overwhelm the Tibetans' votes. The Tibetans' right to external self-determination in theory would be eviscerated in practice. If Chinese settlers were entitled to vote, the Chinese government would have achieved through a democratic electoral process what it had failed to achieve through its occupation.

In sum, a policy of settler infusion not only infringes upon a people's external right to self-determination, but can also assure that they will not be able to exercise this right in the future. The criteria by which the international community judges the legitimacy of a people's external right to self-determination ironically presents incentives for the aggressor country to maintain and increase its settler infusion policies. This is precisely the tactic that the Chinese and Israeli governments have adopted. As one Tibet observer noted, the "object of this [Chinese population transfer] policy is to 'resolve' China's territorial claims over Tibet by means of a massive and irreversible population shift."[44] Meanwhile, as an observer of the Palestinian situation remarked, the Israeli policy of settler infusion is evidence of their intent to destroy the Palestinians' culture and violate their right to self-determination.[45] The more rapidly and systematically China and Israel institute their policies of settler infusion, the more likely these aggressor countries can guarantee that the Tibetans' and Palestinians' cries for external self-determination will be permanently silenced.

E. Population Transfer Violates the "Internal" Right to Self-Determination

A policy of settler infusion also violates a people's internal right to self-determination by undermining their control over everyday political, economic, social, and cultural conditions. The discrimination that buttresses and emanates from a policy of settler infusion constitutes an important factor in the interrelationship between settler infusion and the violation of a people's internal right to self-determination. As one commentator summarized:

> Poverty, homelessness, illiteracy, and increased mortality rates can be the direct results of population transfer programs. In this way, peoples may be systematically reduced to a powerless minority who are treated as second class citizens in their own country and who are denied opportunities to actively participate in social and political processes.[46]

1. General Parameters of the Internal Right. A definition of the internal right to self-determination is difficult to formulate. One commentator has defined the internal aspect of self-determination as the right to self-government and freedom from totalitarianism.[47] Another has emphasized that the notion of "popular participation" underlies the internal right to self-determination:[48] "Where persistent denial of the opportunity for participation occurs, the population concerned may ultimately have recourse to the principle of self-determination in order to ensure meaningful participation in the society in which it lives."[49]

Generally speaking, the internal right to self-determination entitles a people to exercise control over its everyday political, economic, social, and cultural lives. These four realms "are closely and indissolubly linked . . . and each of them can only be fully realized through the complete recognition and implementation of the others."[50] The "political" and "nonpolitical" elements of the internal right to self-determination will be analyzed separately below.

2. "Control" and the Internal Right. The extent of a people's control over their everyday lives indicates the degree to which they enjoy the internal right to self-determination. . . . [S]ettler infusion and its ramifications constitute such an egregious example of a government's systematic and methodical denial of a people's control over their lives that there should be little doubt that such a policy violates a people's internal right to self-determination. "When an unwanted influx of alien people [enters] into the land, economy, and culture of an ethnically distinct people, dominates it politically, exploits it economically, and subjugates it culturally," the host population no longer has control over its status and development.[51]

3. Discrimination and the Internal Right. Discrimination plays an especially large role within the context of a people's internal right to self-determination. . . . As previously described, settler infusion policies are often parts of a larger policy meant to control or eliminate a certain group. Settler infusion policies not only derive from but also facilitate discrimination against host populations. The intent to subjugate might have first motivated a government's decision to implement a policy of settler infusion, and might still be an important element in the policy, as more settlers are infused the dynamic changes. A government discriminates not only to maintain control but also to protect the various interests of its settler citizens. An aggressor government, therefore, will often explicitly reserve for its own people the most important positions in the political, economic, social, and cultural arenas. Additionally, a government often implements a broad array of discriminatory policies regarding taxes, land allocation, education, police protection, health care, and housing.

4. Importance of the Internal Right. Although many observers ignore the internal aspects of self-determination, these are important within the context of population transfers because they affect the protections which peoples enjoy. The international community is more likely to recognize a people's internal right than its external right to self-determination for two reasons. First, many commentators equate external self-determination with secession, and the international community is extremely hesitant to recognize the legality of secessionary movements under current global conditions. Therefore, the international community is unlikely to condemn a policy of settler infusion on the grounds that it violates a people's external right to self-determination. Because the internal right to self-determination focuses upon intrastate democratic processes instead of international affairs, however, there is less likelihood that the exercise of the internal right to self-determination will threaten global peace. Therefore, the international community may be more willing to condemn a policy of settler infusion on the grounds that it violates a people's internal right to self-determination because they need not advocate secession or independence in order to accept that a fundamental right is being violated.

Second, even if a people achieves its external right to self-determination, a government might still deny its members the internal right to self-determination. As one commentator asserted, the international community must ensure that

> peoples enjoy the [internal] economic, social, and cultural aspects of the
> right to self-determination and prevent their [external] political

independence [from] being only a profession of faith beneath which economic domination, social servility and cultural subordination and mimetism subsist.[52]

Take for example, a situation in which a host population exercises its external right to self-determination by deciding through a referendum to merge with its more powerful neighbor. The government then begins to infuse settlers into the territory the host population inhabits. Because the host population has already voted with regard to its international identity, the international community could not assert that the settler infusion policy was illegal on the grounds that it violated the host population's external right to self-determination. However, as noted above, settler infusion policies often lead to discrimination against and exploitation of the host population. Under such circumstances, the international community could assert that the government had violated the people's internal right to self-determination. The internal right to self-determination thus affords a people protection whereas the external right does not.

5. Political Aspect of the Internal Right. The "political" component of the internal right to self-determination indicates the "right of a people living within an independent and sovereign state to freely choose its own government, to adopt representative institutions and to periodically, or at reasonable intervals, elect their representatives through a free procedure."[53] Another commentator has defined the political aspect of the internal right to self-determination as the right to "choose in full freedom, the authority that will implement the genuine will of the people."[54] Settler infusion policies stem from a government's desire for political hegemony. The presence of settlers within a territory allows a government to increase its control over the subject people on the premise that it must ensure the safety and prosperity of its settler citizens. Limiting access to the political process is the most effective means of governmental control.

The Israeli government has acted in precisely such a manner to ensure that the Palestinians do not exercise control over their political institutions in the Occupied Territories and to ensure that they are not free to appoint accountable representatives. Although in the past Palestinians have managed their own municipalities through democratic political processes, these self-governing mechanisms have been completely subordinated by Israel's own institutions. Today, the Israeli Civil Administration, with substantial support from the Israeli military, exercises effective authority over the Occupied Territories. Palestinians are denied involvement in the Civil Administration and do not enjoy voting rights. These Israeli "political" bodies then implement a host of "non-political" policies which further alienate the Palestinians and ensure their dependence upon Israel. The Chinese government has also stripped the Tibetans of their political authority, even within the Tibetan Autonomous Region (TAR). Chinese people dominate the administration of Tibet. Although Tibetans can hold nominal positions of political power, the Chinese Communist Party exercises ultimate authority over the territory. Almost all of the top-ranking officials in Tibet's Communist Party are Chinese, and there has never been a Tibetan First Secretary of the TAR, the highest ranking position within the territory. Furthermore, although Tibetans have been members of the TAR People's Congress, this political body enjoys almost no real power and is not permitted to create new policy.

6. Non-Political Aspects. An aggressor government's control over "political" bodies facilitates its control over the "non-political" aspects of a people's existence. Various U.N. instruments have defined the non-political facets of a people's internal right to self-determination as the right of a people to freely "pursue [their] economic, social, and cultural development." . . . [A]s the U.N. Subcommission on the Prevention of Discrimination and Protection of Minorities recently asserted . . . settler infusion policies limit a people's freedom to control these three aspects of their existence.[55]

[Kolodner discusses in detail the impact of settlers on the economic, social, and cultural aspects of internal self-determination. His summary follows.]

. . . Permeated by discrimination and exploitation, settler infusion policies often violate a people's internal right to self-determination by undermining their control over their political, economic, cultural, and social forms of expression. An aggressor government's control over political bodies facilitates its hegemony over non-political aspects of a subjugated people's existence. The Israeli government, for example, restricts the Palestinians' ability to dispose freely of their natural wealth and resources through its discriminatory and exploitative land management and allocation policies. Similarly, the Chinese government violates the economic aspect of the Tibetans' internal right to self-determination through their discriminatory employment practices and exploitative development policies. China's decision to establish a Special Economic Zone within the TAR may lead to other violations in the future. The Chinese government violates the cultural aspect of the Tibetans' internal right to self-determination through its education and language use policies. Finally, although the social aspect of a people's internal right to self-determination is difficult to define, little doubt remains that Chinese and Israeli policies of settler infusion effectuate some level of social disintegration within the respective Tibetan and Palestinian communities.

a. Population Transfer and the Right to Exist as a People. The right to exist as a "people" forms an inherent component of the right to self-determination. Policies of settler infusion can violate a people's right to exist both literally and legally. Such policies can sometimes literally destroy a people through political, economic, social, and cultural discrimination and exploitation. Under extreme conditions, a government's policy of population transfer might rise to the level of genocide or ethnocide.

These policies, however, do not only potentially effectuate a literal violation of the right to exist as a people; they can also violate the right to exist as a legally designated "people." As the settler population increases, the legal status of the host population may change. More specifically, a government's policy of demographic manipulation can reduce the legal identity of the host population from a "people" to a "minority." The host population, therefore, may no longer possess the right to self-determination; as a "minority" they may possess only minimal cultural rights, such as the right to freedom of religion, the right to attend their own schools, and the right to use their own language. This legal transformation may occur when settler infusion policies produce situations in which the host population becomes outnumbered within their own territory. These policies may then result in the gradual disappearance of the attributes which characterize a particular people, and "may threaten the survival of a distinct people's national or cultural identity."[56] The imprecision with which the international community determines the legal status of a group of individuals additionally facilitates manipulation of the group's legal identity. In sum, even if the international community determined that a government's occupation or its policies of settler infusion were illegal, it is possible that as time passes, these illegal events would produce a "legal" change in the status of the host population.

. . . [T]he international community often employs a two-prong objective and subjective test when determining whether a group of individuals constitutes a "people" for self-determination purposes. The subjective prong examines the extent to which the group self-consciously identifies itself collectively as a "people." Over time, the cultural and social damage wreaked upon a group through settler infusion can affect that group's subjective identity. As demographic manipulation fragments the community, individuals within the group may become alienated from one another and begin to believe they share less in common. As their collective identity fades, so too does their claim to self-determination.

The Chinese settler infusion policies pose a particularly grave threat to the Tibetans' identity. Chinese comprise a majority of the individuals now living in Tibet. Over the past decade, the Chinese have instituted settler infusion policies aimed at reducing the proportion of Tibetans living there. As mentioned above, approximately 7.5 million Chinese and six million Tibetans live in Tibet. There are two million Chinese to only 1.8 million Tibetans in the Tibetan Autonomous Region, and the Chinese outnumber the Tibetans in Tibet's capital, Lhasa, by three to one.

The Chinese policy of settler infusion threatens the national and cultural identity of the Tibetans and slowly deprives them of their right to exist as a people. The Chinese "have carried out a harsh and ruthless policy in Tibet, the manifest purpose of which is the eradication of the Tibetan people's national identity and their cultural, religious, and ethnic personality."[57] The lack of international condemnation of these policies has allowed the Chinese to implement them unfettered. If these policies continue, the Tibetans will soon be reduced to an insignificant and voiceless minority within their own territory and will be forced to relinquish control entirely over their current and future political, economic, social, and cultural conditions.

IV. CONCLUSION

Settler infusion as a form of population transfer has been implemented throughout history as a means to subjugate and oppress. This policy continues today and presents the gravest threat to the identity and survival of some peoples throughout the world. Settler infusion policies can violate a number of internationally-recognized human rights, most notably a people's right to self-determination. Such policies can infringe upon a people's external right to self-determination by undermining its control over its international status, and can violate a people's internal right to self-determination by undermining its control over the political, economic, social, and cultural conditions under which these peoples live. Finally, the demographic changes which accompany these policies can infringe upon a people's right to exist, inherent within the right to self determination, by altering its members' legal status.

Despite the incredible destruction which can flow from settler infusion practices, the international community has only recently begun to examine these issues in depth. Such voices of opposition, however, remain faint. The international community is accustomed to reacting primarily to short-term crises. It possesses an institutional myopia regarding issues such as settler infusion, a policy causing gradual effects which can be equally damaging. This lack of international attention provides aggressor nations with the incentive to continue such practices, because they know that their policies of subtle invasion are unlikely to provoke an international response. Settler infusion policies present the most cost-effective and least controversial means by which a government can invade, conquer, and oppress other peoples and nations. Until the international community systematically addresses this issue, aggressor countries will continue to relocate their citizens into occupied or conflict-ridden territories and thereby violate the host population's right to self-determination.

NOTES

1. *Human Rights in Tibet. Hearing Before the Subcomm. on Human Rights and International Organizations, and on Pacific Affairs of the House Comm. on Foreign Affairs,* 100th Cong., 1st Sess. 116 (1987) (statement of Rep. Tom Lantos).
2. THE RIGHT TO SELF-DETERMINATION, U.N. Doc.E/CN.4/Sub.2/405/Rev.1 (1980) (authored by Hector Gros Espiell), para. 47, at 8.
3. International Federation for the Protection of the Rights of Ethnic, Religious, Linguistic and Other Minorities, Population Transfer 1 (1992) (paper submitted to the 43d Session

of the Subcommission on Prevention of Discrimination and Protection of Minorities) (unpublished manuscript, on file with the *N.Y.U. J. Int'l L&P*).

4. U.N. Subcomm'n on Prevention of Discrimination and Protection of Minorities, Res. 1991/28, U.N. Doc. E/CN.4/Sub.2/1991/65, at 63.

5. U.N. Subcomm'n on Prevention of Discrimination and Protection of Minorities, 34th mtg. at 41, U.N. Doc. E/CN.4/Sub.2/1990/59 (1990); Res. 1991/28, U.N. Doc. E/CN.4/Sub.2/1991/65, at 62–64 (1991); 35th mtg. at 70, U.N. Doc. E/CN.4/Sub.2/1992/58 (1992).

6. Joseph Schechla, *Ethnocratic State Ideology as a Factor in Population Transfer: The Historical Continuum* 2 (1992) (paper presented to the International Conference on the Human Rights Dimensions of Population Transfer, Estonia, Jan. 10–13,1992) (unpublished manuscript, on file with the *N.Y.U. INT'L L. & POL.*).

7. *Id.*, at 3.

8. Alfred de Zayas, *International Law and Mass Population Transfers*, 16 HARV. INT'L L.J. 207, 222–23 (1975).

9. Michael Cernea, *Involuntary Resettlement in Development Projects* 7–8 (World Bank Technical Paper No.80, 1988). In 1980, the World Bank became the first major development organization to require that development projects include plans for resettlement. This section by no means includes all examples of population transfer through forced resettlement. Other instances include the deportation of enemy civilians from occupied territories during war, the deportation of a minority pursuant to a treaty, the expulsion of a minority during peacetime, the internal involuntary transfer of a national minority, and the expulsion of a conquered people without a treaty. de Zayas, *supra* note 8, at 209.

   An additional example of population transfer occurs when a colonizing power relocates people from one of its colonies to another. This transpired, for example, when the British transferred Indians into Fiji and Tamils from Sri Lanka into Ceylon. Hurst Hannum, AUTONOMY, SOVEREIGNTY AND SELF-DETERMINATION 39 (1990).

10. Schechla, supra note 6, at 9.

11. Individuals who are forced to resettle in a new territory will confront many of the adverse consequences already described in the section above on "forced relocation." On the other hand, individuals who decide to relocate on a completely voluntary basis and who are free to return to their original homes may encounter few of the aforementioned difficulties. As will be discussed below, however, most examples of this type of population transfer involve neither completely voluntary decisions on the part of implanted settlers nor entirely dictatorial actions on behalf of States. Rather, governments will offer financial incentives to disadvantaged or disempowered individuals to influence their resettlement decisions. Throughout the discussion, it should become clear that settler infusion policies affect not only the settlers and the host populations, but also impact upon the surrounding communities and, at times, the entire world.

12. U.N. Subcomm'n on Prevention of Discrimination and Protection of Minorities, 34th mtg., *supra* note 5, at 41.

13. Governments employ a variety of means to persuade citizens to relocate. Sometimes they will act affirmatively by implementing financial incentives, providing logistical assistance, facilitating transportation, clearing land, and building infrastructure. Other governments will promote their policies of settler infusion though strategic omissions, for example, by failing to administer economic assistance to an impoverished area of the country or by failing to adequately deal with an overcrowding problem. Through a complex series of positive incentives and strategic omissions, a government can institute substantial incentives to remain in or to leave one's home territory. Thus, it is sometimes difficult to clearly characterize an individual's decision to resettle as voluntary or involuntary. International Federation, supra note 3, at 8; Christy Ezirn Mbonu, *Working Paper on the Human Rights Dimensions of Population Transfer, Including the Implantation of Settlers and Settlements*, U.N. Subcomm'n on Prevention of Discrimination and Protection of Minorities, 43d Sess., Agenda Item 8, U.N. Doc. E/CN.4/Sub.2/1991/47, at 7 (1991).

14. Resettlement itself can sometimes serve as a strategy for development by facilitating

agricultural development of a sparsely-populated area. Mbonu, *supra* note 13, at 2–3. As mentioned above, involuntary settlement can also arise as a function of large development projects. Cernea, *supra* note 9, at 1. However, it should be noted that such benevolent instances of population transfer are rare.

15. International Commission of Jurists, *Israeli Settlements in the Occupied Territories*, 19 REV. OF INT'L COMM. OF JURISTS 35 (1977).

16. U.N. Subcomm'n on Prevention of Discrimination and Protection of Minorities, *supra* note 4, at 71.

17. Hannum, *supra* note 9, at 27.

18. Dov Ronen, THE QUEST FOR SELF-DETERMINATION 7 (1979).

19. U.N. GAOR, 39th Sess., Supp. No. 40, at 142, U.N. Doc. A/39/40 (1984).

20. Michael Van Walt Van Praag, THE STATUS OF TIBET 142–44 (1987). [Much of this section also comes from John Avedon, IN EXILE FROM THE LAND OF THE SNOWS (1986).]

21. Hannum, *supra* note 9, at 424.

22. 5 SELECTED WORKS OF MAO TSE TUNG 73-74 (Foreign Lang. Press, 1977).

23. In 1914, there were 500,000 Arabs in Palestine and only 85,000 Jews. Adam Garfinkle, Genesis, in THE ARAB-ISRAELI CONFLICT 12–13, 15 (Alvin Z. Rubinstein ed., 1991). [Much of this section also comes from other selections in the Rubinstein edited volume as well as HENRY CATTAN, PALESTINE, THE ARABS AND ISRAEL (1969)—eds.]

24. Adam Roberts, *Prolonged Military Occupation: The Israeli-Occupied Territories Since 1967*, 84 AM. J. INT'L L. 44, 79 (1990).

25. Peace Now, Peace Now Settlement Watch Comm., REPORT NO. 5, THE REAL MAP: A DEMOGRAPHIC AND GEOGRAPHIC ANALYSIS OF THE POPULATION OF THE WEST BANK AND THE GAZA STRIP, Conclusions, at 1, (Nov. 1992).

26. Schechla, *supra* note 6, at 25.

27. U.N. Subcomm'n on Prevention of Discrimination and Protection of Minorities, Res. 1991/28, supra note 4, at 63. . . .

28. Mbonu, *supra* note 13, at 2. There may exist examples of completely voluntary population transfers where government policies did not influence the settlers' decisions at all. I am unaware of any such example, however, where an affirmative government policy or a governmental decision to abstain from action did not play a significant role in the mass infusion of individuals into a host population's territory. As discussed above, a decision which appears voluntary may actually be induced as the result of a government's strategically-motivated inaction. A settler infusion which was, in fact, completely voluntary would raise very difficult issues and an analysis of the relationship between population transfer and a host population's right to self-determination would have to be altered accordingly. Such considerations are outside the scope of this Note.

29. Lodi Gyari, *Population Transfer into Tibet: The Influx of Chinese and the Survival of the Tibetan Identity* 5 (1992) (unpublished manuscript presented to the International Conference on the Human Rights Dimensions of Population Transfer, Estonia, Jan. 10–13, 1992; on file with the *N.Y.U. INT'L L. & POL.*).

30. Wang Xiaoping & Bai Nanfeng, POVERTY AND PLENTY, 147, 150 (1991), cited in Gyari, *supra* note 29 at 8.

31. Roberts, *supra* note 24, at 85.

32. Antonio Cassese, *The Self-Determination of Peoples*, in THE INTERNATIONAL BILL OF RIGHTS 100 (Louis Henkin ed., 1981).

33. Amitai Etzioni, *The Evils of Self-Determination*, FOREIGN POL'Y, Winter 1992–93, 22–27.

34. Hurst Hannum, *Contemporary Developments in the International Protection of the Rights of Minorities*, 66 NOTRE DAME L. REV. 1431, 1443 (1991).

35. Hannum, *supra* note 9, at 46.

36. Gros Espiell, *supra* note 2, para. 90, at 13–14. . . .

37. Lea Brilmayer, *Secession and Self-Determination: A Territorial Interpretation*, 16 YALE J. INT'L L. 177, at 179 (1991).

38. Schechla, *supra* note 6, at 24.

39. P.A. Donnet, *Tibetan Traditions Slowly Disappearing*, SOUTH CHINA MORNING POST, Sept. 23, 1985, available in LEXIS, News Library, Allworld File.

40. Mbonu, *supra* note 13, at 10.

41. Al-Haq, PROTECTION DENIED: CONTINUED ISRAELI HUMAN RIGHTS VIOLATIONS IN THE OCCUPIED PALESTINIAN TERRITORIES, 1990, 57 (1990).

42. Claire Palley, *Population Transfer and International Law* 19 (1992) (draft paper prepared for the International Conference on the Human Dimensions of Population Transfer, Estonia, Jan. 10–13, 1992; on file with the *N.Y.U. INT'L L. & POL.*).

43. Justice Michael Kirby, *Population Transfer and the Right to Self-Determination: Differences and Agreements* 7 (1992) (draft paper prepared for the International Conference on the Human Dimensions of Population Transfer, Estonia, Jan. 10–13, 1992; on file with the *N.Y.U. INT'L L. & POL.*). Factors to be considered regarding repatriation include the length of the settlers' stay in the territory, the potential violation of their fundamental human rights, the reasons behind the settlers' decisions to relocate, the settlers' opportunities in their home country, their right to asylum, the international obligation not to increase individual statelessness, and the responsibilities of the government that originally occupied the territory and commenced the settler infusion policy. Palley, *supra* note 42, at 20.

44. Michael Van Walt Van Praag, POPULATION TRANSFER AND THE SURVIVAL OF THE TIBETAN IDENTITY 1 (photo. reprint 1988) (1986).

45. Richard A. Falk & Burns H. Weston, *The Relevance of International Law to Palestinian Rights in the West Bank and Gaza: In Legal Defense of the Intifada*, 32 HARV. INT'L LJ. 152 (1991).

46. Chimi Thonden, International Committee of Lawyers for Tibet, *Population Transfer into Tibet*, at 4 (1992) (paper prepared for the Conference on Human Rights in China, Monterey Park, California, Sept. 19, 1992; on file with the *N.Y.U. INT'L L. & POL.*).

47. Cassese, *supra* note 32, at 94.

48. Hannum, *supra* note 9, at 113.

49. Id. at 115–16.

50. Gros Espiell, *supra* note 2, para. 113, at 22.

51. International Federation, *supra* note 3, at 29.

52. Gros Espiell, *supra* note 2, para. 266, at 64.

53. Asbjorn Eide, *Minority Situations: In Search of Peaceful and Constructive Solutions*, 66 NOTRE DAME L. REV. 1311, at 1336-37 (1991).

54. Cassese, *supra* note 32, at 97.

55. U.N. Subcomm'n on Prevention of Discrimination and Protection of Minorities, Res. 1991/28, *supra* note 4, at 63.

56. U.N. Subcomm'n on Prevention of Discrimination & Protection of Minorities, Res. 1991/28, *supra* note 4, at 63–64.

57. Srinivas P. Gandhi, *Tibetan Decolonization, Population Transfer and International Organizations: A Historical, Legal and Political Overview* 37 (1991) (unpublished manuscript submitted to the U.N. Economic and Social Council, on file with the *N.Y.U. INT'L L. & POL.*).

Conclusion

The Accommodation of Nations in Inter*state* Law: Some Preliminary Conclusions

Thomas Ambrosio

> . . . the Divine design will infallibly be realized. Natural divisions, and the spontaneous, innate tendencies of the peoples, will take the place of the arbitrary divisions sanctioned by evil governments. The map of Europe will be re-drawn.
>
> —GIUSEPPE MAZZINI

THE TENSION BETWEEN states and nations appears to be a durable characteristic of the international system since the ideology of nationalism originated in Europe in the late 1700s. Attempts to resolve this tension within the framework of international law have mostly failed because of the serious implications for international law inherent in the notion of accommodating nations. Historically, as Fowler and Bunck have illustrated, international law was largely restricted to the rules, procedures, and norms governing relations between states—no other international actors need apply. Over time, however, nonstate actors struggled to share the global stage with states. The "rise of nations" phenomenon in particular has put forth the greatest challenge to states since the modern state system was founded following the Peace of Westphalia in 1648. Secessionist movements, ethnic conflicts, and anti-imperialist movements have increased the number of states from some two dozen in the late eighteenth century to nearly two hundred at the turn of the millennium. Since an overwhelming number of states are multiethnic, dealing with this potential threat to their territorial integrity and sovereignty has become imperative.[1]

This essay serves as both a brief retrospective on the progress made thus far and a window onto the future. After briefly examining the developing international law of nationalism, I advance the optimistic view that the state-dominated international system is showing signs of increasingly accommodating nations. In particular, I look at what appears to be growing support for national self-determination in the post–Cold War period, evidenced by a greater willingness to intervene in order to protect national groups, criticisms of Russia's attempt to crush Chechen separatism, and the re-emergence of the notion of minority rights. On the other hand, the pessimistic reality still dominates international politics: Territorial integrity and state sovereignty continues to set the foundation for the interaction between states and nations.

The ultimate conclusion of this essay is that even when states are willing to accommodate nations—though admittedly this is rare—it is done within the structures and rhetoric of the state system. A fundamental rethinking of the status of nations within the international system has not taken place. Instead, there are signs that states are retrenching in the face of the challenge of ethnic groups.

I. THE DEVELOPING INTERNATIONAL LAW OF NATIONALISM

The essays in this volume all examine the tension between states and nations from a variety of perspectives. Their division into three broad sections—the Rise of Nations; the International Legal Challenges Posed by the Rise of Nations; and the International Legal Responses to the Rise of Nations—roughly matches the stages of the interaction between states and nations. At each stage, the situation is inherently reactive. First, the politicization of ethnic groups (thus transforming a cultural group into a nation) is more often than not a reaction to the policies of state leaders (either real, imagined, or feared) aimed at ignoring or repressing a unique and separate cultural identity or population.[2] Consequently, ethnic entrepreneurs mobilize and organize their ethnic group in order to press their claims against the state. As seen in Part II of this volume, nations make a myriad of claims against states, ranging from autonomy, to respect for individual human rights, to outright independence. As Berman has shown, how these claims are framed largely depends on the prevailing concepts and norms of the day. With the overall weakening of state authority, a process which intensified after the Second World War, nations have assumed greater political salience throughout the world. The collapse of ideology as a mobilizing factor in mass politics has caused cultural identities to come to the fore and effectively challenge states as diverse as Canada, the former Soviet Union, India, and Indonesia.[3] Consequently, multiethnic states are compelled to react to these demands and have done so in a number of ways, though in most cases the primacy of the state over the nation is reinforced in both international law and practice. Thus, we have four reactions: the mobilization of the ethnic group in reaction to the policies of states, the framing of national claims in relation to what is acceptable and politically advantageous, the policies enacted by states to defend their sovereignty and territorial integrity, and finally, nations react to these policies and the cycle begins anew.

The dichotomous relationship between states and nations promoted by Barkin and Cronin is conceptually helpful at one level, but requires the more nuanced vision proposed by Berman: The relationship between states and nations is inherently interactive, with both entities affecting the other; i.e., states and state interests are shaped by their need to confront nations and the claims of nations are likewise shaped by their need to play by the rules set by states. While it might appear simple to "make room" for nations on the international stage, as Lâm suggested, this very action has implications not only for the state/nation relationship, but also for the very nature of political organization itself. Exactly how this process will develop in the twenty-first century is unclear, but this much is certain: the future will be shaped by the policies and precedents set at the beginning of the post–Cold War international order.

II. Optimistic View: Increased "Room" for Nations

The successor states to the multiethnic federation of Eastern Europe were nominally constructed along national lines. Where three states stood in 1989, twenty-one national-states are now members of the United Nations.[4] In addition, the international community has recognized the independence of Eritrea, established a transition administrative structure in East Timor, and intervened in Yugoslavia in order to protect the Kosovar Albanians and effectively detach Kosovo from Belgrade's control. In sum, national calls for (*de facto* or *de jure*) independence have been satisfied in numerous cases since the end of the Cold War, thus potentially pointing to a re-evaluation of the state/nation relationship. Furthermore, attempts to crush the Chechen secessionist movement in Russia have drawn international criticism.

Beginning in March 1999, NATO launched an aggressive bombing campaign against Yugoslavia in order to protect the Kosovar Albanians from Serb atrocities and to promote the Albanians' right to self-determination. This action was novel on a number of levels. First, it represented the first time that NATO used force without United Nations Security Council authorization.[5] Second, and most important for purposes of this essay, the war over Kosovo was unlike the case of Bosnia: In the latter case, NATO acted in order to protect a recognized state's territorial integrity against a secessionist movement (or external aggression, depending on one's perspective); the war against Serbia was, at some level, tied to a recognition of the importance of nationalism and national rights. In a statement read by U.S. President Clinton less than a week before the war began, Clinton make a direct link between American involvement and the Kosovar Albanians' right to self-determination: "With our NATO allies and with Russia, we proposed a peace agreement to stop the killing and give the people of Kosovo the self-determination and government they need and to which they are entitled under the constitution of their government."[6] At a speech given at the State Department, Clinton reiterated this theme and argued that "the prospect for international support for Serbia's claim to Kosovo" were being "increasingly jeopardized" by Milosevic's policies.[7]

Eventual independence for Kosovo was and remains the ultimate goal for most Kosovars.[8] On Belgrade's capitulation, a NATO-led force moved into Kosovo in order to set up an autonomous political administration completely free of Belgrade's control.[9] In Security Council resolution 1244 (10 June 1999), the Council identified the "[facilitation of] a political process designed to determine Kosovo's future status, taking into account the Rambouillet accords" as among the civil administration's chief goals. This is significant because the Rambouillet Accords—which Yugoslav President Slobodan Milosevic refused to sign, thus precipitating the war—contained a provision allowing for the "will of the people" to determine a "final settlement" for the province's international status.[10] Given the preferences of most Kosovar Albanians, the possibility of establishing an independent Kosovo is very strong and seemingly sanctioned by the international community. U.N. Secretary General Kofi Annan admitted to a "built-in tension" in the Security Council resolution which makes independence quite possible.[11] In one report, senior U.S. officials privately conceded that Kosovo will become independent sometime in the future.[12]

East Timor is another case in which the international community moved to enforce the principle of self-determination. In Thomas Ambrosio's essay in this volume, the Indonesian invasion of East Timor was generally accepted by the major powers and the U.N. General Assembly. Over time, however, Jakarta's rule became increasingly seen as illegitimate. Indonesian atrocities, the territory's history as a separate Portuguese colony, and the unique national identity of the East Timor people made independence a viable option. Precipitated by a change in U.S. and Australian policy against the Jakarta regime,[13] Indonesia came under intense international pressure to allow the United Nations to hold a referendum in order to determine the province's fate. Upon signing a U.N.-brokered deal on the referendum, Portuguese President Jorge Sampaio proclaimed that "a new phase is beginning, just as we always wanted, with the recognition of the right of the East Timorese to self-determination."[14] On 30 August 1999, over eight percent of the territory's population voted for independence; though the massive violence unleashed by or, at the very least, tolerated by the Indonesian military dampened what should have been a day of celebration for the East Timorese.[15]

After an agreement was reached with the Indonesian government and military, the U.N. Security Council authorized a peacekeeping force to restore peace and security in East Timor, facilitate humanitarian assistance operations, and support the mission of the United Nations Transitional Administration in East Timor (UNTAET) in establishing a transitional administration until East Timor can achieve independence. Under the current timetable, full independence should occur within two to three years.[16] The psychological boost East Timorese independence has given to other secessionist movements in Indonesia raises the possibility that the country might further unravel, a prospect that is feared and taken very seriously in Jakarta.[17]

In its most recent campaign to crush separatists in Chechnya, Russia has faced sharp criticism from the West. Clinton delivered a direct reproach of Russia's policies during the Istanbul meeting of the Organization for Security and Cooperation in Europe (OSCE) in which he said that the there will never be a time when the United States "will ever be able to say we simply cannot criticize this or that or the other action because it happened within the territorial borders of a single [state]."[18] U.S. Secretary of State Madeleine Albright denounced Russian attacks on Chechnya as "deplorable and ominous."[19] Although discussions in Western capitals about the possibility of imposing sanctions against Russia by West was halted by the United States, Albright said that: "There's no question that continued action like this does have a serious effect even on our bilateral relationship."[20] As one sign of the West's displeasure, the International Monetary Fund postponed the delivery of a $640 million line of credit to Moscow in early December 1999.[21]

In contrast to the Cold War period, there has been a sea change in the international community's approach to the issue of minority rights during the post–Cold War era. The rise of nations phenomenon forced policymakers to reconsider the global minority rights regime. The Council of Europe, the OSCE, and the United Nations have taken the lead on minority rights issues. In October 1992, the General Assembly passed the Declaration on the Rights of Persons Belonging to National or Ethnic, Religious and Linguistic Minorities (A/RES/47/135), which identified a number of responsibilities states have toward ethnic minorities.[22] Although this resolution does not have the force of binding international law,[23] it recognizes that forced assimilation is illegitimate and that ethnic minorities must play a crucial and effective role in the decision-making process in their countries of residence. Furthermore, article 2(5) acknowledges the existence of cross-border nations and the need for members of a national group to maintain contacts with their ethnic kin in other countries; i.e., the national entity has a right to establish linkages across international boundaries that aim at fostering a coherent national identity. Possibly the most important element of the U.N. resolution is "a nascent willingness to move beyond recognition of cultural and linguistic rights, and to insist that only enhanced rights of political participation for minorities can adequately protect their interests."[24] While this resolution does not explicitly state what form this participation should take, "it seems clear that the drafters meant something beyond the traditional rule of 'one person, one vote.' "[25] While this certainly does not give international recognition of national groups, it is a significant departure away from the post–WWII system which emphasized individual human rights and significantly downplayed nations.

Each of these issues—*de facto* or *de jure* independence for ethnic groups, criticisms of states attempting to crush secessionist movements, and greater acceptance of minority rights—all point toward increasing international legal relevance of nations. The near absolute support of state sovereignty and territorial integrity appears to be weakening in the face of the rise of nations phenomenon. However, it is important not to take this observation too far: While, on the one hand, there may be some cause for encouragement, state sovereignty remains not only relevant, but on the defensive. The next section will examine how the positive signs illustrated above are strongly qualified.

III. PESSIMISTIC VIEW: STATE SOVEREIGNTY ON THE DEFENSIVE

The implications of *uti possidetis* found in the essays by Ratner and Kingsbury are the first hints that a fundamental reevaluation of the relationship between states and nations will likely not be undertaken in the post–Cold War period. In an official sense, the independence of the former Yugoslav and Soviet republics were not acts of secession. According to the European Community's Badinter Commission, Yugoslavia was not torn apart by Croat or Slovene secessionist movements, but rather "the Yugoslav Federal Republic no longer functions and the Federation itself, since 8 October, has been in the process of dissolution."[26] Disintegration, rather than secession, ended the second Yugoslav experiment: The territory of the former Yugoslavia shifted (at least in an official sense) seamlessly from one state to a number of new states. Once this process was completed, the only question was where to draw the borders between the successor states; "nations" were clearly subordinated to these new states. *Uti possidetis* was employed to hasten the transition to full state sovereignty; thus evincing a clear bias toward traditional notions of statehood. Similarly, the presidents of the three Eastern Slav republics—Russia, Ukraine, and Belorussia—officially dissolved the Soviet Union,[27] contrary to the earlier desires of the United States.[28] Furthermore, the independence of the Baltic states was formally recognized by the vast majority of states only *after* Russian and Soviet authorities recognized their independence.[29] Consequently, there is little to suggest that the proliferation of states in Eastern Europe has heralded a fundamental change in the status of nations.

The United States-led NATO alliance launched a massive military campaign against Serbia and the outcome was the *de facto* separation of Kosovo from Serbia. While this action was sometimes portrayed outside of the West as a blatant violation of Yugoslavia's/Serbia's territorial integrity with the aim of promoting U.S. hegemony in the Balkans,[30] a closer look reveals that there were several purposes behind the conflict. The first identified by Clinton above noted the Kosovars' right to self-determination. However, it was quite interesting that this issue was not mentioned in Clinton's initial address to the American people confirming that the bombing had commenced:

> Our strikes have three objectives. First, to demonstrate the seriousness of NATO's opposition to aggression and its support for peace. Second, to deter President Milosevic from continuing and escalating his attacks on helpless civilians by imposing a price for those attacks. And third, if necessary, to damage Serbia's capacity to wage war against Kosovo in the future by seriously diminishing its military capabilities.[31]

Even in his longer address, security concerns and human rights were cited as the reasons for American intervention, not self-determination or national rights.[32] In fact, in a direct address to the Serbian people, the President stressed that "the NATO allies support the desire of the Serbian people to maintain Kosovo as part of your country."[33]

Throughout the bombing campaign and afterward, the issue of self-determination for the Kosovar Albanians was restricted by the United States' official support for the territorial integrity of Yugoslavia. During a visit to the region in late July, Secretary Albright cautioned the Kosovo Liberation Army against demands for an independent Kosovo.[34] State Department spokesman James Rubin echoed this sentiment: "We have always said we do not support independence for Kosovo, and we do not support independence for Kosovo now."[35] Similarly, U.N. Security Council resolutions during and after the Kosovo war repeatedly reaffirmed that body's support for Yugoslavia's territorial integrity.[36] "Self-administration" and "self-government," rather than "self-determination," were the key phrases in these Security Council resolutions. Human rights violations, rather than national rights or interests, were the primary focus of the resolutions.

A similar position was taken in reference to the crisis in the Caucasus. The United States, while criticizing Russia's handling of its Chechnya campaign, consistently reiterated its respect of and support for Russia's territorial integrity.[37] Again, the criticisms were directed against human rights abuses, rather than Moscow's actions against Chechen self-determination. During the OSCE meeting in Istanbul at which President Clinton condemned Russia's attempt to achieve a military solution, that organization passed the Charter for European Security which stressed the following: "Full respect for human rights, including the rights of persons belonging to national minorities, besides being an end in itself, may not undermine, but strengthen territorial integrity and sovereignty."[38] It was interesting that the phrase "self-determination," found in earlier OSCE instruments such as the 1975 Helsinki Accords, was absent in this Charter.

Furthermore, NATO's criticism of Russia's use of "disproportionate and indiscriminate force" against civilians was tempered by an acknowledgment of Moscow's right to "preserve its territorial integrity."[39]

The resolution of the situation in East Timor likewise did little to alter the balance between state and nation because it was not seen as a case of secession, but rather decolonization; thus, the East Timor case fits well within the traditional concept of "self-determination as independence for colonial possessions" identified by Hannum in this volume. Although the international community provided *de facto* recognition of Indonesian control over East Timor, Portugal remained the *de jure* administering power and the territory was officially considered a Non-Self-Governing Territory, with Indonesia as merely the occupying power. The status of both countries, Portugal and Indonesia, was to be temporary, with the interrupted decolonization process renewed once Indonesian military control was lifted. East Timor is a peculiar case with little to no precedent-setting value, except for such limited cases as Western Sahara (where a colonial territory was effectively annexed by a neighboring power). Independence for East Timor should not be seen as an expansion of the post–Cold War international law of nationalism, but rather unfinished business left over from the colonial period.

Even the more recent minority rights instruments, though calling for an expansion of the relative autonomy of minority ethnic groups, fail to fundamentally address the tension between state and nation. Article 8(4) of the United Nations' Declaration on Minorities includes an oft-repeated refrain: "Nothing in the present Declaration may be construed as permitting any activity contrary to the purposes and principles of the United Nations, including sovereign equality, territorial integrity and political independence of States." Once again, the international community is seen as reinforcing the primacy of state interests over national ones.

The Council of Europe's Framework Convention on the Protection of National Minorities—which came into force on 1 February 1998 and has been described as "the first ever legally binding multilateral instrument devoted to the protection of national minorities in general"[40]—contains many of the same provisions as the U.N. instrument and *is* legally binding on its signatories. However, the Framework Convention was "weakly worded" and "noticeably tamer in its formulation of minority rights than the proposals upon which it was substantially based."[41] It contained a number of clauses that considerably limited its scope either through vagueness or lack of enforcement: Neither individuals nor minorities as groups possess any standing to petition an external body for violations of minority rights and "the drafters of the Convention, concerned with the multiplicity of situations giving rise to minority rights problems, intentionally left states with a broad margin of discretion in determining the means to be used to fulfill their obligations under the Convention."[42] Furthermore, violations of the

Convention's principles are not subject to review by the European Court of Human Rights. Hence, even the most ambitious document falls far short of fundamentally transforming the relationship between states and nations.

What little progress has been made to better accommodate the interests and demands of nations as sparked a sharp reaction in many quarters of the world. Large, multiethnic states such as Russia, India, and China have sharply criticized any weakening of their sovereignty or territorial integrity. In the wake of the successful military campaign against Serbia, the perception was strong during a December 1999 Sino-Russian summit in Beijing that the United States and its allies were interested in intervening in internal ethnic conflicts. Russia and China explicitly supported the other's territorial integrity against Chechen and Taiwanese independence movements, and in a joint statement signed by Presidents Boris Yeltsin and Jiang Zemin both the two sides confirmed their mutual support "regarding the preservation of state unity, sovereignty and territorial integrity" of both states.[43] As one newspaper in India mused: "NATO aggression on Yugoslavia: Today Kosovo, tomorrow Kashmir?"[44] NATO's intervention in Kosovo was seen as potentially setting a precedent for future interventions in ethnic conflicts. Consequently, the Indian government railed sharply against the policy.[45] In fact, Russia, China, and India brought up a failed Security Council resolution describing the NATO air strikes against Yugoslavia a violation of the U.N. Charter.[46] In sum, three of the largest states in the international system have vocally come out against any loosening of the principle of territorial integrity to accommodate national aspirations.

IV. THE FUTURE OF STATE/NATION RELATIONS

Any discussion of the developing international law of nationalism must take into account the state-centric international system. International law *qua* law was originally developed by states for states. Consequently, any changes in international law aimed at "making room for peoples" must be undertaken by states. States obviously have an institutional interest in restricting the erosion of their prerogatives in the international system. Beck's article directly confronts the argument made by Barkin and Cronin that during the interwar period, national, rather than state, sovereignty was ascendant. While there is clearly evidence to support the notion that nations assumed an unprecedented status through the implementation of self-determination in Eastern Europe, the challenges to state sovereignty by individuals and nonstate actors continues to be countered by states. From a constructivist position, as Berman takes in his essay, legal outcomes are part of an interactive process among states, on the one hand, and between states and nations, on the other. Furthermore, these outcomes are also a reflection of the interests and relative power of the main players. Since it remains up to states to develop the international law of nationalism, this law will always be filtered through a state system bent on self-preservation. Nations and peoples that aim at reconceptualizing international law to include a place for them will have to make their case to political leaders on a bilateral basis and through global institutions such as the United Nations. Consequently, fundamental change, if it occurs at all, will be slow and halting.

A key factor which hampers the reconceptualization of the state/nation relationship, in addition to the obvious resistance by states, is the fact that many nations only want the traditional emphasis on state sovereignty and territorial integrity lifted for *them* so that *they* may constitute their *own* state and join the state system as a full member. Rather than seeking to fundamentally alter the balance between nations and states, many nations are merely seeking special dispensation for their national cause (though this is less true for indigenous peoples than for those groups commonly labeled as nations). In fact, newly independent national states have been amongst the fiercest defenders of their territorial integrity and sovereignty. For example, Croatia defended its right to territorial integrity in the face of Serb secession, but actively intervened in Bosnia-Herzegovina to violate the latter's territorial integrity. Serb-dominated Yugoslavia claimed for years that the Serbs in Croatia and Bosnia had a right to self-determination, but they denied that same right to the Kosovar Albanians. It would be safe to say that if a Greater Serbia were established, Belgrade would not countenance any revision of its borders to allow Croats or Bosnian Muslims to secede. The point here is not simply to point out the frequently hypocrisy of nationalist rhetoric, but rather to stress the curious process by which nationalist claims quickly transform into a defense of the state-centric international system.[47] As a result, self-determination for nations more often than not reinforces the state-centric nature of the international system.

Despite these obstacles, the increasing political significance of nations will force state leaders and international legal scholars to deal with the rise of nations phenomenon. As long as individuals owe allegiance to political and cultural entities, an accommodation will have to be reached when there is a disjuncture between them. Fresh perspectives and concepts will be needed in the new millennium in order to avoid, or at least diminish, the violence, political instability, and human misery often associated with the clash between states and nations.

NOTES

1. Ted Robert Gurr, *Minorities At Risk* (United States Institute of Peace Press, 1993); Walker Connor, *Ethnonationalism: The Quest for Understanding* (Princeton,NJ: Princeton University Press, 1994).
2. For example, see Paul R. Brass, *Ethnicity and Nationalism* (London: Sage, 1991).
3. Samuel P. Huntington, *The Clash of Civilizations and the Remaking of the World Order* (New York: Simon & Schuster, 1996).
4. This includes Belarus (Belorussia) and Ukraine which were already members of the United Nations, though were clearly not sovereign. However, a twenty-second state, the Federal Republic of Yugoslavia, has not been granted full U.N. membership.
5. NATO acted under Security Council resolutions in its prior air strikes against Serbs in Bosnia.

6. " 'If We Don't Act, the War Will Spread,' " *Washington Post*, 20 March 1999, A8.

7. John M. Broader, "Clinton Says Milosevic Hurts Claim To Kosovo," *New York Times*, 31 March 1999, A10.

8. Peter Finn, "Compromise Satisfies Residents of Pristina; Many Hope for Eventual Independence," *Washington Post*, 24 February 1999, A17; Peter Finn, "KLA Stakes Claim to Role in Any Kosovo Deal," *Washington Post*, 22 May 1999, A15; Jane Perlez, "NATO Expects Separate Kosovo, Without Yugoslav Police or Taxes," *New York Times*, 11 June 1999, A1.

9. Jane Perlez, "NATO Expects Separate Kosovo, Without Yugoslav Police or Taxes," *New York Times*, 11 June 1999, A1.

10. "Rambouillet Accords: Interim Agreement for Peace and Self-Government in Kosovo," 7 June 1999, S/1999/648.

11. Quoted in Jane Perlez, "Annan Says Quick Elections in Kosovo May Not Help Tensions," *New York Times*, 20 October 1999, A3.

12. Jeffrey Smith, "U.S. Officials Expect Kosovo Independence," *Washington Post*, 24 September 1999, A1.

13. "Australia Upsets Jakarta with East Timor Switch," *Financial Times* (London), 13 January 1999, 5.

14. Richard Waddington, "East Timor Wins Vote on Independence in UN Deal," *The Independent* (London), 6 May 1999, 14.

15. Barbara Crossette, "Annan Warns Indonesians that Inaction May Lead to Criminal Charges," *New York Times*, 11 September 1999, A6.

16. Barbara Crossette, "Annan Says U.N. Must Take Over East Timor Rule," *New York Times*, 6 October 1999, A1.

17. Mark Lander, "New Crisis Frames Even Tougher Test of Indonesian Unity," *New York Times*, 21 November 1999, 1.

18. Quoted in Charles Babington, "Clinton Spars with Yeltsin on Chechnya; President Denounces Killing of Civilians," *Washington Post*, 19 November 1999, A1.

19. Michael A. Fletcher, "Albright Chides Russia for Chechen Attacks," *Washington Post*, 24 October 1999, A31.

20. William Drozdiak, "Big Powers Criticize Russia; Talk of Sanctions Over Chechen Offensive is Blocked by U.S.," *Washington Post*, 18 December 1999, A22.

21. Celestine Bohlen, "Russia Reacts Angrily Over Western Criticism on Chechnya," *New York Times*, 8 December 1999, A14.

22. To quote from the resolution: States have a responsibility to "protect the existence and the national or ethnic, cultural, religious and linguistic identity of minorities within their respective territories and shall encourage conditions for the promotion of that identity" (art. 1 [1]).

    "Persons belonging to minorities have the right to participate effectively in decisions on the national and, where appropriate, regional level concerning the minority to which they belong or the regions in which they live, in a manner not incompatible with national legislation" (art. 2 [3]).

    "Persons belonging to minorities have the right to establish and maintain their own associations" (art. 2 [4]).

    "Persons belonging to minorities have the right to establish and maintain, without any discrimination, free and peaceful contacts with other members of their group and with persons belonging to other minorities, as well as contacts across frontiers with citizens of other States to whom they are related by national or ethnic, religious or linguistic ties" (art. 2 [5]).

    "National policies and programmes shall be planned and implemented with due regard for the legitimate interests of persons belonging to minorities" (art. 5 [1]).

23. Christine Bell and Kathleen Cavanaugh, "'Constructive Ambiguity' or Internal Self-Determination? Self-Determination, Group Accommodation, and the Belfast Agreement," *Fordham International Law Journal* 22 (April 1999): 1345–71 (1353).

24. David Wippman, "The Evolution and Implementation of Minority Rights," *Fordham Law Review* 66 (November 1997): 597–626 (607–8).

25. Ibid., 608.

26. Marc Weller, "The International Response to the Dissolution of the Socialist Federal Republic of Yugoslavia," *American Journal of International Law* 86 (1992): 569–607 (582–83).

27. Michael P. Scharf, "Musical Chairs: The Dissolution of States and Membership in the United Nations," *Cornell International Law Journal* 28 (winter 1995): 29–69.

28. Although President Bush was criticized by many quarters for his address before the Ukranian parliament in the summer of 1991—dubbed the "Chicken Kiev" speech by William Safire of the *New York Times*—it was fairly representative of the feelings of the Bush administration and long-standing U.S. policy. As Bush declared: ". . . freedom is not the same as independence. Americans will not support those who seek independence in order to replace a far-off tyranny with a local despotism. They will not aid those who promote a suicidal nationalism based on ethnic hatred." "Excerpts from Bush's Ukraine Speech," *New York Times*, 2 August 1991, A8.

29. Lawrence S. Eastwood Jr., "Secession: State Practice and International Law After the Dissolution of the Soviet Union and Yugoslavia," *Duke Journal of Comparative & International Law* 3 (spring 1993): 299–349 (321).

30. Yulia Petrovskaya and Dimitry Gornostaev, "The U.S. Has Planned a New Disintegration of Yugoslavia," *Nezavisimaya gazeta*, 13 March 1999, 1, 6, reproduced in *What the Paper Say*, 15 March 1999.

31. William Jefferson Clinton, "Statement by the President on Kosovo," 24 March 1999, 2:15 P.M. EST.

32. William Jefferson Clinton, "Statement by the President to the Nation," 24 March 1999, 8:01 P.M. EST.

33. William Jefferson Clinton, "Videotaped Remarks by the President to the Serbian People," 25 March 1999.

34. Peter Finn, "Albright Class on KLA to Curb Its Claims of Authority," *Washington Post*, 30 July 1999, A23.

35. Quoted in Jeffrey Smith, "U.S. Officials Expect Kosovo Independence; Secession Increasingly is Seen as Inevitable," *Washington Post*, 24 September 1999, A1.

36. See U.N. Security Council resolutions 1239 (14 May 1999) and 1244 (10 June 1999).

37. Tyler Marshall, "U.S. Cautions Russia on Tactics in Chechnya," *Los Angeles Times*, 2 October 1999, A13; Frances Williams, "U.S. to Express Alarm Over Chechnya Deaths," *Financial Times* (London), 2 November 1999, 16.

38. *Charter for European Security*, Organization for Security and Co-operation in Europe, November 1999.

39. *Final Communiqué*—Ministerial Meeting of the North Atlantic Council held at NATO Headquarters, Brussels, 15 December 1999.

40. Peter Leuprecht, "Innovations in the European System of Human Rights Protection: Is Enlargement Compatible with Reinforcement?" *Transnational Law & Contemporary Problems* 8 (fall 1998): 313.

41. Wippman, *supra* note 24, at 612.

42. Ibid., 613.

43. "Russia, China Back Each Other on Taiwan, Chechnya," *TASS*, 10 December 1999.

44. *Gujarat Samachar* (Ahmedabad), 31 March 1999, 18, reproduced as "Indian Newspaper Fears 'Today Kosovo, Tomorrow Kashmir,' " in *BBC Summary of World Broadcasts*, 5 April 1999, FE/D3500/A.

45. Ian Black, "Russia and China Lead International Protests," *The Guardian* (London), 26 March 1999, 2.

46. "Moscow Optimistic About Russia-China-India Cooperation," *Interfax Russian News*, 30 March 1999.

47. What is more amazing is that, at least in the European context, national groups wish to attain statehood in order to relinquish their sovereignty to the supranational European Union.

Index

About the Contributors

Thomas Ambrosio received his B.A. from Trenton State College and his Ph.D. from the Woodrow Wilson Department of Government and Foreign Affairs at the University of Virginia. He has published book reviews and articles in international journals, and chapters in numerous books, and he is the author of *Irredentism: Ethnic Conflict and International Politics* (2001). Professor Ambrosio taught at the University of Virginia and at Western Kentucky University before joining the faculty of the Department of Political Science at North Dakota State University in 2000. He resides in Fargo with his wife, Beth.

J. Samuel Barkin is Assistant Professor of Political Science at the University of Florida. He has published articles on international relations in *International Organization, Millennium,* and *Global Governance,* among other venues, and has coedited *Anarchy and the Environment* (with George Shambaugh, 1999).

Robert J. Beck teaches international law at the University of Wisconsin–Milwaukee. He has also served in the Political Science department of Tufts University and the Woodrow Wilson Department of Government and Foreign Affairs at the University of Virginia. Professor Beck is the author of *The Grenada Invasion* (1993) and *International Law and the Use of Force: Beyond the U.N. Charter Paradigm* (with Anthony Clark Arend, 2nd ed., forthcoming), and coeditor of *International Rules: Approaches from International Law and International Relations* (with Anthony Clark Arend and Robert Vander Lugt, 1996).

Nathaniel Berman teaches international law and human rights at Northeastern University School of Law. Professor Berman's work focuses on international law's relationship to nationalism and colonialism in the 20th century, drawing on cultural studies and postcolonial theory.

Lea Brilmayer is Howard M. Holtzmann Professor of International Law at Yale Law School. Among her published works are *Justifying International Acts* (1989), *American Hegemony: Political Morality in a One Superpower World* (1994), *Conflict of Laws: Foundations and Future Directions* (1995), and *Global Justice* (1999, edited with Ian Shapiro).

Julie Marie Bunck is Associate Professor in the Department of Political Science of the University of Louisville, where she teaches comparative politics and international relations. Professor Bunck has taught government and political science at the University of Pennsylvania, George Washington University, Tufts University, and Colgate University. She has been awarded Fulbright research and lecturing grants to the Central American republics and to Japan, respectively, as well as Ford Foundation and Social Science Research Council–American Council of Learned Societies grants to teach in Vietnam. Among her publications are *Fidel Castro and the Quest for a Revolutionary Culture in Cuba* (1994) and *Law, Power, and the Sovereign State* (1995, with Michael R. Fowler).

Bruce Cronin is Assistant Professor in the University of Wisconsin's Political Science department. The author of several articles on sovereignty in international relations, Professor Cronin has also published *Community Under Anarchy: Transnational Identity and the Evolution of Cooperation* (1999). He is currently working on a book about how and why states protect foreign populations.

Michael Ross Fowler is Associate Professor at the Louis D. Brandeis School of Law of the University of Louisville. A member of the bars of Massachusetts, Maryland, and Washington, DC, Professor Fowler teaches chiefly in the fields of international law and organization, international relations, and negotiation, and he directs the university's Muhammad Ali Institute for Peacemaking and Conflict Resolution. The author of four books, including *Law, Power, and the Sovereign State* (1995, with Julie Marie Bunck), Professor Fowler served in 1995 as the first American international lawyer invited to teach in the Socialist Republic of Vietnam.

Thomas M. Franck is Director of the Center for International Studies and the Murry and Ida Becker Professor of Law at New York University's School of Law. Professor Franck has acted as legal adviser or counsel to many foreign governments, including Kenya, El Salvador, and Bosnia and Herzegovina. As an advocate before the International Court of Justice, he has successfully represented Chad and is currently representing Bosnia in a suit brought against Serbia under the Genocide Convention. Among his more than twenty books are *Nation against Nation* (1985), *The Power of Legitimacy among Nations* (1990), *Political Questions/Judicial Answers* (1992), and *Fairness in International Law and Institutions* (1995).

Hurst Hannum is Professor of International Law at The Fletcher School of Law and Diplomacy of Tufts University. Professor Hannum has served as counsel in cases before the European and Inter-American Commissions on Human Rights and the United Nations; he also has served as a legal consultant to the United Nations in negotiations on East Timor, to the Brcko Law Revision Commission, and to the government of the Faroe Islands on issues of autonomy and political status. Among other publications, Professor Hannum is editor of *Guide to International Human Rights Practice* (3rd ed., 1999), and the author of *Autonomy, Sovereignty, and Self-Determination* (rev. ed., 1996) and *International Human Rights* (with Richard Lillich, 3rd ed., 1995).

Benedict Kingsbury, a New Zealand citizen, is Professor of International Law at New York University Law School. His edited books include *Hugo Grotius and International Relations* (with Hedley Bull and Adam Roberts, 1990), *The International Politics of the Environment* (with Andrew Hurrell, 1992), and *United Nations, Divided World* (with Adam Roberts, 2nd ed., 1993). He is currently completing a book on indigenous peoples in international law.

Eric Kolodner, a graduate of New York University School of Law, is an associate at Cleary, Gottlieb, Steen & Hamilton, currently resident in its Hong Kong office.

Maivân Clech Lâm is Associate Professor at the City University of New York School of Law. The author of *At the Edge of the State: Indigenous Peoples and Self-Determination* (2000), she has written extensively on the rights of indigenous peoples.

Steven R. Ratner is the Albert Sidney Burleson Professor in Law at the University of Texas School of Law. His research focuses on challenges to new states and governments after the Cold War, especially ethnic conflict, territorial disputes, and accountability for past human rights abuses. His published works include *Accountability for Human Rights Atrocities in International Law* (1997 and 2001, with Jason S. Abrams) and *The New UN Peacekeeping* (1995). He has recently served as a Fulbright senior scholar at the Organization for Security and Cooperation in Europe, an expert for the OSCE on language and governance rights of national minorities, and a member of the UN Secretary-General's Group of Experts on Cambodia.

Oscar Schachter is Hamilton Fish Professor Emeritus of International Law and Diplomacy at Columbia University. During his distinguished career, he has served as Legal Advisor and Director of the Legal Department of the United Nations, President of the American Society of International Law, director of Studies and Research of the United Nations Institute of Training and Research, and Co-Editor-in-Chief of the *American Journal of International Law*. Professor Schachter's published works include: *Toward Wider Acceptance of UN Treaties* (1971, with Mahomed Nawaz and John Fried), *Sharing the World's Resources* (1977), *Competition in International Business* (1981, edited with Robert Hellawell), *International Law in Theory and Practice* (1991), and *United Nations Legal Order* (1995, edited with Christopher C. Joyner).